Cambridge Studies in Oral and Literate Culture

ORAL TRADITION AND WRITTEN RECORD IN CLASSICAL ATHENS

Cambridge Studies in Oral and Literate Culture

Edited by PETER BURKE and RUTH FINNEGAN

The series is designed to address the question of the significance of literacy in human societies: it will assess its importance for political, economic, social and cultural development, and examine how what we take to be the common functions of writing are carried out in oral cultures.

The series will be interdisciplinary, but with particular emphasis on social anthropology and social history, and will encourage cross-fertilisation between these disciplines: it will also be of interest to readers in allied fields, such as sociology, folklore and literature. Although it will include some monographs, the focus of the series will be on theoretical and comparative aspects rather than detailed description, and the books will be presented in a form accessible to non-specialist readers interested in the general subject of literacy and orality.

Books in the series

ORAL TRADITION AND WRITTEN RECORD IN CLASSICAL ATHENS

ROSALIND THOMAS
LECTURER IN ANCIENT HISTORY,
ROYAL HOLLOWAY AND BEDFORD NEW COLLEGE,
UNIVERSITY OF LONDON

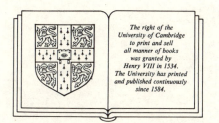

The right of the
University of Cambridge
to print and sell
all manner of books
was granted by
Henry VIII in 1534.
The University has printed
and published continuously
since 1584.

CAMBRIDGE UNIVERSITY PRESS

CAMBRIDGE
NEW YORK   NEW ROCHELLE   MELBOURNE   SYDNEY

Published by the Press Syndicate of the University of Cambridge
The Pitt Building, Trumpington Street, Cambridge CB2 1RP
32 East 57th Street, New York, NY 10022, USA
10 Stamford Road, Oakleigh, Melbourne 3166, Australia

First published 1989

Printed in Great Britain at the University Press, Cambridge

British Library cataloguing in publication data

Thomas, Rosalind
Oral tradition and written record in
classical Athens. – (Cambridge studies in
Oral and literate culture; 18).
1. Ancient Greece. Athens. Literacy
1. Title
302.2'0928'5

Library of Congress cataloguing in publication data

Thomas, Rosalind
Oral tradition and written record in classical Athens / Rosalind Thomas.
   p.   cm. – (Cambridge studies in oral and literate culture: 18)
Revision of thesis (doctoral) – London University, 1986.
Bibliography.
Includes index.
ISBN 0 521 35025 5
1. Greek language – Greece – Athens – History. 2. Oral tradition –
Greece – Athens – History. 3. Oral communication – Greece – Athens –
History. 4. Written communication – Greece – Athens – History.
5. Writing – Greece – Athens – History. 6. Literacy – Greece – Athens –
History. 7. Language and culture – Greece – Athens. 8. Athens
(Greece) – Intellectual life. I. Title. II. Series.
PA227.T47 1988
480'.938'5 – dc19   88–22918

ISBN 0 521 35025 5

CE

To my parents

These are the researches of Herodotus of Halicarnassus, which he publishes in the hope that the memory of what men have done should not be destroyed by time, and that the great and wonderful actions of the Greeks and Barbarians should not lose their due fame.   Herodotus Bk I, Prologue

ἀμνάμονες δὲ βροτοί   Pindar, *Isthmian* VII 13

CONTENTS

ACKNOWLEDGEMENTS

This book is a revised version of a doctoral thesis submitted to London University in June 1986. A Bryce Studentship given by Oxford University enabled me to revise it extensively before submitting it; and the Norman Baynes Prize of London University, awarded for a draft of Chapter 1, made further work on it considerably easier.

I would also like to thank Sally Humphreys for her exacting advice as supervisor, John North and John Davies, who examined the thesis, for their useful suggestions on how it could become a book, and for comments on various chapters at different stages: Riet van Brennen, Tim Cornell, Michael Crawford, Steven Instone, David Lewis, Eric Lewis, Fergus Millar, Oswyn Murray, Nicholas Purcell, Kurt A. Raaflaub; not to mention other friends and relations for their sometimes quizzical support and encouragement, and my brother Mark for his severe criticism of my style at a crucial stage of revision.

To help those unfamiliar with Greek history to orient themselves among the many historical events – not to mention the shifting spectrum of oral traditions – referred to in the course of this book, I have included a chronological table of Greek history at the end. This will also indicate the relative dating of the Greek historians and poets who are relevant to the discussion.

London   R. T.

ABBREVIATIONS

AJA	*American Journal of Archaeology*
AJP	*American Journal of Philology*
Anc. Soc.	*Ancient Society*
APF	J. K. Davies, *Athenian Propertied Families, 600–300 B.C.* (Oxford 1971)
APS	*The African Past Speaks: Essays on Oral Tradition and History* (ed. J. C. Miller, Folkstone 1980)
Ath. Mitt.	*Mitteilungen des deutschen archäologischen Instituts: Athenische Abteilung*
Atthis	F. Jacoby, *Atthis. The Local Chronicles of Ancient Athens* (Oxford 1949)
BCH	*Bulletin de correspondance hellénique*
CAH	*Cambridge Ancient History*
CJ	*Classical Journal*
CPh	*Classical Philology*
CQ	*Classical Quarterly*
CR	*Classical Review*
CW	*Classical Weekly*
FD	*Fouilles de Delphes*
FGH	F. Jacoby, *Die Fragmente der griechischen Historiker* (Berlin and Leiden, 1923–58)
GR	*Greece and Rome*
GRBS	*Greek, Roman, and Byzantine Studies*
HCT	A. W. Gomme, *Historical Commentary on Thucydides*, in five vols.; vols. IV and V completed by A. Andrewes and K. J. Dover (Oxford 1945–81)
HSCP	*Harvard Studies in Classical Philology*
IG	*Inscriptiones Graecae* (Berlin 1873–)
JHS	*Journal of Hellenic Studies*
JRS	*Journal of Roman Studies*
LCM	*Liverpool Classical Monthly*
LSAG	L. H. Jeffery, *The Local Scripts of Archaic Greece* (Oxford 1961)
MDAI (R)	*Mitteilungen des deutschen archäologischen Instituts: Römische Abteilung*
ML	R. Meiggs and D. M. Lewis, *A Selection of Greek*

	Historical Inscriptions to the End of the Fifth Century B.C. (Oxford 1969)
Mnemos.	*Mnemosyne*
Mus. Helv.	*Museum Helveticum*
OGIS	*Orientis Graecae Inscriptiones Selectae* I–II (ed. W. Dittenberger, Leipzig 1903–5)
Par. Pass.	*La Parola del Passato*
PCPS	*Proceedings of the Cambridge Philological Society*
PMG	D. L. Page, *Poetae Melici Graeci* (Oxford 1962)
RE	Pauly-Wissowa-Kroll, *Real-Encyclopädie der classischen Altertumswissenschaft* (Stuttgart 1894–)
REG	*Revue des Études grecques*
Rev. de Phil.	*Revue de philologie, de littérature et d'histoire ancienne*
Rh. M.	*Rheinisches Museum für Philologie*
SGDI	*Sammlung der griechischen Dialekt-Inschriften* I–IV (ed. H. Collitz, Göttingen 1884–1915)
SEG	*Supplementum Epigraphicum Graecum*
Syll.[3]	*Sylloge Inscriptionum Graecarum* I–IV[3] (ed. W. Dittenberger et al., Leipzig 1915–24)
Symbol. Osl.	*Symbolae Osloenses*
TAPA	*Transactions of the American Philological Association*
Tod	M. N. Tod, *A Selection of Greek Historical Inscriptions* (Oxford 1948)
Vansina *OTH*	J. Vansina, *Oral Tradition as History* (London and Nairobi 1985)
YCS	*Yale Classical Studies*
ZPE	*Zeitschrift für Papyrologie und Epigraphik*

INTRODUCTION

We tend to take literacy and its prestige for granted. We regard higher literacy rates as desirable, lack of literacy a sign of backwardness, but without thinking carefully about either the character or advantages of literacy, or the nature of its supposed converse, communication by word of mouth. In the study of the past, the written word is elevated above the oral, the written document generally much preferred as evidence to oral tradition, and written sources given more attention than oral ones, even when the written sources actually derive from oral communication. The reasons for this elevation are, one suspects, more a matter of inherited assumptions and beliefs than of individual thought about the nature of the written word (whose application is in fact exceedingly complex). A strong tradition of historiography and political thought has seen literacy as essential to civilization and liberal democracy. As Gibbon put it, 'the use of letters is the principal circumstance that distinguishes a civilized people from a herd of savages, incapable of knowledge or reflection'[1] – a belief which recurs today, though expressed differently. Nineteenth-century political theorists (and indeed modern ones) could not conceive of liberal democracy without widespread literacy. Since classical Athens was seen as the epitome of both civilization and democracy, it followed that Athenian citizens were highly literate.

Greater understanding of oral communication and tradition are in some ways now modifying these assumptions of the superiority of literacy. Oral communication and oral tradition have more positive associations, and the term 'orality' has been coined to avoid the obvious negative connotations of 'illiteracy'. The value of oral tradition and communication are now more readily recognized; non-written sources have gained respectability for anthropologists and some historians. Yet in some ways we are still not so far from Gibbon's separation of literate civilization and barbarism. To many people oral communication and tradition still suggest primitive characteristics or backwardness – though both are in fact common enough even in the modern world; or else the somewhat idealized world of folklore, folk traditions, the rediscovery of the people's culture, and the like. Most fundamental, the two spheres of literacy and oral communication are usually kept separate, regarded as

---

[1] Gibbon, *Decline and Fall of the Roman Empire*, ed. Bury (1896), vol. I, ch. 9, p. 218.

I

quite distinct, and 'literate societies' strictly distinguished from oral ones, with clear-cut characteristics attributed to each.

Classical Athens of the fifth and fourth centuries B.C. provides a striking refutation of these ideas and divisions. We are forced to think again about the nature of literacy, the role of written record and communication by word of mouth, and the interaction rather than the distinction between the two. For classical Athens had written records, yet it also relied heavily on oral tradition, and indeed the very organs of the radical democracy used oral communication extensively. Athens was in many respects an 'oral society'. A strict division between oral and literate societies is manifestly inappropriate here. The very idea is severely undermined, not to mention the optimistic equation between sophistication in cultural and political achievements and literacy. We are made to reconsider the nature of literacy itself and its relation or interaction with oral communication. In addition, the written histories from Greece were largely derived from oral tradition, so again we need to pay attention not merely to the written texts but to the nature of the oral sources they reflect and the possible influence of one on the other.

Greater understanding of oral tradition and literacy by anthropologists, and of the workings of memory by psychologists, now make it particularly urgent to approach these problems with more sophistication. This book re-examines literacy and the use of writing in Athens against the background of oral communication and analyses the character and processes of Athens' oral traditions and their relation to written historiography. This should contribute understanding not only to specific parts of Athenian history, but to the nature and mechanisms of oral tradition in general, its relation or reaction to the written word, and therefore to literacy itself.

Classical scholars are increasingly aware of the elements of Greek society which depended on word of mouth rather than writing. Milman Parry's work on oral poetry in the 1930s has been the most influential in drawing attention to the unwritten aspects of Greek culture. Through his study of contemporary oral bards in Yugoslavia, he produced the startling and now widely accepted theory that Homer's *Iliad* and *Odyssey*, our earliest Greek literature, were in fact essentially oral poetry: they were the product of a long tradition of oral composition by Dark-Age bards before the poems were eventually written down. While attention still concentrates on 'Homer' himself, it is also increasingly recognized how much the rest of Greek literature was heard rather than read, presented and transmitted orally even if a written text existed.[2] As

[2] Esp. in the sphere of Homeric scholarship: see (e.g.) bibliography of Fantuzzi (1980); Gentili (1984); Morris (1986); on the symposium, O. Murray (1983a), (1983b); Bowie (1986); Kennedy (1963), though old, has useful remarks.

the concept of Homeric oral poetry has rendered the idea of total literacy in Greece irretrievable, there have been repeated attempts to estimate the extent of literacy in the ancient world and some recognition of the importance of the coming of writing to an oral society. Numerous works outside the classical field have tried to generalize about the characteristics of 'oral societies', and they have in some areas begun to penetrate ancient historical or literary studies. Goody and Watt's essay, 'The Consequences of Literacy' (1968) has been particularly influential. They took ancient Greece as a test case to examine the 'effect' of literacy on a previously oral society. Some of these general theories about 'oral societies' can be seen now to have been simplistic or misleading. Increasingly criticized, they imply a strict division between 'oral' and 'literate' characteristics and 'oral' and 'literate' societies that does not bear close scrutiny. However, like Havelock's controversial work on ancient Greece, they have helped focus attention on the 'oral' elements of Greek society.

The most familiar type of oral tradition in Greece is the poetic oral tradition of the Homeric epics. But oral tradition in a wider sense provided most Greeks with a knowledge of their history. The oral traditions I shall be most concerned with are orally transmitted statements from the past or, in Vansina's definition, 'verbal testimonies which are reported statements from the past beyond the present generation' (see further discussion below, p. 10). A simple example of oral tradition by this definition would be an account from somebody's grandparents of something that their parents did. The importance of this wider oral tradition in Greece is now more widely accepted – and it should be stressed that there was no teaching of history for its own sake in schools. Ancient writers often assume oral tradition or memory in the preservation of the past, whether they are scholiasts guessing how the poet Pindar found out about local legends, Xenophon discussing previous conditions in the mines, or Ephorus criticizing narratives of ancient times. The range of such comments is even wider than we usually think, and certainly not confined to historians.[3] For the Greek historians

---

[3] Pindar: schol. on *Ol.* VII 100a, 101, surmising that Pindar asked the local *logioi* or wise men; Xen. *Poroi* IV 14f.; Ephorus: *FGH* 70 F9, declaring that it is improbable that all the deeds or the greater part of the speeches were kept in memory for so great a span of time. Cf. also Isoc. *Panath.* 149f. and *Paneg.* 30, on the truth of things he did not see; Arist. *Rhet.* II 13.12 and 21.9: the old are always talking about the past because they live in memory; Xenoph. fr. 18 Diehl (cf. B1 West, 19–22); Polyb. XXXVIII 1.6, the disasters of the Achaian War. Herodotus regularly mentions *akoē* ('hearing') and *opsis* ('seeing') (esp. II 99, 147, 156), and Thucydides uses *akoē* as 'oral tradition' (I 20.1, 73.2; VI 53.3, 60.1; Hunter (1973), 27, n. 5). The terms expressed a distinction vital amidst predominantly oral communication, between eye-witness accounts and hearsay (see Schepens (1975), but he misses the practical background to the division). Plato presents the most rigorous ancient examination extant of the effect of memory and oral transmission versus

themselves, particularly Herodotus and Thucydides, it is increasingly agreed that they used primarily oral sources and oral tradition.[4] The nature of oral tradition thus becomes a particularly urgent problem for the study of Greek history and society.

Yet there have been very few detailed and sustained attempts to examine oral tradition in the ancient world in its own right. Few go further than mentioning the relevance of oral tradition and perhaps citing a general anthropological work.[5] Often oral tradition – or misleadingly, simply 'tradition' – is mentioned briefly, especially for early periods where it clearly lies behind our sources. But discussion goes no further than wide generalization about the reliability of oral tradition. There is a broad division between 'optimistic' scholars who stress the longevity of oral tradition in societies without writing and the sceptical who assert that oral tradition is all useless fiction.[6] But we must go further than that. Oral tradition does not have a single characteristic degree of reliability (which is what these remarks usually dwell on). Though it is widely held that people in oral societies have extremely long memories, even that is not certain: they do have to have better devices or mechanisms for remembering, which is an entirely different thing.[7] The longevity and

writing on the preservation of the past (*Tim.*, esp. 21e–25d, and *Crit.* 109d–110d, for the story of Atlantis). The Athenian orators regularly assume oral transmission (Ch. 4.1 for references), as do ancient remarks on family tradition (Ch. 2.1). For memory in Greek literature, cf. Notopoulos (1938), Simondon (1982).

[4] Momigliano (1972, repr. 1977) and (1966b); Finley 1965 (repr. 1975), and more recently (1983) and (1985), stressing ancient historians' neglect of written documents. Jacoby pressed the idea of Herodotus' oral sources particularly (*RE* Suppl. ii, 413f.); Murray (1980) and (1987) treats his oral sources in more detail. Cf. also Evans (1982), ch. 10 (very schematic), Hunter (1982), Fornara (1983), and hints in Boedeker (1987), esp. Dewald's article. Other studies try to deal with Herodotus' work as 'oral narrative' or work from that assumption: e.g. Lang (1984), S. West (1985), and Nagy (1987). For 'folktales', implicitly oral, Aly (1921) is still useful.

[5] Cf. for example, Hunter (1982), esp. app. 1 (for both Herodotus and Thucydides); Evans (1982), ch. 10; Cartledge (1979).

[6] For the optimistic, see e.g. Nilsson (1952), Day (1980), 30, Fornara (1971a) citing Jacoby's *Atthis* on the ability of oral tradition to remember chronological data along with events (cf. Rhodes (1976), 227). For the sceptical, see esp. Finley (1965), 26; he also criticizes the 'uncritical acceptance' by modern historians of what they call 'tradition' or 'oral tradition', 'though no one has yet demonstrated a plausible mechanism for the oral transmission of accurate information over a period of centuries' (1983), 209.

[7] Henige remarks ((1982), 67) that belief in such extraordinary memory is 'largely untested and untestable'. There are some indications, though. Cole and Scribner (1981) found that the experience of rote learning of the Koran (in Liberia) did not seem to improve capacity for 'free recall'. Similarly, Baddeley ((1983), 204–7) cites both the work of Wagner in Morocco, confirming that memorizing (here of the Koran) does not actually improve skill in memorizing, and also (p. 207) tests on a South African tribe with a reputation for remarkable memory: the tests showed that in fact their memories were not abnormal except for an immense capacity to remember cattle, which were very important in their social structure. So memory's efficiency depends largely on relevance or interest. Goody (1987), ch. 8 now questions the existence of verbatim memory at all in oral societies.

reliability of oral traditions vary immensely according to certain factors, and these one must consider for each kind of oral tradition separately.

A few more detailed studies tackle directly the peculiar questions raised by oral tradition. Finley's 'Myth, Memory and History' (1965, repr. 1975) is interesting but brief and extremely general. More recently, Oswyn Murray has been examining oral tradition from a particularly Herodotean perspective,[8] and J. K. Davies has applied anthropological findings to the historicity of the Trojan War traditions.[9] Otherwise it is the expulsion of the Peisistratid tyrants, along with Thucydides' own comments on *akoē* ('hearing', therefore 'oral tradition'), which have focused most attention upon oral tradition, and prompted detailed analysis. Yet here analysis of the traditions is still building upon Jacoby's now old-fashioned schema in his *Atthis*.[10] Though the discussion is couched in terms of oral transmission, the traditions have been seen through modern assumptions about ancient political bias and propaganda, and the workings of oral tradition taken for granted. There has been little treatment of other oral traditions or of oral tradition in general outside the narrow circle of memories of the tyranny. Since these memories are often taken to epitomize Greek oral tradition, I have used this complex of traditions as a final detailed test case for the mechanisms and development of Athenian oral tradition (Ch. 5).

So a great deal of our understanding of ancient oral tradition is left to 'common sense'. Yet anthropologists have long been encountering and discussing the problems of oral tradition, and they have developed complex methods for collecting, evaluating and interpreting it. For ancient historians, one difficulty, perhaps, is that it is easier to cite general anthropological works than apply them in detail. Anthropologists treat societies still in existence where researchers can collect 'raw' oral testimonies in great quantity, whereas for the ancient world we have only what was eventually written down. Many anthropologists' remarks about collecting testimonies, details of transmission, or the problems of 'feedback' from published works, seem more relevant to research in the field. In addition, the types of society, interests, narrative motifs, and therefore the very types of oral tradition discussed, seem remote from the oral traditions of ancient Greece. Of what relevance to Greece, for instance, are the lengthy and impressive dynastic traditions carefully transmitted through professional memory-men in certain African states? It is true, we only have written sources from which to approach ancient oral tradition. But that simply makes the study more difficult. There are various ways to approach oral tradition without living informants. The

---

[8] Murray (1980), and at greater length (1987).
[9] (1981), the most detailed treatment so far.
[10] With Fornara, Ehrenberg and others: see Ch. 5 for detailed references.

central role of oral tradition in Greece and the preservation of the Greek past make it essential to try and understand something of its nature.

The anthropological works which treat oral tradition in general are particularly useful, as they discuss the overall problems and principles with which to study oral tradition. Vansina's older work, *Oral Tradition*, was for a long time a standard handbook and introduction (1961; the Penguin edition (1973) has important additions). He has now replaced it by a very different and more complex study, *Oral Tradition as History* (1985). This devotes less time to practical advice for field work and concentrates much more on the processes by which oral tradition is formed (against the rather more severely functionalist approach of his earlier book). This is invaluable. The works by Finnegan and Henige are also extremely useful.[11]

Anthropological studies show the fundamental importance of certain elements to the study of oral tradition. The most important factor in oral tradition is the way the tradition is passed on. This includes several elements: the precise nature and form of the transmission, for example, whether the tradition is passed on in poetic or other fixed form; the group which transmits it, whether a family, dynasty or whole community; and why it is being transmitted (e.g. for status or honour). All these factors bear on the character of the tradition, its 'distortions', whether it is likely to be transmitted accurately or over a long period of time, the tenor or bias of the tradition. For instance, where we find traditions kept by professional memorizers who lay great stress on strict accuracy because they are responsible for dynastic traditions, we may expect fairly accurate transmission over a long period. The reasons behind transmission are also crucial. Even without a narrowly functionalist view of oral tradition, it is obvious that nothing is remembered or passed down for no reason at all. Traditions may, for instance, confirm the prestige and authority of the royal house. Those aims help select and transform the content of the traditions.

So little is known of the nature of oral tradition and transmission in Greece, however, that it is necessary to start at an even more basic level of research. We must decide what evidence is most useful or nearest to oral tradition, in order to isolate oral traditions in the first place. In the complex world of oral transmission it is crucial to devote our attention first to the direct oral traditions themselves. There are no neat and generally applicable criteria for distinguishing oral tradition, though that would be convenient. We must simply look for evidence on how a

---

[11] Finnegan (1977) on oral poetry; Henige (1974) on the 'chronology of oral tradition', and (1982).

certain type of tradition was passed down, where an historian got his information, and use our wider knowledge of the society.

I have therefore tried to find clear examples of direct oral tradition from texts which either directly represent oral tradition or which represent its transmission. The speeches delivered in the Athenian assembly and courts presented a view of Athenian history which expressed Athenian oral tradition (the traditions of the polis or city-state) and actually transmitted it (see Ch. 4). They also include speakers' family history, a valuable source of *direct* family tradition. Comedy also expressed popular tradition. We can only return to the historians after this, and I cannot overstress this. For though they used oral tradition, they may have rearranged their material considerably (as indeed a study of oral tradition suggests) and engaged in extensive research. They may be a source for information contained in oral traditions but not necessarily for any one unaltered tradition. Herodotus in particular cannot be taken as a direct source for 'uncontaminated' oral traditions. This might be tempting, partly because of the surprisingly common image of him wandering around the Mediterranean writing down anything he is told without further inquiry, literary aims or arguments of his own. We cannot evaluate the historian's methods or achievements adequately before we understand what his sources were like.

Inevitably we must concentrate on Athens, and the best direct evidence must be from the better documented classical period of the fifth and fourth centuries B.C. Since there is more evidence for that than for the archaic period (eighth to sixth centuries) or earlier, we can look at certain traditions in depth with external information against which to judge the traditions. Thus, we will be able to discern changes in detail, look at wider questions more adequately, and know more about the character of certain types of oral tradition, what to expect of oral tradition and how to examine it. We can then be more confident about how to treat the oral traditions of earlier periods for which there is so much less evidence.

I should add a word of explanation about my use of the 'external information' derived mainly from the historians. One can often judge the accuracy and changes in an oral tradition by comparing it with the very much more detailed accounts of Herodotus and Thucydides. This does not assume the historians always provide a reliable and historically accurate account, since they may restructure or transform the information they use.[12] But in the cases I discuss, the account of Herodotus or Thucydides is the one generally accepted by historians as most reliable, and Thucydides was himself writing of contemporary events for which

[12] See (e.g.) de Romilly (1956), Hunter (1973), Fehling (1971).

detailed information was available. We must balance the oral traditions against the generally accepted version of events and, as will become clear, the cases are comparatively straightforward.

There are other angles of approach. For instance, memories and traditions depend partly on the customs available for transmitting information, and on the ideals (e.g. of honour) which determine what is thought worth remembering. We can examine the incentives and opportunities for oral tradition and the ideals lying behind it. This I do for family tradition (Ch. 2.1) and rather differently in Ch. 4 where I look at the 'official' Athenian ideals and preoccupations and their reflection in the official vision of the past.

Sometimes we can see how a tradition has changed in the course of time. Even small, apparently minor, changes can illuminate the way traditions change and why they do, and thus the very processes of memory and transmission. Here again, it is important, I think, to concentrate on the later detailed evidence first. One could look at certain common types of oral tradition such as 'migration stories' for which anthropological works can be helpful. But these general, even legendary traditions have undergone very long periods of transmission and change which must be extremely complex. Broad theories about 'official traditions' or 'collective memory' do not adequately explain why and how such traditions formed in the first place or how they changed to reach the much later forms we have. We need a more basic understanding of Greek oral tradition before going on to 'age-old' legends widely known, accepted and enshrined in poetry (and see Chs. 4 and 5 for the immense complexity of the traditions of a community). It is not enough to identify 'oral traditions' – or take tales assumed to be oral tradition – and discuss them only in relation to the contemporary society in which they are found, though that is interesting. Oral tradition by its nature may change, disappear or grow constantly. Its development over the passage of time is not only fascinating in its own right, but also crucial to understanding the character and processes of oral transmission.[13]

Once we have distinguished types of tradition, groups and means of transmission, we can begin to understand the relation between different traditions and how they interact and influence each other. No memory is completely self-contained (this is related to the processes of memory to which I return below). Family traditions give excellently clear and

---

[13] See esp. Vansina's most recent work (*OTH*). Unfortunately much anthropological work has captured oral traditions at one time only. When earlier colonial records of older contemporary traditions exist, they show where traditions have changed and are extremely interesting in explaining why those traditions were remembered and *why* they changed. Or sometimes anthropologists have been able to return much later. Cf. for example, the 'structural amnesia' of the Tiv (Bohannan 1952) (see Ch. 3.2); Firth (1961), 71ff. (Tikopia); Goody (1987), ch. 8 on the Bagre.

comparatively simple examples of such influence (Ch. 2). So we can begin to understand how memories turn into traditions, how traditions form and re-form, the relation between individual esoteric memories and the general traditions of the state; and how oral traditions may gradually become stereotyped expressions of a society's overall beliefs (a characteristic sometimes taken to define oral tradition – see below, p. 10). In short, we may begin to see how historical events and personal reminiscences, if important enough to the society, can become the stereotyped stories with common 'typical' features with which we are familiar from Herodotus.

However, neither classical nor archaic Greece lacked the written word entirely. We cannot simply declare that Greece was primarily an 'oral society' and proceed as if writing and written works did not exist. It becomes increasingly clear that we cannot consider Greek oral tradition alone, completely distinct from the use and application of writing. While very stimulating, many of the studies concerned with either literacy or 'oral societies' tend to leave an impression of a great divide between oral societies and literate ones or between 'orality' and 'literacy'. Some attribute recognizable, even predictable, characteristics to each. So ancient Greece is thought of as an oral society if literacy levels can be argued to be extremely low.[14] The division is clearer in the case of oral tradition. It is a commonplace that oral tradition dies out with the coming of literacy. Anthropologists in the field worry (understandably) about the influence of 'feedback' from written publications into the oral traditions again.[15] The problem has been brought to the fore in classical scholarship by the oral nature of the Homeric epic, the relation between the tradition of oral poetry and our written Homeric text and the possible effects of literacy on the skill of oral bards suggested by Parry's and Lord's findings in modern Yugoslavia. To put it very crudely, the picture often presented is either one of an 'oral society' equipped with flowering oral traditions, minimal literacy and the characteristics often argued to belong to oral societies in general;[16] or one in which literacy is widespread and we need worry little about 'oral' aspects or oral tradition. This division is immensely misleading. It blinds one to the complexity with which the written and spoken words combined and interacted in Greece (I argue this in more depth in Ch. 1.1). Even in our modern world, after all, with its extreme respect for writing, oral presentation has an

---

[14] As Havelock (1982).

[15] Henige (1982), 81ff. gives good examples of 'feedback'; Vansina, *OTH* 155ff. See Ch. 3, p. 189, however, for the possibility that oral traditions sometimes reach their greatest flowering just after literacy arrives.

[16] See e.g. Ong (1982), Havelock (1982); and Finnegan (1977), ch. 1 for a discussion of romantic views of oral tradition.

important role, from television to the lecture hall. This is why my study deals both with oral tradition or communication and with aspects of the use of the written word.

Thus, rather than minimize the 'extent' of full literacy or the purity of oral tradition, we should examine certain fundamental questions about the nature of both literacy and oral tradition that the combination suggests. We should examine not so much the extent of literacy but *how*, and with what degrees of sophistication, it was used (this I do in Ch. 1.2). For literacy and extensive oral communication are not incompatible and they subsist alongside each other even well into the fourth century B.C. Moreover, 'literacy' is not a simple, self-explanatory skill: it develops and changes. We are dealing in the classical period not simply with the presence or absence of literacy but with attitudes which partly govern the use of writing. That greatly affects our interpretation and understanding of the ancient use of the written word. Thus, it is hardly surprising that right into the later fourth century people still knew of the past primarily through oral tradition, and even historians made relatively little use of written documents.

Secondly, a more complex relation between writing and oral tradition may be discerned. It is possible that writing may influence oral tradition – and not simply by killing it. The process of writing down oral tradition may sometimes order and transform it. One area where writing and written scholarship seem to have been applied early to the oral traditions was that of genealogy (see Ch. 3). We can see some of the effects. These findings may suggest further ways of approaching early historiography and the extension of the written word to other oral traditions (see Ch. 5.1 also).

Finally, I return to the definition of oral tradition. How does it differ from the material of 'oral history', the use of living informants for evidence rather than documents? Various scholars stress different elements. These differences raise interesting and complex issues and touch, I think, at the very heart of our understanding of oral tradition. For they involve the processes of its formation.

Vansina's original definition (1973) was 'all verbal testimonies which are reported statements concerning the past'. Thus oral traditions were any reported statements, and they were specifically *about* the past. According to his recent definition (*OTH* 27f.), however, oral traditions are not necessarily about the past, and while transmission is stressed, a prerequisite for 'oral tradition' is that 'There must be transmission by word of mouth over at least a generation.' Oral traditions are 'verbal testimonies which are reported statements from the past beyond the present generation'. I shall be using 'oral tradition' in a similar way, but the implications of alternatives deserve further discussion as they highlight important points about the nature of oral tradition.

Contrast, for instance, Henige's insistence ((1982), 2) that 'oral tradition should be widely practised or understood in a society, and handed down for at least a few generations' and (p. 106) that oral tradition has been transmitted for several generations and has become more or less 'the common property of a society'. That is, oral tradition is very old and generally believed. Recent events belong to 'oral history', and everything that is not a 'tradition' is simply testimony. Henige stresses here the sociological aspects of oral tradition, the 'traditional' elements which imply wide acceptance in a society, rather than the simple element of 'transmission' implied by the most basic meaning of 'tradition'.

One immediate problem arises. At what stage does 'oral history' become 'oral tradition'? How many generations does it take and how do we deal with the intervening stages of transmission between personal reminiscences (which comprise oral history) and the oral tradition of Henige's definition? His definition also neglects the type of 'oral tradition' which is known and carefully transmitted by a narrow esoteric group but not known by the rest of the society. What about family tradition itself? The simple transmission of personal reminiscences to the next generation (and then the next) causes havoc to these categories. Discussing studies of early resistance to colonial rule, for which contemporary witnesses are now mostly dead, Henige adds with some difficulty ((1982), 108): 'For our purposes we can treat such stories as oral history if we argue that hearing about the experiences of one's parents is in itself an experience and can be retold as such even if in some circumstances it might be considered as little more than hearsay.' It seems simpler to recognize that oral tradition and the stuff of oral history form a continuum. Family tradition cuts across the two separate categories and so is particularly revealing for the formation of oral tradition (Ch. 2.1). Henige's (and others') perception of oral tradition seems perilously close to the idea of 'tradition' as something warm, comforting, 'traditional' and accepted without question, which has been criticized most strongly by Finnegan and Finley.[17]

Behind such distinctions between 'oral history' and 'oral tradition', lie, I think, important processes of memory which seem to make the line between the two much more blurred. Recent studies of memory itself and of its role in oral tradition help to clarify the picture. Since the processes of memory lie behind much of my later discussion, it will help to outline the suggestions of that research here. I refer particularly to

---

[17] Finley (1983), 209; Finnegan (1977). Vansina's objection (*OTH* 28) is rather different: a crucial criterion for any sociological analysis of traditions but not for their use as a source for history. There are other emphases: e.g. J. C. Miller (*APS* 2) insists that oral traditions must be deliberate historical statements.

Vansina's discussion on 'Memory and Oral Tradition' (1980), his new general discussion of oral tradition (*OTH*), and Baddeley's *The Psychology of Memory* (1976). The same processes of memory and forgetting, with resulting structuring and simplification, seem to apply both to personal reminiscences and to oral tradition, but with vast differences in degree.

'Oral history' involves personal reminiscences and the actual experiences of informants. So oral historians encounter the problems of individuals' memories.[18] How accurately do individuals remember their own experience? Do old people remember more or less than younger, and are their early memories tinged with idealization? What kinds of information can be remembered accurately at all?

The considerable body of psychological research on memory can help here, though there is still a great deal that is unclear.[19] It is found, for instance, that peoples' memories for repeated actions (e.g. earlier jobs) can be very accurate, but not for separate instances of those actions. Precise numbers are rarely recalled well. Abstract items, motives, thoughts and intentions behind earlier actions are particularly prone to change in later memories. In short, our memories do not simply remember. The very process of recall involves a certain degree of re-forming or re-structuring of the 'original' memory. Psychologists talk of the mnemonic code by which our memories store information. Every memory is 'encoded', as it were: we retrieve it via certain cues, by means of scanning. Information can literally 'slip one's memory' until one finds the right cue. We remember different things according to our different interests. Moreover, the mnemonic code seems to vary from society to society, so that 'memory' varies with culture. Different communities may thus have very different accounts of the same events.

When we recall something, the process of recall may involve further elaboration or structuring, especially if we proceed to description. Vansina gives the apt example of childhood memories which may simply consist of pictures ((1980), 266f.). But the recalling adult may add explanation, description and narrative. Childhood memories also illustrate well how our memories can change gradually through our own later interpretations and especially other peoples' reminiscences of our childhood. Our memories are not completely self-contained. Where our memory coding was inadequate we reinterpret and elaborate, influenced

[18] They are sometimes surprisingly neglectful of the problems. A good introduction to oral history is that of Paul Thompson (1978); cf., however, studies in Bourget et al. (1986) with Wachtel's introduction. For the problems of the reliability of memory in oral history interviews: Henige (1982), ch. 6; Moss and Goldstein (eds.) (1979), esp. articles by Gittins and Baddeley. Cf. Hobsbawm and Ranger (eds.) (1983) for some provocative ideas on the 'invention' of tradition.

[19] Baddeley (1976) and (1983) in more popular form; Lieury (1975); Gittins (1979).

both by our own later ideals and preoccupations and those of our contemporaries in general.[20] This is most vividly described by Halbwachs in his *Collective Memory* (1950, transl. 1980) and confirmed by recent research. For instance, an event might go almost unnoticed at the time because it seemed insignificant. If it later seemed extremely important, we might find ourselves striving to remember it and our reactions to it. But later discussion, description and perception of its precise importance may actually help *create* – or at least improve – our faint recollections. Our memories can be influenced by our own later perceptions and those of our society (or what has been termed its 'collective memory').

These processes seem to be the key to understanding how personal reminiscences can become oral tradition.[21] Personal reminiscences are not all passed on, but edited more or less severely according to the speaker's intentions in telling them. For instance, a person may want to present his life in a manner other people will admire. In the process of telling and retelling, the reminiscences may be improved or gradually restructured in an extension of the processes of individual memory, according to the audience's expectations or interests. The narrative may gradually be improved or simplified. Symbols and other recognized elements of storytelling may be imported. As the 'reminiscence' is retold and passed to the next generation – if it is interesting enough not simply to be forgotten – then the same processes continue and intensify in their effect. As Vansina says ((1980), 272), oral tradition is a memory of memories. The mnemonic code is also collective and varies with culture, as I have said. This seems to be partly why oral traditions vary so much in type and content from culture to culture and how oral traditions may become gradually more and more stylized and stereotyped.

This is a much simplified description of an extremely complex process which is not yet completely understood. But I hope it is enough to indicate how important the restructuring of memory is in oral transmission and to introduce certain crucial ideas which will recur in my discussion of specific traditions (esp. Chs. 2 and 5). I will continue to use 'oral tradition' to denote testimonies which have been transmitted over at least a generation (as Vansina, p. 10) above). But the effect of memory in the formation of both personal reminiscences and oral tradition make me disinclined to separate the two so strictly as to imply a

---

[20] It was first shown by Bartlett that remembering is a reconstructive process: see Gittins (1979), 92f.; Henige (1982), 110f.; Baddeley (1976).

[21] On this, see above all Vansina (1980), and *OTH*, esp. ch. 1. Henige (1982), ch. 6 also has a very useful discussion on memory and oral history. I do not wish to imply, of course, that all oral traditions derive from some 'original event' or genuine memory.

wide gulf between them. In many ways the distinction in Greek historio-graphy between *akoē* ('hearing') and *opsis* ('seeing') – what you saw yourself and what you only heard – is still the fundamental one.

I start, then, by discussing literacy, the use of written record and the relation between literacy and oral communication. Chapter 1.1 re-examines our expectations of what the presence of 'literacy' tells us and the mixture of written and oral methods of communication and record; 1.2 analyses the classical use of documents and archives and the changing sophistication with which the written word was used in the light of that mixture. I then turn to a detailed examination of oral family tradition in Athens, the precise means of transmission, the nature of its memories and the gradual changes it undergoes (Ch. 2). This sets out certain crucial characteristics of Athenian oral tradition in general and some of the processes behind its formation. It involves a somewhat detailed treatment of the direct but neglected evidence. Chapter 3 examines one sphere of family tradition, the preservation of genealogies. Against the conclusions of Chapter 2, I discuss the possible effect of writing and written methods on the oral traditions and the relation of such lists to the early application of writing. Chapter 4 looks at the 'polis traditions' of Athens, particularly the 'official traditions' enshrined in the public funeral speeches. Here we see how beliefs and ideals can influence and eventually create oral tradition. Finally, I turn to the complex of traditions surrounding the 'liberation of Athens' from the Peisistratids, perhaps the best known oral traditions of Athens (Ch. 5). The extent of evidence makes it possible to analyse the layers of tradition and how they change. This re-examination stands as a test case to illustrate in depth some of the characteristics and mechanisms of oral tradition and memory amongst family, polis, and demos.

1

LITERACY, WRITTEN RECORD AND ORAL COMMUNICATION

1.1 Literacy in ancient Greece

A discussion of oral tradition, and still more of its interaction with written record, seems to raise questions about the extent of literacy. For how can we talk of oral tradition in classical Athens in the fifth and fourth centuries when the written word was so plentiful? What are we suggesting about the level of literacy? It is often loosely assumed that oral tradition dies out when literacy becomes widespread. 'Oral' and 'literate' are often seen as opposed characteristics. Romantic views of 'oral society' convey a seductive picture of an intimate 'folk-culture' which is shattered by the insidious arrival of literacy. Behind these views lie certain expectations of literacy and ideas about its use which we are encouraged to take for granted by our sophisticated and highly literate standpoint.

In fact the society of classical Athens was still heavily dependent on the spoken word even in the fourth century B.C. One can still talk plausibly of oral tradition in that century (Chs. 2, 4). Yet the alphabet reached Greece in the eighth century B.C. Many postulate widespread literacy in Athens at least by the fifth century. Other theories assume an extreme picture of Greece as an 'oral society', and the extent of 'literacy' is accordingly minimized. The two pictures would seem to be incompatible. Yet surely the continuation of certain oral practices into the fourth century suggests first that the reality was a great deal more complex; and secondly that we are thinking about literacy and lack of it in a misleading way, influenced by our own preconceptions about literacy. Recent studies of literacy in the modern world help us to consider afresh whether we should not be looking at other aspects of literacy in the ancient world than its 'extent' alone. It is time to re-examine the relations between literacy and oral communication; and – more fundamental – the very meaning of 'literacy' itself.

It is often asked how many Athenians of the classical period were literate. But the way the debate has been posed is misleading. If we use the scanty evidence only to find out about the extent of literacy, we miss much else that it conveys. I would argue that we should consider the place of literacy in Athens rather than its extent. Literacy is not a single uniform skill with only one significant level of competence, and, as we shall see, its use is far from predictable. Common sense tells us that there is little value in considering literacy by itself as an almost theoretical possession, if we do not also consider how it is used. With this shift in emphasis one can attempt a far more sophisticated study of the place of the written word in ancient Greece, its interaction with oral methods of communication, and the development and extension of its use throughout the period.

It is also recognized that much of Athenian life was primarily oral where we might expect the use of writing. So we must extend discussion of literacy to the 'mixture' and interaction of literate and oral processes. Once we recognize such a mixture, and even regard it as normal, then we may see the evidence used for the 'literacy debate' in a rather different light. Much of it is ambiguous when scrutinized only for the extent of literacy. Arguments which postulate extensive literacy because of the mere existence of inscriptions are assuming what they wish to prove – that is, that people could read them. Yet if there was bound to be a mixture of written and oral methods of communication, the evidence makes sense and allows a far more subtle interpretation.

I will therefore approach 'literacy' from the opposite angle to that of the traditional debate. Concentrating first on the uses made of written record and the mixture of oral and written modes, I shall approach the question of literacy in the light of that mixture and the familiarity or availability of written record. This will serve as a background for a more detailed discussion of the development in use and sophistication of documents and in people's reliance on them in the fifth and fourth centuries (Ch. 1.2), and as an introduction to later discussion of the oral traditions of this period and the cases where we can discern the effect of written record upon the oral traditions (e.g. Ch. 3). For the application of writing to certain areas was slow and gradual, and much was left to memory and oral transmission even as late as the fourth century.

The traditional debate on the 'extent of literacy' presents an exaggeratedly simple picture and extremely general conclusions. This is partly encouraged by the slight evidence which forces us to use anything from anecdote to ostracism (see below, p. 18). Had we extensive and detailed information about rural rates of literacy, for instance, school foundations and attendance, types of teaching, and so on, we could tell much of great interest: such a study has been done recently for modern France.[1] But this is clearly impossible for ancient Athens or the rest of Greece. Hence the traditional debate is on its surest footing when books rather than

---

[1] Furet and Ozouf (1982). Cf. also Graff (ed.) (1981) on literacy and social development in the West (and especially his introduction).

literacy itself are discussed. A brief discussion of its shortcomings is an apt introduction to some of the complexities of literacy.[2]

First of all, a fundamental problem in evaluating the extent of literacy from our evidence is surprisingly overlooked. We must argue about literacy from written documents. Yet by its very nature, only written evidence may survive. Oral tradition has only been preserved if it was once written down, and illiterates tend to leave no record. Thus, apart from a few anecdotes and general inferences, our written evidence tells us only about the 'positive' side of the picture, the existence of written record and its use. It does not tell us about those who could neither read nor write, the absence of books, the rarity of written record, and the nature of oral communication – a problem peculiar to the discussion of literacy. Even the attested increase in the number of books in existence from the late fifth century onwards does not, strictly speaking, indicate that more people could read books, unless one can infer a connection between literacy and the frequency of written record.[3] A further problem is not always recognized; as we shall see (Ch. 1.2 below), the presence of written records does not necessarily mean that they were read, even by 'literates'.[4] This cannot be overstressed, and that is why it is particularly necessary to re-examine the general character of literacy and its use. Again, the picture is far more complex. We must appreciate the extent of written records, how far they are used against oral methods, and whether they also had functions other than being read.

Beyond this there are further objections which are interrelated. First, beneath blanket conclusions about 'Athenians' in general, there is seldom much distinction between different sectors of Athens. Secondly, 'literacy' itself is scarcely defined, if at all, and there is almost no attempt to differentiate between varying levels and types of literacy. Related to this, 'literacy' is often felt to be self-explanatory, a 'skill' which needs no

---

[2] The most illuminating studies on ancient literacy are: F. D. Harvey (1966); Turner (1952); Woodbury (1976); and Cartledge (1978) for Sparta, who has a rather more sophisticated approach to literacy. Also Immerwahr (1964); Kenyon (1951); Flory (1980); Greene (1951); Burns (1981). Havelock's works on the oral nature of the Greek society are stimulating, drawing attention to oral aspects of Greek culture: see esp. (1982) and (1986). However, his general theories about 'oral culture' and 'oral mentality' can be questioned by recent research on literacy (see below, p. 24); for specific interpretations, see Ch. 1, n. 61 below. Other non-Greek studies, still primarily interested in the extent of literacy: Baines (1983); Harris (1983) on Romans; Beard (1985) has a more interesting approach; MacMullen (1982) is somewhat disappointing.

[3] Cf. Turner (1952) on increase of books; Kenyon (1951) and Flory (1980) both argue against a general reading public for 'published' books in fifth and early fourth centuries. We can only learn of illiterates (which could simply mean 'not knowing Greek') in Egypt because of the special terminology used on documents made up for illiterates: see Youtie (1971a) and (1971b).

[4] As Knox (1985), 5, takes it, arguing widespread literacy from the archaic period on; Turner (1952), 9f. (more cautiously).

further examination. Thirdly, it is hardly discussed at all what a certain level of literacy actually tells us about Athenian society. This apparently crude demand has rather important implications, both for the ancient attitude to written record and for our own interpretations of literacy levels. Finally, there is little appreciation that types and levels of literacy might have changed during the fifth and fourth centuries.

When we wish to know about 'Athenian literacy', which Athenians, then, are we talking about? We should surely expect different levels and, more important, different uses of literacy amongst the highly educated, the different property classes down to the landless thetes, the women, the farmers who remained mostly in the country, the merchants, slaves, metics and others. Their needs and opportunities for using the written word would differ immensely; so it is probable they possessed different kinds of literacy. Fifth-century farmers in remote demes would have much less contact with the written word than those living in or near the city itself. It has also been noticed – for example in the case of the illiterates on Egyptian papyri – that even when someone has been to school for a while, he soon forgets to read if he does not continue to do so after school.[5] One cannot say generally that 'the vast majority of Athenians were literate' and still preserve much meaning.[6] The particular Athenians meant may also depend on what the writer hopes to learn from the discussion: for instance, how far Athenian literature was disseminated amongst the demos.[7]

An immense range of abilities is often covered by the single term 'literacy': anything from the ability to write one's name or a name on an *ostrakon* or pottery sherd to that involved in reading a literary text on papyrus. It is curious, for example, that the political process of ostracism in Athens – where Athenians wrote out the name of the politician they wanted exiled – is so often quoted as a sign that everyone could read and write (and, it is implied, write more than a name).[8] Yet papyri from Egypt provide many examples of people who could only just write their own name or were 'slow writers' (that is, extremely uncertain ones) and clearly could do no more than that. One town clerk could only manage to seem 'literate' by repeatedly practising his signature.[9] Different degrees

---

[5] Youtie (1971b) on 'slow writers', esp. p. 252; also (1971a).

[6] F. D. Harvey (1966) has a careful discussion of different groups, but concludes very generally. Burns (1981) argues 'widespread Athenian literacy by the end of the sixth century' and attempts to show the effect of literacy on their thought processes – for which he uses the sophists, a tiny minority.

[7] Much depends on who is literate: see, for example, Oppenheim (1975) for the Near East.

[8] See F. D. Harvey's sensible discussion and bibliography cited there for the 'optimistic' interpretation of widespread literacy from this ((1966), 590f.).

[9] Youtie (1971b): he shows how thin a line there is, or could be, between the term 'slow writer' (*bradeōs graphōn*) and a complete illiterate. For the town clerk, pp. 239ff. and p. 260: his practice signatures have been found.

of literacy are demanded and encouraged by the running of a farm, active and energetic participation in the proposing of decrees, and reading philosophical or poetic texts.

Most discussions barely define the term, if at all. Often 'literacy' is defined in extremely vague terms; or it is left as self-explanatory until a case occurs which is obviously rather different and demands a category like 'semi-literacy' or 'minimal literacy'.[10] In fact, it is just as misleading to produce a single definition. For if we take one definition and then proceed to measure its extent for ancient Greece, we are still reducing an extremely complex and varied skill to a single characteristic, thereby almost defining away any variations.[11] The notion of 'functional literacy' used by Cartledge[12] is more useful since it introduces the idea of differing levels of literacy according to the needs of people's everyday activities.

But scholars are often interested in literacy primarily as a means of access to Greek literature.[13] So the literacy they envisage is of a high degree, and the level of literacy needed for trading, for instance, is irrelevant. This kind of conception of literacy and its uses has important implications. For if the question of literacy is reduced implicitly to the problem of whether Athenians read books much, then the whole subject is obscured by preconceptions about the level of Greek civilization. When a scholar insists on a rather 'lower' level of literacy,[14] he is thought to imply that Athenian society was less civilized or cultivated than we would like to suppose. Turner takes an Aristophanic joke about a book to be a 'Philistine' sneer.[15] Yet in a society which heard most of its literature, this cannot be so. Allusions like this can be plausibly explained by the fact that books were still rare enough in the late fifth century, though not unknown, to belong only to the type of 'bookish' people like Euripides.[16] Books may have been associated in particular

---

[10] E.g. Burns (1981) objects to Havelock's view of literacy as 'too demanding'. Goody and Watt (1968) used the term 'restricted literacy', but see below, p. 25, and Street (1984), 61ff., on the use of this term to define away any counter examples. Cf. Schofield (1968) on the use of one level of 'literacy' (in fact the ability to sign one's name) as a measurement.

[11] E.g. Burns (n. 10, above) takes a 'less demanding' definition in order to postulate widespread literacy by the end of the sixth century. But as the definition is widened, 'widespread literacy' means less and less.

[12] (1978), n. 11: used of the ephors to mean literate enough to perform their duties.

[13] Turner (1952) (mostly implicitly); F. D. Harvey (1966), 586 (who also includes people's participation in the democracy). Much, however, was seen and heard (e.g. tragedy) rather than read.

[14] As does Woodbury (1976), arguing that minimal literacy in the fifth century was recent.

[15] Turner (1952), 22f. citing Denniston ((1927), 117–19) on the comic use of 'book'.

[16] Denniston (1927), who also suggests that Aristophanes may be satirizing technical jargon here. One might compare modern jokes about computers. Bookish Euripides: *Frogs* 943, 1409.

with the education of the sophists.[17] But to see them purely as an indication of the level of culture and education – along with literacy – disguises much of interest in the gradual growth and acceptance of written records alongside the old oral methods in this period.

Behind these general conceptions are perhaps two main ideas. 'Literacy' is treated as a self-explanatory term which seems to demand little exact definition or differentiation and as a single skill which, once present, can and will be used for anything almost automatically. Both may have been encouraged or reinforced by the general theories of Goody and Watt and their followers on the consequences of literacy (see below, pp. 25f.) and by the overlapping idea that alphabetic writing is the 'graphic counterpart of speech'.[18] So we may fail to appreciate the very different levels and uses of literacy even in the same society and miss the gradual development in the use of writing. Writing in Greece was not simply the counterpart of speech: it was at various periods used sparingly for some purposes, not at all for others, and there was a slow development in its use and interaction with oral methods (see Ch. 1.2).

This brings us to a more rigorous examination of what exactly we learn from the statement (for instance) that 'most Athenians were literate'. I have already mentioned some of the implications of modern discussions. But the broader conclusions are mostly taken for granted.

Literacy is often connected to the Athenians' level of culture and civilization, as we saw. In the older works there are shades of the idea that the Athenians were rather like us in their use of literary texts. For instance, it was once thought that the notorious line from Aristophanes' comedy, *The Frogs*, about 'everyone having a book nowadays' (1114) meant that they each had the text of the play on their laps![19] This image of the literate and bookish Athenians in its exaggerated form grossly underestimates the extent to which Athenian life was conducted orally, even in its higher reaches. This is more readily recognized now. The Platonic dialogues show how even literary criticism and the detailed

---

[17] Suggested by Woodbury ((1976), 351f.) on *Frogs* 1109ff. Turner (1952), 22f. Hence, perhaps, why books could be regarded as dangerous in Ar. fr. 506 K.–A. (*Tagenistae*), cited by Denniston: τοῦτον τὸν ἄνδϱ᾽ ἢ βιβλίον διέφθοϱεν / ἢ Πϱόδικος ἢ τῶν ἀδολεσχῶν εἵς γέ τις. 'A book has ruined this man, or Prodikos has or at any rate one of the idle chatterers.' (*Adoleschēs*, 'idle talker', is used particularly of the sophists, Eupolis fr. 386 K.–A. (of Socrates); Plato, *Polit.* 299b.) Despite their oral methods of teaching, many sophists did publish written works (and cf. Plato, *Theaet.* 143a).

[18] An expression of Diringer, quoted by Cartledge (1978), 25. Cf. Goody and Watt (1968), 39: the alphabet made it possible to write easily and read unambiguously about anything the society could talk about.

[19] Woodbury explains it more plausibly: βιβλίον τ᾽ ἔχων ἕκαστος μανθάνει τὰ δεξία (1114) ('each one has a book and learns clever things') in the context is a way of assuring the dramatic contestants that, yes, the audience will be able to understand the contest, for 'everyone has a book nowadays, and reading gives him extra polish'. It is perhaps a hint at the new education (as n. 17, above).

discussion of a poem could be conducted entirely orally. Similarly, in the *Laws* (810e–811b), Plato talks of highly educated young Athenians who have learnt whole poems off by heart (this is his section on education). He equates those who have heard much (πολυηκόοι) with those who have learned much (πολυμαθεῖς).[20] To see this kind of evidence only from the one angle of whether it shows anything of reading skills is to miss the point. It reminds us forcibly that still in the late fifth and early fourth centuries a great deal of the literary activity, knowledge and discussion, even among the highly educated, was not necessarily based upon books and 'book learning', although books did exist.[21] A written text often seems to have been an aid to the memory rather than the primary object of study.[22]

If oral and written methods of transmission are combined even at the extreme end of the scale amongst the highly educated and literate, then the extent of literacy is not necessarily related to the level of literary knowledge. Evidence that only indicates 'oral' education and learning – which are generally recognized now – suggests that questions about literacy are couched in the wrong terms. What we should be considering is not so much how 'literate' Athenians were, but how they used literacy or written forms, and so the balance or mixture of oral and written methods. This can also be applied to the more prosaic spheres such as the administration of the democracy. Much of assembly business was conducted orally through speeches and announcements of proposals (see Ch. 1.2.3).[23] Yet, of course, there were also some written records, and some of the speeches were written down. There is no doubt that written record was involved here, but what is significant is the mixture of oral and written modes in many of these activities which we must attempt to grasp. Thus we can understand the combination of oral communication and written record without falling into the trap of declaring Athenians necessarily 'literate' or 'illiterate'. Important implications for the use of written record follow (Ch. 1.2).

Another idea which is sometimes in the background of more recent

---

[20] 'By recitations, making them into great listeners and great learners, who know whole poets by heart.'

[21] Cf. Turner (1952) and below, pp. 22f., on gradual increase of books; also Knox (1985) and Hutchinson (1984), 100, on the reading of poetry from books in the Hellenistic and Roman periods. Kenyon (1951) collects references to consulting books. Havelock recognized the oral elements, but in wildly exaggerated argument.

[22] Immerwahr (1964): in the vase paintings books seem to have a mainly mnemonic role supplementing oral recitation. Writing as a cure for forgetting: Aesch. *Prometh.* 460, 788; *Eumen.* 273; Eurip. fr. 572N (*Palamedes*); cf. Simonides fr. 581 *PMG*. Cf. also Greene (1951) and Woodbury (1976) who points out that any accumulation of books in the late fifth century was confined to intellectuals like Euripides.

[23] Whereas one might expect now that every member of the audience should be issued with a written text to dwell on.

attention to Athenian literacy concerns the theories of Goody and Watt again. Here I refer to their suggestions about the importance of literacy for the rational thought of the Greeks, rather than their general conception of literacy.[24] They claimed that literacy was responsible for the development of rational thought, historiography, the growth of individuality, and democracy. The coming of writing was thus largely responsible for many of the most important features of archaic Greece. 'Literacy' turns out to be what they take to be the 'full alphabetic literacy' of Greece, and this important distinction is stressed to explain why literacy did not have the same effects elsewhere.[25] Though stimulating and very influential, this theory of literacy cannot be accepted as the single and most important factor in the development of archaic Greece, though it may have been an 'enabling factor' in some areas.[26] One may point out, for instance, that the alphabetic system took three centuries to have its 'inevitable' effect in the field of philosophical argument. Cartledge has shown[27] that Sparta's slight use of alphabetic writing does not support the 'technological determinism' that Goody and Watt implied. In fact, one may further insist that the theory is disproved for the Spartan case and questioned for Athens. Recent work on literacy and its effects (which I shall discuss, see pp. 24ff. below) also presents a very much more complex picture, and it transforms our image of literacy. Again we return to the fact that it is not literacy itself which is enlightening, but the way it is used.

Finally, there is the question of change and development. Brought up surprisingly seldom, this has important implications for our whole conception of literacy. Those writers mainly concerned with literacy itself deal with the fifth and fourth centuries together without wondering if the picture might have altered during that time.[28] Yet it is accepted that the use and quantity of books changed considerably over that period.[29] That can even be argued alongside a belief in widespread literacy in the fifth century. Turner's extremely interesting lecture on Athenian books illustrates this well, and I take it as an example only because it gives a very clear idea of the problem.

[24] Also Burns (1981), but he barely goes any further.
[25] Goody (1986) and (1987), which appeared as this book was going to press, has now extended the theory with modifications to other types of writing. See further discussion below, pp. 24ff. and n. 36.
[26] As Murray (1980), 95ff., and (1987).   [27] (1978), 37.
[28] E.g. F. D. Harvey (1966), Burns (1981): perhaps partly because the classical period and the democracy are often seen as a whole, and literacy is linked unthinkingly to both as the high point of Greek civilization. Pfeiffer's picture (1968) of a continuous progress of literacy throughout the fifth century is more plausible.
[29] Turner (1952); Immerwahr (1964) on changes in vase scenes, though from a small selection; Kenyon ((1951), ch. 1): books and the habit of reading were becoming more common at the end of the fifth and early fourth centuries, but not normal till Aristotle.

Turner is looking specifically at books and is not directly concerned with literacy. But he dismisses very briefly the question of literacy in the fifth century, the anecdotes about illiterates and other arguments, and he declares that 'the ordinary Athenian is a literate person' and that there was 'widespread literacy'.[30] Yet, he then discusses 'how books came into common use at Athens'. Attacking Wilamowitz, he shows how rare books were, how 'publication' was achieved through a very few copies and public readings, and how it was only by the first quarter of the fourth century that books were common. That is, there were not many in the fifth century. He also has interesting remarks on people's awareness of writing. So, on the one hand, he charts convincingly the development in occurrence and familiarity of books; on the other, he insists on the blanket statement that Athenians were generally 'literate'. There is a certain confusion about literacy and its significance here, surely encouraged by the modern standpoint of highly sophisticated literacy.

Similarly, the traditional point for remarks on the importance of literacy and perhaps its 'consequences' is that period in early Greek history at which the coming of the alphabet is discussed.[31] This is a significant misplacing – the question of literacy is, as it were, only a matter for historians of archaic Greece – and it cannot but disguise the fact that the use of writing was hardly realized for many areas till the fifth or fourth centuries. Change is recognized for the world of books, but little for other types of record or for the extent of literacy itself. Yet it is probable that the extent of literacy and the depths of literate skills might be connected to the amount of writing available; indeed that the greater availability of written documents was an incentive to learn to read.[32]

I would therefore suggest that we must expect to find a gradual development both in the extent and in the use of 'literacy' of any degree. We must also expect to see changing attitudes to literacy and books during the fifth and fourth centuries. By focusing on the simplistic question of how 'literate' Athenians were, most modern discussion has seen the evidence from only one angle.[33] But as with the remark in the *Frogs* about books, it is precisely the development and change in the use of literacy that produces the ambivalent allusions to writing. Aristophanes was referring jokingly to increasing familiarity with books. The

---

[30] Turner (1952) 9f. I discuss below, p. 61, the assumption that the very presence of documents means that everyone could and did read them.

[31] Murray (1980), 95ff.; Snodgrass (1980), 78ff.

[32] Cf. Clanchy's (1979) plausible theory for the Middle Ages that people did not really begin to learn to read and write until the volume of documents and the need to understand them encouraged them to do so. There, literacy was associated particularly with Latin and the clergy, but the psychology is plausible.

[33] Cartledge (1978) is more sophisticated, attempting to relate the level of literacy to the needs for it.

evidence is frustrating not simply because it is scanty, but also because much of it, particularly that of the late fifth and early fourth centuries seems to suggest that written record was becoming more common and was used for more purposes. Hence the curious allusions to the new phenomenon. Changing attitudes are involved, as well as changes in the frequency of the written word. Recent studies of literacy in the modern world help to interpret this picture.

In the last few years suggestions have been made about the use and 'effect' of literacy which differ radically from the views presented by Goody and Watt and by others who postulate certain fundamental characteristics for oral and literate societies. Ruth Finnegan in particular has shown in her study of oral poetry how the schematized characteristics of 'oral poetry' which are supposed to set it apart from literate poetry are often either absent from oral poetry or are not confined to it alone. She makes a strong case for blurring the sharp distinctions often made between 'oral' and 'literate'.[34] More recently (1981) she has argued against the 'technological determinism' implied by Goody and Watt which lies behind much discussion of the effects of literacy against the characteristics of 'orality'. She stresses how frequently one finds a combination of oral and written means of communication side by side: this questions the existence of a great divide between oral societies and literate ones. She also suggests that one should concentrate on the uses of literacy rather than the technology alone. If we examine the different uses made of writing, its 'consequences' are clearly not the result of the mere adoption of writing, as if writing were simply a neutral skill or technology.

In a different field, the medievalist M. T. Clanchy has done an extremely interesting study on the gradual adoption in medieval England of an administrative system based on written record rather than primarily oral means (*From Memory to Written Record*, 1979). He discusses in depth the previous oral methods and mentality, their influence on the way writing was adopted and the frequent mixture of both. He shows the gradual formation of an attitude or mentality that was more 'document minded' (see below, p. 36). Thus he illustrates in practice many of the features of literacy that Finnegan and Street argue on a more theoretical level.

A similar approach to that of Finnegan, elaborated and extended, is argued by Brian Street, in his *Literacy in Theory and Practice* (1984). He gathers together and discusses studies that concern literacy, examining in particular the ideas or assumptions about literacy that lie behind, even if not supported by explicit theorizing. He thus roughly divides them up

---

[34] (1977), esp. ch. 2.

into two groups which he calls the 'autonomous model' and the 'ideological model': this useful distinction clarifies a great quantity of muddled ideas about literacy. The autonomous model comprises views which involve the technological determinism Finnegan mentions: literacy is regarded, whether implicitly or not, as encouraging by its very nature the qualities of rationality, logic, and individuality. Its 'effects' are independent of a society's character and customs that exist already (i.e. autonomous). It is a neutral skill, as it were, which by its mere introduction may have predictable uses and effects.[35] Studies which see the use and effects of writing as influenced by the customs and beliefs of the society come under the 'ideological' model: the adoption of writing is partly affected by 'ideology'. Street argues strongly for this latter mode, and he supports it by his own fieldwork in Iran.

Goody's theories have been particularly influential in the exposition of the autonomous model – though he has now slightly modified his views.[36] Street painstakingly dissects his argument in 'The Consequences of Literacy'. We see how Goody is forced to confine his theory to the 'full' alphabetic literacy of ancient Greece, for the rational and logical mentality he sees in Greece as the result of literacy does not appear so clearly in other societies which are 'literate' or were 'literate' long before Greece. These others therefore have 'restricted literacy'. One might add that on this argument large areas and sectors of the Greeks should also come under this same category of 'restricted literacy'.[37] Moreover, as Street points out, Goody himself exaggerated his case, using phrases which do suggest determinism (one need only think of the paper's title), even though he warns us against taking literacy as the one significant cause. His followers have taken it as an absolute cause.

I have already briefly discussed the theory in relation to archaic Greece: as soon as one looks closely at it, it breaks down. Yet, along with the whole 'autonomous model', it can perpetuate a conception of literacy which surreptitiously influences – or even confirms – our own preconceptions about writing. I am thinking particularly of the idea that once writing is known it will be used for anything; or that its advantages will be seen immediately and that it will quickly supersede oral methods. Several

---

[35] I.e. Goody's 'technology of the intellect'.

[36] Modified slightly in (1977) towards seeing the effects of literacy more within the context of the society. In his recent study (1986) he examines much more closely the use of writing in the ancient Near East, which was merely a foil to ancient Greece in 'The Consequences of Literacy'. But as the title shows, he still stresses inherent characteristics and effects of writing rather than the question of why different societies use writing so differently. Further modifications and refinement of arguments in (1987), esp. chs. 9 and 10.

[37] As Street comments ((1984), 63), it looks as if only Aristotle actually fits the theory! See esp. pp. 50f. on Goody's argumentation.

studies correct this, including Clanchy's (which Street puts under the ideological model). They deal with periods or societies which provide a great deal more direct evidence than we have for ancient Greece. Thus interpretations can be more subtle. They suggest that there is a far more complex relation between literacy and its 'effects' and the character of the society in question. The written word is used, adapted or ignored partly according to the society's customs and beliefs that exist already: alphabetic literacy is not a neutral skill which transforms a society adopting it and which by its very nature induces a more rational mentality. The effect of literacy is related directly to the customs and attitudes of that society.

Some examples will clarify this and show its strength. For instance, some studies of modern literacy seem to show that the learning of literacy is associated with the ability to argue logically and to categorize – that is, rational thought is produced by literacy.[38] These surveys seem impressive. Yet on closer examination it is clear that the rationality is not caused by literacy alone but by the whole system of education at school and, even earlier, at home. So such children are 'rational' not simply because they are literate but because they have been educated in a certain way.[39] It is probably, in fact, impossible to find a case where the effect of literacy by itself can be studied without being disturbed by many other factors. Literacy cannot be isolated like that, and particularly not from education.

Even different sectors of the same society or country may have different reactions to the written word, different beliefs about it: literacy can thus be said to produce differing 'effects' and different mentality. One American study[40] has looked at 'mainstream' children and children from a black, Christian, working-class area. Each group learned different ways of using and approaching the written word. In the working class area, for instance, literacy was used strictly for instruction and moral precept, and it was associated only with stories of real events. The middle-class children, however, were used from early on to associate books, and therefore the written word, with fiction. So, one might add, was Edmund Gosse, son of two Plymouth brethren, who describes in *Father and Son* his horrified discovery of fiction. Such a difference in approach is clearly connected here to cultural values, beliefs and institutions: 'literacy' does not have an automatic connection with 'truth'.

Brian Street himself has done much work on literacy in Iran. In one large mountain village he examined the varying forms literacy takes. The

---

[38] One of the best known is the Russian psychologist Luria: see Ong (1982).
[39] Street (1984), ch. 1, and Cole and Scribner (1981).
[40] S. B. Heath (1982) and (1983) for which see Street (1984), 121ff.

literacy taught in the Koranic schools (maktab), associated with religious texts, in fact introduces characteristics usually connected with literacy by the 'autonomous model'. Perhaps particularly intriguing are the 'hidden skills' which pupils learn through this 'maktab literacy': the understanding of the complicated conventions of layout and lettering for the religious texts and their commentaries. It teaches certain skills and encourages certain attitudes to the written word, and it is intimately linked to the culture and beliefs of their society.[41] However, another type of literacy developed there in the economic expansion of the 1970s when there were openings for commercial enterprise. This 'commercial literacy' involves use of the written word specifically for commercial purposes, the signing of cheques or labelling of boxes.[42] This is 'literacy', too, but a different type from that associated with the Koranic texts. Yet the adoption of commercial literacy seems to have been easier because the religious maktab schools and maktab literacy had already introduced some familiarity with writing. Some of the skills so encouraged could be adapted well to commercial needs. In fact, maktab literacy had taught some to read but not write, but even that could be adapted.[43] Street explains the village's success in commercial enterprise and their adaptation of commercial literacy partly by the presence of the religious type of literacy. In some other areas, the modern education introduced by the government had had little effect. But in the mountain village, both the use and the effect of literacy were closely related to the 'ideology' of the village, the character of the existing maktab literacy and, in fact, the very structure of the village itself.

One may compare some modern literacy campaigns. Some have been conducted under the mistaken assumption that literacy is a neutral and autonomous skill which would automatically improve someone's lot in life. But the teaching of Western literacy with little relevance to the life and needs of the people being taught has sometimes had little effect. It was forgotten very fast, and the teachers had to set up what they called 'literacy environments' to keep this kind of literacy going.[44]

Clanchy's study of medieval England presents a comparable picture of literacy and the uses of written record. I will have occasion to refer extensively to his more detailed discussions of the medieval use of documents in Ch. 1.2. For the moment it is interesting to note that in medieval England, too, the use and later extension of literacy clearly depended largely on the customs and beliefs already there. For instance, there already existed a tradition of scribal activity at the time of the Norman conquest. This was mostly for religious purposes; much secular

[41] Street (1984), sect. 2; p. 153 on maktab literacy.   [42] Street (1984), ch. 6.
[43] Street (1984), esp. pp. 172, 175.
[44] Street (1984), ch. 7; 'literacy environment' in Tanzania, p. 194.

business was conducted orally where we might expect the use of writing. When the Norman rule introduced an administrative system which relied more upon written record, the new uses of literacy were still heavily influenced by the old, primarily religious uses of literacy. The Domesday Book, for example, was decorated, and indeed almost treated, like the Bible, which was most people's idea of a book. But the familiarity with the written word in other contexts already actually eased the transition to an administration which made greater use of writing and to a gradual acceptance of the written word for other forms of communication and validation.[45] The change was very slow, and oral and written methods subsisted alongside each other for a considerable time. Here too, literacy, its uses, its adaptation and people's attitudes to it were related to their beliefs and their previous uses of it.

These detailed studies show what varied forms literacy may take. They suggest that one cannot automatically attribute certain characteristics or effects to literacy. Its uses may vary a great deal within the same society, and they vary according to the beliefs, attitudes and actual organization of that society. Adaptations in the use of literacy are partly influenced by previous familiarity with writing. Literacy cannot be isolated completely as a separate skill. Nor do the literate practices in a given society necessarily conform to our idea of how literacy is 'naturally' used.

This brings us to a further crucial point concerning the mixture of literate and oral modes. Above (pp. 23ff.) I was mainly discussing the use of written methods. What of the oral ones? Just as the use of literacy is influenced by cultural values, it is also influenced by previous oral communication.

It is clear that when literacy is introduced or its use extended, the oral methods may influence the adoption of literacy and may even continue to exist alongside the written record. Clanchy shows how gradually oral methods of proof or validation gave way to writing in medieval England. Often they continued together: an object like a sword, for instance, was an older way of proving rights to land – the object was the symbol or memorial. When written record came to be required as proof it was still accompanied by the oral memorial in many cases.[46] Some examples illustrate particularly well how the two methods were combined: a knife might have writing on it and an additional label attached. It thus preserved both the material object as memory of the conveyance and a parallel written record which was still not regarded as enough on its own. Clanchy also suggests that the seals on charters may have been regarded as symbolic objects of memory which were (also) inscribed.[47] Written

[45] The whole picture is further complicated by the use of Latin for writing on the Continent. England was unusual in having a tradition of writing in the vernacular as well.
[46] Clanchy (1979), 202ff.   [47] Clanchy (1979), 20f.

record was used within an oral framework. The oral methods did not at once become obsolete and forgotten.

Similarly in ancient Greece, we see exactly the same combination of written and oral modes in the cases where a merchant uses both a written contract (*syngraphē*) and witnesses.[48] This does not show that the merchants were more, or less, literate.[49] The point is, rather, that there is a combination of both modes of validation. The *syngraphē* has begun to be used, but it is still used in an oral context, parallel to the use of witnesses. The witnesses, the oral method, are still trusted, perhaps trusted more than writing, while written record had only just acquired legal status (see Ch. 1.2 further). This case is expressive of the slow, gradual process by which the use of writing was extended to new contexts and partly adapted according to the older oral usages.

Behind both types of example lie attitudes to writing which influence its use. Simple distrust of the new medium is very important. Clanchy gives interesting examples in which men of the Middle Ages voice their distrust of the new extended use of writing. In some respects they were right. Against the oral methods involving witnesses or symbolic objects, writing was not necessarily the superior proof we might expect. Certainly it was not always regarded as such. Forgery was easy in a period where neither document layout nor scribal writing were uniform, and cursive signatures were not used. We must remind ourselves that oral methods of validation could be, or could be regarded, as perfectly efficient. The use of writing as the 'superior' method was by no means obvious – though neither should we be so naive as to think that oral methods were foolproof.[50] The same is true for classical Athens (Ch. 1.2).

In fact, the mixture of oral and written methods so well illustrated for the Middle Ages may be very much more common than is usually recognized. As Ruth Finnegan has argued, it is indeed very difficult to find a purely oral society now; most have a mixture of both literate and oral practices. If one challenges the basic division between pure oral or literate types of society, a mixture begins to appear as fairly normal.[51] One can then examine the combination and interaction of the two modes without omitting one aspect of it or defining it away. Such a 'mixture'

---

48 [Dem.] xxxv 10–14; other references: F. D. Harvey (1966), 610.
49 See F. D. Harvey (1966), 608ff. and bibliography: he argues against Hasebroek's view that merchants were illiterate because they used witnesses and few documents.
50 Cf. Street (1984), 116–18, though he is extreme in his approval of the oral methods themselves. Clearly personal witnesses are valuable for a recent case (though they, too, can be bribed), but for an event beyond living memory it is not enough to trust 'collective history' to preserve knowledge, when oral tradition can change so fast. Moreover, 'collective history' would not preserve the deeds of many private individuals.
51 Finnegan (1981) and (1977) for the 'oral' character of oral poetry; cf. Alexiou (1984/5) for related problems in the study of 'folklore' (for modern Greece).

clearly existed in classical Greece beyond the occurrence of poetic oral performances. If we recognize that a mixture of oral and literate modes is a frequent and understandable occurrence – and an acceptable term – we can better understand the combination of oral and written processes without misinterpreting the evidence from too literate a standpoint. We can also appreciate better the uses of written record – particularly some aspects which otherwise seem inexplicable – and the continuation of certain oral practices long after written record had become widely used in many other areas.

Let us return to ancient Greece. Three crucial points will now be clear: the use of literacy and written record is not obvious or predictable, and therefore it is not enough to observe the presence of literacy without considering its uses; its use is linked closely with the customs and beliefs of the society; and there is a complex mixture of both oral and written processes which persists long after the initial introduction of writing. In Ch. 1.2 I shall look closely at the particular case of the Athenian use of documents, archives and documentation – the gradual process by which Athens became more 'document-minded'. Here we may make some brief and preliminary observations of Greek literacy and the written word on a more general level.

While we cannot simply discuss the extent of literacy, we can see the levels and types of literacy in relation to people's needs for written record, their previous familiarity with it and their deeper attitudes to writing. Here are some suggestions. Sparta had little use for written record, and accordingly the level of 'literacy' there seems, on any estimate, to have been fairly low.[52] There was little familiarity with the written word. Presumably the Mycenaean Linear B script was forgotten without regret precisely because once the palace administration it was used for had disappeared, there was little further need for it.

In the case of Athens, one may suppose that more and more Athenians learnt to read and write or became more fluent once the democracy was established and the public documents that went with it became increasingly numerous. It is often suggested that 'most Athenians were literate' because of the democracy, but precise causation and period are left vague;[53] Goody suggested that widespread literacy actually caused democracy. However, it may have been the other way round, as the examples above suggest. The vast increase in public documentation under the radical democracy from the 460s probably had considerable effect (rather than being caused by widespread literacy), and there was greater need for active citizen participation. So, by the second half of the

---

[52] Cartledge (1978) finally suggests that it was because Spartan society did not develop 'the social arts which depended on popular literacy'.

[53] E.g. F. D. Harvey, (1966), 598ff.

fifth century, most Athenian citizens who lived near the city could probably read or write in an elementary fashion – like Aristophanes' sausage seller who 'could read, but not very well'. But this elementary literacy could have varying uses. The democracy's use of documents must have affected most Athenians' idea of the written word. Books were still very rare in the mid-fifth century. Thus, apart from the highly educated, most Athenians' contact with writing – as opposed to the products of writing like poetry – was through private and public inscriptions, 'memoranda' or casual graffiti (i.e. non-inscribed writing).[54] Literacy must have been mainly pragmatic. One may speculate on the attitudes to the written word and its uses that these formal inscriptions and laconic graffiti might have fostered. Certainly they are hardly the 'graphic counterpart of speech'.[55]

One should also notice how closely writing must have been associated with the temples, particularly in the archaic period. Some of our earliest public inscriptions are sacred laws, and many other inscriptions of public interest, like treaties, were displayed in the precincts of temples. Whatever the precise significance of this connection, it seems plausible to suppose that written record would be most familiar in early Greece from its presence in the temples (and where there would be dedications, too). It is therefore intriguing that one of the earliest known prose works, that of Heraclitus, was said to have been deposited by him in a temple – like a set of laws or an inscription of public importance. The previous associations of the written word set this in a rather different light. One may also notice that when Athens set up its first central archive in the Metroön, the Metroön itself was in part a shrine (Ch. 1.2.1).

If we consider other attitudes to written record and their effect on the way writing is used, certain examples immediately spring to mind. Sparta provides an extreme one. Athenians thought all Spartans were illiterate.[56] This was not actually true, and the Spartans probably learned as much as they needed.[57] However, Sparta's legendary founder Lycurgus was said to have forbidden the writing down of laws, regarding education as a better compulsion than law. Whatever the historical status of this story, it certainly reflects an attitude to written record in

---

[54] Schools are often cited in this context – the earliest around 500 – but there is no indication that they were for everyone, and there was no democratic theory of education at Athens. Aristotle (*Pol.* VIII, 1338a) regarded writing as useful for money-making, the acquisition of knowledge, political life.

[55] Cf. Aly (1929) on early Greek prose style. A familiarity with inscriptions perhaps explains why vase paintings often show the grid-pattern *stoichedon* style on the book rolls they illustrate (Immerwahr (1964) therefore suggested that early books were written in *stoichedon*).

[56] Isoc. *Panath.* 209; *Dissoi Logoi* 90 F2 10 DK.

[57] Cartledge (1978) and (1976), and Plut. *Lyc.* 16.10; *Mor.* 237a.

Sparta that must be connected with the extraordinary dearth of written documents.[58] There was also a strict prohibition of named tombstones (Plut. *Lyc.* 27.3), which exempted men who had died in war.[59] One need hardly stress here how Spartan attitudes to written record determine what is recorded and, in the tombstone rule, reinforce their general ideals.

Cartledge, in fact, suggests that the rule about named tombstones seems to endow the written word with a 'quasi-magical potency'. However, if that is true, it can hardly be confined to Sparta, though we are perhaps more ready to accept it of Spartans than of Athenians. Under the Athenian democracy there was a convention that public commemorative inscriptions did not name the generals – thus reinforcing the communal achievement (Ch. 4.1). And it is remarkable how many of the earliest graffiti consist mainly of proper nouns, either claiming an object as someone's property or cursing someone else.

In contrast to Sparta, however, it was believed in Athens that written laws were a mark of democracy, as is well known (e.g. Eurip. *Suppl.* 433–7). But it is equally true that 'unwritten laws' were the fundamental laws of the gods, and this suggests rather ambivalent ideas about written law.[60]

Other remarks about writing can be interpreted convincingly in the context of an increasing use of the written word. I have mentioned Aristophanes' jokes about books that suggest both that books are familiar to the audience and that they could still be regarded as a joke. Presumably they were becoming more common, yet were still associated with unusual and 'bookish' people. More intriguing is the possibility broached by Woodbury and others (n. 17 above) that books were especially connected with certain of the sophists. If this were so, it would then be the particular influence of the sophistic movement which was increasing familiarity with the written word in the form of books.

Plato distrusted the written word as a means of true education.[61] He presents his reasons at length in the *Phaedrus* (274b–279b): writing is but a reminder, it cannot defend itself (275c–276a). The written word is merely an image of knowledge, and it should only be the recreation of old

---

[58] Plut. *Lyc.* 13.1ff.; cf. *Mor.* 227b and *Mor.* 221b, Spartan laws on bravery were unwritten. See Cartledge (1976), 33ff., and now Gagarin (1986), 56–8.

[59] Perhaps also priestesses who died in office, but see Cartledge's note 71 (1976) for the possible alternative, women in childbirth.

[60] Cf. Arist. *Pol.* III, 1287b; 'Customary laws (οἱ κατὰ τὰ ἔθη) have more weight and relate to more important matters, than written laws, and a man may be a safer ruler than the written law, but not safer than the customary law.'

[61] Thus it is puzzling that Havelock (1963) argues that while the Presocratics were poets of an oral culture, Plato championed the written word. He is misled by an extreme and schematized view of Athens as an oral culture (cf. the excellent review by Solmsen (1966)).

age, used as a memorial (276a–d). He says much on the disadvantages and inadequacies of writing and declares again (278a) that even the best of writings are only a memorandum for those who know; the wise man does not rely on writing. Here, then, we have a coherent exposition of the disadvantages of writing as a mere image of the truth. We must surely see this, too, as a belief perhaps formed and held against the increasing use of writing for educative purposes and as a substitute for the skills of discourse and discussion.[62]

Nor was Plato alone in this feeling, and it is interesting after Goody's suggestions to see the propounders of philosophical thought attacking the use of writing. Oenopides, the mathematician, rebuked a young man who had a great many books, saying μὴ τῷ κιβωτῷ, ἀλλὰ τῷ στήθει ('not in a bookshelf, but in the heart') (Diels – Krantz 41 fr. 4). Antisthenes also expressed the view that knowledge should be in the soul, not on paper, when a friend complained he had lost his notes (*hypomnēmata*).[63] Such an attitude may indeed have been encouraged in reaction to certain sophists.[64] But even so, it cannot be seen merely as a narrow philosophical wrangle. In the wider context of an increase in the amount of written record and a development in its use, it also expresses a reflection on writing itself. If the sophists were partly responsible for the greater quantity of books and increased use of writing, then the attitudes and reactions to them include reactions to the use of writing and may have had some effect on it. We are reminded of the resistance to written record in medieval England, though in different circumstances. The extension of written record and literacy is much affected by attitudes to it, and it is crucial to recognize that a body of highly educated philosophical thinkers opposed extension of its use.

So, if we re-examine the nature of 'literacy' itself, instead of taking it for granted and measuring its presence and effects, it appears to have a very complex relationship to the society in which it is found. Its uses, advantages and 'effects' are closely related to, or determined by, the cultural values, beliefs and customs already there – including previous oral methods of communication. It is misleading to talk of 'literate society' and 'oral society' as if each were an easily defined and recogniz-

---

62 Compare also the prejudice, shared by Plato (*Phaedr.* 277b–278b) against the writing of speeches, as opposed to their composition and delivery without writing: Hudson-Williams (1951). For writing as a mnemonic aid, which even Plato admits as useful (*Crit.* and *Tim.*), Flory (1980) points out the interesting parallel with a musical score.

63 D.L. VI 5: 'You should have inscribed them on your mind (*psychē*) and not on paper (*tois chartiois*).'

64 As Turner suggests, (1952), 23; also Xen. *Mem.* IV 2.8–10. Several philosophers right into the Hellenistic period published nothing: e.g. Zeno of Citium and Carneades – like Socrates. In fact books may not have been that common even then, as Sandbach (1985, 3) suggests.

able type with predictable 'oral' or 'literate' characteristics. In the case of ancient Greece itself we should be careful to avoid equally the idea of an extreme 'oral society', cosy and traditional, and the presumption of highly sophisticated uses of literacy such as we now take for granted.

That is not to say that writing does not have certain advantages – advantages that perhaps enabled Goody to connect literacy with the development of rational thought. It is important not to go to the other extreme and imply that the written word offers no advantage at all against oral communication.[65] Plato points out its mnemonic value, and one must insist that a written text does enable the complex ideas of individuals to be preserved far more easily than oral tradition could. It also enables successors – as well as distant contemporaries – to examine, criticize and build upon someone's work more easily, as did the Presocratic philosophers. The Greek tradition of philosophical speculation could be refined and passed down in a manner that oral transmission surely could not have achieved. Laws and documents fixed in writing could be referred to more easily (though see Ch. 1.2) and were less liable to the fluidity of memory and oral transmission with which much of the rest of this book will be concerned. Moreover, unlike the spoken word, the written word can be preserved accidentally. But these characteristics of writing are potential only. The use made of them depends enormously on the society. The mere presence of writing is not enough to prompt its widespread use. Moreover, written and oral methods of communication or validation may exist side by side for a considerable time after the influx of writing. The old oral methods are not abandoned immediately, if indeed at all. The increase of books in late fifth-century Athens actually aroused opposition and criticism.

1.2 Written documents and archives

Vast numbers of inscriptions have survived from fifth- and fourth-century Athens. They record on stone anything from the laws and decrees of the democratic assembly to honours granted to individuals or dedications to the gods. An invaluable source, they are, apart from papyri, the main 'documents' for the ancient historian. Sometimes they refer to the archives, archive copies and, in short, to the documents not preserved for us on stone. In this area it is particularly easy to assume

---

[65] As Street (1984), 116ff. As he points out (p. 99), the fixed text can actually encourage a great deal of interpretation and therefore malleability: a text written down does not necessarily have a meaning that is forever fixed, as Goody and Watt argued (and Goody (1986) modified). However, an oral tradition of parallel character would probably be even more malleable and have no check at all. Goody (1986) and (1987) has further suggestions on the advantages and potential of writing.

that we are dealing with the kind of written document familiar to us in the modern world – and that our intuitions about written records, literacy and the very use of writing are applicable. Surely written documents and archives belong to a highly 'literate' context?[66]

Yet, against our modern ways of thinking about written documents, there are puzzling or inexplicable features in the classical use of documents. These can only be understood against the background of oral communication and with the recognition that the uses of writing are not obvious and predictable but influenced both by attitudes to it and by non-written features. The relation between inscriptions and archive documents, for instance, is curious. There are occasions when an Athenian orator relies on oral transmission and his audience's memory where we might expect a reference to written record. It is not clear that Athenians actually read inscriptions much. Many of these characteristics have been noticed separately. But they are often explained elaborately from a modern standpoint well acquainted with a sophisticated use of the written word; the oral nature of many aspects of Greek society and its methods of conducting business is neglected. There are important oral or unwritten elements in the classical methods of proof or of disseminating information even where a written version did exist: this must alter our interpretation of the role of written documents and perhaps indeed of their content. An extreme example is the continuing use of witnesses during the fourth century for the validation of contracts even when written contracts had begun to be used (see Ch. 1.2.1 below). The importance of witnesses as an oral method of proof and validation in a society which was not entirely dependent upon the written word would seem to be quite understandable.[67] Written proof was not as 'natural' as we might think, and witnesses remain in use. Athenian preference for witnesses has been elaborately explained, for instance, by a liking for publicity connected with the ideals of the polis.[68] Yet if we see the development of the written contracts from the other way round, as an addition to the oral methods of validation which were already accepted, then the way in which documents are incorporated into the system becomes understandable. Written record only gradually becomes acceptable as proof.

One must first recognize that there is a mixture of oral and written elements in classical Athens and that in some areas written means of

---

[66] Our distinction of 'documents' from other types of writing was not often made: orators talk of *ta grammata* (simply 'letters' or 'writing') (below, Chs. 1.2.3 and 1.2.4), referring to the archives, and *biblion* could refer to a document as well as a book (Flory (1980), 20). Hence technical translations (e.g. 'archives') are misleading.

[67] Cf. Humphreys (1985a), and above, Ch. 1.1.

[68] Pringsheim (1950), 43; cf. Finley (1952), 22 and n. 62, with further elaborate explanations: but he does not realize the possibilities of proof without writing.

validation or communication are either replacing the oral means or supplementing them. But written documents, even when they do begin to be used, are often still duplicated by oral communication, oral proof or non-written symbol. Thus we should expect that Athenians only gradually become prepared to use written documents extensively rather than oral communication and indeed to trust written documents at all. (Clanchy's expression 'document-minded' aptly denoted this attitude, avoiding the misleading connotations of the words 'literate' or 'literate mentality'.) If documents are only just becoming familiar, then they may not be used in the manner we consider obvious. One can discern attitudes to written documents which invest writing with more significance than their written content alone would imply. Or we may find that certain documents are inadequate on their own without the accompaniment of oral elements, their written content unsophisticated or minimal. There is a grey area between the implied extremes of 'oral' and 'written' procedures where documents do exist but their presentation and use is coloured (or accompanied) by oral elements or other elements which we do not associate with written documents. Moreover, the mere existence of documents does not necessarily imply reference to documents after they are made, their preservation and future use. Here, too, the classical use of written records is comparatively undeveloped.

We may start by looking at certain areas where it is clear and widely accepted that changes are taking place in the use and storage of written documents against the previous oral methods (Ch. 1.2.1): these show a gradual change in attitude to the written word in the first half of the fourth century. Then, some examples are examined where written documents seem to be treated in ways which we would take to be more characteristic of non-written methods of communication or attitudes (Ch. 1.2.2) and the use of written documents for reference, their oral propagation and their preservation in archives (Ch. 1.2.3). Finally (Ch. 1.2.4), we turn to the growing use by the orators of written documents in their arguments and in particular their use of 'historical decrees'. In much of this section, I refer to diverse types of written documents and examples to build up a general picture of the use of written record: inevitably it cannot be complete, and I have concentrated on areas which are most illuminating for the overall picture.

The work of Clanchy has already been mentioned to illuminate the mixture of oral and written procedures. He goes on to trace in detail the slow development in the medieval use and organization of written documents. It takes more than a century in medieval England for people to become really 'document-minded', even though written record was already familiar from religious works, and there was a scribal tradition in England of writing in the vernacular. Many of Clanchy's points about the use of documents or archives reinforce or confirm some of our impressions from the classical evidence. In particular, they may correct modern assumptions about documents that are encouraged by our own extreme familiarity with the written word.

For instance, Clanchy shows that in the Middle Ages the collecting of documents into archives was clearly a very gradual one. Early 'archives' were not archives in our sense at all, but often miscellaneous collections of pieces of writing and material objects, and they might not even be gathered into one place. Documents and books were at first kept wherever they were useful. It took some time for the idea to grow up that written documents could all be kept together or the idea of an archive as a place where documents were collected and organized so that they could be and were consulted again later (complete centralization was never, of course, achieved). Still slower was anything approaching an 'archive mentality'. By this (for want of a better expression) I mean the assumptions we now take for granted about archives and archive keeping: that any documents not completely ephemeral should be kept – anything of practical value and anything that could conceivably be of interest to later researchers. For us archives are storehouses of the past.

Early medieval collections of documents were also a curiously assorted bunch. The non-written types of records, like knives, would be mixed up with the 'proper' documents on parchment. A collection of documents need not be one of uniform 'papers'. In fact, we must be especially careful, with our uniform habits of writing, not to assume a standard material for documents – like papyrus – especially where we no longer have the originals.

Moreover, there is an immense difference between making documents, keeping them as records, and referring to them later. As Clanchy said of the medieval use of documents; 'Making documents for administrative use, keeping them as records and using them again for reference were three distinct stages of development which did not automatically and immediately follow from one another.'[69] This realization is crucial and cuts through much confusion surrounding ancient documents. As I said, the simple presence of inscriptions could have immense significance of other kinds. The medieval evidence confirms our suspicions. The form and content of the documents made may also determine whether they are used as records later. When the use of documents is at an early stage, documents may be made which are not, in fact, much use as long-term records, since the wrong kind of information has been included, partly through inexperience of what kind of information would be needed later. For example, Clanchy argues[70] that the Domesday Book itself suffered

---

[69] Clanchy (1979), 124ff., ch. 5 and ch. 6 on libraries, esp. p. 147; quotation from p. 125.
[70] Clanchy (1979), 18ff.

from this inadequacy. Though a powerful symbol of royal authority, it was apparently not used much for reference by contemporaries. It only became useful as a record by the 1250s when it could be a good source of archaic titles to land. It was founded upon a misconception of how to use writing in administration. However, as the Domesday Book illustrates so well, a written document may have had an immensely important function even though it was seldom read. Written records may have a significance other than that carried by the written words alone. The medieval evidence also reminds us, with its great accumulation of scribal documents, that as documents became more common, there were gradual changes in layout, presentation, and the use of a cursive hand; written documents became more sophisticated and easier to use as their presence became more familiar. It is particularly important to bear this in mind when we approach classical evidence for documents, since that mostly consists of formal stone inscriptions.

One final point: I may sometimes imply a sharp contrast between the ancient use of writing and our modern attitudes. But a sharp dichotomy between 'oral' and 'literate' methods is not meant (see Ch. 1.1); even we are not entirely lacking in oral transmission and tradition and thus dependent on written documents alone.[71] I merely wish to clarify or emphasize modern scholarly preconceptions behind interpretations of ancient documents and to separate more clearly different types of methods or attitudes in what may sometimes be an over-simple manner.

1.2.1 The encroachment of the written document

Athens probably first established a city archive at the end of the fifth century. When the new council house (*bouleutērion*) was built, the old one became the 'Metroön' or city archive. It housed the official documents of the boule and assembly.[72] It also contained the shrine of the

---

[71] Not only do we use the spoken word extensively where the written one might do, but television and radio increase our dependence on the spoken word again. However, the contrast I intend should be quite clear, and I shall not qualify throughout. As for oral tales in modern society, see, for instance, Brunvand (1981) on urban legends.

[72] Its main contents were the decrees. By the time of Lycurgus and Dinarchus (late fourth century) it also contained copies of the laws: see Wycherley (1957) no. 482 (Harpokration). Athen. IX (below, n. 79) is not enough to prove that records of lawsuits went there, too. Official documents, such as the letter of the Amphictyones (e.g. *IG* II² 1132), also found their way into the archive. The difficulty about using much later evidence to produce a systematic list is that archival practice might have changed: for example, we know archives began to take private documents in the Hellenistic period, so the deposit of Epicurus' will was symptomatic of later use (and see Clay (1982) for Epicurus' works there also); then it also housed certain accounts, for which we have third-century evidence, *IG* II² 847 (Boegehold (1972), n. 13) and lists of ephebes, first century A.D. For full collection of references see Wycherley (1957).

Mother of the Gods (hence its name), a fact often neglected.[73] This was Athens' first building devoted to documents and thus its first central 'archive'. What happened to documents before this is controversial: it is either supposed that there were no documents at all except upon wood and stone (and thus no archive) or this view is attacked without the substitution of another coherent picture.[74] In fact some documents on inscriptions were displayed earlier in the old *bouleutērion* (see Ch. 1.2.3 and p. 75, n. 193, below). It is usually agreed, however, that the Metroön itself marked a significant change and that it was the first central archive.[75]

The date of its beginnings may bear on the reasons for its establishment. Two inscriptions of around 405 B.C. refer to documents ἐν τῷ δημοσίῳ, 'in the public archive'. The Athenian decree thanking the Samians refers to names recorded in the archive which are to be erased;[76] and the decree of Patrokleides of 405 (And. 1 73ff.) instructs people to erase certain types of documents 'everywhere, any that may be in the archives (*en tōi dēmosiōi*) and any copies there may be' (1 79).[77] (The phrase *en tōi dēmosiōi* used of document transcription was originally thought to refer to public display on *leukōmata*, whitened boards, but it has been shown conclusively now to denote the Metroön or city archive.)[78] Two literary references are less decisive. An anecdote about Alcibiades erasing a law suit in the Metroön is too colourful to be reliable.[79] Andocides, on the other hand, seems to show that the

---

[73] Wycherley (1957), 150–60 for references to the Metroön; Homer A. Thompson (1937), 215–17 on archives; Boegehold (1972); Posner (1972); Curtius (1868) is still useful. It is not clear how the shrine was incorporated or added, how important it was, or whether the 'Metroön' referred to a whole precinct and altar as well as the old building: but directions such as 'in front of the Metroön' (e.g. *IG* II² 140, 34f.) suggests it was simply the building, which included shrine and archive.

[74] Kahrstedt (1938), appendix, pp. 25–32, thought there were no archives whatsoever before 403: see, however, pp. 73ff., below.

[75] Separate records still continued to be kept by the relevant boards of officials, so the term 'central archive' needs qualification.

[76] *IG* I³ 127, l.27–30, ἀν] αγεγραμμένον ἐν τῷ δημοσίῳ: the new restoration argued by Boegehold (1972), 25, n. 12.

[77] Cited by Boegehold as indicating a single archive. They now disprove older theories (incl. Kahrstedt's) which connected the Metroön strictly with the revision of laws in 403/2. Andrewes (1976), 14 interprets *pantachothen*, 'from everywhere', in the decree of Patrokleides too legalistically.

[78] Klaffenbach (1960), esp. 11ff.; Boegehold (1972). The previous view is that of Wilhelm (1909). MacDowell's note on And. 1 79 does not consider possible reference to the archive. It seems unlikely that the phrase could simply denote 'in public' – cf. Isocrates' use of *en tois koinois* to denote that (*Paneg.* 180).

[79] Athen. IX 407b–c, quoting Chamaileon of Heracleia Pontica, fourth to third century B.C. In fact, it may have nothing to do with the archives at all; he was probably doing what Strepsiades wanted to do to the wax notice of the indictment, Ar. *Clouds* 769ff. (Kahrstedt (1938), 27). There is no evidence that indictments were deposited in the archives (Boegehold (1972), 27).

'*bouleutērion*' (i.e. when the boule still used it) housed documents as late as 409 B.C. For he has the decree of Menippos read out (II 23f.): 'For it is still, even now, inscribed in the *bouleutērion*.' It is curious, though, that the decree is still there, for Andocides cites it as revoked and is perhaps surprised at this himself.[80]

The Metroön, then, was in use by 405 B.C. and was probably established at some time in the last decade of the fifth century. Let us set aside for a moment any possible connections with other developments of that decade, and the complex question of the revision of the laws and the system of law-making. The late fifth century seems comparatively late to establish the first city archive. This is several decades since the beginning of the radical democracy and the vast increase of documentation which it brought,[81] a century since Cleisthenes' reforms and two centuries since the laws were written down by Solon. Classical Athens associated written law and the publication of its written documents with the democracy, yet it lacked a specific place for the democracy's documents until the end of the fifth century. Even taken at face value this suggests that the preservation and organization of the city's documents was in a rudimentary state in the fifth century and probably well into the fourth. But its implications are neglected. It emphasizes that writing, and even documents, can exist without the sophisticated organization of documents we are used to expect. And it indicates the crucial difference between documents and archives and between the use of documents and their systematic preservation (to this I return below, Ch. 1.2.3). The Metroön was perhaps established now because the accumulation of inscriptions and other documents had reached a point where some order was urgently needed. It is probably also connected with the creation of the board of magistrates (*anagrapheis*) in 410 to revise and codify the laws and thus, perhaps prompted by recent oligarchic activities, with a general move towards greater order in written documents and records. The revision of the laws was necessary partly because they were scattered over the city and it was becoming impossible to tell what was still valid. The chaotic nature of the city's documents may have pointed to the need for a better system.[82] The beginnings of the Metroön were a significant step in the organization of written documents towards the end of the fifth century.

Certain other landmarks in the use of the written word have long been noticed. But, discussed primarily within the context of the Greek legal

---

[80] See Ch. 1.2.3 further, on this haphazard keeping of documents. Kahrstedt (1938), 31 insists the decree came not from a document but a stone stele – believing that no archive existed before 403; but ἐγγέγραπται used there does not usually denote an inscription.

[81] Davies (1978), ch. 4; Schuller (1984).

[82] Boegehold (1972); Harrison (1955), primarily concerned with the complex procedure of law-making, which I cannot go into here.

system, their wider significance has been neglected. I refer to the gradual change from the use of witnesses to written contracts in the business sphere, from oral testimony to written, and from oral to written pleas, all of which takes place in the courts in the first half of the fourth century.

The written contract first appears in our evidence in the first decade of the fourth century (Isoc. *Trapez.* XVII 20) and more frequently there-after.[83] But not till much later in the fourth century do we find a written contract apparently made without witnesses (Hyp. *Ag. Athenogenes*, i.e. 320s). Before this, witnesses were present as well and they duplicated the proof of the written contract. As Pringsheim has put it: 'We are in a transitional stage in which documents did not yet replace attestation, but only helped to prove it'; and he recognizes that the oral agreement was still felt to be the important element of the contract.[84]

This extension in the use of business contracts may reflect the expanding commercial life of the fourth century. Such written documents were especially suitable for the fluid world of traders and trade in which stable and visible real estate had little part.[85] Commercial needs certainly encouraged the growing use of written contracts. However, oral validation continues alongside written. So the change is also expressive of the gradual extension of the written word, its slow accept-ance in place of the old and trusted use of witnesses. For one cannot simply label dependence on oral witnesses as primitive and suitable to a rural or village community[86] – this hardly describes Athens in the second half of the fifth century. Rather, we must recognize the increasing use and familiarity of the written word in other areas of Athenian life now – and with that familiarity, a growing sophistication in people's use of documents. The use of witnesses was old and trusted, written contracts were comparatively new. Why should people trust them? In addition to sheer force of habit, these early documents were not as foolproof as we might assume. Cursive writing did not yet exist, nor did characteristic 'signatures', though seals (essentially non-written tokens) may have compensated.[87] In the legal context at least, there were clearly few precautions except witnesses connected to the actual writing of a docu-ment, even once documents were used. This is surely precisely because the widespread use of writing for these purposes was very recent. Hence, it is no surprise that questions of authenticity mostly revolved round the

---

[83] See, above all, Pringsheim (1955), repr. (1961), vol. II, 401ff. Also Finley (1952), 21ff.; Gernet (1938).

[84] Pringsheim (1961), vol. II, 403f. A contract is also left with a trustee without witnesses, Lyc. I 23.

[85] Pringsheim (1961), contrasting it with the use of *horoi* for land.

[86] Pringsheim (1961), vol. II, 402. Trade had hardly been parochial before this.

[87] On seals, see Bonner (1908).

reliability of the witnesses, not the document (e.g. Arist. *Rhet.* I 15, 1375b).[88] Moreover, it probably took some time to develop a standard format for a contract that seemed authoritative. Written documents were themselves unconvincing in certain ways, partly because such documents were new. The witnesses were to persuade both the courts[89] and the parties to the contract themselves that they had used a reliable form of validation. Wider attitudes – as well as the very form of the written document – are involved than legal requirements alone.[90] We are finding a new acceptance of writing as proof as people become more 'document-minded'. We must accept that such changes were occurring in the early fourth century.

A similar change takes place in the form in which pleas (*graphē*: literally 'writing') were handed in to the courts.[91] By the time of Demosthenes, complaints at the initial *anakrisis* ('preliminary hearing') were presented in written form, but a careful analysis of the terminology used in earlier orators and by Demosthenes himself reveals that before this, pleas were initially made orally and presumably only written down by the clerk. Amongst the great variety of terms used, none indicate the handing in of written pleas by the litigant at first. Then they gradually give way to phrases such as *graphēn apopherein* ('to hand in an accusation') in which *graphē* indicated a written document – though oaths still continue as well in the *anakrisis*. (The term *graphē* has a wide range of technical uses.) There are signs that writing in some form was used in recording complaints earlier than 425;[92] but the verb used is in the middle, *graphesthai* ('to have something written'). So the *graphē* or complaint itself was at first written by a clerk or magistrate, as we might expect of the earliest use of writing for legal purposes. The shift is from oral pleading confirmed by an oath to a written document actually handed in by the litigant.

Calhoun argues that, since all pleas were to be handed in in writing by the time of Demosthenes, the change was enforced by law. It must have come after Lysias, thus he puts it in the 370s and sees it as part of a great

---

88 Calhoun (1914) and Bonner (1905), 80: both note lack of documentary precautions and the absence of expert evidence on handwriting, but this is a very modern comment. There are, however, two cases where slaves recognize their handwriting: [Dem.] XXIX.21 and [Dem.] XXXIII.17. For wills, see Thompson (1981) and Is. I 25, on additions to wills held by archons.

89 Not simply the courts, as implied by Pringsheim (1961), vol. II, 405.

90 Cf. Calhoun (1914) who, however, takes the oral methods simply as an archaic survival; see Clanchy (1979), ch. 1 and Ch. 1.1 above for the combination of oral and written methods of validation for a long time in medieval England.

91 Calhoun (1919); Harrison (1971), 98f.

92 E.g. Ar. *Clouds* 759–74, *Knights* 1256, and see Calhoun (1919). An Erythrean law, *Inschr. Erythrai*, I no. 2 (before 454) has *syngraphein*.

reorganization of the judicial system.[93] This is quite possible. But as with the adoption of written contracts, we should not explain it only by immediate Athenian history. It also signifies a new acceptance of the value of the written word.

Similarly, it was shown long ago by Bonner[94] that evidence did not have to be presented in court in writing until the fourth century: the early orators Antiphon, Andocides, Lysias and Isocrates have nothing of written testimony. The first evidence for the reading out of testimony in court occurs in Isaeus (v 2), probably about the time of the Corinthian War (late 390s); thereafter in Demosthenes and Aeschines. Here there is definite evidence for a decree requiring testimonies in writing (Dem. xLv 44).[95] The witnesses probably did not have to write their testimonies themselves. The main aim was perhaps to fix testimonies in writing so that they could not be changed.

These three changes involve a move towards written documents as an acceptable form of validation: writing either supersedes or duplicates the previous oral forms. The change can be placed fairly precisely within the first half of the fourth century, and, in the case of written contracts, they do not seem to be treated as valid on their own until the 320s. We meet evidence for this transition in the legal sphere. But we cannot, therefore, see the shift only as a development in the law-courts and relegate it to the sphere of legal procedure.[96] Legal procedure here must reflect a wider acceptance of the written word; and we must remember that in the case of written contracts the usual judgement in the courts is only a final judgement on the validity of such a contract. Most contracts did not reach conflict in the courts, and the most important aspect of validation was for the two parties to be satisfied themselves about their method. Hence the very slow and comparatively late use of written contracts and the fact that they were still covered with witnesses as well for most of the fourth century. As Aeschines said (1 161) in the mid-fourth century once written contracts were becoming common; 'We make contracts (*syngraphai*) with one another through distrust, so that the man who sticks to the terms may get satisfaction from the man who disregards them.'[97] But

---

[93] Calhoun (1919) dates it more precisely to 378/7 but only from a presumed connection with the foundation of the Second Athenian League; cf. Rhodes (1980), 315.

[94] Bonner (1905), 46f.; cf. also *RE* col. 2038 *Martyria* (Latte); Leisi (1907).

[95] 'It is because of this that the law requires people to give evidence in writing (*grammateion*) so that it is impossible to remove any part of what has been written or add anything to it.' It is interesting that the courts of the Areopagus, Palladion and Delphinion cling to the older practice.

[96] As Rhodes (1980), 315.

[97] He is actually trying to argue away the possibility of prostitutes' contracts and the objection that there was neither contract nor witnesses for Timocrates' activities. Cf. Eurip. fr. 582N, a tablet is to avoid fraud or deceit, or Antiphon's canny argument that one only uses written messages to conceal something or 'when they are too long to

witnesses continued as a double check, and the reliability of the document could depend on the character of the witnesses themselves. A passage in Isaeus (v 25) perhaps illustrates the confusion possible amidst these double forms of proof. Talking of a written compromise agreement about property made in court, the speaker says that on his side they wrote down some points in the document and obtained witnesses for others. But his opponents 'affirm the validity (*kyria*) of the parts to their own advantage even if they are not in writing, yet deny the validity of what is against their interests unless it is in writing'.[98] This implies some doubt at the time about which method to use, which was more 'valid' and what one could get away with in the courts. If we imagine a system which had long relied on witnesses rather than writing, we can appreciate better the changing ideas about writing and about what can be accepted as valid proof amongst a wider circle of Athenians.[99]

Alongside the establishment of an official city archive these changes imply that written documents are gradually becoming more common in various spheres. It must be stressed that the transition from oral to written methods of validation is not a simple matter of 'technology'. The written word is only now becoming acceptable as proof. On the literary side books were increasing by the late fifth century: this aroused criticism from Plato and other philosophers defending the value of the spoken word (above, Ch. 1.1). Thus the legal acceptance of the written word as proof is not an acceptance which was long overdue, its trust in witnesses an archaic survival. We are seeing both an increase in written documents and in familiarity with writing and readiness to accept it. Alongside this is a growing awareness of the value of written records. This cannot happen overnight. There are many indications (Ch. 1.2.2) of a mixture of oral and literate methods of communication subsisting together even once writing has begun to be used in certain areas – and I do not want to imply that the change was uniform or that writing ever took over completely. We should therefore expect that documents were not always used or regarded as we might assume from our highly literate and 'document-minded' standpoint. Though Athens in the early fourth century was becoming more document-minded, many characteristics of even the fourth-century use of documents are not those we would associate with the use of archival records, archives and modern archival assumptions in general. Indeed, some are quite opposed to them. Certain aspects of the

remember' (*Herod.* 53). Writing might also compensate for the lack of other bases of trust (like that of neighbours).

[98] Plato, *Laws* 953e specifies that written contracts must be witnessed, and the number of witnesses varies with the sum involved.

[99] Because of the huge juries of the demos, their decisions would also reflect wider attitudes the more readily. See Humphreys (1985b).

Athenian use of the written word will illustrate some of the implications of this section.

1.2.2 Between 'oral' and 'literate'

When we look more closely at certain types of written record and the way they are regarded, some features emerge which one can initially describe best by saying that they do not correspond to our modern attitude to documents; they are misunderstood if seen through our preconceptions derived from modern archive use. We find a mixture of oral and written communication and record: the significance of documents sometimes lies mainly in their non-written aspects. Occasionally we can go so far as to say that the written document is being treated as an iconic or material symbol, despite its written content. In other cases this is less clear, but their treatment is connected with the fact that the use of such documents was comparatively recent and unfamiliar. Preservation or reference are haphazard and unsophisticated, often supplemented by oral transmission or other non-written aspects (this will become clearer below, p. 55), rather than written methods. In particular, the classical use of archive documents is very different from modern archival assumptions. This forces us to reconsider Athenian written record from a rather different perspective and the use of writing as influenced partly by oral methods of communication. I shall concentrate on the relation of the inscriptions to the archive copies, the visual and symbolic as well as written significance of the inscriptions, the practice of copying and obliterating written documents, and finally the peculiar use of the mortgage stones (*horoi*) in Athens. These apparently miscellaneous aspects of the written records all help build up a picture of the classical use of documents, the grey area between supposedly 'oral' and 'literate' methods, and the mixture of oral and written modes of record and communication that persists throughout the period.

First the relation of inscriptions to archive documents. This shows particularly clearly how modern scholars tend to approach ancient documents from modern documentary usage and how this misconceives ancient written record.

Are the inscriptions the inferior copies of archive originals, the archive versions the authoritative texts – as is usually assumed or even stressed? Robert declares, for instance, that the documents on stone are not the archives; they may be the copies of the archives, but they are not the originals.[100] Such a statement obviously applies to modern archive copies, but it raises several problems if applied to the classical world. After all, it does not account for the ancient habit of referring to

---

[100] Robert (1961), 459; cf. Weiss (1923), 357, similarly.

inscriptions as if they were authoritative. In fact, it imports modern archival assumptions, and it ignores the possibility of development in the practice of ancient archive keeping. One can never assume that the later Hellenistic practice was followed in the fifth and fourth centuries.[101] Such development is very clear in the classical period – when archives were so simple – and it bears exactly upon changing uses of the written word.

Thus in the classical period there are many cases where reference is made to the stone inscription (the stele) rather than to the archive original. Many examples where an orator refers to an inscription and not an archive version will be mentioned below in other contexts. Even more telling are the epigraphic instances where the inscription demands obedience to the stele itself. The treaty between Athens and Chios of 384/3 refers to 'the writing on the stele' (Tod II 118, lines 21f.). The wording of the treaty between Athens and Keos of 363/2 (Tod II 142) suggests that it is the stelai which will make the oaths valid (*kyriai*),[102] an instance which is not unique. We even find a case where the secretary of the boule is to make a copy of an inventory not from an archive original but from a stele (*IG* II/III² 120). There are other examples.[103] Stelai are referred to as if they were authoritative, whether they record treaties, laws, public lists or decrees.[104] We must rid ourselves of the idea that 'proper' documents could only be on paper or papyrus. The stone inscriptions were in any case the most certain means of preservation. We must also recognize that, at least in the classical period, archive originals were not felt to be more authoritative than the public stele.[105]

---

[101] E.g. stone versions of accounts of temple treasurers cease at the end of the fourth century; *horoi* disappear in mid-third century, which points to the final development in Athens, later than in many other places, of archives' use for private documents: see n. 72 above; Weiss (1923), 384; Posner (1972), 93ff.; Lambrinudakis and Wörrle (1983) for some Hellenistic archive regulations.

[102] (ll. 17–22) 'So that the oaths and the alliance . . . should be valid (*kyria*), the generals of Ioulis should inscribe the oaths and the alliance on a stele and set it up in the temple of Apollo' (and the secretary of the boule is to put a stele on the Acropolis).

[103] See below for examples in orators: esp. Dem. xx 127, a copy of the stele is read out; [Dem.] LVIII 56; Lys. I 30; Lys. xxx 17; Aristotle (*Ath.Pol.* 54.3) supports his point about secretaries by citing their presence at the head of stelai of alliances and proxeny decrees. Cf. also *Syll.*³ 581, l. 96: so that the stele should be visible for all time; in a Samian inscription (*Ath.Mitt.* 72 (1957), 242, no. 65, lines 15ff.) the stele of the decree and *synthēkē* is expressly said to be put up 'in order that they should be consecrated (*kathierōthēi*) and remain valid (*kyria*) for ever'; the inscription for the fifth-century expedition to Brea (*IG* I³ 46, ll. 20ff.) demands obedience to the stele; cf. also the Hecatompedon inscription, *IG* I³ 4; and the Tean curses (ML 30, B l. 35). See Heuss (1934) for other epigraphic examples (with n. 104).

[104] Heuss (1934) argues that the stone publication is the true text for treaties only, because they are intended as 'international' documents; but he neglects rhetorical and other evidence.

[105] So Heuss (1934), 250ff. (treaties); Boegehold (1972), 24. Compare, too, the idea that the decree should be visible 'so that anyone who wants' may see it (see ch. 1.2.3 below), implying that the stone carries the only text that matters.

In fact, to apply the concept of original and copy to ancient documents is anachronistic. In addition to the practice just outlined, the term *antigraphon* ('copy') is used in the epigraphic evidence of both an archive version and the public version on stone. It carries no derogatory implication that a 'copy' is not authoritative.[106] As Klaffenbach has pointed out,[107] we must abandon the modern concept of authenticity and the modern requirement of exact verbatim correspondence down to the very punctuation.

But if this is so, one may perhaps go further and connect these attitudes to authenticity and copies with the fact that it was only in the fourth century that Athenians began to be more document-minded. Precise differentiation between original versions and inferior 'copies' or insistence on absolute verbatim accuracy would seem to be the product of a highly developed literate mentality,[108] an extreme familiarity with the written word and a very firm sense of its importance (which therefore requires the actual words as well as the sense to be preserved). Such an attitude would be surprising in classical Athens. Indeed, one may wonder if a concept of accuracy that demands exact repetition of even the punctuation can exist without the printed word.[109]

As for the actual content of 'copies', the casual nature of much ancient copying is well known.[110] For instance, the differences between Thucydides' copies of the Peloponnesian treaties and the actual Attic inscription (*IG* I³ 83) are notorious, though the variations are slight.[111] There

---

106 Perhaps both were thought of as copies of the oral version: e.g. *Syll.*³ 915.20, ἀναγράψαι . . . ἀντίγραφα τῶν συνθηκῶν εἰς στήλην λιθίνην, 'Inscribe copies of the treaty on a stone stele', where the 'copy' was on stone. The decree of Patrokleides (*And.* 1 77–9) speaks of the names to be obliterated in the '*dēmosion*' and 'any copies'. See also n. 114 below for an example where only one copy exists.

107 Klaffenbach (1960), 34–6.

108 By 'literate mentality' I do not mean to suggest the exaggerated claims made for literacy discussed in Ch. 1.1: simply to denote a literate way of doing things by using writing, a familiarity with written as opposed to simply oral methods; compare, e.g., our modern assumption that if we are discussing a text we should all have the text in front of us.

109 It is worth thinking about inconsistency of spelling from this point of view. 'Bad spelling' in graffiti (e.g. Lang (1982)) is often taken to show that the writer was particularly ill-educated or slow: e.g. Immerwahr (1964), 41 n. 3 (graffiti on vases); Cartledge (1978), 32 (frequency of error in Spartan graffiti); Chadwick (1973), 35–7 (the lead letter from Berezan). But it is a comparatively recent development in modern Europe for a country to try to maintain a single system of 'correct spelling', and dictionaries are an essential tool for that.

110 And the similar character of ancient quotation. Comparable factors may be present to some extent: cf. Lattimore (1958), esp. 9f., on the practical difficulties of writing and looking things up in the ancient world; and Kenyon (1951), 67–9 on reading difficulties. Copying from a text in writing might be more accurate. Presumably the scribes copying ancient literary manuscripts must have had a rather greater respect for the original text and copies of it.

111 Gomme *HCT* on Thuc. v 47; but also D. M. Lewis (1980), 277 and Andrewes *HCT* v p. 457 on new evidence concerning the relation between the texts.

are examples where the epigraphic 'copies' themselves differ from each other.[112] Small variations in unimportant words did not matter. Surely this is not simply a quaint peculiarity of Greek copying, but partly symptomatic of a broader characteristic of the classical use of written documents.

It is also remarkable that the epigraphic copy could be regarded as authoritative even though it was incomplete and in effect an 'excerpt' from the spoken decree. It is recognized that certain inscriptions must be abbreviated versions of the original decree if, for instance, they obviously omit elements which must have been in the decree.[113] For some this confirms the importance of the archives and the belief that the archive copies constituted the original and authoritative texts (above, p. 45). But we have seen that the stelai are regarded in this way: clearly they could be authoritative even if they were slightly abbreviated.[114] Again we find a use of the written word which is opposed to our modern archive mentality, which indicates a different perception of the written word, and which probably reflects the comparatively unfamiliar use of written documents.

Even where we seem to find insistence on the verbal accuracy of a written text, it may not be the strict insistence that we might expect. One such case provides a perfect example of the mixture of oral and written methods (here, of transmission) even where an exact text is demanded. Plutarch tells us that the late fourth-century politician Lycurgus arranged for the texts of the three great tragedians to be kept ἐν κοινῷ (literally 'in public', 'in common'), perhaps in the Metroön (*Vit. X Orat. Lyc.* 841F). It was unlawful for actors to depart from these texts and they had to consult them if they wished to perform the plays. This seems to be approaching the establishment of one accurate and authoritative text. It

---

[112] E.g. inscriptions on the Athenian treasury at Delphi which duplicate a text at Athens: Colin (1933), 248f. and references; *IG* 1³ 78. Plut. *Vit. X Orat., Mor.* 852 gives the decree of Stratokles (307 B.C.) in memory of Lycurgus: contrast *IG* 11² 457 (the Teubner text of Lycurgus, pp. 13–17, puts both together), with M. Osborne (1981), 172–4.

[113] E.g. Boegehold (1972) cites *IG* 11² 1612, 154ff., where the sums are missing, and *IG* 11² 1013, 63, where the rubric ἐκ τοῦ αὐτοῦ ('from the same place') seems to indicate that the following lines are taken from the same text as the previous ones. Cf. Meritt (1967), 118ff.; Klaffenbach (1960). Yet at the same time one should note how little excerpted inscriptions often are: e.g. instructions for publication are written out on the stele, or amendments are added at the bottom of the initial decree, written out without altering parts of the original decision which are now superseded – e.g. *IG* 1³ 46, expedition to Brea.

[114] As recognized by Meritt (1967), who explains the Greek type of copying by their interest in content, not in wording or form; Boegehold (1972), 24. Cf. also the fourth-century addition of a law to an older stele: *IG* 11² 140, 31–5 (353/2 B.C.) – to be added to the former law of Chairemonides (probably from 403/2) on the stele in front of the Metroön. Nothing is said about any archive copy, and one wonders if there was one.

seems suitable in the late fourth century, partly because of the greater attention to records by then, partly as a sign of increasing traditionalism and reverence for the great fifth-century figures (whose bronze statues were also to go up).

But when we look more closely, the presence of these authoritative texts does not enforce accurate transmission of the text to the actors: for when actors wish to perform one of the plays, the secretary is to read the text out aloud to them. The new law said 'that their tragedies be written out and kept in a public deposit and that the secretary of the polis read them out to the actors who are to perform them'. So there is a written text to keep to. But in effect its transmission is oral, read from the text, and the accuracy is that ensured by reading a text aloud, not the absolute accuracy enforced by learning straight from a written text.[115]

This Lycurgan institution epitomizes much that is characteristic of the classical use of the written word: even when a text is available and adherence to it required, its transmission is not necessarily through the written word itself, but it can be oral with the text as a distant mnemonic aid. It exemplifies the mixture of oral and written modes and the use of written record I have been discussing. Written texts may exist without the attitudes to them we take for granted.

The public inscriptions are often referred to by the orators. Here again, the stelai form the authoritative text. But the rhetorical citations show more than this: the stelai are often so closely associated with the events they record that they actually are the treaty, the peace or the disgrace. They are also cited in a similar way to the monuments – tombs, temples and other memorials. This suggests that the public inscriptions were regarded as memorials as well as written documents. They therefore had a significance quite independent of whether they were read much by most Athenians. For, more than documents, they were also stone memorials or symbols of the honour, treaty or decision that they recorded – material objects which were a reminder and symbol of the decision they recorded, as well as documents with written contents.[116]

Certain inscriptions were an assertion of superiority or honour just as statues or trophies could be. Demosthenes (xx 36f.) cites the decrees granting tax immunity to Leucon, ruler of the Bosphorus: stelai have been set up in the Bosphorus, Piraeus and Hierum. 'You yourselves . . . have set up inscriptions, copies of all these.' 'Those stelai', he continues, 'are the covenants of all that you have received or granted. It is worse to

---

[115] Cf. Finnegan (1977), 52–8 on variations in detail and the common occurrence of slight differences in the detailed 'texts' of oral poetry; and now Goody (1987), chs. 3 and 8. These are particularly clear with the use of the tape recorder.

[116] Cf. Clanchy (1979), ch. 1, and above, Ch. 1.1. Cf. the fascinating models of hands, symbols of friendship, discussed by Herman (1987), 53–4, and generally, chs. 3.3–4.

repudiate them while they still stand than to pull them down.' It is the stelai themselves that he cites, not simply their written content, or a remote decree in the abstract. The stelai themselves are the covenants. Later (xx 64) he speaks of the list of benefactors, some no longer alive, 'but their deeds survive, therefore it is fitting to allow these stelai to hold good for all time . . . then when they are dead, the inscriptions will be a memorial of our character and paradigm to others of our benefactions in return'. The sentence slips between decrees being read out, inscriptions and the actual honour; the stelai are memorials and paradigms. It is not enough to be friendly with Athens; the stelai – the material proof – which show the contrary must be removed. Thus Demosthenes (xvi 27) rejects the Megalopolitans' plea, admittedly unscrupulous, that their friendship is based not on stelai but on mutual advantage and demands that they destroy the stelai of their treaty with Thebes. Not only do stelai provide an authoritative text; they symbolize the friendship so strongly that they actually are the friendship. It is the material symbol which is being referred to, not so much the document or the writing itself.

Disgrace was embodied in the public stelai recording the terms of the Peace of Antalcidas, made by the Persian king with the Greek states (386 b.c.). Isocrates was not writing for the assembly and was self-conscious that he was 'writing' speeches. Yet even he sees the clauses of the peace and its terrible iniquity in terms of its appearance on the stele and its copies all over Greece. He declares (*Paneg.* 176) that the clauses on the islands' autonomy 'have long been overridden and lie on the stelai in vain' (πάλαι λέλυται καὶ μάτην ἐν ταῖς στήλαις ἐστίν). He laments the shame of their publication (§180): 'And he forced us to write them up on stone stelai and deposit them in our temples, a far finer trophy than those of battle.' It is particularly interesting that he likens them explicitly to a trophy: a powerful visual symbol of defeat.

One can compare the orators' use of memorials (*mnēmeia*). They are the visual counterparts of many of the historical events the orators so often cite. They are used directly as arguments in themselves, and the orators do not need to stress that everyone will know of them. We meet a recurrent call to consider the memorials left by the Athenian ancestors, proof that fourth-century Athenians must emulate them: the Propylaia, Parthenon, stoas and docks,[117] or more vaguely ancestral tombs and trophies.[118] These visual memorials are comparatively stable foundations of *philotimia* ('love of honour', 'ambition'). Orators stress that

---

[117] E.g. Dem. xxiv 184, xxii 76, xxiii 207.
[118] It becomes a more frequent platitude in the course of the fourth century as the gulf from the fifth grows clearer.

they are for memorial and emulation.[119] Or they can be used for moral proof. Aeschines' notorious reference to Solon's statue in Salamis was meant to show that all the great orators spoke with their arms inside the cloak.[120] The functions of memorial and example are obvious for such *mnēmeia* as the Stoa Poikile and the monument at Thermopylae, an object of pilgrimage (Isoc. *Phil.* 148). They are in a sense unwritten symbols of memorial; the significance of the visual, material object is clear. The *mnēmeia* are also mentioned when examples are not intended, to signify the event or honour: for instance, 'Will you set up in the agora the statue of any ambassadors Philip sent?' (Dem. xix 330), or 'Arcadia has set up Philip's statue in bronze and garlanded it' (xix 261) (that is, they have gone over to Philip, king of Macedon).

Certain inscriptions are used in exactly the same way to stand for the honour or treaty itself, memorials with powerful non-written significance. (The decorative grid-like *stoichedon* style perhaps reinforced this.)[121] I do not mean to suggest that their written content was irrelevant; but like other tangible memorials in some ways, they are not purely documents whose written content is all that matters. If one sees Athens in the early fourth century as a society which is only just beginning to be aware of the importance of the written document in other spheres, one can better appreciate the mixture of symbolic (unwritten) and written aspects in these great stone inscriptions. Even the clause that sometimes occurs at the base of an Athenian inscription describing the purpose of its erection is perhaps ambiguous; a stele is said to be erected 'so that anyone who wishes may see it' (*skopein*) – but not necessarily read it. One probably cannot press this far.[122] But again it may express the significance of the stelai as visible memorials as well as precise written documents.

The widespread practice of obliterating documents can be seen from the same angle. In a way the written document is the transaction or

---

[119] Dem. xxii 76 again; [Dem.] lix 94, the picture in the Painted Stoa. For the idea that their ancestors left the memorials as deliberate examples for later erring descendants, cf. Dem. xv 35: they set up trophies not for you to wonder, but that you might imitate their virtue (*aretē*); Din. ii 24; cf. Dem. xxii 72 on the inscriptions (*epigrammata*) on the crowns: they are tokens of envy (*zēlos*) and ambition (*philotimia* again) (thus they have both written and symbolic significance).

[120] Aeschin. i 25, (note exaggerated introduction) scorned by Dem. xix 251. Cf. [Dem.] xxv 34, where the wickedness of sycophants is argued from the fact that there are temples and altars to Athena, Justice, and others, but none to sycophants.

[121] Though it prevented word division at the end of the line and therefore presumably inhibited easy legibility, it went on well into the third century (R. P. Austin (1938)). Used by Flory ((1980), 20) as a reason for few reading the inscriptions, though one should be careful of judging the difficulty of reading something by our own standards.

[122] See below, Ch. 1.2.3 and n. 151 for examples. Clanchy (1979), 202ff. discusses medieval changes in describing the absorption of written matter: usually verbs of 'hearing' are used, but by 1300 documents are also 'seen' as well as heard.

decree that it records. Obliteration is also directly opposed to an archive mentality.

Demosthenes (xvi 27) demanded that Megalopolis destroy the stelai, their treaty with Thebes, as I mentioned above. The decree of Patrokleides (And. 1 77ff.) gave elaborate instructions that inscriptions and copies should be destroyed. The speaker of Dem. lvii (64) declared that his opponents stole the shields he had dedicated to Athena and 'chiselled out' the decree which the demesmen passed in his honour – here both the non-written memorials and the written stele are obliterated. Andocides (1 103) evokes those who benefited from the amnesty of 403, and 'for whom you destroyed stelai, you made laws invalid and you erased (ἐξηλείψατε) decrees'.[123] Complete destruction was evidently intended, for the copies in the archives were to go as well as the public inscriptions. It is perhaps significant that our two earliest references to the Metroön are to the destruction of documents in it. Clauses on obliteration specify that this applies to all copies everywhere, in an obvious attempt to be complete. But completeness was not always achieved. Even inscriptions from the time of the late fifth-century oligarchy survived, though they were supposed to have been destroyed (cf. the decree of Patrokleides).[124] But this must have been extremely difficult if one considers the nature of the archives and the locations of the stelai. Systematic obliteration sometimes had to rely upon non-official knowledge of where the relevant writings were, as is suggested by an obliteration clause in one decree; this adds the possibility, εἴ τις ἄλλος οἶδεν – anyone else who knows where the documents are.[125] However, this is partly a question of the system of storage and preservation of documents to which I return (Ch. 1.2.3) – both were probably more haphazard than we often assume.

Such obliteration is evidently the converse side to the treatment of stelai as if they were themselves the honour, the treaty, and so on. If stelai (or other documents) are symbolic memorials or actually are the enactment, then their obliteration destroys the enactment that the writing records. There is even a hint of the semi-magical in this treatment of writing, for instance in the obliteration of the deme honours by the man's opponents cited above. And when Alcibiades returned from exile

---

[123] Cf. obliteration of Pausanias' hubristic inscription on the Delphic tripod, Thuc. 1 132. The Thirty destroyed inscriptions on the Areopagus (*Ath.Pol.* 35.2); official destruction of the stele recording the alliance with Alexander of Pherae in 368 (361/0), *Syll.*³ 184, 35–40; Samian honours, *IG* I³ 127, 27–30. The laws inscribed on the Stoa Basilea were possibly erased by the oligarchy of the Thirty and reinscribed after 403: And. 1 84 and Atkinson (1939), 40; Fingarette (1971) (on the confused revision); Clinton (1982).

[124] Andrewes (1976) on erasure of names and documents connected with the oligarchy.

[125] *IG* I³ 52 (Callias decrees), 9ff., esp. 11–13, 'after having searched the tablets (*pinakia*) and the documents (*grammateia*) and wherever else anything is written; these written documents (*ta gegrammena*) should be produced by the priests and the *hieropoioi* and by anyone else who knows of them'.

in 407, the stele which recorded his condemnation was cast into the sea and the curse withdrawn.[126] Moreover, the practice seems to continue with vigour into the fourth century, well after the establishment of the Metroön. Obliteration in the fifth century has been taken (wrongly) to be a sign that there were no archives before 403,[127] but clearly we must consider the practice from a broader point of view.

Obliteration is also indicative of the classical attitude to archives as well as documents. The archive copies are destroyed along with the public stelai as a kind of *damnatio memoriae*. This is quite contrary to our assumptions about the use of archives. It is worth reflecting how far modern archives accumulate 'records' of business or administration which have been finished with but which might conceivably need to be referred to again and how far documents are kept 'just for the record' – because they may some day be of interest to someone, probably an archivist or historian (this concern is likely to be very recent). Ancient documents are not regarded automatically as records for the future. Archive copies can be destroyed without any feeling that, though defunct, they should be kept as 'records'.

Compare also the obliteration of documents for other, purely administrative, reasons. The instances above were connected with political honour, shame or political change; the obliteration removed an unwanted document. The circumstances surrounding the documents of the oligarchy were highly charged. But there was probably also widespread destruction of purely administrative documents as soon as their immediate usefulness was over. (One can assume that this was more frequent than our sources reveal, precisely because of the comparatively ephemeral nature of these documents.) The circumstances of some of these types of obliteration contrast strikingly with modern practice, particularly in the recording of debts.

Thus Aristotle tells us of the routine of the official *poletai* and the *apodektai*, a board of financial magistrates (*Ath.Pol.* 47.2–48.2). He outlines the elaborate system by which the *poletai* record on tablets the taxes or contracts that they lease out. They write on whitened tablets the name of the man leasing the taxes, and the price of the lease, and hand it to the boule (47.2). For those who must make a payment every prytany,

[126] Plut. *Alcib.* 33.31; D. M. Lewis (1966), 188f. suggests it was bronze because of the association of bronze with *atimia* ('dishonour').

[127] An important argument of Kahrstedt (1938), 30: see below, Ch. 1.2.3. But it was not, in fact, less frequent in the fourth century and these later examples cannot be dismissed as empty demonstrations: as well as those above, cf. Philoc. *FGH* 328 F135 (Dion. of Hal. *Dein.* 11) on the demolition of the stele of the Peace of Philocrates; *IG* ii² 43, 25ff. (= Tod 123), Aristoteles' decree of 377 on the Second Athenian Alliance: destruction of stelai in Athens which are 'unfavourable' to cities ready to join the confederacy. It is not specified which they were! (D. M. Lewis (1966), 186f. has suggestions.)

there is a separate tablet for each payment.[128] These are brought to the boule and kept by the public slave. When a payment is made, the public slave takes the relevant tablet from the *epistylia* (some kind of pigeon-hole or shelf) and hands it to the *apodektai*. They delete the sums paid before the boule (καταβληθῆναι καὶ ἀπαλειφθῆναι), taking care not to 'delete anything prematurely' (προεξαλειφθῇ) and return the tablets to the public slave (48.1).

The records are therefore essentially temporary mnemonic aids, kept only until the payments have been made. They are deleted as the leaseholders pay each instalment, and the sign of the payment is that there is no record left of the debts – a system involving neither written receipts nor permanent record of the leaseholders. Once the full payment has been made, presumably the only record of the transaction is that of memory.[129]

Finley has called this whole procedure one 'designed to fulfil a police function', pointing out the 'impermanent' and 'unreliable' nature of Greek public record keeping.[130] But these latter terms misplace the emphasis.[131] We see here the use of written documents as a mnemonic aid and a check on default: as a document, but not necessarily as a record for long-term reference, to use Clanchy's distinction. In fact like the public stelai, the tablets also physically represent the debt in a way: this is simply a different use of writing. Clearly it was not thought desirable to keep permanent records of the transactions. Indeed what practical use could they have? Proof of repayment lay in the absence of written records, not more documents (as we would like), and probably it would occur to no one to keep further records. The process emphasizes the absence of an archive mentality which would keep anything that could possibly be of use and which sees proof only in writing.[132]

---

128 The connection of these with the whitened tablets in §47.2 is not clear: apparently there is an official record and a separate document made for each prytany, and all is cancelled at the end.

129 Contrast modern expectations that proof of payment should be in writing, e.g. in the form of a receipt or a written comment against the record of the original debt. Proof of payment in Athens is the complete absence of writing. Perhaps people were afraid that records could enable officials to collect the money again, but the essential difference lies in what we regard as the best proof. Bankers, on the other hand, were remarkable for their keeping of detailed banking records which marked when loans were paid out and other transactions. See esp. [Dem.] XLIX 5 (and *passim*); Finley (1952) 22; Bogaert (1968) and (1976).

130 Finley (1952), 14 and n. 17, repeated (1982). It is interesting that Posner (1972), 101f. assumes that the system was like our modern accounting system, marking 'paid' against the sum.

131 Indeed Finley is unnecessarily puzzled by the very similar use of *horoi* – on which see below, p. 55.

132 Many of the purely administrative decisions which were not recorded on stone or which were for immediate and temporary use were probably simply thrown away when their

One may compare the earliest known published document of the *poletai*, the record of the sale of property of the men condemned for the irreligious mutilation of the Hermae and profanation of the Mysteries in 415 (*IG* I³ 421–30): is this exceptional or the first beginnings of careful record of the transactions of the *poletai*? Why was this published on stone? Surely not simply because the permanence of stone was thought necessary to protect those who bought the property[133] – in fact the purchasers' names are not even given. But the inscription must have had a powerful exemplary function, perhaps symbolic of the public disgrace of the perpetrators and the maintenance of public order in their punishment. Thus, the insults to the gods are seen to be avenged.

Here, then, are several cases where the written word is used in a manner opposed to our archive ideal, often close to non-written symbols. These practices show a use of documents as memorial, example, disgrace or honour, and mnemonic aid, but not necessarily as record. Often the destruction of the document signifies the end of the transaction it recorded, the end of the honour or agreement. This is sometimes connected with the extremely close identification of the written document and the transaction it records, of which it is in a sense a memorial. So, from the point of view of an Athenian enquirer or historian, a great deal of information, whether important or ephemeral, would simply not have existed in written form.

It is illuminating at this point to compare the practice of putting up 'mortgage' *horoi* (stone markers) on mortgaged land which seems to start in the early fourth century.[134] This epitomizes the mixture of written and non-written elements in the ancient use of written documents and provides an extreme case where the mixture in fact explains the curious character of the written inscriptions. The presence or removal of the *horoi* indicated whether the debts had been paid (rather like the tablets of the *poletai*). They also carried very brief inscriptions which record a minimal amount of information. But it was the physical presence of the *horos* which signified the debt. So the marking of a debt involved both the presence of a material object, put down before witnesses, and a slight written addition: thus, both visual and written methods of marking the transaction.

content had been followed. Officials under indictment had their records removed when the charge was cleared up: they were not put in the archive (Boegehold (1927), 27).

[133] As Rhodes on *Ath.Pol.* 47.2. (D. M. Lewis points out that the purchasers' names are not given); Finley ((1982), 707f.) takes it simply as the 'police function' again. See D. M. Lewis (1966), 186f. for comments on the layout and order of the document and its slight attempts at accounting. *Poletai* accounts were not put on stone, so far as we know, till 370: Meritt (1960), 25, no. 33.

[134] Main works on the *horoi* are Fine (1951) and Finley (1952); also Gernet (1938). More recently, Millett (1982).

If you wished to see if a man was in debt, you looked on his land for *horoi*. In the Phainippos case ([Dem.] XLII 5), his opponent says he looked for *horoi* and could find none; therefore Phainippos could not have had the debts he said he had. It was crucial to ensure that they were not removed. Apollodorus declared that Timotheus tried to defraud his creditors by digging up the *horoi* on his estate ([Dem.] XLIX 12) – clearly an attempt to invalidate the creditors' claims. The stones form an unwritten memorial or physical object that symbolizes the debt. In the Middle Ages, material objects were used as mnemonic aids or symbols of a transaction: later, they were often accompanied by writing, but they could be regarded on their own as sufficient evidence of an agreement. The point about this type of memorial is that its very presence signifies the transaction. Though the *horoi* also carry a written notification, it is their presence or absence which shows if the debt is paid. The writing is secondary, next to the symbolic object and the memory of witnesses. Hence the speaker of [Dem.] XXV 69 declares that the *horos* is like a writing tablet (*sanis*) deposited with the goddess.[135]

In this sense the mortgage *horoi* can be seen as related to the other kinds of *horoi* that abounded in Attica. Boundary *horoi* were crucial markers between neighbours' lands. Misers, we are told, would check regularly that they remained in place, and there were penalties for tampering with them.[136] Other types of *horoi* marked a tomb or shrine or called attention to the nature of a particular object, rather than being purely boundary stones. The ones that have been found and published are, of course, inscribed: some simply say *horos*, others ὅρος μνήματος (marker of tomb) or more specifically ὅρος ἱεροῦ (temple marker).[137] In these cases it is more obvious that the stones are markers or memorials whose main significance lies not in the written message they carry but in their physical presence.

The mortgage *horoi* can perhaps be seen, then, as a development or adaptation of these numerous other *horoi*. They have the same name, and they could consist of any available stone, even a large boulder which could take an inscription.[138] The conclusion seems inescapable that when the custom of placing mortgage *horoi* began in the classical period, it was

---

135 Cf. Finley's incredulity (1952), 16f., though he concedes that Apollodorus' argument must have carried weight: a vivid example of a highly literate interpretation made from a familiarity with extensive official recording of all sorts of transactions.

136 Misers checking *horoi* in Theophrastus, *Characters* 10.9, Plato, *Laws* 843c (against neighbours encroaching); penalties suggested, *Laws* VIII, 842e–843; inscription from Chios, *SGDI* 5653.

137 There are many fifth-century ones: *IG* I² 854–907 (also II² 2505–641), and Fine, (1951), ch. 3 on *horoi*, p. 41 and n. 40, p. 50 (with bibliography there).

138 See Fine (1951), 42–6 on the crudity and variety of the actual form of *horoi* and their inscriptions: one is simply a huge boulder. Gernet ((1938), 307ff.) realizes the possibility of tradition to explain their primitive character.

adapting the previous custom of placing *horoi* as boundary stones or markers.[139]

Here we come to the significance of the written message on the mortgage *horoi*. If these *horoi* have a mnemonic function based on their mere physical presence, then their curious inscriptions appear in clearer perspective. These are laconic. They usually only name the creditor, not the owner of the land holding the *horos* who had contracted the debt. Most are undated.[140] The message is extremely simple: usually creditor, sum of money and the formula for the type of obligation. So the inscription is not a document that is complete in itself. For it is supplemented in effect by the information that the stone's position gives about the owner of the land (not inscribed) and by the knowledge of the witnesses. They would presumably have a rough idea of the date when the debt was marked and possible other details. Thus, written, oral and symbolic methods are combined to make the transaction secure; the written part of the communication is incomplete by itself and omits what seems to us crucial information.

Some *horoi* mention a written contract and the person who has possession of it. Obviously we should not assume that all other *horoi* were duplicated by a written contract.[141] In other words, there was some development of the process to include a separate contract as well as the *horos*. We can compare this with the increase in the use of written contracts (*syngraphai*) in other spheres which occurred during the fourth century; as the advantages of the *syngraphē* became apparent and more and more people used one, even the system of mortgage *horoi* sometimes adopted it.[142] The balance of written and oral types of validation that existed for most cases is therefore tipped in some instances more towards the written side, as the system is elaborated. It is tempting to wonder whether there were also early mortgage *horoi* which did not even have the slight and formulaic inscription. The *horos* is essentially an unwritten marker of a debt confirmed by witnesses. Our extant mortgage *horoi* are all inscribed, but I would tentatively suggest that *horoi* marking loans might also have been used with even less written markings – perhaps

---

[139] The relation of Solon's *horoi* to the later ones is unclear, esp. since the very significance of Solon's is still controversial. They were probably a mark of subordination of some kind, and were meant to be permanent: cf. Gernet (1968), 360–70, who stresses their primitive nature and so continuity in symbolism with the later ones. Such continuity is vague, since *horoi* were used as other kinds of markers (e.g. shrines) in the intervening periods.

[140] Only 21 carry an archon's name, and they are between 363/2 and 259/8.

[141] Finley (1952), 25–7. There are only three examples of deposit with government officials.

[142] Finley (following Gernet (1938), repr. (1955), esp. 30–2) suggests that the need for written documentation was less urgent in the case of land than other businesses since land was stable.

simply the description '*horoi*':[143] the non-written methods of validation could have been adequate, and the inscriptions of even the classic type are themselves not complete as documents without information provided by oral means.[144] It is otherwise very surprising that this 'primitive' system suddenly began in the early fourth century just at the time when written documents were becoming more frequent in other spheres.

The *horoi*, then, are a non-written type of record: their inscriptions are a secondary element still reinforced by the oral method of using witnesses and the presence of the stone. In a society which was used to purely oral validation of contracts, we may recognize the inscriptions as slight additions to the visual symbol, perhaps merely mnemonic aids. It is not because the *horoi* could not really give protection against fraud that they had such scanty written content.[145] The use of writing for these purposes was comparatively new and unsophisticated. So the information the writing gave was incomplete: it had to be supplemented orally, just as the whole transaction was validated by oral methods.[146] The need for mortgage *horoi* has been partly connected with developments after the Peloponnesian War, when it became more common for strangers rather than kinsmen or neighbours to acquire land: written and visual signs of indebtedness were needed when transactions extended beyond the close circle of family or neighbours.[147] This must be a significant element in their increasing use. However, it must be borne in mind that the evidence for that dating is largely the body of full *horoi* themselves – which begin in the early fourth century. What if similar transactions with even slighter written documentation were being used earlier, as seems very probable from the background of the mortgage *horoi*? What if 'mortgages' were sometimes almost completely oral? At any rate, the whole process is expressive of a primarily oral mode of conducting business. The simple, laconic document is the kind of document used where written documentation is new or unfamiliar,

---

[143] Whatever the precise use of the Solonian *horoi*, their removal also signified the removal of the obligation: Solon simply says he has taken up the *horoi* (fr. 36.6 West). There is little reason to think they were inscribed.

[144] It is generally agreed that the inscribed *horoi* we have are after the Peloponnesian War: i.e. fourth to second century and most in the latter half of the fourth (Fine (1951), 48). Fine's explanation was that land was not legally alienable till the Peloponnesian War: against this, D. M. Lewis (1966), 181f. and Finley (1968). Obviously one cannot push back the phenomenon indefinitely, but such dating assumes that only *horoi* with the formulaic inscription were mortgage *horoi*.

[145] As Finley (1952), 18f.

[146] Indeed one wonders if very early written contracts could have resembled these inscriptions in their extremely slight content.

[147] The speaker of Dem. XLII does not know Phainippos' neighbours and is afraid they will be on Phainippos' side: this illustrates well how the *horoi* would be neutral testimony, removed from merely oral testimony and links of trust.

unwritten types of communication or validation predominant.[148] The use made of writing was influenced by previous, oral means. Again, we cannot assume a use of the written word that is akin to ours.

We have been looking at examples in the Athenian use of written documents where written and non-written (oral or visual) elements are combined: where the document has a significance derived from its appearance or position as well as the written content, or the written element relies on oral methods of validation or communication. There is no sharp dichotomy here between oral and written processes, nor a regular development away from the oral means. Rather, I would emphasize the grey areas in between, the elements which are neither strictly 'oral' nor entirely 'literate' to the modern mind. The older oral processes influence or govern the way writing is adapted; writing is reinforced by oral validation. In fact, such written documents may be 'incomplete' on their own without information preserved orally. The mortgage *horoi* are an important and extreme example, probably an adaptation of the common use of *horoi* as markers. Their written message is primitive partly because the unwritten elements were primary, partly because the use of writing in this area was new and little developed.[149] It is less tempting to see the *horoi* as proper 'documents' than the sophisticated public inscriptions of Athens. But these, too, are not simply written documents whose use and significance we can take for granted. They also have a non-written significance as memorials, material objects representing the act they record, exempla cited like other uninscribed memorials. The significance of the uninscribed memorial may be shared by the inscription,[150] and the obliteration of certain inscriptions suggests that they were more than just documents. This has important implications for the Athenian use of records and archives.

Moreover, the classical approach to copies of written texts and the actual process of copying suggest an attitude to the written word which is not the literal one we take for granted. Again, this is a grey area in the use of the written word which is related to the oral nature of much of Athenian communication and business even where the written word was involved. In short, fourth-century Athenians were only just beginning to

---

[148] Finley (1952), 15 and Fine (1951), 15ff. both explain the *horoi* system by the absence of formal notice and official recording of hypothecation in Athens. But both are facets of the same phenomenon – of widespread non-written methods of validation and relatively undeveloped use of written record.

[149] Cf. perhaps the custom of dedications with very short inscriptions – the object is 'explained' simply by the written name of dedicator and divinity; or the common occurrence among archaic inscriptions and graffiti where the object 'speaks' in the first person, proclaiming that it is the property or memorial of someone.

[150] The same symbolic aspect may apply also to the great written law codes: Humphreys (1985b), Finkelstein (1961) on Mesopotamian law codes.

be document-minded. We must see their use of the written word as influenced by the oral methods of conducting business and against the constant background or oral communication and other non-written means of proof.

In the written content of documents, too, certain peculiar features may similarly be related to their non-written significance or to a relative lack of sophistication in making documents which were quite separate from their oral context. Some oddities of Greek documents deserve more attention. I mentioned the custom of inscribing additions at the bottom of a decree without noting which part of the decree was now invalid. Occasionally one can discern changes in the form of documents which indicate that document-making was becoming more familiar and, with that, more sophisticated. The order of the tribute lists, for example, changed from the rather haphazard order in which tribute was collected to a more ordered grouping by area. The archon lists themselves are extremely laconic, omitting information we think vital (see Ch. 3 and Appendix), and so are the casualty lists. The record of the sale of property in 415 B.C. has curious gaps – if we regard it simply as a 'record' of the whole transaction. Such observations could be extended much further (e.g. pp. 79f. on the 'dating' of decrees). They remind us that the production of documents coherent and self-sufficient in their own right is not necessarily easy and obvious, that the use of the written word could develop in its sophistication, and that we can see such development in classical documents. We must also remember that the making and publication of documents need not primarily have been to display 'records'. Publication might have a primarily religious or exemplary function. Many 'records' simply were not kept at all (see p. 82).

So did Athenians of the fifth and fourth centuries refer to the documents, inscriptions and archives? How much of this information was in fact transmitted orally in spite of the written text? What was the character of the archives and the nature of record keeping? We can now look at these questions with the background knowledge that in many areas, even in the fourth century, writing was only supplementary to oral transmission, documents new and comparatively unfamiliar, and the contents of written documents sometimes simple or inadequate without the oral or symbolic elements that accompanied them.

1.2.3 Preservation, reference and archives

In the classical period it was regarded as a mark of the Athenian democracy to have written laws and published decrees. Inscriptions sometimes specify that their publication is on stone in order that 'anyone who wants may see them'.[151] This ideal certainly encouraged the numerous and often ostentatious inscriptions, written publications of the democracy's business. But how far did Athenians actually read them? Were they used as a source of reference? And were the archive documents treated in the same way?

First, it is common sense that the mere presence of documents, even public ones, does not prove that they were read or used.[152] But that is reinforced by recognition of the symbolic character of the stone stelai which is not impaired if the stelai are not carefully read. A more complex point is related to the development of a system which relies more upon written documents and an archival mentality. Clanchy's distinction between documents and records is a fundamental one. The making of documents, their preservation and their later use for reference are stages which do not necessarily follow each other.[153] The observation confirms and reinforces the impressions one gets from ancient Greece: there were so many inscriptions, yet archives developed comparatively late and there is little explicit evidence that people read the inscriptions, some that they did not. The oral repetition of the contents of many written records (below, on public dissemination) also reminds us that Athenians could know the content without reading the text. The inscriptions might indeed inhibit free alteration or misinterpretation of their message, but so could the oral traditions of the assembly. Consultation of the written word might not always be thought necessary. Here the evidence of oratory is essential, for it tells us how written documents were regarded in practice, beyond the ideal itself and the presence of the inscriptions.

Public dissemination

The oral dissemination of information was essential to the democracy. Business and persuasion in the assembly were conducted by the spoken

---

[151] E.g. And. 1 84, decree of Teisamenos: the laws are to be inscribed on the wall (of Stoa Basilea) where they were before, 'for anyone who wants to see' (σκοπεῖν τῷ βουλομένῳ); Dem. xxiv 17f., new statutes before the Heroes; *IG* i³ 84.26 (418 B.C.), and others (see Meritt (1940), 90); also Eurip. *Suppl.* 433–7. Aristotle disapproves of Sparta for not ruling according to written law, *Pol.* 1270b28–1272a36. Contrast [Dem.] LIX 76, Theseus' law erected in a certain temple open one day a year, so that not many could see the writing! The calendar of the Salaminioi said explicitly that it was put up so that the archons should know what each party was to pay, *Hesperia* 7 (1938), 1, no. 1, lines 80–5. A late inscription from Roman Egypt specified clear letters for the inscription itself, *OGIS* 665, 12f. Gagarin (1986), esp. ch. 6, discusses the emergence of early written law.

[152] As Flory (1980) points out; Stroud (1978) sometimes blurs this distinction in his useful collection of evidence for the survival of archaic documents. Havelock (1963), 39f. takes the inscriptions purely as a source of reference in case of dispute. It is obviously absurdly optimistic to think, with Nouhaud (1982), that the passers-by and orators would read inscriptions and thus acquire 'a basic historical knowledge'.

[153] Ch. 1, n. 69, above.

word. But even where written documents existed and were published on stone, they were propagated by the spoken word also. The orators almost always assume that information will be transmitted orally, often by older men (see further, Ch. 4.1). Rumours are deliberately spread by one's opponents in the agora.[154] Particularly telling, oral transmission or memory are sometimes relied on even for recent cases where one might expect a document to be consulted. The speaker of Dem. XLVII attempts to prove that he is right about the boule's decision and the plaintiff's agreement to pay a fine (§44): 'I ask those of you who were in the boule in the archonship of Agathokles to tell the facts to those by you, and I will bring as witnesses all those I could find who were in the boule that year.' Proof here rests upon people's memory. Dinarchus (I 42) says that if any in the court were among those included in the 300 when Demosthenes brought in his law about trierarchs, then they should tell their neighbours that Demosthenes will alter anything for a bribe of three talents. Though this obviously involves rhetorical manipulation of the 'facts', we find the same assumption of oral transmission.[155]

The process of passing decrees involves written notices posted beneath the eponymous heroes, as is well known.[156] Other types of information were posted in writing, such as challenges and denunciations.[157] This presupposes that people could read them. No suggestion is ever made to the contrary (though orators are careful never to talk down to their audience). Perhaps more important, however, is the fact that the written notice was only part of the process of informing the members of the assembly. For hearing the proposals in the assembly was just as essential. (The ancient preference for reading aloud would also help those who found reading hard.) Demosthenes puts it neatly (XX 93f.): proposed laws have to be exposed in front of the eponymous heroes, before the assembly, 'so that each of you may hear them often and examine them (*skepsamenos*) at leisure, and if they are just and expedient, may make them law' (§94). Thus they hear the proposal several times in the

---

[154] E.g. Dem. XXIV 15, Dem. XXI 104. Cf. the process, rather like the Roman *flagitatio*, described by Aeschin. I 60: Pittalokos sat by the altar of the Mother of the Gods, a crowd gathered, and Timarchus had to lie to him (Pittalokos), so that his own crimes would not be spread around (ἀνακηρυχθῇ).

[155] Cf. recent cases often alluded to by orators: e.g. Dem. XXVII 58 (some of you saw the money for it was counted out in the agora); Dem. XL 11 (you all know how Plangon swore the opposite, 'for the matter became much talked about'); [Dem.] LIX 91 and 116 (explicit statement that they know what the orator is alluding to).

[156] Dem. XX 94; XXIV 18 and 23; Aeschin. III 38f.; and And. I 83f.

[157] Challenges, Dem. LVI 18 (probably posted on the eponymous heroes); earlier publication of those who failed to pay what they had promised for the war, Is. v 38; a denunciation about a contract for a merchant ship is put in front of the meeting place of the board, until the secretary is bribed to cross it out, [Dem.] LVIII 8. A notice was probably put up listing those chosen to go on military expeditions (Ar. *Peace* 1179–82), possibly duplicating a proclamation (*Peace* 311f.).

assembly, but they may study it 'at leisure' on the written board. The essential posting in writing is supplemented by frequent readings. In fact, if people could not, or did not, read the proposal they could catch up quickly. The Athenian democracy could rely – and surely knew it could – on those who could read telling those who could not and on the efficiency of oral publication in the assembly, a far quicker way of circulating information than the written word alone. We even have glimpses of a body of information concerning historical decrees which was made familiar through citation in the assembly (Ch. 1.2.4, below). The same is true of the regular business of the democracy.[158]

The formal means of oral transmission by proclamation was also widely used. Again, like much else we have been discussing, proclamation often duplicated a written document; a written document might still continue alongside the oral publication. A herald was used to ask whether anyone wished to lay claim to the estate of Hagnias, an opportunity which Theopompus did not take up ([Dem.] XLIII 5).[159] The orator Demosthenes was to have his crowning and proclamation in the theatre, on the motion of Ktesiphon. Aeschines insisted, however, that this treated proclamations as a source of profit, for the laws decreed that crowning should take place before the assembly only (III 32ff., 154, 246). He contrasts the iniquity of Demosthenes' crowning in the theatre and the presentation of the war orphans. Aeschines even goes further to proclaim (§246) that it was not merely the *palaistra*, schools and music that educate the young, but far more τὰ δημόσια κηρύγματα, the public announcements of the people, which can only corrupt when people hear that wicked men are to be crowned. Through Aeschines' demagogic rhetoric we glimpse the importance, perhaps exaggerated, of the public proclamations.[160] Compare the ritual proclamation by the archon when he entered office about the security of property (*Ath. Pol.* 56.2) – probably a traditional survival. A herald also keeps order in the assembly.[161] And it is startling to read in the *Ath. Pol.* (§62.2) that the

---

158 Cf. Plato, *Theaet.* 173d on the philosophers who know nothing of the city's affairs: 'They neither see nor hear the laws or the decrees whether they are spoken (*legomena*) or written.'

159 When parents withdraw their son's name (Dem. XXXIX 39), however, the terms used (ἀποκηρῦξαι ('announce') with ἐξαλεῖψαι ('obliterate')) are technical and probably quite early: Harrison (1968), 75ff. and 79, n. 1.

160 His crowning mentioned proudly by Dem. XVIII 83. Cf. Aeschines' exploitation of the democratic significance of the Metroön (below, pp. 69ff.). The educational aspect of decrees, however, does develop in the late fourth century, especially under Lycurgus (Humphreys (1985)).

161 Ar. *Ach.* 43ff.; cf. heralds in wartime proclamations, Thuc. IV 105 (for Brasidas), Xen. *Hell.* V 4.10; *Hell.* II 4.20 (for initiates of Eleusis). The herald apparently summoned the council to the *bouleutērion* and lowered a flag, And. I 36; also mentioned by Suidas, the flag's use is unclear.

nine archons receive four obols each for maintenance and to support a herald and a piper.

Obviously we should not underestimate the role of heralds and official proclamations in transmitting information, even though they might repeat what was also published in writing.[162] As for the actual business in the assembly, Aristotle tells us that in his day one secretary was purely responsible for reading documents in the assembly and council (*Ath. Pol.* 54.5). This is not in itself remarkable, for someone had to read them out. But again, it reminds us of the role of the secretaries in communicating the contents of the written documents (orally) to everyone else.[163] I have already remarked on Lycurgus' rule about the authentic texts of tragedy – which was enforced by a secretary reading the text aloud to the actors; similar to this is the early role of secretaries or magistrates in writing down the complaints in court. Such instances do not necessarily indicate a low level of literacy. They remind us, first of all, that much of the more complex side of documentation was often dealt with by secretaries; secondly, that they provided a bridge between written documents and oral communication. Their role is part of the mixture of written and oral methods of transmission.

How often were the inscriptions themselves actually read or referred to in detail? Stelai are, as we saw, regarded as being or symbolizing the enactment they record. The stele honouring the 'tyrant-killers', Harmodius and Aristogeiton, was one of the best known of the city's inscriptions (Dem. XXI 170), but was it actually read? What of the others? Evidence is slight, and some of the rhetorical references are simply to the stelai as paradigms and memorials. What seems to emerge is that certain stelai were well-known memorials, but that most were neglected and one had to know where to look to find and cite the relevant document. Oral transmission in the assembly could have compensated to some extent. It will be useful to draw the evidence together.

Texts taken from stelai are sometimes read out. The speaker of [Dem.] LVII 56 has the decree of Moirokles read out with the words: 'Read out the stele.' Lysias (I 30) reads the law from the stele on the Areopagus: 'Also read out that law from the stele on the Areopagus.'[164]

A stele clearly set up for reference is the list of the Plateians granted citizenship, as is assumed by the speaker of [Dem.] LIX 105. He reads the original decree honouring them with citizenship, then adds that they had undergone scrutiny and the names of those passed were inscribed on a stele and set up on the Acropolis near the temple of the goddess, 'so that

---

[162] In some of these examples the herald may be an archaic survival.

[163] The secretary of the boule was at first an elected officer and close to an eponymous official; probably a sign of the secretaries' importance, below, pp. 81f.

[164] As Lys. XXX 17, we must perform the sacrifices on the *kyrbeis* and stelai.

the gift should be preserved for their descendants and that each might be able to prove his relationship'. (The visible stele seems to be distinguished from the decree whose location the orator does not give.) The stele was meant as a source of reference, and in a later inscription of 338/7 (*IG*II/III² 237) citizenship is actually proved by referring to the decree (line 17): 'The decree in which the grant was made is inscribed on the Acropolis.'

The list of public debtors in the Acropolis, probably a wooden tablet, was – and was meant to be – frequently consulted.[165] Arguments about public debtors revolve around the one list. The speaker of [Dem.] LVIII 14–16 seems to have gone up to look for his opponent's name on the tablet. Triumphantly he found that of his opponent's grandfather, which was the same. He cannot be sure which it was, but declares that it still debars Mikon. A little later (§18) he adds how he was planning to take a copy of those on the tablet or *grammateion* (the one on the Acropolis is assumed).[166]

The stele of benefactors was used for consultation and, according to Lysias, people tried to get themselves added to it. Lysias (XIII 70–2) tries to prove that Agoratos did not help murder Phrynichus, nor, like Thrasyboulos and Apollodorus, was he made an Athenian citizen. Lysias reads two decrees honouring the benefactors to prove this and adds (§72) that if Agoratos had helped in the murder; 'He should have been inscribed as being made an Athenian on the same stele, just like Thrasyboulos and Apollodorus.' He adds that some bribed their way on to the stele of benefactors. It is not clear if the decree was on the same stele, but the stele is certainly referred to as proof. It also has an exemplary function: as Demosthenes said of the stelai (XX 64), 'it is proper therefore that these stelai remain valid (*kyrios*) for all time', so that they form both a memorial (*mnēmeion*) and a paradigm.[167] The stele of traitors was also exemplary. Lycurgus says, probably wrongly, that it was made from the bronze statue of Hipparchus, 'so that they could leave

---

165 Probably a wooden tablet in the temple of Athena. The terms used are *engraphein* and *grammateion* ('tablet'): e.g. [Dem.] LVIII 16, 'the writing on the tablet', and §18. Cf., however, Dem. XLVII 22, a stele for those who owe equipment to the city; [Dem.] XXV 99, alluding to the registration of public debtors up there: Boegehold argues curiously ((1972), 26f.) that this was 'an archive'.

166 Possibly copies in the central archive, too (Boegehold (1972), 27), but that rests on an overliteral reading of the decree of Patrokleides. Cf. also [Dem.] LVIII 50, an erasure for a portion of debt; Dem. XLVII 21f.: note that the copy was evidently meant to be crucial.

167 *IG* I³ 102; ML 85 is probably a different decree (the one read by Lyc. *Leocr.* §§112–14 yet another): Agoratos is merely a 'benefactor', only Thrasyboulos is made a citizen. Its relation to the two decrees cited by Lysias is hard to determine (see ML). Lines 28–30 specify that the secretary of the boule should inscribe the benefactors on a stone stele on the Acropolis.

for the rest of time an example for descendants of their attitude to traitors' (*Leocr.* 1 117–19). Lycurgus reads out the inscription on the base of the stele (*hypogramma*) and the list itself with great relish.[168] It obviously had powerful paradigmatic force, though there is no clear evidence for people going up to read it. Leodamas apparently had to defend himself against the accusation of Thrasyboulos that his name had originally been posted on the Acropolis (ὅτι ἦν στηλίτης: literally, 'that he was inscribed on a stele') but that he had erased it in the time of the Thirty – he refers to the list of traitors. Leodamas tried to argue that the Thirty would have trusted him more had his hatred for the people been engraved in stone (Arist. *Rhet.* II 1400a32–6). Argument probably revolved as much round supposed erasures as over the visible names on the list. Other stelai of deserters and those tried for homicide or guilty of massacre or attempted tyranny are mentioned in the 'decree of Patrokleides' (And. I 78), though it is not clear what form these records took.

It is striking that so many inscriptions here are lists. Reading lists demands a much lower level of literacy than lengthy decrees and less perseverance. It is easy to pick out a name – though names might be ambiguous, too.[169] Early documents often take the form of lists (see further Ch. 3). Essentially, lists provide a different calibre of information from many inscriptions. They could also be altered easily and we hear much about fraudulent additions to certain ones.[170] The main safeguard lay in the interests of the other people on (or off) the list and general public knowledge (Boegehold (1972), 27). Clearly they were referred to comparatively often and were more accessible by their nature than many other types of inscription.

The democratic principle of access to the laws is exemplified in practice by the man who makes the notorious visit to the *exegetai* or sacred expounders[171] to ask their advice on what to do about the murder ([Dem.] XLVII 71). After visiting the *exegetai* he goes and checks on the stele, then with his friends: 'I heard this from the *exegetai*, and examined the laws of Drakon from the stele.' It is an interesting but tantalizing

---

[168] The decree is questionable. No one was honoured with a statue after the tyrannicides till Conon (Dem. XX 70). Lycurgus is our only authority for the story about melting down the statue; but the tale is attractive, and one can see how it could have grown up on the basis of the stele of traitors clearly visible, the inscription on its base and Hipparchus' name on the list. The next stage was perhaps the invention of the decree itself.

[169] For the problems of identical names on lists (not inscriptions here), see [Dem.] XXXIX *passim*.

[170] Lys. XVI 13 and XV 5, for erasures from military lists; the list of cavalry under the Thirty was corrupt, Lys. XVI 5–7; Lys. XIII 72 asserted that the list of benefactors included some who had bribed the orator.

[171] *Atthis*, esp. 243, n. 44: the *exegetai* advise him on his legal position, because he evidently needed it, not because that was their usual business.

single example of an ordinary citizen checking on his legal position himself.[172] Another instance where the public law is called upon is described by Andocides (see below), but there the reference depended on knowing where to look in the first place.

To this one can only add rhetorical references to the stone inscriptions of peace treaties, but they, too, are indecisive. For instance, Isocrates (*Paneg.* 120) compares past and present treaties as they are inscribed – one will best understand the difference, 'if one reads alongside each other the treaties made in the time of our power and those now inscribed' (εἰ παραναγνοίη τὰς συνθήκας τάς τ᾽ ἐφ᾽ ἡμῶν γενομένας καὶ τὰς νῦν ἀναγεγραμένας).[173] But this docs not show he had actually read either; what he says of the terms is vague and could well be common knowledge. Andocides' *On the Peace* is more concerned with detailed argument. He compares the terms of the truce after Aigospotamoi in 405 and the suggested terms of the peace with Sparta in 391. The terms of the truce are those on the stele (III 12): 'Consider the provisions from the writing itself (*ta grammata*), comparing that which is engraved on the stele with the conditions on which you can make peace today. For there it is written . . . ', and he compares the terms in detail. (It is interesting, incidentally, that the stele is still up.) It sounds as if he consulted the stele itself.[174]

Thus explicit evidence for many Athenians reading inscriptions is sparse. An orator like Andocides might read a treaty in detail from a stele, though his elaborate explanation implies he was doing something unusual. It is telling that even in this scanty collection the public documents to which reference seems most assured are the lists of public debtors, traitors and others held up for public example. Other inscriptions may have been read by a few Athenians, and sometimes a copy had to be made from one for the courts or the assembly. But consultation of the inscribed decrees – and apparently the laws, too – was not a deeply ingrained habit. Even for the epigrams in the Hermes portico, Demosthenes (XX 112) only hazards that 'perhaps you have read them'. Yet this was an important commemorative inscription. Oral transmission is

---

[172] It is perhaps this the speaker of Hyp. *Ag. Athenogenes* 13 is pretending he has done: he has, he says, been 'examining and studying the laws night and day', neglecting all else.

[173] He refers to the Peace of Callias, whose authenticity has been doubted. This passage suggests that it was at least inscribed by 380. Cf. also his horror at the public stelai, *Paneg.* 176 and 180. *Anagegrammenos* usually means 'inscribed' and '*publicly* recorded' (Sandys, at Gagarin (1986), 51 n. 2), but not always; used of writing on a *sanis* (wooden board), Aeschin. III 39, and in the decree of Teisamenos, And. I 83f.

[174] For the importance (only) of the stelai as the authoritative versions: Aeschin. III 70, on what is written about the allies in the decree: 'They also added in their resolutions (*prosegrapsan*) that any other Greeks who wished could within three months have their name inscribed on the same stele along with the Athenians and share in the oaths and agreements.' Less reputable: [Dem.] XII 8.

relied on, rather than written records, for the results of recent trials or details of cases within living memory.[175] Clearly, there was not a developed habit of referring to written documents where oral tradition would do. Classical Athens was not as 'document-minded' as we might expect, and the literate habits of looking to writing for proof or reference were not widespread in the early fourth century. This was beginning to change by the middle of the century (see below, Ch. 1.2.4), but for the time being, it was hardly surprising that inscriptions were little used for reference.

It is worth considering an incident involving references to a stele that is described by Andocides (1 116). Though isolated, its implications are supported by what we have seen so far. In Andocides' version of his trial at the Eleusinion, there is a surprising and sudden reference to a stele nearby. Kephalos reveals that the 'ancestral' punishment for Andocides' alleged misbehaviour was invented. The inventor was one of the Kerykes. Kephalos declares that the true punishment is given on 'the stele at your feet' (ἡ δὲ στήλη παρ' ᾗ ἕστηκας) and that it is only a fine. The stele is read out, and this is found to be true. Andocides is thus saved from the death penalty.

This story suggests that the stelai lying around were often neglected, as indeed one would expect of the numerous inscriptions. But the neglect might include fairly important ones, even those specifying punishment. Negligence could even perhaps be deliberate when someone wished to press for severe penalties. But if necessary, and if someone knew where to look, everyone would cluster around an inscription and read it out. Moreover, it is the public stele, visible and accessible, which makes this possible at all: we are far from a picture of a clerk automatically checking through archive copies. The impression is one of rather haphazard and casual reference to the written records. The tale vindicates the democratic principle of access to the law. But in this case the principle required that one knew where to look. The man who consulted the *exegetai* knew where to find the law of Drakon. But people could be at the mercy of experts and interpreters who knew where the relevant inscription was or who used their authority to disregard the written records altogether. This was surely a common problem. The written documents could be a safeguard against arbitrary judgement, if one could find the right ones. What we know about the arrangement of documents and inscriptions will confirm that these could be hard to find.

Archives and records

Still less is there evidence that ordinary Athenians, or even the rich Athenians of the court cases, consulted the records in the Metroön. We

175 See above, p. 62.

can only assume that, just as orators could cite decrees which the clerk found and read out, one could consult the records when it was necessary for administration and government. But that may not have been as necessary as we would think. For some needs of administration the officials concerned would have a copy of the decree of instructions, just as Demosthenes and the embassy had their own copies (Aeschin. II 101). Other documents, as we saw, were meant to be preserved only as long as the obligation or debt existed.

A passage of [Dem.] xxv 99 is usually cited as a sign that many ordinary people went to the Metroön to look things up. Unfortunately the speech is at least of the late fourth century. But the very interpretation itself is doubtful. The speaker asks how the jury could possibly go into the Metroön if they did not uphold the laws in this current trial – surely they could never enter it individually with a clear conscience, in the presence of laws which were still valid, if they did not collectively confirm them now.[176] But he seems to see the visit in a symbolic and semi-religious light, for he then imagines the jury going up to the Acropolis at the beginning of the month to pray – where Aristogeiton and his father are registered: how can they do that if they give a verdict contrary to their oaths and 'the writings' (*ta grammata*) up there (i.e. the list of public debtors). The visits are to the two places which embody the traditions of the state which the accused is defying, but the speaker is not envisaging consultation of the documents there. The Metroön did contain a shrine to the Mother of the Gods as well as the archives.

Such evidence clearly does not help us much. More interesting are signs that the significance of the public archives was only beginning to be realized properly around the middle of the fourth century. The man who realized this and began to make far more sophisticated use of its documents seems to have been Aeschines. He is the first to exploit the public records as part of his demagogic rhetoric. He also uses documents from the Metroön in a way which seems to be new. Thus, there are two closely related elements in his citation of documents: one is his awareness of the archive's significance as a place of storage, the other is the way he actually uses its documents.

Aeschines alone of our extant orators exploits the past decrees fully for chronology. We are familiar with the common rhetorical habit of quoting a decree with almost no commentary from the speaker, as if its import were clear. But Aeschines is self-conscious and emphatic about what he is doing, as if he were using these documents in an exceptional

---

[176] οὐ γὰρ δήπου ἕν ὑμῶν ἕκαστος ὡς ἐπὶ κυρίους τοὺς νόμους πορεύσεται, εἰ νῦν μὴ βεβαιώσαντες αὐτούς· *epi* here can mean 'in the presence of'. Wycherley's translation (1957) is unusual in not making 'consultation' explicit.

way.[177] According to his argument in his speech on the embassy
(343 B.C.), his opponents are misrepresenting the chronology of the
events. Thus he declares (II 89): 'For in the public documents of the
people you preserve for all time the dates and the decrees and the names
of those who put them to the vote.'

And he reads aloud the decree of the boule, discussing how it shows
the date of the embassy. He emphasizes this repeatedly in the same
speech (II 58, 92, 96, and 135 for other events). In *Against Ktesiphon* (III
24) he dramatically varies a familiar topos and declares that the 'public
documents of the people' (*dēmosia grammata*) convict Ktesiphon by
showing the dates of Demosthenes' magistracies. Aeschines' argument is
unique because he explicitly and emphatically links the argument about
the course of events with the public documents which prove the dates.[178]
He seems to show a realization about their possible use that is new.

It is also he who, characteristically, is the first to exploit the public
records as part of his rhetoric. Other orators used them to produce the
decrees and letters they wanted to quote (though see below); Aeschines
presents them as the great guardians of the oppressed, preservers of
records unaltered and thus a bulwark of the demos. In all the references
given above (except II 96) the *dēmosia grammata* are cited as providing
the information. The democracy guards these records for ever there (II
89, already quoted). The idea is presented more epigrammatically
elsewhere (III 75): καλὸν ἡ τῶν δημοσίων γραμμάτων φυλακή · ἀκίνητον
γάρ ἐστι. 'The preservation of the public documents is a fine thing since
they remain unaltered.' For it enables the demos to discern those who
have been rascals before, but who now claim to be honourable. He
mentions the documents as sources also at III 24 (above), III 187 for the
rewards and epigram for the party from Phyle (who helped restore
democracy in 403), and for the results of the congress of the Greeks in
371 (II 32). These are our first references to the Metroön in the literature
– the document quoted by Andocides (I 73ff.) is obviously not relevant
here.

It is intriguing, then, to see that the only references to the Metroön in
Demosthenes occur in *De fals. leg.*, also in 343, and *De corona* (§142).
The second is for 'writings' (*grammata*) there which incriminate Aeschines. The first introduces the Metroön in a deliberate manner similar to
that of Aeschines: it is cited for the affidavit of Aeschines' refusal and a

---

[177] Demosthenes uses chronological arguments from documents slightly, but less explicitly:
XVIII 155, the dates of the transactions are read out. Cf. Is. VI 13, who works out that
the opponent's story cannot be true from the date of the Sicilian expedition; contrast
the chronological vagueness of, e.g., Dem. *Ol.* III 3, Philip's siege in Thrace, 'three or
four years ago'.

[178] Cf. his deliberate stress on written record, III 201; II 66, the decrees stand 'as they were
written from the start', unlike the sycophant's words.

decree in his name (XIX 129) – 'in your public documents (*koinois grammasin*) in the Metroön, of which the public slave is in charge'.

It is thus tempting to see Aeschines as the orator who first realized the full significance of the public records in demagogic rhetoric and their place in the democracy. More than that, he used the records with a much greater sophistication, extracting more information from them than was usual. As we shall see, it was easier to make documents than to use them later, and consultation of archival records can be regarded as a further step from the recognition that written documents are useful. One may thus see Aeschines' particularly extensive use of the archives as a sign that he was more 'document-minded' than most Athenians and had a clearer idea of the meaning of documents as records. In fact, this seems to have been recognized by his contemporaries. For Demosthenes abused him as 'accursed' and γραμματοκύφων (XVIII 209) in a passage making fun of all the past deeds Aeschines cited (§§206ff.): 'γραμματο-κύφων' means someone who is hunched over records. He is also called a *hypogrammateus* ('junior clerk') (XIX 70): this, too, is an insult, which is interesting. In fact, Aeschines had been a junior clerk and then a secretary (*grammateus*) 'with maintenance in the Prytaneion for two years' (Dem. XIX 249; cf. §237). Demosthenes' observations have an element of truth. Aeschines' peculiar style of using the public records was indeed noticed at the time. Surely it was encouraged by his secretarial activities: these alerted him to the extraordinary potential of the documents stored in the archives – a potential neglected or unnoticed by others.

After Aeschines, the Metroön's democratic significance was emphasized. Lycurgus (I 67) gives a hypothetical example of someone destroying just one law in the Metroön to show that the scale of an offence does not matter. Dinarchus (I *Ag. Demosth.* 86) mentions a decree deposited 'with the Mother of the Gods, who stands as protector of all written contracts (πάντων τῶν ἐν γράμμασι δικαίων) for the city'. One is reminded of the passage in [Dem.] XXV 99, written after Chaeronea which was quoted above. The Metroön has completed its elevation as guardian of the records of the democracy. Whereas for Aeschines it helped the demos reveal past deceit, it is now seen in almost religious terms, as guardian of the supports of democracy, law (*nomos*) and justice (*dikē*). (Dinarchus continues extravagantly that it would be impious to make these records invalid or give a vote which did not conform with the actions of the gods themselves.) The place itself can now be a paradigm in its own right. It is impossible not to see here a sudden and growing recognition of the role of written records themselves, and most important, the records of the democracy.

It is not surprising to find such recognition of the value of archives, and thus of records, only in the mid-fourth century. It is one thing to produce written decrees, put them up in stone and (probably) deposit the original wooden tablet in the archive; quite another to refer systematically to the archive copies once their immediate relevance has passed. This awareness is an expression of the increasing importance of the written word, its recognition as proof alongside the older oral methods, and thus of the usefulness of its preservation.[179]

This brings us squarely to the problem of reference to the archives and how it was actually organized. By now it will be clear that we have almost no evidence for the arrangement and organization of the Metroön, nor even of Athenians looking anything up there.[180] We certainly cannot assume that the later ordering of documents in the Seleucid empire and Ptolemaic Egypt was present in Athens so early, and we should expect a far more primitive system.[181] However, a general picture does emerge if one considers several related aspects of Athens' preservation of documents. We know something of the distribution of inscriptions and a little about the kind of document that went into the Metroön; considerable evidence has now accumulated for the directions for preservation that occur on inscriptions elsewhere in the Greek world. We have some idea of what kinds of documents were not kept at all or went to other places than the Metroön. There are interesting groups of curious documents, like the *horoi* and the 'cavalry archives' recently discovered in lead. I cannot pretend to be complete, but by collecting these pieces of disparate information together, we can see a coherent picture. If we look at this evidence without preconceptions drawn from modern archives, and with the knowledge that in many areas the Athenians were not very document-minded, then certain elements fall into place. What we find is that preservation is often haphazard and inconsistent, even for documents that had to go into the Metroön; other documents are kept in a variety of different places; and from what little we know of the contents of the Metroön, it would in fact be difficult to refer systematically to documents. Perhaps most important, we even catch glimpses of certain kinds of written records that were made but not in fact used.

Clanchy's distinction between making documents, keeping them and referring to them once they have been kept, prompts us to wonder how far we can seriously talk of 'archives' at all in the ancient world. The

---

[179] The use of archives in Athens and the rest of Greece broadens in the late fourth century. Whether influenced by knowledge of Near Eastern archives that came with Alexander's conquest (Posner (1972)) or not, the development had already begun before this.

[180] Except for inference from the production of documents in speeches: but these were needed less in the earlier speeches (see Ch. 1.2.4.).

[181] Posner (1972) tends to assume a sophistication and order not found till much later; similarly for the contents of the Metroön, see above Ch. 1, n. 72.

concept of an archive is not one that necessarily appears as soon as written documents begin to be produced – if one takes an archive to denote at the very least an organized collection of documents which was meant to be referred to. Often what we call 'archives' in the ancient world are simply collections of documents. Even Posner, writing on 'ancient archives', admits that one perhaps cannot speak at all of archives in the proper sense of the word.[182] The Greeks did not distinguish between current records and those which were no longer needed regularly for business (this distinction he connects tentatively with the recognition of the research value of records), and the idea of concentrating in one place documents produced by different groups was one alien to them. Thus, the ancient preservation of documents might be unsophisticated. Nevertheless, he and others often take for granted archival practices more appropriate to the modern world and its stress on documentation.[183] The very use of the word 'archive' is bound to be misleading. Moreover, the kind of archives that existed in classical Greece must be connected with the way documents are used and how they are regarded. Jacoby's warning is often ignored: 'There still seems to be a tendency to overestimate both the amount of documents and particularly their easy accessibility in the state archive.'[184] It will be clear by now that the lack of certain kinds of records in Athens is expressive of wider attitudes and methods of using the written word.[185]

First, let us return to the question of how documents were preserved before the Metroön was set up. Our knowledge is sparse, but enough to suggest certain important points.

It was argued forcibly by Kahrstedt[186] that Athenian documents were publicly displayed on stone or wood or not written at all before the establishment of the Metroön, that is in the high classical period of the fifth century: there was no archive as such before 403/2 (a date which, as we saw above, must be modified). Most important are his arguments behind this date, which point to aspects of Athens' use of documents or inscriptions which we have been discussing already. So he points out how

---

[182] Posner (1972), 5f. Note also how *grammateia* ('tablets') or *grammata* ('letters') are often used for collections of documents where we would use 'archive': Boegehold (1972), 23 on *grammateion* for 'archive', and p. 35, n. 66 above.

[183] E.g. Posner (1972), 114, citing a law against bringing false documents into the Metroön, deduced from Lyc. 1 67 and §4 of the second hypothesis to Dem. XVIII.

[184] *Atthis* 205.

[185] Finley (1982, transl. 1985) points out that documents and archives are a function of the society which keeps them (or fails to do so), discussing the lack of statistical information for the ancient world. But he goes no further in explaining their rudimentary state. He also argues (1983) that ancient historians were indifferent to documents partly because of the paucity and rudimentary state of the archives. But the two are facets of the same attitude.

[186] Kahrstedt (1938), upheld by Hignett.

many documents from before 403 are cited as stelai (the list is impress-ive);[187] how the laws of Solon and Drakon are cited according to the divisions of the actual blocks – implying that there were no 'original copies' in the archives, therefore that there were no archives; the frequency of obliteration of inscriptions in the fifth century which (he insists) is less common in the fourth; and the rarity of citations of documents in the orators before 403.[188]

These are extremely important observations: but as we have seen, they are not characteristics confined to the fifth century alone. They must therefore tell us something about the classical approach to documents, archives and inscriptions in general. It is not enough to refute Kahrstedt by arguments which continue along the same lines as his, without really explaining the features he has pointed out.[189] Many of these, as we have seen, are indicative of a different attitude to documentation, one that sometimes includes oral or unwritten elements alongside the written ones. Archives are not an obvious and natural accompaniment to written documents. Thus it is clear even on Kahrstedt's view that an archive, archival system and accompanying attitudes to records could not simply arise overnight – that is, in 403/2. The state archive would be likely to retain unsophisticated elements when it was set up, elements that were related to the previous use of the 'stone archives'.

Kahrstedt's discussion has sometimes been taken to imply that the Athenian democracy before 403 managed entirely without written docu-ments,[190] but that cannot be the case. That interpretation is itself surely prompted by a modern concept of the separate and authoritative archival originals. Separate officials kept documents which were relevant to their own business – though whether they were preserved for long or sys-tematically is another matter.[191] The inscriptions themselves were the

---

[187] Stelai of treaties, Thuc. v 18.10; 23.5; 47.11; tomb and stele on Acropolis of Peisistratids, Thuc. vi 55.1; Athen. vi 234E mentions a stele of a decree proposed by Alcibiades; Ar. *Birds* 1044ff. takes the duties of the allies to be on a stele; stele for Arthmios of Zeleia, references in Ch. 1.2.4; for Harmodius and Aristogeiton (Dem. xxi 127); for the Plateians ([Dem.] lix 104f.); stelai in the decree of Patrokleides (And. 1 78), stele of Demophantos (And. 1 95ff.). And several on archaic cult or laws: Lys. 1 30, law from Areopagus; Lys. xxx 17 and And. 1 116 (cult); [Dem.] lix 76, law about king's wife; cf. also the decree when Skamandrios was archon, probably of 510/9, still known in original form in 415, And. 1 43, Cadoux (1948), 113, Lys. xiii 27; *IG* i³ 84, 21ff., which is to be inscribed on the wall rather than deposited in the archive. See Stroud (1978a) for survival of archaic documents.

[188] See, however, below Ch. 1.2.4 and n. 243.

[189] As (e.g.) Boegehold (1972), Stroud (1978a), Bradeen (1963), 205, criticizing Kahr-stedt's view as too strict; Atkinson (1939), esp. 40ff., claiming simply that there was no important change with regard to archives in 403.

[190] E.g. by Klaffenbach (1960), 29ff.

[191] Deme lists, for example (below p. 82); cf. Jacoby, *Atthis* 383, n. 27, though he perhaps exaggerates the organization of the 'archives' of different boards; Stroud (1968), 28f.

most permanent type of document possible: these were the democracy's documents as much as any archive versions.

However, there are also signs of deposit of documents in the old *bouleutērion* (council house): the *bouleutērion* was used for some kind of record storage before the Metroön was set up.[192] For instance, a decree about first fruits to be dedicated to Eleusis (*IG* I³ 78, *c.* 423/2) specifies first that a tablet (*pinakion*) should go to Eleusis and also to the *bouleutērion*; an addition at the end stipulates that two stone stelai of the decree should be made for the temple at Eleusis and the Acropolis (lines 48–51). A decree of Cleonymus in 426 (*IG* I³ 68) about the *eklogeis* (tax-collectors) may stipulate an inscription in the *bouleutērion* (lines 54ff.). The assessment decree of 425/4 orders the decree and assessment of each city to be recorded on two stone stelai, one to be set up on the Acropolis, one in the *bouleutērion* (*IG* I³ 71). An updated proxeny decree (*IG* I³ 155) almost certainly provides for a stele on the Acropolis and a wooden tablet (*sanis*) in the *bouleutērion*. There are others, as well as the decree of Menippos which Andocides says is still in the *bouleutērion*.[193]

It is thus clear that documents in some form were put in the council house before the Metroön was formally established as an archive, though we cannot know how many. They were probably regarded as the documents belonging to the boule, just as other officials kept their own documents. Sometimes they were on a *sanis* or wooden board which duplicated the stone stele. So far one can affirm that the *bouleutērion* contained copies of at least some important decrees, perhaps even the sole copies of others.

But the variety of arrangement is striking even from these few references. Sometimes the stele goes on the Acropolis, the *sanis* in the *bouleutērion*, sometimes stone stelai go to both (as *IG* I³ 71). This may have been related to people's ideas about the relative importance of certain decrees: some perhaps were felt to deserve two stone copies. In

---

[192] Meritt (1977) shows that double record in the *bouleutērion* and on the Acropolis was made at least by the mid-fifth century. The examples in H. A. Thompson (1937) are discussed by Kahrstedt (1938) and then Harrison (1955), 28, but Harrison omits those which refute his argument. Cf. indications of 'archives' or rather storage of documents apart from stone inscriptions cited by Meritt (1977), 21: plaques or boards for those in arrears of tribute or for tribute assessed and paid, from 448/7 and 426/5 (mentioned in inscriptions).

[193] *IG* I³ 27, proxeny decree of *c.* 448: stele on Acropolis and in *bouleutērion*; *IG* I³ 165, pre-420 B.C., honorary decree: stele on Acropolis and probably *sanis* in *bouleutērion* (shorter restoration, however, in *SEG* XXVI 19); stone stele and deposit in *bouleutērion* in *IG* I² 87, 40ff. and 171 (446/5–405/4), both heavily restored, also cited by H. A. Thompson (1937); also see Meritt (1977). David Lewis has pointed out to me that for proxeny decrees the family might well have kept a private copy of the text, and they were often put up by the individual himself (cf. also *IG* I³ 48 where the priest makes a private copy).

fact, it is worth wondering why particular decrees were considered deserving of stone at all – why, precisely, were they important?[194] It seems clear at any rate that there was no fixed system. The methods of displaying documents may even have depended on the ideas of individuals in the assembly. For in the decree about the first fruits at Eleusis (*IG* I³ 78) it is an amendment that adds (or substitutes?) two stone stelai to the two wooden *pinakia* already decreed.

This is a characteristic shared by other ancient 'archives', many of them from Hellenistic times. A collection of epigraphic instructions concerning publication and storage of documents by Klaffenbach reveals almost every conceivable combination of stele, *sanis*, temple archives and walls. Such instructions document the use of archives, but they also illustrate extraordinary variety in preservation: for instance a stone stele and a copy on the wall of the *dēmosion* at Corcyra, apparently without a wood or papyrus copy.[195] One suspects that the variant (even within the same city) often depended upon what people felt at the time about the significance of the document.[196]

A related question concerns the positioning of the Athenian public stelai themselves. A great many were to be placed 'on the Acropolis', but nothing more specific was instructed. Was there actually a system? How did anyone know where to look – especially once a new decree had ceased to be recent news. (Cf. the stele at the Eleusinion which saved Andocides, mentioned above, p. 68.) Then there were stelai 'in front' of the *bouleutērion*: this apparently continued right through the fourth century.[197] Andocides said that the 'decree of Demophantos' was in front of the (old) *bouleutērion* (I 95). Were such stelai necessarily duplicated by archive copies inside the building, too? Stelai were also put up 'in front of the Metroön' (e.g. a *nomos* set up in 353/2, *IG* II³ 140, 34f.) and decrees were added to stelai which were already standing (above, n. 114).

Yet 'the stele of Demophantos' was repealed even before Andocides quoted it. Demosthenes (XX 159) refers to it as well known and already

---

[194] Cf. D. M. Lewis' interesting observations, (1973), 193f., that the tribute lists record Athena's sixtieth, not the whole tribute, and that loans to Athena, not total expenditure, get recorded on stone.

[195] *IG* IX 1.692, lines 14ff., *SEG* XIII 384. Or the combination of temple and *bouleutērion*; or simply on the archive wall at Delphi: *FD* III 4, 153, lines 17f., 'the letter in the archive (ἐν τῶι ἀρχείωι) on the wall' (apparently without another copy). See Klaffenbach for others; Rhodes' formulation ((1972), 31, n. 6) of archive practice is too rigid and clear-cut. Cf. M. J. Osborne (1981) for modern bafflement at imprecision about numbers of copies and where they were to go.

[196] Cf. also the phenomenon of the so-called 'archive walls' in Hellenistic cities: S. M. Sherwin-White (1985) stresses their overall theme.

[197] *IG* II² 298 (336/5); II² 487 (*c*. 304/5), honorary decree cited by M. A. Thompson (1937); also a letter in the *bouleutērion*, of the fourth century, [Dem.] VII 33.

mentioned by Phormio, 'remember the stele of Demophantos'. Lycurgus (§124) cites the same decree when he says: 'Also hear the stele in the *bouleutērion.*' He adds that the ancestors inscribed the decree on a stele and put it in the *bouleutērion* as a reminder to the boule. Presumably it had eventually been moved inside. But this anti-tyranny law was not, so far as is known, re-enacted after the fall of the Thirty, and in any case it is the pre-403 stele which is cited. So, stelai which were null and void in legal terms could remain in place and even be cited repeatedly. Obviously the decree of Demophantos had a powerful paradigmatic force. Certain documents, especially stelai, were evidently preserved carefully and cited not for archival reasons or a feeling that all past decrees should be kept, but because they provided revered examples. This must partly explain the preservation of the early sixth-century laws of Solon on the archaic stele-like *kyrbeis* and *axones* (revolving wooden blocks) after they had been rendered legally obsolete by the revision of the laws at the end of the fifth century.[198]

In addition to such variety, it is also striking that stone stelai are to go into the *bouleutērion.* We cannot, of course, dismiss them as not proper documents:[199] they are copies of the public stelai and must have whatever function the ones on the Acropolis have, though for the perusal of members of the boule. However, they must alter our idea of ancient storage of documents and the physical appearance of archives. The documents preserved must have been extremely bulky; in fact, rather than of 'storage', one could better speak of 'enclosed display'.

Nor is this only the early practice of the fifth century. For there is some evidence that stone stelai were also put in the Metroön: for instance the decree of the Amphictyones (278/7 B.C.) and their letter to the boule and demos were put on stone and into the Metroön.[200] No doubt there were others, but this is enough to make the point.

---

[198] For the physical existence of Solon's *axones* in the fifth and fourth centuries and even after, see Stroud (1978a), 26f. and (1978b). There were still supposed to be remnants of the old wooden *axones* in the Prytaneion in Pausanias' time (I 18.3) and in Plutarch's (*Sol.* 25.1). I cannot go into the problems of the 'laws of Solon' here: there was clearly confusion about them in the fourth century. Some of the modern confusion, on the other hand, may arise from the assumption that Athenians, especially scholarly ones, would necessarily have studied the *axones* carefully had they existed.

[199] There is a confusion in ideas relating to archival documents: the fact that a document is on wood or stone often seems to be regarded as a sign that it is not an archive document, as if archive documents should only be on papyrus (e.g. Boegehold's argument ((1972), 29) against Kahrstedt, stressing evidence for 'papers', χάρται).

[200] *IG* II² 1132.2; there is a faint possibility that they went into the temple part itself, and this, too, upsets our neat idea of an archive. Aeschines (III 187) cites an epigram on a stele (and perhaps the decree, too) in honour of the party from Phyle: the 'reward' is to be seen in the Metroön, and this seems to be the decree itself; later (§190) he also reads the epigram. For stelai also in *bouleutērion* in the first century B.C., see H. A. Thompson (1937), 215 and n. 5.

Clearly the classical archive had great variety in the appearance and bulk of its documents, as well as in the relation of its documents to publicly displayed ones. We must remember the diverse types of writing material for documents – in fact, even in Egypt where papyrus was so plentiful, private individuals kept 'archives' of sherds which have been found.[201] Moreover, from the physical aspect of the records alone, we must clearly blur the line between archives and collections of documents in Athens. Not only was there great variety in the type of material used for records; both the *bouleutērion* and the Metroön contained a form of written record (stelai) which had a symbolic and visual significance as well as that of a document. In some senses the classical archive was an accumulation of different kinds of record like the medieval one.[202] And the later archive in the Metroön clearly inherited certain features from the earlier and less sophisticated collection.

How easy was it to find these documents in the archives? Obviously this question bears on the infrequency of consultation. In the *bouleutērion*, if the tablets and stelai were on the walls, reference was mostly a matter of knowing where to look. For the Metroön itself, most ideas about its arrangement are surely over-optimistic. Again, we know extremely little; for the arrangement of the documents we must largely rely on chance information about the contents. We have no evidence about the overall size and arrangement of the fourth-century Metroön: in the Hellenistic building the documents were probably kept in two rooms, while the goddess guarding the archives was in a third. For the fourth century we only know that the Metroön included a shrine.[203] Thus the documents were in fact closely associated with a temple, an association perhaps inherited from the earlier connection between temples and public documents (see p. 31).[204]

It has been suggested that the documents themselves were stored in yearly batches under the archon year and different prytanies. This is inferred from the fact that many documents do not have dates and therefore the exact dates of each must have been obvious to the keeper of the archive from the place where they were stored.[205] However, this is not only speculative, but optimistic, and the reasons for this are illuminating for the general level of sophistication in documents.

---

[201] Posner (1972), 157ff.; Wilcken (1899). They were probably kept in big jars.

[202] For an example of a Near Eastern 'archive' cluttered up with furniture and other objects, see Posner (1972), 122 (Persepolis).

[203] See n. 73 above for possible extension of 'Metroön' to include a wider area than the building alone.

[204] See H. A. Thompson (1937), 216f. on similarity of the Hellenistic Metroön to the library at Pergamon. It was traditional for libraries to have a statue of the goddess Demeter.

[205] Curtius (1868), 23f. (from Boeckh); Posner (1972), 112f. and n. 64.

First, the suggestion assumes that an exact date was thought necessary (even aside from the immensely complex problems of the Attic calendar and the prescripts of Attic decrees).[206] If this were so, then the form of the documents could be said to be inadequate on its own, since complex archival organization would be necessary to preserve the desired information.[207] More probably the system was far more haphazard and 'dating' vaguer. If the form of the documents is inadequate on its own, this suggests a situation akin to that of the mortgage *horoi*, though much less primitive: the written document was meant, or was assumed, to be supplemented by external information preserved orally (or else through the archive arrangement). Thus, the form was not enough by itself to create a record that could be used in the future, though it could create a memorial.

Apart from this, however, the form of the prescripts (and superscripts) at the top of decrees varied and developed throughout the fifth and fourth centuries. A recent detailed study of Attic prescripts by Henry[208] comes to the conclusion that in the classical period, and indeed later, a secretary was never bound to include all the elements that were available: he had considerable latitude in what he decided to include. Henry explains this by the absence of modern standardization and by the lack of any expectation of verbatim accuracy (one can also point to the temporary nature of the post of secretary – see below, pp. 80f.). This, then, brings us back to the ancient idea of copying, the lack of that exaggerated respect for the written word which demands absolute fidelity, and thus to the overall explanation of these features. If the use of written documents is comparatively unsophisticated or undeveloped, there may be variations, inconsistencies and omissions of the kind of information that we might consider essential in a document.[209] This may be partly because no one had realized what information was essential for a document to continue its usefulness in the archive. Meanwhile, there is no absolute standard format. That said, however, it is also clear that different

---

[206] Rhodes (1972), 'Additional Notes A' has a concise summary.

[207] Cf. the complex system of hero years described by *Ath.Pol.* 53.4–7: year classes were divided between 42 heroes and also dated by the archon year in which each person enrolled as ephebe. The system helped the calling up of a certain age-group for military service or to be arbitrators etc. It was evidently to deal with the fact that most people did not know their age and there were no birth certificates: giving each year group an archon and hero compensated for this. Ignorance of one's age is not simply the product of illiteracy (*pace* Duncan-Jones (1977) discussing the Roman period).

[208] Henry (1977).

[209] E.g. Henry (1977), 32, on truncated prescripts; 43ff., on omitted items (fourth century). He also argues (1979) that archon dating in the fifth century does *not* become a regular rule from 421 onwards. Clanchy points to elements in medieval documents indicating that, though the documents were being made carefully, it was not realized for a while what information was necessary in writing for them to be useful as records in future: e.g. most twelfth-century charters were not dated ((1979), 231).

systems of dating decrees did actually come into use in the fourth century and these were sometimes very exact (e.g. in giving the day of the month).[210] So in some cases greater precision was developing in the production of documents. The sophistication of both the documents and their storage may therefore have changed gradually. But the two are interrelated. Both the form of the documents and the actual storage must be related to an overall degree of complexity in using the written word: if documents seem naive as documents, their 'inadequacies' were not necessarily balanced by the complexities of the archives. In fact, in classical Athens the documents were more probably supplemented by the spoken word.

The Metroön may have had some kind of shelves, like the *epistylia* (shelves with pigeon-holes) for the tablets of the *poletai*[211] or niches for papyrus rolls, a practice used in Hellenistic libraries. But it probably also contained jars. It has been seriously suggested, with some likelihood, that the tablets of decrees were stored in jars.[212] It seems to be supported by the anecdote about Diogenes the Cynic who found a home in a jar in the Metroön (unless it was in the temple). Moreover, the use of jars as document containers was probably common. The written documents for cases which were to go before an arbitrator were put separately in jars, one jar for each side. The jars were sealed and handed over to members of the Forty: thus to 'file' a case was to put it in a jar and seal it (Arist. *Ath.Pol.* 53.2).[213] The use of jars rather than shelves may have been more frequent than we would suppose.[214] If there were storage jars in the archive, reference would not be straightforward, and they would imply again a more haphazard and confusing system than one would expect from the neat systems of the Hellenistic libraries.

So one probably had to go through an official to look anything up in the Metroön. What officials were there? The main official in charge of the archive was the secretary of the boule (the same as the secretary of the prytany).[215] The changes in the secretariat in the 360s probably had some

---

[210] See Henry (1977). The inclusion of the *epistates* (president of prytany) in the prescript was not necessarily a means of dating to the exact day (Henry (*ibid.*), 26).

[211] *Ath.Pol.* 47.5; Wilhelm (1909), 248.   [212] Posner (1972), 112.

[213] Storage jars for private documents have also been found in Ptolemaic Egypt (Posner (1972), 157f.) and all over the Near East.

[214] For the use of *kibōtoi* ('boxes'), cf. the temple 'archive' at Locri Epizephirii of numerous bronze tablets (Franciscis (1972)). In Athenian treasury inventories, objects are moved around in *kibōtoi*.

[215] Rhodes (1972), 134ff. and Ferguson (1898), chs. 3–4: the terminology was not rigid in the fourth century. *Ath.Pol.* 54.3 on the secretary of the prytany 'who is in charge of the documents (*grammata*), keeps the decrees which have been passed, checks the transcription of everything else (ἀντιγράφεται) and attends the boule.' Aristotle comments that the post was once held by distinguished men who appeared on the stelai. The growing importance of fifth-century secretaries may be related to the strengthening of the democracy, see Davies (1984), 115.

bearing on the efficiency of the archives and recognition of their importance. For until 368/7 or slightly later, the secretary served only for one prytany (i.e. a month), and he was a member of the boule; by 363/2 the secretary (now usually called the 'secretary of the prytany') served for a year, and he was chosen by lot. In either arrangement the post is temporary and brief; probably most of the archive work was done by the lower assistant or *hypogrammateus* and, more important, the public slave (*ho dēmosios*) who is actually mentioned as being in charge of the records.[216] However, the change may reflect some recognition that the growing complexity of the records required an official who had more time to grasp his duties. Indeed, Rhodes has suggested that the Athenians were now 'beginning to treat their records more seriously' and the month-long secretaryship was not enough to cope with the work. So this may be a move towards greater efficiency and professionalism.[217] But not entirely, for the secretary is now chosen by lot and Aristotle (*Ath.Pol.* 54.3) seems to think the secretary was now less powerful. This is a long way from a professional keeper of records. The lower assistant and public slave were the only permanent personnel.

So far, then, we have seen that behind the inscriptions and other written documents lay numerous means of oral transmission. Public inscriptions were consulted: but our evidence suggests that apart from the lists of public debts, traitors or benefactors consultation was rare. Lengthy decrees often had a commemorative function which was not impaired if they were little used for reference. The laws were surely consulted more often. But part of the problem in consulting any document was knowing where to look. The Metroön was used far less. It was not until the mid-fourth century that the value of its records seems to have been properly realized. This is hardly surprising. It is after all comparatively easy to keep documents. It is a rather different step to use them again, find them and consult them. The archive's organization was simple, if not haphazard, without catalogues or important permanent keepers. With its combination of stelai, wooden tablets and large jars, it did in some ways continue the methods of keeping documents (including stelai) in the old *bouleutērion*. The Athenian archives may have been more akin to an accumulation of documents than highly organized archives. Both the degree of system and the frequency with which records were later consulted are related to the overall degree of familiarity with documents. As we have seen, Athens was extending the use of the written word and its preservation during the first half of the fourth century. The two elements are facets of the same phenomenon. Sophisti-

[216] Dem. XIX 129; also *IG* II² 463, 28f.; 583, 5–7; *IG* II² 120, 10ff. (certainly 353/2, Schweigert in *Hesperia* 7 (1938), 286).
[217] Rhodes (1972), 138.

cated use of the documents once they are kept as 'records' seems to become evident in the mid-fourth century.

Many records were not preserved at all. Certain types of document were destroyed as soon as the transaction they signified was over. The keeping of accounts was rudimentary or faltering, and there seems to have been no single text which collected together the entire revenue (or expenditure) of Athens.[218] This is hardly surprising if certain types of financial records were obliterated as soon as the transaction was completed. Other types of record were never made in the first place – for instance, there was no land register and no list of those eligible for agonistic liturgies, the obligatory financing of certain polis contests.[219] There was no central register of citizens.[220] Some of this kind of information did not need written documents but was transmitted by oral means. Everyone in each deme knew who owned what land. Written documents concerning different officials were kept separately. For instance, the deme registers were kept individually by each deme and it was the deme's responsibility to make sure it only included deme members: the information in the list was partly confirmed by the general knowledge of the deme, not purely dependent on a written text.[221] No doubt there are many other examples. The crucial point is that documents were made and often kept, but that certain documents were often supplemented or duplicated by orally transmitted information. If they repeated information everyone knew already – perhaps serving as a mnemonic aid – they did not require frequent reference. Or else they might be kept, but kept with a very simple idea of what precisely their use was: either inadequate, therefore, as records without further information or seldom consulted.

There seems to be an example of precisely this phenomenon in the recent finds of 'cavalry archives' in the agora: they may form a final – and perhaps conclusive – illustration of this section's theme.[222] The collection is of great interest for my discussion, for its material, lead, makes it one of the few archives (if not the only one) where we can actually tell from

---

[218] Finley (1982); cf. D. M. Lewis (1966) on the stelai of the sale of property and the 'accounting' visible there. Strepsiades is seen in the *Clouds* doing his accounts. On ancient accounting, see de Ste Croix (1956) and Macve (1985).

[219] There was, however, a list of trierarchs: Ar. *Knights* 912f. and schol.; Davies (1984), 24; also *IG* II² 1928ff., the *diadikasia* documents, and Davies (1984), app. I.

[220] Hansen (1986), ch. 1.4: except the deme register, *lexiarchikon grammateion* and the list of those who could attend the assembly, the *pinax ekklesiastikos*, which were kept separately in the demes (see next note), and the bronze stelai for each year class, which recorded those eligible for military service. See his appendix v for sceptical discussion of the 'hoplite *katalogos*' (list of hoplites).

[221] Cf. Weiss (1923), 369–83 on lists; Hondius (1922); [Dem.] LVII and Dem. XXXIX on confusions in deme record-keeping; Whitehead (1986), 35, n. 130, 97ff., 104f.

[222] Braun (1970); Kroll (1977).

the documents alone if anyone used them. The 'archive' consists of lead tablets rolled up with a single name on the outside. Inside each tablet we usually find the same man's name with a description of his horse and its price. There is no date. Some tablets are from the fourth century, some from the third. Thus apparently every cavalryman had his own lead roll with a brief description of his horse and its value.

What is most peculiar about these tablets is that all have been tightly rolled up and were found in their original state (as one can tell because they are made of lead). It is thus very doubtful if any had ever been consulted. What were the tablets for, then? Various explanations have been offered, particularly for the presence of the evaluation of the horses, and they probably have some truth.[223] Yet the most complicated tries to show why the tablets have not been consulted; this involves a complex system of insurance for the horses which was updated each year. The tablets would then only have to be consulted when a horse died in battle and the insurance was to be paid.[224] There are in any case difficulties in this idea. But there may be a simpler and more plausible explanation. There are numerous reasons to keep records of cavalrymen's horses, but a complex insurance system need not be the only reason for the records being unopened. Perhaps they only recorded what everyone knew already. Or the records were in fact too crude (and they are very crude indeed) to be of much use as records without other information that could be supplied orally. Or it was simply felt appropriate to have a record of each horse (which included its value) and of its owner, even if the record was not going to be consulted much. We might be seeing here an instance of the keeping of records in a context where they did not actually need to be used.

These tablets form an extremely rare example of a collection of documents whose material enables us to tell if they were used or not. They seem never to have been opened. I would like to take them as an instance of an 'archive' or collection of documents that was carefully made and rolled. But the nature of the documents, their content, or their context amidst much oral transmission meant that they did not actually need to be consulted. I suspect that the same was true of other ancient records, an expression of the incipient nature of classical record keeping.

1.2.4 Documenting the past
The use of 'historical' documents from the past has obvious relevance to

---

223 Habicht (1961b), esp. 135; Braun (1970), 267–9. Kroll objects to Habicht's explanation (connected with *dokimasia* ('scrutiny') of horses in Arist. *Ath. Pol.* 49.1) because of the valuations, but surely valuations can be part of a horse's essential description.

224 Kroll (1977), 97–100: though at the same time he points out that Harpokration indicates that the money paid out against the horse was a *fixed* amount. He believes the values

historiography, but again, I shall concentrate first on the appearance of such documents in other spheres, primarily in the ordinary business of the democracy. Their relation to the general increase in documents is therefore all the clearer.

Historical decrees were often cited in the fourth-century assembly to provide examples from the past – mainly Athens' glorious fifth-century history. For instance, the punishment of Arthmios of Zeleia for treachery was written upon a bronze stele placed prominently on the Acropolis (Dem. xix 271f.). It is cited four times as a paradigm in our extant orators alone, three times as if from the stele – Dinarchus introduces it with 'consider this stele' (ii 25; also Dem. ix 41f., xix 271f., Aeschin. iii 258). It was a familiar part of the rhetorical arguments from the past. Other material was certainly widely known from the assembly. For example, Dinarchus quotes a Theban decree (i *Ag. Demosth.* 25), apparently passed by Thebes at the end of the fifth century to help Thrasyboulos and the exiles at Thebes to seize Phyle: Thebes would turn a blind eye if any Athenians marched through their territory bearing arms. Dinarchus calls it 'the decree often read out before you', though we know little more of it. So a decree was familiar in the assembly which has left no trace in our earlier sources.[225]

The notorious decrees which purported to date from the Persian Wars over a century ago were equally well known in the fourth-century assembly. Demosthenes (xix 303) reminds the assembly how Aeschines read out the decrees of Miltiades and Themistocles from the Persian Wars and the ephebic oath: apparently his audience needed no further explanation. The Peace of Callias is called 'this peace so talked about (θϱυλουμένην) by everyone' by Demosthenes (xix 273). He may be referring to the excessive use made of it in the assembly. The Plateian Oath (Lyc. i 80f.) and the Salamis decree, condemning a man who had spoken treason (Lyc. i 122; story alluded to by Dem. xviii 204), were probably also well known from patriotic citations. Whatever their historical status, these documents were effectively propagated through the assembly.

These decrees are probably best known in their guise of fourth-century 'forgeries', a formulation which was convincingly argued by Habicht (1961a) shortly after the publication of the Themistocles decree. He noticed that a crop of decrees supposedly dating from the Persian Wars started to appear around the mid-fourth century. Bringing them together, he argued from inconsistencies and anachronisms (many of

---

were changed every year but in that case we should find erasures on the tablets – for that is one of the virtues of lead. They are so tight that some cannot be unrolled.

[225] Cf. however, Diod. xiv 6.3, Plut. *Lys.* 27.6, *Pelop.* 6.5, which may suggest that some fourth-century historian included it – unless it was extracted from the orators.

them already noticed) that the group was forged expressly for political propaganda in that period. Only the ephebic oath, he believed, went back to a genuine fifth-century text.[226] The others were essentially fourth-century products, even if based on some genuine tradition. Thus the Troizen decree, so full of anachronistic details, is clearly a much later fourth-century fabrication.[227] The Plateian Oath is an amalgamation of various other oaths.[228] The decree about Hipparchus is colourful but unlikely (see above, n. 168). The Salamis decree seems a complete invention from Herodotus (IX 5), but has been altered in an attempt to legalize the council's action.[229] The Miltiades decree, in fact alluded to by Kephisodotos earlier than Habicht's dating,[230] was for the emergency expedition to rescue Euboia in 490. We know too little to say more than that the circumstances are not improbable.[231] Of the others, the Peace of Callias and the decree of Themistocles arranging Athens' military preparation before the Persian invasion, the circumstances and controversies surrounding them are well enough known.[232] The Arthmios decree may well be genuine (though Habicht thinks not): a simple and basic original can be recovered behind all the rhetorical paraphrases.[233] Perhaps, though genuine, it was only noticed again when it could become a suitable paradigm in the fourth century. These last three stand out from

---

[226] Lyc. I 76 quotes it; Dem. XIX 303 says Aeschines read out the oath from the temple of Aglauros, apparently referring to a public copy. See also Siewert (1977).

[227] Habicht (1961a); see also Jacoby on Cleidemus *FGH* 323 F21.

[228] Its authenticity is expressly denied by Theopompus, *FGH* 115 F153: his denial is not decisive since he is not impartial and F153 and 154 criticize all the achievements Athens boasts about. A rather different version of the oath appears on the Acharnai stele, which indicates that other such documents (now lost) were around: Tod II 204 (who omits the clause about not rebuilding, which may be authentic), and Robert (1938), 293–316 on differences; cf. Siewert (1972). It has only the Athenians' oath, not the Greeks'. According to David Lewis, the lettering is Lycurgan.

[229] In Herodotus the councillor was stoned to death simply for speaking treason; there was no question of a trial, and the deed is more savage since he had only advised submitting the proposal to the assembly. In Lycurgus it is a case of judicial murder, and he stresses the example as in the decree, rather than the stoning itself. Dem. XVIII 204 also mentions the man (but calls him Kyrsilos, not Lykides) and his wife's fate, but there is no decree. Only Lycurgus and Aristeides (II pp. 286f. (Dindorf)) have the boule's decree and correct date. The slightly divergent traditions are understandable and serve the same patriotic aim: the main difference is the provision of a suitable decree.

[230] Arist. *Rhet.* III 10, 1410a10; probably in 357/6.

[231] It had gathered anachronisms by Plutarch's time, and it may bear complicated relations to later criticism of the Athenian abandonment of Euboia in 490: Habicht, and Munro, *CAH* IV 237f.

[232] For the Themistocles decree, see esp. Jameson (1963) and Meritt (1967), and the bibliography in ML. For the Peace of Callias, see the excellent summary of the controversy and important references in Meiggs (1972), 129ff. and app. 8; most recently, Meister (1982).

[233] Meiggs (1972), 508ff.: it is anachronistic only if one assumes (with Habicht) that Arthmios is outlawed from the allies' territory as well as Attica, and that Zeleia was in the Delian League at the time.

the rest for they were publicly inscribed,[234] publicly endorsed and visible, whatever their character.

Habicht's article has been immensely stimulating and influential. However, we should not lose sight of the wider context in which these decrees appear. Habicht's collection of documents is not an isolated phenomenon. Orators cite other historical documents as rhetorical examples. Surely the very citation of these kinds of written document must be connected with the wider changes in attitude we have been discussing. Explanations of the appearance of the 'forged documents' have stressed immediate political needs. Their timing is usually connected with political events for which their 'lessons' are appropriate. So Habicht linked them with the disaster at Olynthus since the documents seemed to start around 348 B.C. But some decrees were in fact cited before 348, so more recently they have been connected with the external policy of Athens in the 370s.[235]

Such dating obscures a crucial element. The immediate politics must explain why a certain decree is cited in a particular speech. But why is a decree cited at all? Historians of the ancient world are so familiar with the use of Greek decrees as historical evidence that it is easy to miss the extraordinary nature of their use here. Why do the orators bother to cite precise decrees at all? So often they are content with patriotic calls upon the great ancestors of the Persian Wars and the days of Athens' superiority. These oral traditions were clearly adequate, though they seem repetitious and trite to us (see, for instance, the conventional content of the public funeral speeches, Ch. 4). So why should it suddenly seem necessary to quote actual decrees connected with these achievements? Clearly these historical documents and their citation must be seen against the increasing respect for written documents in the first half of the fourth century and the development of rhetorical technique in citing written documents.[236]

Other fifth-century documents or material were quoted by orators around the middle of the fourth century or a little before – not merely the famous 'forged documents'. There are other exemplary decrees.[237] And a crop of epigrams starts appearing around the mid-fourth century.

---

234 Inscription of Peace of Callias implied by Isoc. *Paneg.* 120, i.e. in 380 B.C.

235 Robertson (1976); Davies (ICS seminar, 1985) would push it further back still, to the 390s. Kephisodotos had already quoted Miltiades' decree (n. 230 above), Isocrates referred to the Peace of Callias in 380 (see previous note).

236 I shall not, therefore, be so concerned with the authenticity of specific texts nor the immediate political background to their citation, which have been discussed at length elsewhere.

237 The decree of Demophantos became a rhetorical example (Dem. xx 159; Lyc. I 124); the decree about Phrynichus being tried for treason posthumously, Lyc. I 113f. (Lysias (xiii 70–2) used a similar decree on the same subject for factual proof about Agoratos); Aeschin. iii 187, the decree for the Phyle party, which is contrasted with the deserters from Chaeronea; the list of Plateian citizens, [Dem.] lix 105; Lyc. I 120 on those who

Aeschines quotes the epigrams on the Hermae for victory against the Persians in 475 (III 183; Dem. XXII 112). Epigrams on the Spartan dead at Thermopylae and for the Athenians at Marathon are quoted later by Lycurgus (I 109), as is one in honour of the democrats from Phyle (who opposed the Thirty in 404–403) which was accompanied by a decree from the Metroön by Aeschines (III 187).[238] Epigrams may be less dependent on a written text than decrees, but their appearance is the more striking because of that. Why were they not quoted before? Poetry is also quoted at length, particularly that of Solon.[239] Apparently all kinds of material, most of it documentary, must now be brought forward and quoted in order to prove the virtue of the Athenian ancestors. There were certainly relevant patriotic decrees and epigrams which Isocrates, Lysias or Andocides could have quoted. Yet they did not do so.[240]

We should also compare the orators' practice in using documents of any kind. This reminds us of the extension of the written word for testimonies in court (Ch. 1.2.1). We can discern a slight increase in their use of documents as the fourth century progresses. Thus Antiphon, in the late fifth century, quotes no documents at all, yet witnesses are called fairly frequently. Andocides quotes three decrees and three laws in *De myst.* (I) and otherwise only one other.[241] All these are strictly related to his own case and play no paradigmatic role. Lysias, surprisingly, quotes decrees only in *Ag. Agoratos* (XIII): all of them are relevant to Agoratos himself, including the famous decree rewarding the killers of Phrynichus (§§70–2).[242] These earlier speeches rely heavily on witnesses, little on recent decrees and not at all upon historical exempla in the form of

withdrew to Decelea; the decree about Harmodius and Aristogeiton, Dem. xx 127; the Theban decree, Din. I *Ag. Demosth.* 25; Aeschines' quotation of the Hermae epigrams, III 183 (questioned by Wade-Gery (1933), who thought they came merely from a book of epigrams, but it is quite improbable that Aeschines should have quoted prominent epigrams as visible if they were not – see Gomme, *HCT* I pp. 288f.).

[238] For this, see Raubitschek (1941) on epigraphic fragments which, in so far as they can be read, confirm Aeschines' accuracy.

[239] Dem. XIX 255 (343 B.C.), extensive quotation of Solon; also in Aeschines, Lycurgus and Dem. XVIII and XIX: on quotations of poetry in oratory, see Perlman (1964). All (extant) rhetorical quotations of poetry occur in seven speeches, and the addition of poetic citations emphasizes that the debate is, in fact, about a relatively small number of speeches treating expressly patriotic issues (incl. Aeschin. III and his speech mentioned by Dem. XIX 303). Habicht argues from Theopompus that Aeschines also cited the Plataean Oath in 348. The rest of Habicht's examples all come from the one complete speech of Lycurgus in 330, except for references to Arthmios' stele from Dem. IX, XIX, Aeschin. III again and Din. II 24 (324 B.C.) (and stoning of Kyrsilos in Dem. XVIII 204).

[240] Cf. esp. Isocrates' extensive use of *exempla* from the Persian Wars. And. I 77 quotes the amnesty decree of Patrokleides which begins by mentioning that of the Persian Wars: had he lived in the late fourth century he might perhaps have quoted the very decree from the Persian Wars, too, to add a suitable historical example.

[241] And. I 17, 83, 85, 87, 96, of which 83, 87 and 96 are laws. Also II 23, a decree (before 403).

[242] Witnesses are numerous and there are occasional citations of a law.

documents taken from that period.[243] This must be indicative of an earlier practice of rhetoric. Written documents were simply not incorporated into the argument as much as they were in later oratory.

We have already seen that even when documents are cited, they are used with varying degrees of sophistication. Aeschines drew particularly unusual and complex arguments from the public documents, but that was new. (He was also notorious for his citations of historical documents, as Demosthenes' criticisms imply (xix 303).) Often documents were produced as an argument in a manner which seems naive to us. These variations must partly be connected with the fact that extensive written documentation was comparatively recent, the use of documents undeveloped. That was increasing in the ordinary business of the assembly and courts (Ch. 1.2.1, above). Citation of documents concerning the deeds of the ancestors, however, is symptomatic of the same growing respect for the written word. It was no longer enough simply to refer to the achievements of the ancestors, remembered in the old oral traditions. It was more impressive if their achievements could be documented with the written word, in fact by the precise texts of their decrees.

In fact, the orators hint that they feel their words are not enough and that the written documents (*ta grammata*) of their ancestors constituted more certain proof. The contrast is sometimes explicit. So Demosthenes (ix 41f.) introduces the Arthmios decree by stressing that the proof is in their writing, not his words: οὐ λόγους ἐμαυτοῦ λέγων, ἀλλὰ γράμματα τῶν προγόνων τῶν ὑμετέρων, 'repeating not my own words, but the written words of your ancestors'. Lycurgus introduces the Plateian oath thus (i 80): 'For though the events of that time are ancient, we may discern their virtue (*aretē*) clearly enough in these written words (ἐν τοῖς γεγραμμένοις).' (Here there is no antithesis between their writing and his words.) The point of the example of the Salamis decree was in the decree itself, not the action it led to (Lyc. i 122).[244]

Alongside this tendency to want written proof, there is at the same time a feeling that the ancients were too virtuous to need writing. This is the other side of the coin. If the mid-fourth century is a world where written memorials are beginning to be used as paradigms for future

---

[243] Kahrstedt (1938) used the extreme rarity of documents cited before 403 as a sign that there were no archives: in eleven speeches before 403 only one decree occurs, while in And. i, which is later, there are several. Relevant speeches include [And.] *Ag. Alcib.*, Lysias, *On the Subversion of the Ancestral Constitution*; Ant. *Murder of Herodes*, *On the Choreutes*; And. ii; Lys. xx (*For Polystratus*), xxiv (defended as genuine, Dover (1968), 189.)

[244] Cf. also the stress on writing in Aeschin. iii 113, the oracle, oath and curse from the original war against Cirrha are still inscribed; Aeschin. iii 192; Dem. viii 5, the oath we took and the terms on which we made peace 'are published in writing for all to see' (ἔστιν ἰδεῖν καὶ γεγραμμένα κεῖται). Cf. And. iii 12, an isolated earlier example.

generations, the ancestors were naturally so virtuous that they had no need of those paradigms. Thus, Demosthenes adds to his citation of the Arthmios decree (IX 41) that, of course, that generation did not need these *grammata*: καὶ γὰρ ἄνευ τούτων τῶν γραμμάτων τὰ δέοντ' ἐφρόνουν. 'For even without these written words, they knew instinctively what was appropriate.'[245] Aeschines (III 181f.) compares his opponent Demosthenes with the heroes of the Persian Wars, Themistocles, Miltiades, Aristides, and the democratic heroes of 403. He challenges him to show if anywhere there stands written an order to crown those men (for there is not); 'For they thought that they should be honoured not in writing but in the memory of those they had served.' They relied on memory alone. Here the antithesis between honour and honour with crowning has become one between writing and memory. One is reminded of the words Thucydides wrote in Pericles' Funeral Speech (II 43.3) that the memorials of the dead would be not merely stelai, but 'unwritten memory' (*agraphos mnēmē*). Written records were increasingly felt to be necessary, but these fourth-century orators could regard them as characteristic of their own contemporary decadence. The late fourth century was excessively preoccupied with Athens' past glories, it is true. But the 'historical documents' are not so much a symptom of the need for exhortation and example, as of a desire for example in the form of written documents. The fourth century had paradigms enough in oral tradition, but they were no longer sufficient.

What, then, of the 'forged documents' and their origin? They are usually linked with historiography. They are taken to have originated with an historian, and their appearance in oratory becomes an instance of rhetorical use of the historians. However, this does not really explain their presence: the problem of their sudden appearance is transferred to the historians and left there. The precise timing of their appearance in the speeches of the assembly is related merely to immediate political events. But as we have seen, the use of historical documents at all in oratory is related to the orators' general awareness of the written word and increasing use of other written documentation. So in that sense such development is internal and not tied closely to historiography. Oratory had its own need for documentation already.

We should also consider the historians' use of documents in the same context. The citation of written documents is not the preserve of historians alone. Ancient historians' relative neglect of written evidence is not simply explained by the paucity or inadequacy of ancient documents.[246] The two aspects are facets of the same phenomenon. The

---

[245] Printed in small type in the Oxford Classical Text, it is one of the passages in the expanded version of the speech by Demosthenes.
[246] As Finley (1983) (= 1985, ch. 2).

historians' methods are partly symptomatic of more widespread changes of attitude.

We recognize that they used documents infrequently, if at all.[247] Thucydides cited contemporary documents only in Book v, probably realizing that the exact texts were necessary. He made slight use of older inscriptions for his research on the Peisistratids, and his careful citation and argument suggest again that it was unusual to extract historical information from inscriptions.[248] Herodotus frequently quotes short inscriptions or epigrams, but primarily as commemorative memorials, not to extract historical information from them. They serve as commemorative illustration of what he has just narrated.[249] It is hardly surprising to find a fairly simple use of written documents like this, symptomatic of the relatively unsophisticated approach to written documents of the time (it is only with Aeschines, after all, that we first find detailed argument from past decrees). What is remarkable is not so much that Herodotus lacks complex epigraphical methods,[250] but that he tries to extract new historical information and complicated theories from certain types of written record. His use of the 'Cadmeian' inscriptions of Thebes (v 59–61) and others which supposedly dated from before the Trojan War are less a sign of naive credulity than an interesting attempt to illuminate really distant periods from which – unlike the recent past – little oral tradition survived. For oral tradition was quite adequate for recent history. Perhaps we see here the difference between using written record to illustrate or commemorate what everyone knows already from oral transmission and using it to illuminate areas of the past where oral tradition gives out.

Inscriptions were not used extensively for historical information and argument until Aristotle. Craterus' *Collection of Decrees* (the ψηφισμάτων συναγωγή, probably late fourth century) was a new and unusual idea.[251] As for the fourth-century Atthidographers, it is unlikely that they used documents to alter the received view. Their originality, as Jacoby stressed, lay in rationalizing the legends and reinterpreting accepted facts.[252] Thus, so far, their aims do not seem so remote from those of the orators who cited exemplary decrees simply to illustrate

247 E.g. Finley (1982) and (1983); Momigliano (1972).
248 References in n. 187 above. His contemporary, Cratippus, said that Thucydides deliberately abandoned the use of speeches later on (Dionysius of Halicarnassus, *Thuc.* 16), an absence often taken, along with the documents' presence, as a sign of incompleteness.
249 There is a useful detailed discussion of all Herodotus' citations of inscriptions in S. West (1985).
250 As S. West (1985) stresses: she explains the lack, however, rather by the nature of Herodotus' literary oral narrative and general characteristics of an 'oral society'.
251 Jacoby, *FGH* 342 and commentary. Cf. Polemon (2nd century B.C.), nicknamed 'tablet-glutton' (*stēlokopas*) (Herodicus at *Ath.* vi 234d).
252 Jacoby, *Atthis* 204f. This is, indeed, what Isocrates is particularly proud of.

broad and accepted patriotic beliefs of the past – but not to draw detailed or unusual inferences from them. The methods of the *Ath.Pol.*, in using extensively both documents and poetry to elucidate Athens' past, seem to be expressive of the increasing interest in documents and documentation. In fact, the initial impetus for such interest could equally well have come from the orators and politicians as from historians.

We might suppose that this greater attention to written record encouraged some people to search for relevant inscriptions and decrees in the archive.[253] Not all the historical documents the orators quote are certainly 'forgeries'. Even some of Habicht's collection seem to be taken from inscriptions.[254] More attention was being given to the old inscriptions lying around.

But what of the other documents whose anachronisms are glaring, which have little basis in any original document and were probably elaborated from Herodotus' narrative or other historians? They are also to be seen partly as a product of the increasing use of written proof as opposed to oral. That seems clear from what we have seen of the general increase in the use of the written word. But we can perhaps go further. For in that case, how would they have been regarded in the fourth century? They are clearly forgeries in the modern sense, since they are not the original documents or even copies of them. But would they have been regarded strictly as forgeries in classical Athens? Fourth-century Athens did recognize fraudulent additions to documents, false wills and additions to lists. But the line would perhaps be more blurred in the case of historical events of the past which everyone accepted as true.

There are various aspects to this. First that of documentary anachronism. We might have an example of an historical decree quoted in the fourth century in which some elements look as if they derived from the original, much earlier, decree but where there are additional inaccuracies and anachronistic phraseology and detail (as it has been argued of the Themistocles decree). We have seen that strict verbatim accuracy was not generally demanded of documents. If little importance was attached to the precise wording – even of an old decree – anachronisms could get incorporated slowly, perhaps partly from an assumption that the document should be 'updated' to make it look like a 'proper' decree. The gradual accretion of anachronisms to the conventional formulae of old decrees would probably not have been regarded as inexact or fraudulent at all, especially without a strong sense of the historical importance of older phraseology.[255] Moreover, without a highly sophisti-

---

[253] But much depended on what they wanted to find and the use that was to be made of the past at all: cf. Finley (1971), Plumb (1969).

[254] E.g. the Arthmios decree, the epigram for the party from Phyle, the epigrams on the Cimonian victories (Aeschin. III 183) and (?) the Peace of Callias.

[255] Meritt (1967) recognizes the relevance of this for the Themistocles decree.

cated treatment of the detailed implications of written documents, or awareness of historical change in their format, anachronisms would not necessarily seem anachronistic.[256]

What about the fraudulent decrees which seem merely elaborated from a tale in Herodotus or some other narrative, but no documentary source? Here one would think documentary forgery could be recognized clearly. But again, the line between false and 'true' might have been blurred. This was another grey area between the reliance on oral tradition and communication and the use of written record. The circumstances of forgery in the Middle Ages seem to confirm these suspicions. For 'forgeries' in the Middle Ages become rife just when written documentation was becoming more common and in some areas essential. Oral methods of validation were no longer accepted, and institutions, cities and monasteries had to produce written proof of their status and privileges for the Norman administration. Clearly some charters could have been invented quite cynically (in fact 'forged'). But what if a monastery, say, had traditions of its foundation and rights which had been passed down orally and which everyone 'knew' to be true? Or the traditions were also confirmed by one of the symbolic objects which acted as memorial and non-written proof of the claim. The monastery is forced to produce written proof, so it embodies the traditions it knows to be 'true' in written form. The truth of those claims was not in doubt. But the society still relied heavily on the spoken word and non-written proof, its use of the written word was still undeveloped, though encroaching steadily on the oral forms. Was there much difference in their eyes between continuing in their belief in the oral traditions and transferring them to document form?[257]

These may be extreme examples where institutions were compelled to produce written proof. But it is at least worth wondering how far the inventors of the fourth-century historical decrees (whoever they were) thought they were merely transferring oral traditions or historical narrative to written documentary form; or whether they classed their activities in the same bracket as the additions to the lists of debtors or traitors that were openly recognized as false. When the priests of the sanctuaries – often much earlier – added the names of legendary figures to the temple offerings thought to have been dedicated by them, their activities and motives may have been still more blurred (e.g. Hdt. v 59).

Whatever the ancient interpretation, however, the connection of such

---

[256] Cf. Syme's comments (1972) on literary 'fraud and imposture': the term 'forgery' is hardly applicable until the existence of literature as such is recognized, the 'genuine' as well as the 'spurious'.

[257] Clanchy (1979), 117ff. and 248ff. Thus he sees the forgery or renewal of documents as 'essentially a product of the movement from memory to written record' (p. 254).

'forgeries' with increasing regard for written proof is clear. The need for written documentation of the past seems to be a development of that. The Greek historians' comparative disregard of written documents in favour of oral tradition is not simply a choice on their own part, but symptomatic of attitudes in other spheres. Even in the fourth century, Athens was only partially document-minded, familiar with oral methods of proof and record. Written documentation of the past, as opposed to oral tradition alone, may not have been a concern of historiography alone. In assembly rhetoric as well as the late fourth-century historians, it is a logical development from the increasing use and demand for written record in other walks of life and the increasing sophistication with which the written word was used. Accompanying it was a feeling that oral tradition alone might no longer be adequate.

*

Far from being a static or neutral skill, literacy has a development and a history. The use of literacy in any society, as in ancient Greece, may be influenced partly by previous oral methods of communication and record, partly by attitudes to the written word, partly by 'ideology' in general. The case of classical Athens reminds us forcefully that the role of the written word in the development of a society might be very much more complex and faltering than we would assume. It also encourages us to think more carefully about our own expectations of contemporary literacy.

We should never ignore – or underestimate – the background of oral communication, of non-written methods of proof and record which both exist alongside the written word in classical Athens and may actually influence its use. This is particularly important for the study of the classical world for which scholars stress the survival of written evidence so much. Both written and oral methods clearly exist together in many spheres of life in classical Athens, and we should take both into account. This removes the dichotomy which so often hovers in the background of modern scholarship between 'oral' and 'literate'. The 'grey areas' in between, where both oral and written methods or very simple written methods are used, cannot be overemphasized. This has been proved for classical Athens, where we may even discern the extension and growing sophistication of the written word. We should therefore assume that oral methods of communication were even more important in earlier centuries and in many other classical city-states.

Our approach to Greek, as well as Athenian, documents is deeply affected. We have traced the extension of the written word into spheres previously reliant on non-written methods and the adaptation of the written word to the older oral methods. The oral context may alter the content and significance of the written word considerably. The sophistication of its use varies considerably. Some documents are inadequate without parallel non-written proof or memory. Others have non-written significance as well as written. They are not simply written documents in our sense, and we may misinterpret their content, omissions and their very importance if we take them to be that. Modern historians of the ancient world rely so much on the evidence of written documents in the form of inscriptions that they can easily ignore the wider importance of the stone inscription beyond its written message alone: for instance, the significance of the stone's setting, the reason for its erection in the first place, even the frequently curious form of the 'documents' written out. The use of writing develops as it becomes more familiar – though I do not wish to imply this was uniform. Many of the peculiar characteristics of ancient documents may reflect the incipient character of ancient record keeping. Similarly with the absence of certain documents. The amount of ancient literature that has perished and of inscriptions being discovered makes the historian acutely conscious how much written evidence has been lost. But again, we must also appreciate how much was simply never written down at all, what types of document that would be useful now were never made, and the attitudes to the written word that lie behind this absence.

Perhaps most interesting – especially since it is so strange to us – is the slow realization of the use of documents and archives for later consultation. We cannot assume attitudes to these documents that we would normally take for granted. If oral transmission was dominant and the written word not revered simply for its own sake, even in the fifth century, later reference to documents, once they were made, was not so necessary or obvious. For instance, ancient Greek historiography cannot be interpreted from the presumption that historians used written record in our manner. Greek historians were not necessarily more sophisticated in their treatment of documents than their contemporaries. It is only by the mid-fourth century that we begin to find explicit recognition of the importance of past documents as records to be consulted – and with that, detailed examination of precise wording to elicit new information.

For the recovery of past history itself it is therefore not surprising that oral sources were thought the best. The historians' relative inattention to the written documents which we stress so much was linked to wider contemporary attitudes to the written word. Closely related to this, the inscriptions recorded matters of more interest to modern scholars than to most Greek historians. It is when the oral traditions about Athens' earlier superiority were fading that we begin to find a conscious stress on written documents as providing more forceful evidence for the past. With this, a different kind of historiography was becoming possible.

2

FAMILY TRADITION

We have seen, then, that the use of writing extends only gradually and at different rates in different areas of Athenian life. The growth of documents in some areas from the early fourth century on does not necessarily pervade all walks of life; nor did it necessarily render oral tradition less accurate or extensive. Oral transmission, therefore, could subsist alongside 'literacy', and the two were not necessarily incompatible. Oral communication was in fact still very important in the fourth century B.C., as our sources show. But how, and in what form, was the past remembered, when so little trust was placed on written record for knowledge of the past? I now turn to oral tradition, its formation, character and workings, in the specific case of ancient Athens. I start with family tradition. For against the wider traditions of the whole community, family tradition is comparatively simple, we have clear and direct evidence for it, and Greek family tradition seems to have suffered almost no interference from writing. It is a clear and apt introduction to some of the problems of oral tradition, the importance of transmission for its character and reliability, and the reasons behind its fluidity. We may see clearly how ideals and beliefs help transform traditions. Since family tradition is the corner-stone to our understanding of Athenian traditions – and to the mechanisms of oral tradition in general – it will be necessary to re-examine the ancient evidence in some detail. For it is in the detail, so often skimmed over, that we may find the most revealing hints and most fascinating examples of how the oral traditions preserved – or changed – the past.

In the later, highly literary, age of Augustan Rome, the only surviving descendant of the fifth-century Spartan general Brasidas saved himself from imprisonment by Augustus by referring to Brasidas' achievements in the late fifth century. He referred to them as they were described by Thucydides and even cited the book number (Plut. *Mor.* 207F). By then, family tradition relied heavily on earlier written sources and a great family's classical past was probably almost entirely preserved by written literary material rather than oral transmission.[1] Nothing could illustrate

---

[1] Herodes Atticus in the Second Sophistic period claimed descent from Miltiades and Cimon, openly proud of Militiades' triumph over the Medes and Cimon's punishing them for their hubris (Philostr. *Herod. Att.* 546f.): this is the conventional historian's version

more clearly the contrast with classical family tradition. For Brasidas' descendant, the written text preserved the information in stable form and provided proof to his educated contemporaries. Moreover, it was that of an historian who had researched the contemporary events thoroughly. A classical Athenian family, however, knew of its ancestors mainly through oral tradition. In fact, older poetry might mention one of its historical ancestors, or celebrate its legendary ancestors more fully, thus preserving the family's past through more than oral tradition alone. But oral transmission within the family was assumed and accepted. Their traditions were very different from the historian's narrative of Brasidas' descendant. For oral tradition is peculiarly dependent on the way and form in which it is transmitted, on customs and other mechanisms which might preserve traditions. The very nature of transmission would transform the material of family memories.

Family tradition may have been crucial in preserving knowledge of past Greek history and an important source for the historians. Finley suggested that the great families were responsible for preserving almost all the memories of the archaic age, for only they would have had the interest to remember events and the prestige to impress that memory on to public opinion.[2] When Jacoby emphasized that most of Herodotus' sources must have been oral, he drew attention to the possible use of 'family sources' and attributed much of the narrative to certain great families.[3] Both claims probably have some truth, recognizing the difficulty of preserving the past by oral means. Even so, little attempt has been made to examine what ancient family tradition actually contained or to pursue the implications of such oral transmission. The content and 'bias' of family tradition have been assumed, and it is usually viewed merely as a minor adjunct to historiography. So far as I know, only Bethe's imaginative and now rather old work has systematically examined ancient family tradition in its own right, discussing the role of the Roman ancestral masks (*imagines*) in Roman family tradition and the differing Greek ways of remembering their ancestors.[4] But even he neglected the ways in which the traditions were passed on orally and thus how such variations in custom and transmission might have affected their contents. For the precise form in which oral tradition is passed on is crucially important.[5] This cannot be overstressed, since oral tradition can differ vastly in the material it preserves and its reliability. We must

which gives Cimon, as well as Miltiades, his rightful recognition. Contrast oral tradition, Ch. 4.1.

[2] Finley (1965); repr. (1975), 28.

[3] Jacoby (1913), 413f., and *Atthis*: his methods are continued by Fornara and others (see Ch. 5).

[4] Bethe (1935); Haedicke (1936) is also interesting.

[5] See esp. Vansina, *OTH*, *passim*.

examine very carefully the basic mechanisms of transmission (e.g. poetry) and the motives for its preservation (such as prestige).

A detailed discussion of this transmission has a further advantage as well as helping us understand family tradition. In family tradition we can perceive more easily than in other types the very process by which oral traditions, orally transmitted statements from a previous generation, are formed and re-formed. The history of a family is based around a small and comprehensible unit, and in contrast to the more complex, general history of a centralized state, it deals mainly with individuals. So when selection and distortion occur, they are more readily intelligible than in the formation of the wider polis traditions. The stages of transmission and distortion are those of a small number of individuals. They can be understood in terms of individual memory and transmission, comparatively uncomplicated by general and often misleading ideas such as the 'collective memory'. We can perceive how family tradition grows up from the reminiscences of one relative to another. They are passed down with selection and alteration to one generation after another. We see the gradual selection and attentuation of the family history, the progressive deterioration of calibre for more distant ancestors and the eventual blank after some generations. We also see how individual traditions are influenced and actually changed by the general polis traditions which impose a simple version of the salient episodes of Athenian history.

As individuals' memories are gradually transformed into family history or 'family tradition', we are forced to admit their relevance to the formation of oral tradition. Family history spans the conventional categories of 'oral tradition' and 'oral history' (composed of participants' reminiscences) in a clear and unavoidable manner.[6] People may have reminiscences, but if they repeat them to their sons, are those reminiscences 'traditions' yet or merely 'extended reminiscences'? As outlined in the introduction, such an example can produce far-fetched attempts at redefinition in order to preserve the 'father's reminiscences' as oral history, not oral tradition. Family tradition forces us to consider the one as growing from the other and thus the very processes of memory and selection behind the formation of oral tradition. Not all oral traditions develop from actual historical incidents, but many do. In family tradition we can recognize this process of change and development.

The very idea of family tradition is clothed in confusion. Modern assumptions about its character and provenance have included other

---

[6] See Introduction to this book and Vansina (1980), 271, on the particular case of family tradition, often ignored. It seems otherwise neglected by anthropologists except in the guise of genealogies (very common in African tradition) or dynastic traditions, including king-lists, where the family traditions become the main traditions of the state.

types of tradition under the term. But the group transmitting memories is crucial in oral tradition, and we must distinguish different groups carefully. I shall use the term 'family tradition' to denote those traditions about a family that are handed down within the family – that is, the small unit of close relations around the nuclear family and their ancestors in direct line.[7] This corresponds to the anthropological category of 'esoteric tradition': its transmission is entirely in the family's hands, even if outsiders may know of it.[8] We must distinguish that from knowledge about wider Greek history passed down within the family. This can overlap with esoteric family tradition. The more important the family, the more likely it is that considerable knowledge of the past will be remembered through the family's own part. Finally, there is popular tradition about well-known families. In the guise of 'folk-tales' (e.g. about the tyrants) these may have a lively existence quite independent of the family's own traditions. In Athens there was a surprising quantity of such traditions (see below, p. 109, and Ch. 5). One should not be misled by conventional historiographical source criticism into identifying folk-tales with family traditions. An outstanding example is the story about how Alcmaeon gained his wealth (Hdt. vi 125), usually taken to be straight from an Alcmaeonid source (see Ch. 5.5).

These distinctions resolve some confusion and overlapping. For it is often assumed that anything concerning a particular family must belong to their family tradition (sometimes reinforced by conventional reckoning of 'bias').[9] Or it is simply taken for granted that an important family will preserve the 'family history' and that we know what sort of family history this would be. Or else it is thought that an individual's beliefs about his ancestors will be historically 'true'. It is salutary to remember that the historian Herodotus (v 57.1) cited family tradition only once and then to contradict it.[10] On the other hand, clearly, a city's history is often, in effect, that of its ruling aristocratic family. Presumably that family's

---

[7] Greek has no specific term for 'family' other than *oikos*, which also denotes 'household'. When Thucydides refers to Themistocles' family tradition (1 138.6), he cites merely 'the relations' (οἱ προσήκοντες). Family traditions do not branch out laterally very far, as we shall see.

[8] Vansina (1973), 34: but compared to his examples the Greek family traditions seem hardly to merit a term which implies such systematic and jealously guarded transmission! Cf. Finnegan (1977), 270, on owning poetry: in Hawaii an heir might have to produce the family chants to prove his position.

[9] Most especially in Jacoby's division of Herodotus' Athenian history into family sources, often ignoring a passage's actual tenor (see Ch. 5 on Alcmaeonids). He takes Herodotus' mention of the Cimonian family grave (vi 103.4) as one of those details 'which could scarcely be of interest outside the family'. This is almost certainly untrue.

[10] Thucydides cited Themistocles' relations for the whereabouts of his bones (1 138.6), however, and Plato comments, perhaps jokingly, that the children of the gods must be a reliable source for what happened in their own family (i.e. relations of their ancestors) (*Tim.* 40d–e).

preserved tradition would be impressed on the general traditions of that area to become its main traditions. There is some overlapping – much knowledge of earlier history was passed down by a relative from his own experiences – but at least such overlapping will be clear. We can thus be more precise about the content of different types of tradition, the effect of transmission, the extent to which the past is remembered only in so far as the ancestors participated, and so the transformations such memories undergo.

We must start with direct evidence of family tradition actually uttered by a member of the family or embedded in poetry commissioned by the family. Only after looking at this direct evidence, so neglected by modern studies,[11] can we approach the indirect evidence of historiography. Family tradition appears frequently in the oratory of the late fifth and fourth centuries where a speaker presents to the people (the demos) what I have called his 'family defence'. This is a plea for voters' sympathy in which a speaker asserts his democratic ancestry, the service given by his ancestors for the city and its democracy. One can assume a speaker is presenting a version of family history acceptable to his family and transmitted through them.[12] These are the traditions of wealthy, and sometimes aristocratic, Athenian families. The only other direct evidence for a family's tradition lies in commissioned poetry such as the epinician or victory ode, expressly celebrating a family member. Tombstones have limited use, for usually they record only the contemporary who has just died. Unless a tombstone shows simultaneous knowledge of past ancestors, it is not a record of 'tradition' but an attempt to create it. It may indicate what was thought memorable and so what could be retained later if memory failed. Usually only the literary evidence can tell us what a family knew and thought about its past. Historical and legendary genealogy was also part of family tradition, but here we find the rare intrusion of written, scholarly speculation into family history. Since this brings up quite different questions, I reserve discussion of ancient genealogy until the next chapter (Ch. 3).

From this direct evidence we can concentrate on the actual character and content of family tradition.[13] I first examine transmission and the possibility of customs or devices which helped preserve family tradition (Ch. 2.1). This may also serve as an introduction to the way one should, in general, consider the transmission of oral tradition. It is crucial to

---

[11] Even by Bethe (1935), who concentrated deliberately on poetry.

[12] Indeed, as I shall argue, this kind of defence may actually have created a new type of family tradition.

[13] It may be very different from information collected by researching historians. What an historian may extract by careful questioning relies certainly on memory, but may well differ from that spontaneously produced.

consider whether there were any customs, legal requirements or 'mnemonic devices' which encouraged or helped preserve memories or which might even create a formal occasion for transmitting family tradition. Funerals may often be an occasion for celebrating family tradition. Or family tradition may be embedded in other, often surprising, places.[14] Sometimes traditions are formally attached to the tombs: the tomb is a mnemonic aid, a material object to which traditions are connected.[15] Customs and material objects may reinforce knowledge of individual ancestors; or else they may only encourage attention to the ancestors as an amorphous group without propagating family tradition.[16] Then I discuss more fully the family traditions of classical Athens, the kind of memories they preserved (Ch. 2.2). We can see the reasons for their preservation and the inevitable changes they undergo. Thereafter I turn to the chronological span of the family traditions and the reasons for those limits (Ch. 2.3); finally the strengths, weaknesses and eventual transformation of certain traditions (Ch. 2.4).

2.1 Transmission

Most knowledge about the family past was preserved orally in the classical period. A noble family might have the written text of a poem composed in its honour.[17] But family tradition was generally not preserved in writing, still less by 'archives', which could not have existed in any form approaching our modern conception of family archives.[18] Family history was not conceived of in terms of written documents. Apart from a few isolated allusions to earlier poetry,[19] or to memorials, the assumption that the traditions were preserved orally is overwhelm-

---

[14] Even lullabies: in New Zealand they may contain praise of the baby's heroic ancestors encouraging him to be worthy of them – see Vansina (1973), 189.

[15] Vansina, *OTH* 46 and (1973) (royal tombs). Cf. dead kings 'preserved' by impersonation, see Bloch (1981).

[16] Bloch ((1981), 139) gives an example of ancestor cult where the ancestors' bones are deliberately mixed up: the ancestors are important, but not as individuals. This reminds us that ancestor cult can exist without knowledge of, or attention to, individual ancestors.

[17] Irgoin (1952), 8 thinks that it was the archives of the recipients' families which largely preserved the poems of Pindar. (This, however, neglects the interests of victors' cities.)

[18] See Ch. 1.1. At most, a family perhaps kept isolated documents like contracts, if they were made (and not deposited with a third party); but they were probably not kept together. The 'archive' would include material objects – important gifts in earlier periods or the democratic memorials Aeschines mentions (III 47), Ch. 2, n. 22 below. Nor was family history preserved by central archives (*pace* Rosenmeyer (1949)).

[19] In Plato's family the earlier ancestor Dropides was probably remembered partly because he was mentioned in Solon's poetry (*Tim.* 20d–e): see Ch. 3.1 and *Charm.* 157e, where the house of Critias is said to be eulogized (ἐγκεκωμιασμένη) by various poets. The idea that a family's early history was chronicled in poetry (e.g. Shear (1963)) is not borne out by the evidence.

ing. Fourth-century speakers never feel the need to justify what they say by citing a written source as Brasidas' descendant did.

The picture in Plato's *Laches* is typical. In a discussion about education (179a–180b), Lysimachus and Melesias tell Laches how they decided not to treat their sons as others do, allowing them to do just what they wanted. They have meals with them and tell them of their own fathers' deeds (the sons' grandfathers) (179c), 'all the things they achieved both in war and in peace, when they were managing the affairs of the allies and the polis'. They have much to say of the achievements of their fathers, Aristeides and Thucydides, son of Melesias, but nothing of their own. They are ashamed and want their sons to grow up worthy of the names they bear (179d) and to emulate their grandfathers.[20] Oral transmission through the family is taken for granted, and it is through casual conversation. We may compare the interesting remarks of Aeschines (II 74ff.), which, though not strictly about family tradition, show the ready acceptance of transmission through the family. He declares that Athenians must imitate only their ancestors' wisdom, not their ill-judged actions, such as the Sicilian expedition. He defends this remarkable harangue by the fact that the misfortunes of Athens were in his blood.[21] His own father, not a stranger, told him about those misfortunes, and he outlines his father's democratic credentials. The oral family testimony is his bulwark for dangerous criticism of the Athenians' previous actions. Oral tradition within the family is both assumed and accepted as reliable. Moreover, it seems to be passed down quite informally in casual conversation (cf. also Aeschin. III 191, his talks with his father).

There is little suggestion of more formal transmission, even in aristocratic families. Poetry might crystallize the legendary ancestors. There are occasional hints that memorials and tombs might reinforce family memory.[22] The speaker of Is. v (41–2) offers proof of his ancestors' many public duties in the offerings in temples and the tripods and statues on the Acropolis. They must have reinforced the family tradition, but here they seem merely to complement the informal oral transmission. This casual

---

[20] It may also be significant that the conversation does not reach beyond the grandfathers, though admittedly Plato's interest is in distinguished fathers and their sons. Thucydides' father Melesias was a famous wrestler and trainer (probably of Pind. *Nem.* IV, VI; *Ol.* VIII: Wade-Gery (1958), 244f.). *Meno* 94d mentions with some sarcasm Thucydides' 'great family' (οἰκία μεγάλη). We know nothing of the father of Melesias I, nor much about Aristeides' father, Lysimachus I.

[21] A characteristically original and extreme inversion of many of the conventional topoi and accepted views of Athenian history: cf. the official traditions (Ch. 4).

[22] [Dem.] LVIII 66: his grandfather won a crown for the city at Olympia; Lys. X 27f. cites the trophies in temples of victories won by his father; cf. also Aeschin. III 47, the gold crowns that could be kept at home and not dedicated were intended to ensure that the honoured man's descendants were also loyal to the democracy. Cf. Dem. LVII 37, the maternal uncle of the speaker is buried in the public tomb, having died in Sicily.

transmission, contrasting with many other types of family tradition, must be stressed. Traditions not embodied in any more stable form were bound to be much more fluid, changeable and short-lived than those enshrined, for instance, in oral poetry or funeral customs. This explains much about the character of Greek family tradition, and the contrast with Rome should make us especially wary of thinking about it as at all similar to Roman family tradition. A closer look at other possible mechanisms which could encourage family tradition confirms this impression.

First the customs surrounding funerals and the tending of tombs. The great aristocratic families of Rome had the *imagines*, or masks of their ancestors, and the *tituli*, inscriptions or labels beneath, which were added later and gave the name and offices of each man represented by the *imagines*. Above all, in the great public funeral the *imagines* were displayed and a family member delivered the funeral oration (*laudatio funebris*). In this the dead man's achievements were described, then those of the ancestors. As Polybius remarked, the ancestors' virtue was thus kept fresh in people's memories, and the young were encouraged to emulation (VI 53f., esp. 54.2–3). The achievements enumerated were those thought worthy of memory by the Romans. They were historical and detailed, mainly concerned with offices and victories. We are seeing here very different ideas about what constitutes 'praise'. Thus an ever-growing family tradition with biographical elements for each ancestor was remembered and perpetuated with each funeral, a great formal and ceremonious opportunity to parade the ancestors. Praise and celebration, moreover, were in the hands of the family, and it was a valuable opportunity to assert their prestige. The *imagines*, tangible memorials of each ancestor, preserved the memory of each individual from early on and probably encouraged the individual *tituli* attached to each. They enabled the family tradition to preserve the memory of each ancestor and reproduce it at the funeral. The whole combination of funeral customs and preservation of the *imagines* is a striking illustration of how customs or institutions could encourage family tradition and provide an opportunity for its propagation. It also shows how tangible objects could encourage, and even make possible, the memory of individual ancestors in a series. The *imagines* form in effect mnemonic devices, whatever their original purpose.[23]

---

[23] See generally Bethe (1935); Vessburg (1941), 97ff. and Boethius (1942) on the masks. Most attention has been devoted to their relation to Roman portraiture. The relationships were preserved by *stemmata* (Pliny *NH* XXXV 6), now identified (Vessburg (1941), 103; Zadoks-Josephus Jitta (1932)) as large wall-paintings with painted portraits (not interconnected shrines with masks, as once thought) – i.e. family trees with portraits. On the *laudatio*, see Vollmer (1891) and (1924); Crawford (1941). Since Dionysius of Halicarnassus called the *laudatio* an old Roman invention (V 17.3), it must have differed

The Roman case helps by contrast to clarify our impressions from the sparse Greek evidence. Very little indeed is known about the archaic funeral, still less how far it involved celebration of all the ancestors. The magnificent seventh-century aristocratic funerals before Solon may have involved attention to the ancestors' tombs (we cannot know if family tradition was also paraded).[24] But sumptuary legislation at Athens seems to have tried to prevent just the kind of aristocratic self-assertion that we see in the Roman funeral. Extravagance of funeral, tomb and mourning could reflect superiority. These Solon expressly tried to curb (Plut. *Sol.* 21; Cic. *De leg..* II 59ff.). Set dirges (τὸ θρῆνειν πεποιημένα) were also forbidden, as was visiting of tombs other than that of the person being buried (Plut. *Sol.* 21.6). So, whatever this implies about attention to the ancestors, it was limited by legislation. It is doubtful that even aristocratic funerals before the classical period stressed their magnificence through their recent ancestors (like the Romans) rather than legendary ones.

Tantalizing hints about later sumptuary laws imply further anti-aristocratic moves, introducing a certain 'democratic' element to the preservation of the past. They also imply that there used to be funeral speeches in the archaic period. For Cicero associates a prohibition of private funeral speeches with the other sumptuary laws of the late archaic period and these, in turn, can most convincingly be associated with Cleisthenes who introduced the Cleisthenic democracy in 508/7 (*De leg.* II 26, 64–5).[25] 'Some time after Solon' (*post aliquanto*), prompted by the extravagance of the tombs, sumptuary laws about tomb size are introduced, 'speeches in praise of the deceased were also forbidden except at public funerals, and then they could be made only by orators officially appointed for the purpose' ('nec de mortui laude nisi in publicis sepulturis nec ab alio, nisi qui publice ad eam rem constitutus esset, dici licebat'). The period is extremely vague. But the passage does suggest that sixth-century aristocratic families had private funeral speeches and that these were curbed at the end of the sixth century.[26] What could they have contained? We cannot assume that 'praise' necessarily meant the detailed exposition of a man's deeds.[27] If the later public funeral speeches of Athens (*epitaphioi*) were built on archaic precedents,[28] they

---

from the Greek encomia. The *imagines* surely encouraged the *tituli*, the *tituli* helped develop the characteristic Roman epitaphs (Stuart (1928), ch. 8) and *laudatio*.

24 Humphreys (1980), Alexiou (1974), esp. 14ff.

25 Plut. *Sol.* 21, Cic. *De leg.* II 59ff.; and most recently Stupperich (1977), 71ff., 219ff.

26 Cicero's source, Demetrius of Phalerum, is himself trying to justify his laws by precedent. For the date of the introduction of the public speeches over the war-dead, see p. 207.

27 As Stuart (1928); see 'Encomium', *RE* v, col. 2581–3 (Crusius).

28 Stupperich (1977), 225.

might suggest the tone and contents of the praise. But they devoted more attention to extravagant and general praise of the virtue of the deceased than to their precise 'biographical' deeds.[29] Even in classical Athens the epitaphic topic of the 'ancestors' consisted mainly of mythical achievements (see Ch. 4.1). Perhaps this reflects an earlier funeral custom of celebrating legendary ancestors. As Momigliano remarked, Greek funeral orations and songs in honour of the dead did not apparently give rise to anything approaching biography.[30] Perhaps legendary ancestors rather than the recent past were celebrated at archaic funerals. Whatever the subject-matter, however, such speeches were henceforth banned.

Moreover, this type of praise was now confined to those receiving public burials, benefactors of the polis, and the praise was in the hands of a special orator. So the aristocratic families lost their authority to glorify the family through praise of an individual at his funeral. Praise was now in the state's hands.[31] The one mechanism so powerful in Rome for the memory and perpetuation of family tradition at funerals seems to have vanished from Athens by the fifth century.

The *threnos* or dirge itself seems to have contained little or nothing about ancestors' achievements. The scanty fragments, mainly by Pindar and Simonides, consist almost entirely of philosophical and consolatory reflection, possibly impressed on the genre by Simonides.[32] While they might not be representative, the very slight evidence for narrative in the *threnos* does not indicate much concern with family tradition either.[33] Both the *threnos* and the *goos* ('lamentation'), sung by relations, were primarily concerned with death and grief, as befitted the women.[34] Such

---

[29] Similarly the relation of the public funeral speech to the grave elegy, which it is sometimes thought to replace, would suggest the same absence of 'narrative' or historically significant detail; see Stupperich (1977), 225; cf. Aly (1929), 32f.

[30] Momigliano (1971b), 24. He sees the funeral orations and songs in honour of the dead as 'potential biographies', but it is possible that they hardly contained any biographical information at all, confirming his point about the lack of interest in biography before the fourth century. (There was more of this interest in Asia Minor than mainland Greece.)

[31] Stupperich (1977), 73 and 219ff. therefore thinks the epitaphic ceremony of the Pentekontaëtia was instituted before the Persian Wars. But Cicero's language is too imprecise to indicate that particular institution, and there were obviously public burials of some kind before this. Cf. Wallace (1970), 102f., and Ch. 4.1.

[32] Perhaps connected with the origin of elegy (A. G. Harvey (1955)). Reiner (1938) collects all the fragments.

[33] Pindar fr. 135 Snell, Schol. Pind. *Ol.* 1 127a, cited by Harvey (1955), indicates narrative (if that) of the myth of Oinomaos. Simonides apparently told of the disaster which overtook the Thessalian family of Scopades (cf. Hdt. VI 127.4) when a roof collapsed (*PGM* 24, Favor. ad Sim. fr. 6D, and schol. to Theocr. XVI 36). But (*pace* Reiner (1938)) this remarkable event does not indicate conventional attention to family achievement. Nothing is known of the content of Pindar's *threnoi* for the Alcmaeonid Hippokrates, probably in the 480s but possibly long after his death (A. E. Harvey (1955), 169).

[34] There are occasional hints that encomia of some kind were included in the lamentation for the dead, but this may partly be a matter of definition (see A. E. Harvey (1955), 169f.), since there was little or no narrative. Reiner's examples ((1938), 116f.) consist of

poetic commemoration did not preserve memory of the achievements of the deceased, nor those of the ancestors.

Did the tombs themselves encourage or preserve family tradition, either by their inscriptions or because they were tended by the family? Archaic epitaphs are notoriously laconic and the deceased is usually presented as a heroic type, detached from his family and the period in which he lived. Later classical epitaphs tend to commemorate domestic virtues and stress the unity of the nuclear family but again, not the position of the deceased in a long line of forebears.[35] In the period of *c.* 500–430, moreover, funeral monuments were forbidden, another blow to the preservation of family memories. Large groups of family tombs – though never common – also give way to very much smaller ones in the classical period. The large archaic groups probably fostered knowledge of the ancestors, but oral tradition would still be necessary for anything more. However, they are not well documented. There are two examples (found so far) of large family groups in the classical period in Athens where the members buried were listed as they were interred. One inscription listed eleven members extending over six generations in five or six different hands. They were a family of priests (*manteis*), which probably explains this unusual series.[36] This kind of span and deliberate collection of family burials was very rare in the classical period. That implies even less reverence for the distant ancestors or for a long series of generations that would stress the family's continuity.

The bare arrangement of tombs may tell us more about family respect for unity or continuity than about family tradition itself. Legal requirements are perhaps more helpful. Every Athenian archon was asked at his *dokimasia* ('scrutiny') before taking office where his family tombs (ἠρία) were, the names of his father and mother and their fathers, and if he treated his *goneis* well (*Ath.Pol.* 55.3) – *goneis* are usually parents. So, required knowledge of ancestors extended only to the grandfathers and no further. Further evidence for family tradition confirms that the third generation was often the limit of family knowledge (Ch. 2.3). The duty to look after one's *goneis* and tend their tombs when they died involved close relations, not distant ancestors

extremely general praise of virtues. The later encomium of Evagoras by Isocrates says remarkably little about Evagoras.

[35] Contrast the Megarian's description of his achievement in war which is so unusual (ML 51). Lattimore (1962), ch. 8 briefly treats biographical themes in epigrams. For the genealogical inscription of Heropythos (*SGDI* 5656), see Ch. 3.

[36] Tomb of Meidon of Myrrhinous: Humphreys (1980), 114ff.; she argues against the nineteenth-century idea of family tomb cult, 'far from being destroyed by the state . . . the idea of a visible tomb for every man and the continuity of all *oikoi* may have been generated by it' (p. 123). A few inscriptions commemorate several generations, but names added with each generation do not presuppose much knowledge except the name for previous generations.

never met.[37] *Goneis* and the charge of ill-treatment of *goneis* (*kakōsis goneōn*) could refer to grandparents as well as parents and even great-grandparents, as Isaeus asserted in one cunning piece of pleading (VIII 32). But they are essentially live *goneis* who must be treated well when they are old, buried with due respect when they die and tended when in their tombs. Charges of *kakōsis goneōn* reflect the natural concern that infirm parents should not be left in want and without proper burial. Contrary to some over-literal interpretations of Isaeus VIII, this duty has nothing to do with the tending of tombs of distant ancestors.[38]

There seem, then, to be no customs or requirements in the classical period which involved knowledge about ancestors beyond the grand-father. Such knowledge was either left to chance or some other need to preserve family tradition. There were few built-in mechanisms to reinforce continuing memory. Under the democracy, those that existed were systematically reduced.

The epinician ode commemorating the victor, his family and his city was more appropriate than the dirge for family tradition. The family tradition deemed suitable, however, was primarily that of the legendary period. We hear almost nothing of a family's recent past or that of the victor except for his other victories. For instance, Pindar's ode for Aristagoras of Tenedos (*Nem.* XI) praises Aristagoras and his family, then turns to their legendary ancestry from Peisander, contemporary of Orestes, and Melanippos. The ode is sung in Aristagoras' honour as he becomes Prytanis of Tenedos, but despite this unusual occasion and the connection with local politics, the praise and commemoration is devoted to victories in the games and mythical ancestry. The very rare hints of other elements of the recent past are conspicuous for their vagueness and lack of straightforward glorification.[39]

---

[37] The yearly festival of the Genesia kept by all Greeks (Hdt. IV 26) implied no special knowledge of ancestors and probably involved only the tombs of recent relations, not distant ancestors (Jacoby (1944b)).

[38] Lacey (1968), 37 cites Is. VIII as proof that the Greeks stopped in their genealogies at the great-grandfather because of the legal and accepted limitation of the family. But as Isaeus says, he is only enumerating the *goneis* who could possibly be alive: 'The *goneis* are the mother and father and the grandfather (*pappos*) and the grandmother, and the mother and father of these *if they are still alive*. For they are the source of the *genos*.' *Goneis* are the parents in most references. *Kakōsis goneōn*: Din. II 17f., Dem. LVII 66–70, Xen. *Mem.* II 2.13; Dem. XXIV 105–7; Plato *Laws* 930e–931 extends respect for *goneis* to grandparents – but only while they are still alive. Other references in Wyse (1904) on Is. I 39.5. For continuing care of the tombs of *goneis* in Genesia, Xen. *Mem.* II 2.13, Plato *Laws* 717d–e; cf. Soph. *El.* 277–81, Lys. XXXI 21, Dem. XXIV 107, Lyc. I 144.

[39] *Isthm.* IV 14ff.: in the midst of his praise of the Kleonymidai, Pindar regrets the four who all fell in battle in a single day. (*Isthm.* III, for the same Melissos, mentions more conventionally the ancient glory of Kleonymos in the chariot race, line 15.) Character-istically oblique, this is hardly open glorification for participation in a famous battle. The battle of Plateia, often suggested, is far from certain: the family knew which it was and it needed no further commemoration. *Isthm.* VII hints that the victor's uncle died in battle

This concentration on the legendary past in a genre devoted to praise and commemoration would itself be indicative of what was thought worthy of praise and memory. But it reflects a widespread characteristic of much aristocratic family tradition of the late archaic and early classical period. As Bethe pointed out, the Greek aristocrat, unlike the Roman, was almost exclusively concerned with his heroic ancestors. A family's prestige was connected primarily with Homeric or other legendary ancestors rather than the deeds of recent, historical ones – with the partial exception of victories at the games.[40] This would determine the preoccupations of family tradition. The demands of the Athenian democracy altered this emphasis. But otherwise, legendary ancestry carried immense prestige. Moreover, it was crucial because a family's first origins were regarded as the most important elements of their past. These often altered to reflect later changes in prestige and status (on this, see further Ch. 3). When Pindar celebrated Agesilaos of Syracuse as an Iamid, a famous family of seers, he did this with the beautiful myth of the origin of the Iamids (*Olympian* VI). Nothing is said of the family's recent distinguished past, not even of the recent exceptional grant of Spartan citizenship to the Iamid seer Teisamenos (Hdt. IX 33–6). However, that Spartan element has been incorporated into the origin myth in the form of the woman Pitane. Recent honours and their causes are omitted, but the myth of origin is there and the honours have been translated into mythical terms.[41] We probably cannot overestimate the place of legendary ancestors in aristocratic traditions. As for the recent past, again, it was not crystallized in poetry, and as a lesser source of prestige, it was therefore remembered less carefully.

Our picture of family tradition has been fragmented and often negative. There were few mechanisms which propagated family tradition, and ideas of family prestige seem to have rested primarily upon the legendary past, which was what poetic commemoration emphasized. The recent past was correspondingly neglected. The overall impression is clear. The Greek aristocrat derived more prestige from his legendary past, a habit eventually adopted by hellenized Romans in the second and first cen-

for his fatherland (23–30), but so obliquely that guesses about the occasion have ranged over a span of more than fifty years. Cf. also *Pyth.* VII to Megacles of Athens for a victory which we know was only a few years after his ostracism: line 19 mentions envy of noble deeds.

[40] Bethe (1935), 54–6 gives other examples from Pindar. Victory at the games could be respected by all Greeks, not merely the citizens of one city.

[41] The woman 'Pitane' is clearly inserted into the legendary ancestry of the Iamids, an Arcadian family: thus Pitane bore Euadne, who bore Iamos. 'Pitane' is also the name of a Spartan village, so the legendary woman Pitane represents a Spartan element in Iamid legendary ancestry. Two Iamids, Teisamenos and his brother, gained Spartan citizenship in the early fifth century, which must explain this (and see Ch. 3.2 for further points). First argued by Wilamowitz (1886).

turies B.C.[42] Apart from poetic commemoration, they relied on an informal transmission of family history, the most fluid and short-lived type of oral tradition.

This seems to change with the Athenian democracy. The neglected evidence of family tradition in Athenian oratory of the late fifth and fourth centuries in fact presents family history that was peculiar to Athens. The assertion of democratic ancestry before the people (*demos*) was an essential part of Athenian democracy. A speaker justifies himself by his ancestors' patriotic behaviour in fighting the tyrants or other enemies and his ancestors' service to the polis. He does not bother to cite his Homeric ancestry. Even the aristocratic Andocides did not mention his mythical ancestors, Odysseus and Hermes, elaborated by Hellanicus (*FGH* 323a F24), for they were inappropriate. He risked only the boast that his family was the oldest (I 147) and instead proclaimed his ancestors' struggle against the Peisistratid tyrants. A different kind of family tradition is emphasized here, linking the family to the recent past and the history of Athens according to patriotic polis tradition. It is, therefore, tempting to see the democracy as promoting the memory of a new kind of family tradition more concerned with the recent past. In this, service to Athens is of overwhelming importance, and even non-aristocratic families could claim it. Families in other city-states (e.g. Sparta) might similarly remember their recent ancestors' service to the polis, probably in war. But the need to defend oneself before the popular courts in Athens created a particularly strong reason for preserving recent family history and an opportunity – perhaps the only formal one – to present it. There was now more cause to remember historical family tradition which attached itself to the centralized democratic polis. In the rest of this chapter I shall be concentrating mainly upon this type of democratic family tradition, its preoccupations, limits and eventual transformation.

2.2 Classical family tradition and Athenian history

What did Athenian family traditions of the classical period record? How did the needs and ideals of the democracy affect family tradition? Did the old type of legendary tradition disappear completely?

In fact, both families and the popular traditions continued to celebrate legendary ancestors enthusiastically – but not before the democratic institutions themselves. This reminds us of the complexity of oral tradition. Aristocratic families continued to preserve their legendary past. In Plato's *Alcib.* I the distinguished family of Alcibiades is discussed

[42] Wiseman (1974).

and its legendary ancestry mentioned as well as the conventional democratic achievements (104, 112c). Plato makes fun of the man who boasts of his ancestors going back to a legendary hero (*Theaet.* 174e–175a), implying that the legends had popular appeal outside the family as well.[43] A distinguished family might have a tradition of its origins. Herodotus' sole citation of family tradition is for the Gephyraioi, whose version of their origins he immediately contradicts (v 57). An interesting passage in Plato's *Lysis* (205b–e) suggests more. According to Socrates, Lysis' lover went far beyond the usual matters that 'the whole city celebrates' about Lysis' eminent family, its wealth and victories. The lover sings of traditions which are more old-fashioned (κρονικώτερα), 'the kind of things old women sing', such as a story about Lysis' ancestor, descended from Zeus and the daughter of the hero of the deme (i.e. 'village', 'ward'), entertaining Herakles. Socrates' remarks are suggestive but tantalizing. Presumably the family still preserved the tradition about its legendary ancestor: it is interesting that the ancestor has acquired a democratic character in the mention of the deme, which must be fairly recent. But while dismissed as antiquated, these legends are also said to be 'the kind old women sing'. Were there still stories about the legendary ancestors of great Athenian families, which were sung and propagated by 'old women' and thus had popular circulation? The scale of such traditions is quite impossible to gauge, but the role of women in preserving the oral traditions is probably far more important than the sources suggest.[44] Apparently popular traditions about legendary ancestors still continued in the late fifth and fourth centuries. So did family traditions.

It is interesting to compare other popular traditions about such families. Popular gossip and comments in oratory concentrated on their wealth and financial problems, as well as more scandalous gossip. Callias' family (prominent in the fifth and early fourth centuries) attracts most attention and that for the way its wealth has been gained and lost.[45] Such

---

[43] Cf. Menander fr. 612 on the tiresome enumeration of *pappoi*.

[44] There are occasional hints: in Plato, *Hipp. Mai.* 285e–286a, Socrates says that Spartans enjoy Hippias' multifarious knowledge and that they make use of him, 'as children do of old women, to tell them agreeable stories' (πρὸς τὸ ἡδέως μυθολογῆσαι). In *Rep.* (II 376c–383c) Plato implies that most stories now told by nurses and mothers should be discarded, for instance those about Uranus and Kronos. An interesting passage in *Crat.* (418b–c) presumes that women preserve a more old-fashioned speech, 'especially the women who most preserve the ancient language (*phonē*)'. Lysistrata (Ar. *Lys.* 1126f.), however, derived her 'education' from the *logoi* or tales of her father and older men. See Scobie (1983), 16ff. for female story-telling, mostly marvellous tales of various kinds.

[45] The son of Callias II, Hipponikos, reputedly the richest man in Greece, Lys. xix 48; And. I 130 pairs him with the highest fortune of Athens; most admired of his contemporaries, Isoc. xvi 31. And. I 130 also mentions the widespread rumour that he had an 'evil spirit' (ἀλιτήριος) in his house consuming all his wealth (i.e. Callias III). More scandalous gossip about Callias III, his extravagance and final poverty: And. I 124, 129; [And.] IV 13f.; Ar. *Birds* 284–6, *Frogs* 432–4, fr. 583 K.–A.; Eupolis' *Kolakes* and

comments are what 'everyone knows' or straightforward gossip and rumour (e.g. And. 1 130). The family's political activities are barely mentioned,[46] yet when Xenophon presented the speech of Callias (III) at Sparta (*Hell.* VII 3.4), he inserted boasts of the family's record in serving Athens in war and by making peace. We can presume their family tradition was similar in tenor to those we find in oratory. Popular tradition about the family revelled in semi-moralizing financial and sexual gossip, but the family's own traditions would be very different (cf. Ch. 5.5 further).

Otherwise family tradition as it was told within the family had the same patriotic tenor as family defence before the demos. The grandsons of Aristeides and Thucydides, son of Melesias, heard what their grandfathers did 'in war and peace' and were expected to emulate them. One remembered and boasted of those matters which were approved by the rest of the city and which showed one's own family had played a good part in its past.[47]

The family traditions presented in the courts (mainly in the fourth century) as plea or defence represented the family's service to Athens. The need to show that your family had an impeccable background of support for Athens encouraged, and even created, a new kind of family tradition and the one formal opportunity to present it. The kinds of achievement expressed in this form indicate something of the ways in which prestige and honour were attained in classical Athens, thus what family tradition remembered. Nevertheless, we receive an impression of family tradition that is in fact curiously archaic, even aristocratic, compared with the changed conditions of the classical democracy. This tells us both about classical family tradition and the democracy in which it thrived.

Autolykos; an example of a very rich man whose property came to very much less than expected, Lys. XIX 48. A popular moral theme runs through the allusions. On how the wealth was gained; later literary sources (Plut. *Arist.* V 7f., schol. Ar. *Clouds* 64, Suda λ 58, Herakleides F59 Wehrli = Athen. XII 536f.), supported by the nickname *lakkoploutoi* in comedy, provided a source in Persian gold or money held in trust during the Persian Wars: a typical explanation of 'folk-tale' (see further p. 267) which ignored the probable prosaic source in the mines (Nepos, *Cim.* 13; Xen. *Poroi* IV 15).

46 Though cf. Dem. XIX 273 on the notorious tale (*logos*) of how they treated Callias II who negotiated 'that peace which everyone talked about': they nearly executed him for taking bribes, but fined him 50 talents instead. The scarcity of information may not be a sign that the family kept out of public life (as *APF*, p. 258): apart from the peace itself, Hipponikos, son of Callias, died as general at Delium, unless he is being confused with Hippokrates: cf. Thuc. IV 101.2.

47 Cf. *Alcib.* I 104 and 112c on Alcibiades' distinguished family which had produced Pericles and Alcibiades' father who died in battle (i.e. the conventional democratic points of approval). Other aspects: family friendship remembered, Plato, *Laches* 180e–181c; the burial of a recent famous ancestor – Thuc. I 138.6, with Ch. 2, n. 10 above; poetry which celebrates or mentions ancestors, *Charm.* 157e, *Tim.* 20d.

The patriotic service of such family tradition consists mainly of military achievement, death in battle, liturgical generosity and embassies, and victories in the games.

Thus the civic side of patriotic duty thought worth remembering was that of lavish generosity and ostentation. Victories in the games brought honour (*timē*) to the city, as one descendant reminded his audience (Lys. xix 63). A victory in the early fourth century was said to bring the city a crown ([Dem.] lviii 66). The Alcmaeonids boasted proudly of their ancestor Alcmaeon's victory (Isoc. xvi 25). Victories could be thought more important than liturgies because they involved unnecessary expense (Lys. xix 63). The munificence that went with chariot victories had long since ceased to bring political power.[48] But even in the fourth century they still conferred prestige and honour on both city and victor.

However, the most important civic duties were the liturgies, the public services performed by the wealthy, the *chorēgiai* (providing a chorus) and the trierarchies (fitting out a trireme, which might also involve military action). They are stressed as a sign of a family's patriotism[49] and openly expected to bring corresponding favour in the courts, just as lavish expenditure was used in the fifth century to gain political prestige. The speaker of Is. v (§41) said his family performed every kind of choregic office, paid *eisphorai* (a property tax) and never ceased being trierarchs: the 'witnesses', dedications for their choregic victories and other signs of their wealth, lie on the Acropolis. He then adds the family deaths in battle. The speaker of Lys. xxv 12f. declares that he performed more liturgies precisely to gain favour in court.

While liturgical expense is repeatedly stressed, mere office-holding in the democracy seems, astonishingly, to be inappropriate. Participation on embassies is cited. This *is* seen as service to the city. Andocides declares how his uncle Epilykos arranged 'the peace with the Persian king' (iii 29: see Ch. 2.4.2). The speaker of Is. xi (§8) proudly adds, 'when Hagnias was preparing to set out as ambassador on that mission which had such favourable results for the city'.[50] In the speech of Callias already mentioned (Xen. *Hell.* vii 3.4), Callias boasts of his ancestors, chosen by Athens as generals in war and peace-makers when they wanted peace (presumably this referred to the notorious Peace of Callias, as well as their proxenies). Plato's relative Pyrilampes is distin-

---

[48] Davies (1984), 99ff.

[49] E.g. Lys. xxvi 21f., xix 56f., Is. v 41, to take only those referring to 'ancestral' generosity. The speaker of Isoc. xviii 58 says the demos owe him favour (*charis*) for one liturgy especially.

[50] Usually identified with the Hagnias mentioned by Harpokration and Hell. Oxy. who was killed by Spartans while on an embassy to Persia. Hell. Oxy. ii 1 dates the embassy to 396: *APF* 2921, W. E. Thompson (1976); but cf. Humphreys (1983b).

guished for his service on numerous embassies (*Charm.* 158a).[51] But here again, an embassy tended to involve private wealth, since the city contributed only a small allowance. Moreover, it had aristocratic overtones, for it could involve a family's contacts in another city and the older system of proxenies. The citation of embassies carries clear aristocratic implications.

What of the more mundane civic offices, service as archon, member of the council (*bouleutēs*), legislative official (*thesmothetēs*) or treasurer? Often the subject of accusations of bribery, they are not entirely ignored in popular oratory.[52] Sometimes a man's office is mentioned but not usually as part of a plea for sympathy because of his service to the city. One man is mentioned as having been in office (ἄρχων), but while it may add to his stature, it is incidental to his death in Sicily (Lys. XXVI 21).[53] Andocides reveals the posts or liturgies he has held not as a defence of his civic virtue and service to Athens (which comes elsewhere) but as proof that he had not been regarded as impure at that point (1 132): he was gymnasiarch for the festival of the Hephaistia, chief of a sacred embassy (*archeotheōros*) (both liturgies), then treasurer of Athena.[54]

This cannot be a mere accident of our evidence. The emphasis of such declarations of ancestral service to Athens is clear. Offices involving neither military command nor conspicuous use of private wealth were not regarded as useful proof of service. They were not worth flaunting along with the military successes and liturgies. Yet the ideal of participation by all citizens in the democracy was one of its basic foundations in the classical period.[55] When Demosthenes declares that Aeschines and his father have never been 'useful' (*chrēsimos*) to the city, his list of

---

[51] In other allusion to deeds in war and peace (e.g. *Laches* 179c) those in peace time are probably largely on embassies.

[52] Aeschin. III 62 asserts that Demosthenes' position on the boule was acquired by purchase; he accuses Timarchus (1 107) of taking bribes when he was *logistēs*, of diabolical behaviour when on the boule (1 109) and of having bought a magistracy in Andros; [Dem.] LIX 72 deals with Stephanos' machinations to acquire the archonship. Cf. F. D. Harvey (1985) on bribery.

[53] [Dem.] XLIII 42 names Euctemon 'who was archon basileus' (also in testimony §§43 and 46), but this is in a witness testimony about family relations, far from a rhetorical boast. Yet it is interesting that this is remembered of a grandson of Bouselos, that is, in the same generation as Makartatos' grandfather. [Dem.] LIX 65 mentions two men in passing as thesmothete and son of the archon Nausinikos. Cf. death in military office, Is. v 42f.

[54] Chosen by lot, Arist. *Ath.Pol.* 8.1. His ancestor Andocides was treasurer of Athena in the mid-sixth century, but we know this from an inscription, *IG* I² 393. Cf. Dem. XXIX, 7ff., on offices one might have to hold.

[55] Arist. *Pol.* III, 1281b, Jones (1957), ch. 3. Nor were members of the boule insignificant men. Rhodes (1972), 4ff. argues that the trierarchic class was probably over-represented in the fourth century.

suggestions is instructive[56] (xix 281f.): 'Has the city ever received from any of them in their whole life so much as a horse, or a trireme, or a military expedition, or a chorus, or a liturgy, or a tax contribution (*eisphora*), or any sign of goodwill (*eunoia*), or any valiant deed whatsoever?' Though this is perhaps a rhetorical, persuasive definition, it coincides neatly with the usual marks of 'usefulness' that are produced in court. The common denominators are financial expense and military service, with vague goodwill to the demos thrown over all. Magistracies, service in the administration, are not included.[57]

Can we understand this neglect of the mundane offices of the democracy? It is not enough to suggest that magistracies were too ordinary to be included; or that the speakers were mainly wealthy men who were therefore most impressed by their own generosity.[58] Certainly financial generosity provided entertainment, security and defence. Compared to the fulfilment of duty in administrative office, it was obviously more dramatic. The use of the lot for apportioning offices – except for the generalship – may also have devalued their prestige. Yet, even so, one would think such offices could still be a sign of a democratic citizen. However, the idea of the relationship of lavish expenditure ($\mu\varepsilon\gamma\alpha\lambda o$-$\pi\varrho\acute{\varepsilon}\pi\varepsilon\iota\alpha$) and compensating favour (*charis*) from the city is a survival of the older forms of expenditure which were expressly meant to gain political influence and office.[59] The rest of these 'democratic' defences have a similarly aristocratic tinge. In short, we see here an aristocratic and heroic picture removed from the prosaic features of democratic

---

[56] But see Dover (1974), 296ff. on 'usefulness'. Jones (1957), 145, n. 35 takes the list to show the proper qualifications for high office, but it is only the usual abuse that a man and his family have not served the city and, it is implied, are not *dēmotikoi* (supporters of the people). Cf., however, Dem. xix 237.

[57] Cf. Dem. liv 44; also Is. iv 27, a good citizen ($\sigma\pi o\upsilon\delta\alpha\tilde{\iota}o\varsigma$ $\pi o\lambda\acute{\iota}\tau\eta\varsigma$), as his clients are, is never absent, except where the demos commands, nor useless (*achrēstos*) when here, 'but they serve in expeditions, pay their property tax (*eisphora*), do everything else they are told to, and, as everyone knows, they behave decently (*kosmious*)'. Aeschin. iii 169 'defines' the *dēmotikos* as a man of free birth and with ancestral good service (*euergesia*) to the demos.

Other rhetorical arguments comparing different services: Ant. *Tetr.* i β 12 (c. 420), boasts of generosity to the city; answered *Tetr.* i γ 8. Lys. xix 12 insists the estate is small because of numerous liturgies, but stresses that his father never *sought* office (i.e. liturgies), thus the generosity was altruistic. Lycurgus (i 139f.) distinguishes expensive gestures and actions which protected everyone's welfare: probably a new distinction that he tried to promote, Humphreys (1985c). Cf. Aristotle's criticism of the system, *Pol.* 1309a17, fr. 17 Rose; Demetr. fr. 136 Wehrli.

[58] Perlman ((1967), 164) thought the stress on wealth proved that the audience was wealthy, too; cf. Jones (1957), 36f.; contrast Davies (1984), 88f.

[59] Davies (1984), 96 – this *charis* represents an attenuated survival of a previous form of spending for political motives: 'In terms of this older mechanism *charis* was nothing less than the primary basis both of election to office and of preponderant political influence.'

government, a conjunction of vast generosity with military service and victories at the games which brought honour (*timē*) to the city.

This is not simply a narrow indication of what persuaded the courts – though that in itself is remarkable. Rather, it seems to be part of a wider picture, in which many of the traditional values of virtue (*aretē*) and the *agathoi* continued to subsist during the classical period (*agathoi* literally means 'good men', but usually denoted the aristocracy). Analysed by Adkins,[60] the old idea of the *agathoi* (i.e. aristocracy) was transferred to some extent to the ideal of the good citizen, the *agathos politēs*. With it went the persistent approval for many of the old manifestations of the *agathos*, such as the provision of liturgies which earned favour and the other elements of character that went with traditional *aretē*, such as courage, risks, success. Against these, the quieter, 'cooperative values' had greater recognition with the new needs of administration under the Athenian empire. But confusion, and indeed inherent conflict, continued. The good citizen, *agathos politēs*, inherited many of the traditional characteristics associated with the aristocratic *agathoi*.[61]

We can now see rather more clearly why the simple holding of civic and administrative office was not the mark of a 'useful citizen' who had served his city. Alongside the aristocratic and heroic character of the services that were boasted of, the 'quiet' duty of holding democratic office was unimpressive and its virtue belonged to a scale of values which was at variance with much of what was still considered prestigious. The 'quiet values' were hardly considered an essential characteristic of the good citizen.[62]

This has important implications for family tradition. Current values, current sources of prestige and honour helped determine what a man said of himself and his family in court and thus what was remembered in family tradition. Office-holding alone was not thought prestigious. *Philotimia* demanded other marks of prestige.[63] The descendant of Cleon, the fifth-century demagogue, boasted not of Cleon's administrative or civic role, but of his military success at Pylos ([Dem.] XL 25). This would imply that family tradition did not keep careful memory of offices, even archonships. Again, the contrast with Roman families is striking. In the Athenian evidence, we are very far from the Roman *cursus honorum* or 'ladder of offices', and the Roman preoccupation should not mislead us into expecting a similar knowledge of office-holding in the Athenian

---

60 (1960), chs. 8, 9 and 11; cf. also Raaflaub (1985), 308ff.
61 The 'Old Oligarch' makes much of this paradox.
62 Though compare the hint of some 'quiet virtues' in Is. IV 27.
63 Cf. Dover (1974), 230 on sources of *philotimia*, 'love of honour', (which do not include office-holding), and Whitehead (1983); Arist. *Eth.Nic.* 1095b25.

family. Their equivalent seems to be victories in the games and liturgies. The archonship may have been remembered more carefully as a genuine sign of honour before it was filled by lot. The Philaid genealogy elaborated by Pherecydes (early fifth century) says that it was in Hippokleides' archonship that the festival of the Panathenaia was established. Even so, it is not the archonship alone which is noted in the genealogy so complimentary to the family, but the act accomplished during the archonship (*FGH* 3 F2: see Ch. 3.1). Miltiades' later archonship during the tyranny was, like that of Cleisthenes, left unmentioned by the family tradition. We should be very cautious of expecting extensive and detailed family knowledge of archonships. We can be virtually certain that at least in the classical period civic offices were not an important part of family tradition. Moreover, family traditions that extended to the sixth century were loath to remember archonships then, too, however prestigious they had been. For they implied collaboration with the tyrants.[64]

Most family tradition recorded achievement in war when it was not concerned with *philotimia* in peace. When a descendant boasted in general terms of his family's past, military achievement and command were prominent. For instance, the speaker of Lys. x (27f.) says of his father, who is unknown and who died under the oligarchy, he 'was often general and underwent many other dangers at your side'. Compare Andocides, who boasts of 'other offices' (ἄλλας ἀρχὰς), too (1 147): 'They [his ancestors] have commanded countless expeditions and have won you many victories by land and sea, and they have held many other offices.'[65] Similarly, almost all specific incidents mentioned in these traditions are those of war. Often an ancestor is said to have died for Athens at a certain place (which is named), perhaps the only thing said of him. The battles implied are often hard to locate and mostly minor ones. Nevertheless, such memories are detailed and impressive against the generality of the official traditions. Military action against external and internal enemies was evidently well remembered.

Thus the speaker of Is. v (41f.) turned from financial generosity to ancestral death in battle: his great-grandfather died at Eleusis as gen-

---

[64] Thuc. VI 54.7 quotes the memorial set up by the younger Peisistratos recording his archonship. See further, p. 169 and appendix on the archon-list.

[65] Cf. Lys. XVIII on behalf of Nicias' brother Eucrates, made by Eucrates' sons, (*c.* 393), esp. §2–3 on Nicias, with extraordinary vagueness: as strategos he took many cities and won many trophies 'which it would be too much trouble to enumerate'. True, this reminds us of the victories, but I doubt if a Roman general's nephew would have missed the opportunity to cite them all explicitly.

eral,[66] his grandfather as phylarch at Spartolos,[67] and a son of that grandfather as trierarch of the Paralos at Cnidus.[68] The only non-genealogical information given in Dem. XLIV (9ff.) is of a death at Methymna, four generations from the speaker. Similarly in Dem. LVII (37f.), beyond relationships of the speaker's maternal relations, we only hear that his mother's brother was one of 'those who fought and died in Sicily' and was buried in the public tomb. The mother's nephew died at Abydus serving under Thrasyboulos (in 388).[69] Of the three original brothers in the family of Is. VII (three generations from the speaker), one died in Sicily, another in Athens. A father-in-law's death is cited proudly in Lys. XIX 16, 'when the sea battle in the Hellespont occurred' (i.e. Aigospotamoi). The unknown father of the speaker of Lys. XXVI (21f.) died in command ($\check{\alpha}\varrho\chi\omega\nu$) in Sicily.[70]

So positions of command are occasionally mentioned, though mainly for the achievements – or death – attained in that position. These family traditions produce several generalships: generals, unlike archons, were elected for ability. Thus, Cleon as general captured many Spartans alive at Pylos ([Dem.] XL 25)[71]. But not all these generalships can be historical. Andocides said that his two ancestors were both generals in the 'victory against the tyrants' at Pallenion (I 106: see Ch. 2.4.2 below). The younger Alcibiades says that his two ancestors 'as generals' led back the demos from exile and expelled the tyrants (Isoc. XVI 25f.). Quite apart from their other doubtful features, it is suspicious that both family traditions attribute the main responsibility for the expulsion of the tyrants in the late sixth century to their two ancestors, both generals. Thus, four generals are provided for the expulsion alone. This is too

---

66 Sometimes emended to Halieis (as Thuc. I 105.1). But there is ample room for an incident at Eleusis and it sounded impressive: perhaps in the Corinthian invasion of Megara (Thuc. I 105, in 458/7) or at the time of the revolt of Euboia, *c.* 446, when the Peloponnesians advanced to Eleusis and Thria (Thuc. I 114). These latter movements are confusing (cf. ML 51, recording an episode hard to fit into the logical and concise narrative of Thucydides). Insignificant 'battles' are precisely what family tradition remembered.

67 Spartolos: Thuc. II 79, Plut. *Nic.* 6.3, a disaster for the Athenians. See Wyse (1904), *ad loc.* on the link with Olynthus in the text.

68 Almost certainly the battle of 412/11 (Wyse (1904), 405) rather than the more famous one of 394, since the date of the battle was 22 years before the speech (in 389?). But the audience would probably understand the famous battle of Cnidus, since they could not make careful calculations from different parts of the written text as we can.

69 Introduced as proof that the speaker's parents were both citizens, these deaths show both citizenship and the family's service to the city.

70 Patriotic military action alone is occasionally cited: the speaker's father was 'fighting with Thrasyboulos' (one of the great democratic heroes of fourth-century oratory), Lys. XXXII 7; father connected with Conon 'who was general round the Peloponnese', Lys. XIX 12. There seems to be no examples like this further back.

71 Others: Lys. X 27f.; Lys. XVIII for Nicias' generalships; And. I 147; Aes. I 27; Xen. *Hell.* VI 3.4 (Callias).

much of a coincidence, whatever the families' status at that stage. Obviously their descendants assumed their ancestors were the generals leading the whole enterprise, when they claimed they liberated Athens. Whatever the technical position of the generalship at that early period,[72] later descendants and audience would understand the kind of generalship they knew. We should expect this sort of simplification and improvement in family tradition, particularly in the oldest traditions. Cleon's generalship was historical, so were those of Nicias (Lys. x 27f.). No one has questioned the accuracy of the speaker of Is. v 41f. who gave his ancestors' posts with detail that suggests he was telling the truth.[73] But further back we find conflation and elaboration.

It is striking how most of these traditions of military service are presented in a timeless historical vacuum (except for those about the tyrants' expulsion). The place of death is mentioned, but not the war or campaign it occurred in. An ancestor simply died, for instance, at Methymna (Dem. XLIV 9ff.). *We* can try to work out the date, campaign and context. But all those were unnecessary for the death to have its proper force before the demos. Nor can one believe that the audience would always know the campaign. A death 'in Sicily' suggested the great Sicilian expedition of 415, not necessarily correctly (as implied by Dem. LVII 37f., see p. 116, above).[74] But how could people know the context of a death at Eleusis or Spartolos? These men died a heroic death for the city. Clearly, next to that, the historical significance of that death was irrelevant.[75] How long would it be remembered even by the family, when the heroism itself was enough? This attitude is obviously related to the ideals expressed in the public funeral speeches over the war dead. There, too, the dead were treated as heroes in a timeless series of Athenian successes (see Ch. 4.2). These official ideals influenced Athenians' ideas of what was memorable and thus their own family traditions, the individual counterparts to the official public commemorations of the dead. The glory of death in battle is that of the Homeric hero, and the

---

[72] Hauvette-Besnault (1885), 48f. and Davies (1984), 122f. on the families which had held the generalship and their financial position. It is very improbable that the generalship, an established institution of yearly generals, existed before Cleisthenes' reforms; generals were probably appointed in an *ad hoc* manner if necessary. Nor is it even certain that they would have had the title *stratēgos* which the literary sources give them: Hauvette-Besnault (1885), 6ff.; Sealey (1960), 173 (taking And. 1 106 at face value); Fornara (1971a), 1–10; Badian (1971), 26, n. 68.

[73] Though for the 'general' at the battle at Eleusis, the Spartan invasion of 446 is usually ruled out because Andocides III, grandfather of the orator, is taken to have been general then (ML 51)! Cf. above, Ch. 2, n. 66.

[74] There were other expeditions to Sicily and reasons for dying there.

[75] Nor was there much need to distinguish battles from minor skirmishes, victories from defeats.

ideal, transferred to the democratic polis, is clearly still powerful.[76]

Nevertheless, we should not underestimate how family tradition could preserve memories which would otherwise be forgotten. The official and general polis traditions remembered only the broadest outlines of the past, much simplified and improved (Ch. 4). But even these brief family defences record little-known incidents that would certainly have been forgotten in the wider traditions. Methymna, Eleusis, Spartolos, Andocides' Pallenion, and the late fifth-century Cnidus were hardly the great rallying points of Athenian history. A family had an interest in remembering details which the general traditions did not (and we should not emend their testimony to a better-known battleground).

We can therefore suppose that when a historian tried to research the past from oral tradition alone, he had to rely considerably on the knowledge of families or participants. The polis traditions propagated a general and simple picture. The detail which filled it out, and memories which perhaps contradicted the official patriotic vision, resided largely amongst the esoteric traditions of the family. Here the distinction between 'tradition' and 'reminiscences' is also important. What we have been discussing are family traditions which were highly selective portions of family history deliberately passed down. For a while other memories would continue. A father would remember much more than the reminiscences of his bravery in the Peloponnesian War which he deliberately told his son as inspiration. But the casual reminiscences would be forgotten fast through the inevitable processes of memory. The traditions deliberately passed on, worth remembering for some reason, continued longer. This immensely simplified picture at least explains the increasing selectivity of memory and tradition as time progresses. It reminds us that an 'enquirer' like the historian Herodotus could well probe deeper and find out more than people would present spontaneously and as part of their 'tradition'. A son's testimony that his father died at Methymna would be enough for the demos in court. Herodotus might demand to know more and the son might manage to remember the circumstances. But because the heroic death itself was enough for prestige and respect, the circumstances would eventually become forgotten, and only the death at Methymna would be passed down to the next generation.

So family tradition could preserve individual memories rather different from the polis traditions. How, then, did a family envisage Athenian

[76] Cf. the extreme reticence of dedications commemorating a victory which do not always even specify the place of victory, let alone the wider context: the epitaph for the fallen at Koroneia does not mention the place of battle and attributes the defeat to a demi-god; see Peek (1938), Bowra (1938). As often remarked, the classical epitaph dwells on the timeless and ideal features of the deceased (Ch. 2.1 and Bethe (1935), ch. 7).

history in general when it had its own tradition of patriotic service (i.e. family tradition about the past of Athens)? What kind of accounts would an historian hear from individuals or leading families whose ancestors had played a marked role in Athenian history? There is little direct evidence, but what there is is very striking. Some family traditions of resistance to the tyranny or the Thirty give enough description to show how their unique memories are combined with the conventional prevailing view of events in the polis tradition (Ch. 2.4). Andocides, however, produces an equally remarkable version of Athenian history during the Pentekontaëtia, the period between the Persian Wars and the Peloponnesian War (479–431). Understandably quite neglected as evidence of the actual events, it is a unique example of an Athenian aristocrat's version of his city's recent history in which his family played some part. It tells us much about family tradition and oral tradition in a wider sense and sets Thucydides' exasperated remarks about the Pentekontaëtia in perspective.

Andocides' 'account' of the Pentekontaëtia (III 3ff.) and his briefer analysis of the Athenian empire through its acquisition of ships and walls (III 37ff.) provide the only references in oratory to some important aspects of Athenian history. The first passage was regarded by Aeschines as good enough to be borrowed almost verbatim when he needed a summary of the period (III 172–6). Its greatest significance lies in the fact that it is a product of Andocides' own knowledge and of his family tradition. There is little justification in thinking that it has a written source, and there was no need for one.[77] Indeed, on close scrutiny, its extraordinary inaccuracies and selectivity are intimately related to the part Andocides' family played in the events. His family tradition has given rise to an image of Athens' past based round his family's role.

Andocides' family was old and prominent. The family believed that their ancestors helped expel the tyrants (I 106: see Ch. 2.4). We also learn from Andocides (III 29) that his maternal uncle Epilykos was 'on the embassy to arrange the truce with the Persian king'. Here, family tradition again records with pride a piece of information apparently forgotten in all our literary sources, even by the orators so keen to cite the Peace of Callias. An inscription supports it, reinscribed in the fourth century (ML 70), and together they bring to light an embassy to the Persian King Darius in 424/3, on which Epilykos and Herakleides

---

[77] That Aeschines' passage is straight from Andocides is betrayed by the way Aeschines incorporates Andocides' father into his version (§174). A common oligarchic source proposed by Matthieu (1914), followed by de Romilly ((1963), 283), is unnecessary. There is little in Andocides' description that can be identified as oligarchic, indeed he is concerned with the immense benefits to the democracy. W. E. Thompson's theory (1967) that Hellanicus is the source is also unnecessary.

went.[78] As Andocides says, it was soon rendered useless by the alliance with Amorgos, and it was probably merely a renewal of the Peace of Callias.[79] Yet is was remembered proudly by one of the few men who had family reasons for doing so. Andocides' next example to prove that Athens always chose the weaker for its friends was the Sicilian expedition. He declares (III 30) – to our astonishment – that it was undertaken to help Egesta, though Syracuse had offered friendship and peace. It is not irrelevant that Epilykos died in Sicily (I 117).

His longer section on the Pentekontaëtia (III 3ff.) must derive largely from his family and other general traditions. Andocides' birth is usually put not long before 440,[80] and certainly he can have had no direct memory of the period himself. The scrambled series of half-truths can be closely linked to his own family's participation. For his grandfather Andocides was on the embassy of ten who went to Sparta to negotiate the Thirty Years Peace in 446: he is proudly mentioned when Andocides argues the beneficial effects of peace (III 8). We also know, but not from family tradition, that as general Andocides had invaded the Megarid in 446/5 and escaped being cut off by a circuitous withdrawal from Pegae to Boiotia (ML 51). He also helped in the siege of Samos.[81] Thus we might expect Andocides to have a fairly good knowledge of that period from his own family's activities.

This is his account of the main events of the Pentekontaëtia (III 3ff.). Each section is complemented with puzzling and wildly inaccurate details about the building of ships and walls.[82]

> At about the time of our war in Euboia, then, when we held Megara, Pegae and Troizen, we were seized with a desire for peace. We recalled from exile Miltiades, son of Cimon, who had been ostracized and was living in the Chersonese, as he was *proxenos* (official representative) for the Spartans, to send him to Sparta to make overtures for a truce. On that occasion we made a peace with Sparta for fifty years, and both sides kept the truce for thirteen years . . .

[78] See Wade-Gery (1958), 207–11; Meiggs (1972), 134f.; Meiggs (1984), 37 for new confirmatory evidence.

[79] The family connection with the later peace means that it cannot be used as evidence against the existence of the Peace of Callias.

[80] He was young in 415 (II 7) and over 40 at his trial, still expecting to have children (I 148, in 399); the *Life* puts his birth in 468/7, which must be wrong.

[81] Androtion *FGH* 324 F38; perhaps also on the Athenian expedition to Corcyra in 433/2 (Thuc. I 51.4; cf. *Life* §2) but the text is uncertain. See Gomme *HCT* I, 188f., and *FGH* 323a F24, commentary.

[82] W. E. Thompson (1967) has a detailed discussion of the intervening details, but see n. 77.

Then we went to war about Aigina, and after both sides had suffered badly, we again desired peace. Ten men were chosen from all Athenians to go as deputies with unlimited powers (*autokratores*) to negotiate peace. Amongst them was Andocides, my grandfather. They made peace with the Spartans for thirty years . . .

Then we went to war again on account of Megara . . .

Andocides has divided the period into two wars, the first 'in Euboia', the second 'because of Aigina' (and a third 'about Megara', the Peloponnesian War). They are punctuated by two peaces. The first, negotiated by 'Miltiades, son of Cimon', recalled from exile, was for fifty years and it lasted thirteen; the second was negotiated by ten men including his grandfather, and it was for thirty years.

Andocides has apparently inverted the main features of each 'war'. His first war has elements which seem to belong to the later period just before the Thirty Years Peace (446/5) (according to Thuc. 1 114). It is introduced, 'at the time of our war in Euboia when we held Megara, Pegae and Troizen . . . '. Yet the war in Euboia must be connected with the very serious Euboian revolt (447/6) which the Athenians under Pericles were suppressing when Megara revolted. Pericles has to return in haste from Euboia to prevent a Peloponnesian invasion of Attica. This was just before the Thirty Years Peace in which Athens gave back Nisaea, Pegae, Troizen and Achaia (Megara had seceded anyway). That signified the end of Athens' mainland empire. But in Andocides' version Euboia's revolt has been remembered with its own peace negotiations – though its critical importance had lain in coinciding with the Megarian revolt.

Andocides' 'fifty years peace', which ended the war 'about Euboia', seems to correspond in fact to the five-year truce (*c.* 450) mentioned by Thucydides (1 112.1). Perhaps it was upgraded by its association with 'Miltiades, son of Cimon', which is also wrong. The main burst of fighting with Aigina actually occurred before this truce, though for Andocides the second war was 'over Aigina'. Thus he has transposed events closely connected in time just before the Thirty Years Peace to about fifteen years before.

Andocides uses the mainland possessions, especially Megara, as a time marker. This unusual recognition of the mainland empire betrays some knowledge of the significance of the Thirty Years Peace which relinquished such ambitions. We remember that Andocides' grandfather helped negotiate the peace and had invaded the Megarid in 446/5. Andocides' peculiar choice of 'events' thus becomes more intelligible. He says nothing of the fighting in Boiotia nor of the fighting in the east;

his family was not so involved there.[83] But family involvement perpetuated memory of the importance of the Megarid and the Thirty Years
Peace. The fragile memories of the Athenian past preserved by his
grandfather's participation have been strung out into two full-scale wars,
each equipped with a peace. The 'peace' his grandfather negotiated is
roughly accurate, the other very inaccurate. Aigina itself was very
important in the negotiations of the Thirty Years Peace. It was granted
autonomy while remaining in the Delian League. This probably explains
the fact that Aigina has become a 'cause' of the second war that the peace
put an end to; and this may reflect more than Andocides' family
tradition. Just as the Peloponnesian War was in popular tradition 'about
Megara',[84] so the war, 'about Aigina' may reflect something of popular
tradition.

This is our only clear indication of the kind of image that might have
been held by the aristocratic houses of Athens' history about fifty years
before. It is true that this one case might not be typical. Yet Andocides
makes remarkably detailed use of the past in his arguments. It is
unlikely that he was particularly ignorant; indeed, Aeschines used this
very passage when he needed a similar account. If anything, Andocides was probably more knowledgeable than most because of his
family's prominence. His family tradition is lengthy and impressive
compared to most others. This view of recent history is probably
representative, and we should at least consider its full implications.

For the sheer preservation of the past with historiographical accuracy,
obviously it is not encouraging. Was this the kind of account Herodotus
had to grapple with in the 440s and 430s when he was enquiring into the
history of fifty years before? It exhibits extreme confusion of chronology.
Events (here wars and peace treaties) are duplicated and in the process
are made to seem more similar than they were – for the five years' truce is
promoted to fifty years' peace. There is a simplification in the mention of
'Miltiades, son of Cimon' which is intelligible as an approximation to the
better-known Miltiades, the great hero of the Persian Wars, an interesting sign of ignorance about Cimon, one of the most prominent men of the
Pentekontaëtia.[85] Of the two wars, an element which seems more
appropriate to the second period, Euboia, has been transferred to the
first, thus breaking its crucial connection with events of the second war.
The two periods of war have been reduced to an extreme simplicity,
involving two areas only which were important at that time. It is the more

---

[83] Though his grandfather helped besiege Samos.
[84] E.g. Ar. *Acharnians*, And. III 8f.
[85] On the disappearance of Cimon in oral tradition, see p. 203.

striking that Andocides' two wars seem mainly composed from his grandfather's experience in one single period.[86]

However, even this account is unusual in its detail and knowledge compared with other oratory and the official tradition itself (see Ch. 4). This suggests that family knowledge and family tradition could help preserve information about Athenian history that was comparatively independent of 'official tradition' and propaganda; but that it nevertheless preserved an image of the past centred around the involvement of the family's ancestors. Moreover, the traditions might be vastly simplified and distorted. Memories within the family about wider Athenian history were individual compared to the wider polis traditions, but they might also be highly selective and eccentric.

2.3 The limits of family memory

How far back did classical family traditions go? This is often asked of oral tradition in general: how far can one expect an oral tradition to last, how long do oral traditions remain accurate? But there is no general rule for the life-expectancy of oral tradition even within the same society. The preservation of oral traditions depends on a huge variety of factors which can be reduced essentially to a question of whether there was any reason to remember them. Their accuracy depends partly on the form in which they are transmitted. There are famous examples of oral traditions being passed down apparently without much change for many generations, usually in poetry. Mnemonic devices help crystallize traditions.[87] As we have seen, however, Athenian, and indeed Greek, family tradition depended for its preservation on more nebulous reasons for memory which did themselves select and alter the traditions.

The family traditions of the Athenian rhetorical defence are peculiarly useful because in a 'family defence' the speaker is anxious to prove that as many as possible of his ancestors had been patriotic citizens, and he cites as many remote ancestors as he remembers.[88] (There was no regular and semi-legal 'limit' either to family tradition or to the family itself.)[89] The traditions of these wealthy Athenians set in perspective the longer traditions of the great aristocratic families and the few genealogies which

---

[86] Andocides' hurried account of the Peloponnesian War (III 8f., 29–31), however, is recognizable, if simplistic, with all the main stages present; his main errors may partly be encouraged by the rhetorical points he is making.

[87] It can be argued that a tradition is reasonably reliable because its transmission has been exact – Vansina (1973), esp. Ch. 2, though the idea of an archetype for narrative traditions he now questions.

[88] The Alcmaeonids, however, had particular reason to omit their first known ancestor: see Ch. 2.4.3 and Ch. 5.4, below.

[89] Above, Ch. 2, n. 38.

extended to an Homeric ancestor (Ch. 3). There are two elements to the question: how far back any tradition extends, however transformed, and how far back we find memories which are reasonably accurate. In discussing accuracy I may have to anticipate later detailed treatment. It is least misleading to count in generations initially, as precise years are impossible to determine. Since the material is probably unfamiliar, I shall have to go into some detail.

In many cases family history seems to extend for only three generations to the speaker's grandfather. Considerable knowledge about uncles, fathers and brothers may contrast with the dearth of knowledge about older ancestors. It is a salutary thought that these are primarily men of the wealthiest classes in Athens, neither poor nor nonentities.[90] For instance, a descendant of Cleon introduces a family defence indirectly in speaking of his mother's ancestry ([Dem.] XL 25). His mother first married Cleomedes, 'whose father, they say, led your ancestors as general, took many Spartans alive at Pylos, and was held in the greatest esteem of all in the city'. He also mentions his mother's father Polyaratos who 'was held in great honour' by the Athenians.[91] The speaker's fine ancestry goes back to his maternal grandfather and (amusingly) to his paternal grandfather Cleon, the late fifth-century demagogue so reviled by most of the ancient writers. Perhaps Cleon was enough, and there was no need to remember further back. There is a span of just over seventy-five years since the capture of Pylos which is mentioned.[92]

In a case about citizenship (Dem. LVII) the speaker Euxitheos includes a detailed account of his family. His father (§18) was captured in the Decelean War (i.e. during the last decade of the fifth century) and taken to Leuctra. He names his mother's father (Damastratos (1) Meliteus) and tells us that his mother's half-brother Amytheon fought and died in Sicily (we are meant to understand the great Sicilian expeditions of 415). A nephew of hers fought and died at Abydus with Thrasymachos (§38). Attempting to prove his mother was Athenian he cannot go further than his maternal grandfather. Little seems to be known of Damastratos beyond his name, which is hardly impressive. The family tradition extends barely to the grandfather and at least seventy years to Amy-

---

90 Contrast Bethe's suggestion ((1935), 38) that it is only the ordinary (i.e. poor) man whose family memory extends to only three generations: the 'natural' man does not concern himself with his ancestors.

91 [Dem.] XL 24; possibly public honours of which no record has survived, rather than the two offices he is known from inscriptions to have held (*APF* 11907), but I doubt it refers to anything so specific.

92 Date of speech in early 340s: Schaefer (1885–7), vol. IIIB 224; Blass (1887–98) differing only by a year, 347 B.C.

theon's death.[93] The same limit of three generations and about seventy years to the earliest external event also holds in the case of Isaeus VII. The speaker (Thrasyllos II) explains the inheritance of the property by three sons, of whom one is the first husband of the speaker's grandmother (§5) (she has already had recourse to the courts). The name of the father who originally bequeathed the property is not given. But alongside much detail of quarrels, marriages and his grandfather's conduct which are relevant to the case, the speaker also adds for effect the death in Sicily of Thrasyllos, one of the three original brothers, and of Mneson, another son, in Athens.[94]

One is reminded of the scene in Plato's *Laches* (179a–180b) where the boys are told about their famous grandfathers; or of Plato's family knowledge which was accurate as far as the third generation, then moved suddenly to a remote ancestor mentioned by Solon (see below, p. 170). Aeschines, too, began his attack on Demosthenes' family from his grandfather Gylon (III 171), an interesting and rare example of tradition against a family.[95] Other allusions to family history or straight pieces of family defence do not even reach the grandfather.[96]

Thus, even a member of the exceedingly wealthy trierarchic class might have a family tradition that extended for no more than three generations. This hardly involves complex transmission. It could even run directly from grandfather to grandson (there is often said to be a particularly strong link between these two generations).[97] Moreover, boys often took their grandfather's name, which emphasized family continuity, and you had to know your grandparents' names to take office. In Aristophanes' *Birds* (281–3), the hoopoe's pedigree is explained by an analogous one, the 'Callias–Hipponikos–Callias' genealogy, which is clearly meant to be a parody of a genealogy.

What is remarkable is not that family tradition could extend with ease to the grandfather, but that it often went no further. In fact the

---

[93] The earliest 'biographical information given here. Damastratos must have been born before 460 and may not even have lived into the fourth century, *APF* 3126.

[94] Also (§9) that his stepfather made a will when about to start for Corinth on military service – probably the Corinthian War.

[95] He says Gylon betrayed Nymphaeum in Pontus to the enemy; in Bosphorus he was rewarded by the tyrants and married a Scythian woman (probably towards the end of the fifth century, Schaefer (1885–7) vol. 1, 264, 268). Dinarchus (1 *Ag. Demosth.* 111) said of Demosthenes that he had no ancestral *doxa* (good repute) handed down from his forebears. Unfortunately we do not know Demosthenes' answer; cf. Dem. XXVIII answering accusations that his grandfather was a public debtor.

[96] Of the father's generation: Lys. x 27f., his father was general many times and was killed by the Thirty; Lys. XII 4, Lysias' father was persuaded by Pericles to come to Athens; Lys. XIX 12ff., father's connection with Conon and his services (55–7 and 63), and father-in-law (16); Lys. XXXII 7, father; Aeschines' father and uncle (II 77f. and 147; III 191).

[97] E.g. Halbwachs (1980), 63.

implications of this go far deeper. For *progonoi*, which we conventionally translate as 'ancestors', could refer merely to the grandfather's generation. In English an 'ancestor' tends to be rather more remote, probably outside living memory.[98] In Greek the terms *pappos* (usually 'grandfather') and *hoi progonoi*, the ancestors, could be used of the same man. Aeschines, for example, said of Demosthenes (III 172): 'From his grandfather (*pappos*), therefore, he would inherit enmity to the people, for you [the people] condemned his ancestors (*progonoi*) to death.' The 'ancestral' slur on the family was that of the grandfather.[99] Similarly *pappoi*, literally 'grandfathers', express the kind of inherited propensities that were 'ancestral'. The Birds (Ar. *Birds* 374) cannot at first believe that men can help them, since they were 'enemies to the Birds' *pappoi*'.[100] *Pappos* could be extended to denote previous generations,[101] *progonoi* denoted anyone from the legendary heroes to the grandfather who was actually within living memory. The 'ancestors' could mean merely the grandfather, and ancestral characteristics could be only three generations old.

This usage confirms the very short span for family memory that we see in the direct evidence. Surely the oral nature of transmission encouraged this. The earlier generations faded into oblivion so fast that there was seldom a much deeper, much older layer of ancestors to contrast with the recent generation of grandparents. Past events or generations known by oral tradition became ancient or 'ancestral' very fast.[102] Without written record or a 'bookish' and historical sense of chronology, chronological data are very unstable. The 'telescoping' or compression of chronology is common, especially when one isolated, much older ancestor was remembered for some reason alongside the very recent ones, and the ancestors in between were forgotten (see Ch. 3 in more detail). For now, it is enough to stress that much family tradition, even that of rich families, was extremely short-lived, barely reaching an 'ancestor' who could have

---

[98] *O.E.D.*: [a forefather] 'usually more remote than a grandfather'.

[99] Aeschines has already (III 169) defined 'public service (*euergesia*) from one's ancestors' as a necessary sign of the *dēmotikos*. Din. I *Ag. Demosth.* 111 similarly for Demosthenes (Ch. 2, n. 95 above).

[100] The sycophant (Ar. *Birds* 1451) later explains cheerfully that informing is a 'family tradition' (lit. 'of one's *pappos*'): παππῷος ὁ βίος συκοφαντεῖν ἐστί μοῦ; *Lys.* 653, 'the so-called ancestral (*pappōos*) fund; cf. enumerating one's *pappoi*, *Theaet.* 174e–175a.

[101] As *LSJ*: as grandfather, Hdt. III 55; as ancestors generally, *Theaet.* 174e, Menander fr. 612; referring to specific further generations, Arist. *Pol.* 1275b24, 'to two or three or more *pappoi*'; and Dionysius of Halicarnassus IV.47, 'tracing the family back to the third *pappos*'. Cf. Ar. *Birds* 765 (with pun).

[102] Perhaps analogous is the way *palaios* (lit. 'ancient') can be used of comparatively recent events well within living memory (though *palai* may also mean 'former'): Dem. XIX 191 (Conon); Dem. XXI 78, '*palaia*' of Demosthenes' youthful action for patrimony; Is. VIII 6.

been known personally to the descendant repeating the tradition. We must imagine a picture of the past particularly hard for historians, in which grandfathers constituted 'the ancestors' (*progonoi*) as much as a legendary hero, a past of extreme chronological vagueness and fluidity and one which might from the family's viewpoint be a void more than three generations back.[103]

Other family traditions, however, extend further,[104] to the fourth or fifth generation, and in the remarkable case of the Alcmaeonids, to the seventh. At this point we can begin to see family tradition becoming dramatically inaccurate.

The speaker of [Dem.] LVIII (66f.) presents a family defence which extends four generations to his grandfather and great-grandfather Aristocrates, who, he says, razed Eëtioneia and restored the demos (i.e. democracy). Aristocrates performed this achievement about seventy years before the speech.[105] But, as we see below (Ch. 2.4), the family tradition has been remarkably changed during that time. The speaker of Isaeus V (41f.) also extends his family tradition back to his great-grandfather. His ancestors performed every kind of choregic office, and some died fighting for their country. Of these, his great-grandfather died at Eleusis. Whatever the precise reference of a battle 'at Eleusis', we are here at the limits of the family tradition.[106] The death of Dikaiogenes is usually put in the mid-fifth century (from the death of his son), and the speech dates from the early 380s. So the span of memory is about sixty or seventy years from the earliest external 'events', four generations in family terms. The memorials of choregic victories mentioned have not prompted a much longer span than other traditions.[107]

We find family traditions of five generations, but little seems to be known of the ancestor in the fifth generation except his name. The family descended from Bouselos is mainly described for the complex inheritance case of [Dem.] XLIII (*Ag. Makartatos*). Information about the family is mostly genealogical, as was needed for the case, and much more may have been known. But it is interesting that this lengthy tradition goes back to an ancestor who gave his name to the family and that the descendants of Bouselos all have a common tomb (*mnēma*) which 'is

---

[103] The absence of an easy and memorable dating system and of history teaching in schools exacerbated this tendency.

[104] Some ten or eleven examples in extant oratory where the speaker is of the family in question concern family tradition of over three generations.

[105] *APF* 1904; the speech was probably delivered c. 341 when the speaker was a young man (§§1–2).

[106] On the family, *APF* 3773, Wyse (1904), 402ff.; pp. 115f. and Ch. 2, n. 66 above.

[107] Cf. also the advice about impiety cited by the speaker of [Lys.] VI 54 from Diokles, his grandfather, son of Zakoros, a hierophant. The great-grandfather is remembered by his unusual office and presumably gives weight to his son's advice.

called the *mnēma* of the Bouselids, a large enclosed area, just as the ancients used to have' (XLIII 79). Surely this is why the tradition is quite long. A family must remember its eponymous ancestor above all, and the family burial place reinforced this. Dating is difficult and the occasions of the court cases themselves are uncertain, but we can probably say that the family tradition extends over a century back to Bouselos, though knowledge of him may indeed be purely genealogical.[108] Similarly, the litigious family of [Dem.] XLIV may also be said to extend its family tradition five generations to Euthymachos. Most information given is genealogical, probably encouraged by the manoeuvring for the estate. Apart from this, we only hear that Euthymachos' son Archippos died at Methymna serving as a trierarch. So genealogical information is plentiful for the five generations, if not necessarily right. But the only further information is from the generation of the plaintiff's grandfather, four generations from the speaker who is the plaintiff's son. The family tradition spans a century or more,[109] but its quality may not be impressive. Though Euthymachos left a considerable estate we only find out about his sons (§§9ff.).

So some family traditions extended for four or five generations, but the information about the oldest ancestor mentioned is either inaccurate or very slight. The complex property cases may be misleading as they are primarily concerned with genealogy. They do, however, indicate a detailed tradition of genealogical ramifications, surely encouraged – and preserved – by the lengthy inheritance wrangles.[110] But where we can check genealogical information given by other, aristocratic families (below, p. 130), it turns out to be extremely inaccurate so far back. By counting the length of a tradition by generations, we get a good impression of the chains of transmission, where more precise counting of years would be very schematic.[111] Yet, when we can estimate roughly the number of years since the earliest event mentioned, such events fall

---

[108] See *APF* 292: Bouselos is five generations from Makartatos, six from speaker, and the speech is in the late 340s. Bouselos can only be dated vaguely: his son Euboulides (1) was treasurer of Athena in 441/0 (ML 55.10–11), which puts Bouselos' active life in the first half of the fifth century. Is. XI (for the same dispute) only gives us a little more, on Hagnias' embassy (§8).

[109] Euthymachos can only be dated from Archippos' death (*APF* 5638), and his *floruit* is thus put at *c.* 450 (Kirchner's date is rather earlier). See Davies, *APF* 5638 for details: he puts the battle at Methymna before 428. We also hear of Archiades who died unmarried, as his grave shows ([Dem.] XLIV 18).

[110] Not necessarily accurately, despite the detail: cf. [Dem.] XLIII 18, where the speaker cunningly says he will not put up a written family tree because it would be unfair to those at the back!

[111] Cf. [Dem.] XLIV where the speaker is acting for his father, therefore adding another generation to the count, and where the other branch of the family produces four generations to the three of the first branch. As for variation in generation length, I have recently met (in England) a grandfather who was thirty-two.

surprisingly often to about sixty or seventy years before the time of the speech. Knowledge of up to five generations implies a tradition of over one hundred years, but for both the families of Bouselos and Euthymachos the scantiness of information makes a smaller span more realistic. Family traditions barely extend beyond seventy years unless they are particularly remarkable. This is the rough span of 'living memory' – the rough span of time for which there were people still alive who had witnessed or experienced the events in question.

Compare the family tradition given by the speaker of Lysias xxvi (21f.) in the early years of the fourth century. He asserts in very general terms that his ancestors fought against the tyrants. This should indicate a remarkable tradition of about a hundred and twenty years, but his vagueness suggests strongly that he had no specific knowledge about his sixth-century ancestors at all and the claim was wishful thinking.

> In the case of myself, or my father or my ancestors, he [his opponent] will have nothing to say which shows hatred of the people (*misodēmia*). For he cannot say that I took part in the oligarchy (since it was later than that that I was declared to have reached manhood); nor my father (since he died in office in Sicily long before the revolution (*stasis*)); nor were my ancestors subject to the tyrants, for they were continually in faction against them the whole time.

So, for both his father and himself he gives careful chronological proof that they could not have participated in the oligarchy. But the activity of 'the ancestors' is vague and stereotyped, and there is no corresponding 'proof' for them, only further description. Can he have known anything about them at all? He produces the conventional assertion of anti-tyrant action that was helpful in the aftermath of the oligarchy (see Ch. 2.4 and Ch. 5). No special details or 'anomalous' elements suggest genuine memory amidst the conventional catch-phrases. Either a dim family tradition has been worn down into the stereotyped form of the polis traditions or the 'tradition' was simply invented according to conventional models. No ancestors are mentioned between the father who died in Sicily and the end of the tyranny nearly one hundred years before. So the supposed family tradition that had lasted for one hundred and twenty years and an undisclosed number of generations was probably not a genuine one at all.

This family defence suggests – as do the others – that the period of the tyranny was just beyond the range of most family traditions by the early fourth century. Memories for over one hundred years were very rare. This brings us to the two remarkable family traditions of Andocides and the Alcmaeonids which did have comparatively detailed memories of their ancestors' participation. But in each we find a combination of unique or 'anomalous' elements which show that genuine memories have been preserved and stereotyped elements which show how the traditions have undergone considerable transformation. I shall only discuss them briefly here, anticipating my later conclusions.

Andocides cites his great-grandfather Leogoras and Leogoras' father-in-law: they defeated the tyrants at 'Pallenion' which heralded the return of the people and the end of the tyranny (I 106, II 26). So the tradition purports to extend to the fifth generation from Andocides. But 'Pallenion' is almost certainly a confused memory of the battle of Pallene of *c.* 546 (see Ch. 2.4.2). Thus the tradition actually retains the memory of an event of over 150 years ago. But it has translated it to the period of the fall of the tyranny two generations later (about 100 years ago) and transformed its whole character. This transposition of two generations makes a mockery of any literal calculation of a tradition's 'age', still more of any general expectations for the survival rate of oral tradition. A tradition might indeed survive for as long as 150 years, but it may do so in a completely different guise from its original character. Similarly with the genealogical knowledge expressed. The texts mentioned above give two different relationships for the same Leogoras, and one (II 26) is usually emended to make Leogoras Andocides' great-grandfather (see n. 140 below). But since the tradition has transposed the battle to a period two generations after, are we calculating the position of the real Leogoras or the 'fictional' one of the tradition? Amidst this confusion, it seems most probable that the family tradition itself was no longer sure of the exact position of Leogoras in the family tree. Could Andocides have written both texts giving different relationships? Even in this exceptionally old family tradition, genealogical knowledge seems to be at least shaky by the fourth or fifth generation – despite their firm belief in their Homeric ancestor.

We find a similar confusion for the Alcmaeonids. The family defence presented by the younger Alcibiades (Isoc. xvi 25ff.) starts with Alcmaeon, the first Athenian to win the chariot race at Olympia. This takes us back seven generations from the famous Alcibiades, eight from his son, and the chariot race is about two hundred years from the time of the speech.[112] By now it is clear how remarkable such a time span is. Alcmaeon was their eponymous ancestor (Ch. 2.4.3), who would therefore be remembered carefully, and the family had been important in the archaic period. But they could, in fact, have gone back even further to Megacles (1), who had been associated with the origin of the family curse.

---

[112] The victory is usually dated to 592: Moretti (1957), 68, no. 81. Schol. Pind. *Pyth.* VII 14 give a date for a victory of Megacles which seems to refer to that of Alcmaeon.

And this they do not do. The family probably 'forgot' him in order to suppress memory of the curse, and they surely named themselves after Alcmaeon for the same reason (Ch. 2.4.3 and Ch. 5.5). As for the rest of the tradition's accuracy, it was clearly drastically reshaped from very early on, and the family's version of the expulsion of the tyrants bore little relation to Herodotus' detailed narrative. Moreover, the genealogical relationships expressed by the younger Alcibiades are inaccurate. The remarkable span of tradition is counterbalanced by extreme distortion and transformation.

The aristocratic families retain the longest traditions with the most complex content. They had illustrious ancestors worth remembering, an interest in maintaining continuity, and their nobility (*eugeneia*) required distant ancestors. But what is striking is that even their traditions do not go back further. They had traditions of legendary ancestors but there was apparently a void between the recent past of four or five generations from the present and the Homeric hero (see Ch. 3 for further implications of this). Most traditions extended for three or four generations only, some not even to the fifth century, and often the earliest specific events alluded to fall about sixty or seventy years back. The continued relevance of the period of the end of the tyranny probably encouraged slightly longer memories – since length of memory depends on relevance as well as the simple lapse of time. Family tradition was partly encouraged and confirmed by the polis traditions and the demands of the democratic audience. But by the early fourth century that period was at the very limits of family memory. Distortions and gross inaccuracies are increasingly visible from the third generation back. In concrete terms this may mean that by the end of the fifth century memories dating back to the period of the Persian Wars were fading fast and will almost have disappeared by the middle of the fourth century.

2.4 Memory and transformation

Certain longer traditions force us to consider not just fluidity, emphasis and lifespan, but the wholesale transformation of the content to fit very strong general conceptions about Athens' history, indeed the patriotic polis traditions themselves. I turn to three particularly striking family traditions: that of the family of Aristocrates ([Dem.] LVIII 66f.); that of Andocides in his own speeches; and the tradition about the Alcmaeonids in Isoc. XVI 25–7. This is the nearest we have to the notorious Alcmaeonid tradition so often discussed without this passage; it therefore deserves to be examined first, alongside other family traditions and apart from other wider traditions of the tyranny. We have external evidence for each family which helps us to discern the changes they have undergone. Each one represents some genuine memory of ancestral achievement. We can tell this partly from 'anomalous' elements in their tradition that we know from other sources are either misplaced or do not prove what they are thought to. But they are each set in a conventional and simplified narrative which represents a landmark of Athenian democratic history, the ending of the tyrannies of the Thirty (404–403 B.C.) and the Peisistratids (end of sixth century). We thus find a combination of genuine individual memories and the wider, stereo-typed polis traditions. Each family tradition has undergone considerable transformation and has ended up with an impeccable record of demo-cratic action against tyranny. This can partly be explained in terms of the process of memory and transmission, as individual memories are reinforced or slightly changed by other traditions around them. They throw much light on the problems and characteristics of oral tradition – and it is thus essential to examine every one of them closely. The effect and argument are cumulative. As we analyse these family traditions consecutively, they turn out to have many features in common. They begin to reveal parallel characteristics and transformations of memory which illuminate and explain each other and therefore the workings of oral tradition in general.

2.4.1 The family of Aristocrates

I start with a family tradition that is complemented and largely contra-dicted by the evidence of an historian contemporary with the events it refers to. The tradition about Aristocrates, son of Scelias, produced in [Dem.] LVIII 66f., probably in *c.* 341, has a counterpart in the detailed narrative of Thucydides' Book VIII. Discussions of the original events have understandably paid slight attention to this passage of family defence. Its surprising content is barely noted, if at all. But its impli-cations for the character of oral tradition are extensive and astonishing. It is particularly striking both because it is comparatively late and because it is duplicated by Thucydides. It is all the more important to grasp the scale of the deformation.[113] Family tradition and memory have created a glorious, spotless democratic past from a far more ambiguous reality.

The speaker, possibly an Epichares (*APF* 1904), gives as his final argument to the assembly the service rendered to the city by his grandfather Epichares and by Epichares' uncle, Aristocrates, son of Scelias (66f.). The speaker first proudly cites the victory of Epichares, his

---

[113] Andrewes (*HCT* v, 295) comments laconically that 'the speaker of [Dem.] LVIII, being a grandson of Aristocrates' nephew, naturally made him a democratic hero and credits him with warlike exploits as well as the destruction of Eëtioneia'. On Nouhaud (1982), see Ch. 2, n. 132 below.

grandfather, in the boys' footrace at Olympia: 'My grandfather Epichares was a victor at Olympia in the boys' footrace and won a crown for the city, and he died with good reputation amongst your ancestors.' Unfortunately we know nothing more about Epichares than what we are told here.[114]

We continue with the fine democratic deeds of Aristocrates:[115]

> On behalf of which [the polis], Aristocrates, son of Scelias, the uncle of my grandfather Epichares, whose name my brother here bears, performed many fine deeds when the city was at war with the Spartans. He razed Eëtioneia to the ground, into which Critias and his followers were about to receive the Spartans, he destroyed the *epiteichisma*, and he led the people back from exile (κατήγαγε δὲ τὸν δῆμον). He suffered himself dangers not like those we are incurring, but dangers in which even disaster is glorious, and he stopped those who were plotting against you.

So, his many glorious deeds 'when the city was at war with the Lacedaemonians' are mostly left unspecified. The speaker concentrates on a series of actions which cluster around the final years of the Peloponnesian War. Aristocrates razed Eëtioneia, into which Critias and his followers were about to receive the Spartans. He destroyed the *epiteichisma* (what this refers to is unclear) and led back the people, stopping those who were plotting against them. To anyone familiar with the final years of the fifth century, this seems to be a muddle of the two periods of oligarchy that Athens suffered at the expense of its democracy in the last decade of the Peloponnesian War. The first, in 411–410, was named the 'Four Hundred' after the number of oligarchs involved. A moderate oligarchy, it was eventually forced to include the 'Five Thousand' citizens in government, which thus created a mild oligarchy, before full democracy was finally restored. The second oligarchy, imposed by Sparta on Athens in its defeat (404 B.C.), was extremely narrow and very severe, nicknamed the 'Thirty Tyrants'. We know about these oligarchies from good historical sources. But how was the passage intended and understood in the mid-fourth century?

It is virtually certain that for an audience in the 340s, sixty or seventy years after these events, this passage could only be taken to refer to the final events which brought back the democracy after the Thirty, so

---

[114] Victory dated tentatively to 396, Moretti (1957), 114, no. 368.

[115] The rediscovery of *IG* I², 772 (Shear (1973), 173–5) ends the controversy about the patronymic Scelias and identification of the dedicator. It clearly belongs to the later Aristocrates, not his grandfather (dedication mentioned by Plato, *Gorg.* 472a–b) and has *Skelio*. Other texts have two *l*'s, and neither spelling can be produced consistently by emendation (also Ar. *Birds* 126 and fr. 25 Dem.). Clearly it was spelled either way.

frequently recalled in fourth-century patriotic oratory. The razing of Eëtioneia is described in Thucydides' detailed and reliable account (VIII 89ff.) as part of the fall of the earlier oligarchy of the Four Hundred, and the speaker would have had to mention the Four Hundred if he had meant the first oligarchy. The restoration of democracy after the first oligarchy was barely mentioned in fourth-century oratory, except in the immediate aftermath of the Peloponnesian War.[116] Attention shifts to the more decisive events of the very end, the tyranny of the Thirty, the battle of Aigospotamoi and the destruction of the fleet, and finally 'the return of the demos'.[117]

The fortification of Eëtioneia is connected here in family tradition with Critias himself and the intended betrayal to the Spartans. Critias was the most notorious of the Thirty tyrants and seems to have had little part in the government of the Four Hundred.[118] There was a threat of Spartan invasion at the end of the first oligarchy, as Thucydides tells us (VIII 90f.), but the Spartan threat and actual occupation of Athens at the very end of the war was far more notorious.[119] The speaker was probably referring to that. The destruction of the *epiteichisma* is more puzzling. It is a separate episode from the razing of Eëtioneia, which was in any case only a wall (90.3). An *epiteichisma* is properly the building of a fort on the enemies' frontier, and *the epiteichisma* would seem to refer to the one best known to the Athenians, that of Decelea,[120] whose occupation by Sparta was a terrible blow to Athens. Can the speaker really be asserting that his ancestor destroyed Decelea, which was relieved of Spartan troops only in 404 by the Spartan King Agis himself (Xen. *Hell.* II 3.3)?

Finally Aristocrates 'leads back the demos from exile' (*κατήγαγε τὸν δῆμον*). The phrase is the one commonly used in fourth-century oratory of the glorious return of democracy after the Thirty, accomplished by

---

116 The 5000 are mentioned only in Lys. xx 13–16 on Polystratos; Lys. xxx 7, the speaker was not in the Four Hundred and not even in the Five Thousand; Lys. xII, closely concerned with the last decade of the war (see below, p. 137).

117 E.g. (from many references) Isoc. xvIII 17f., Aeschin. II 77 and 176, III 181, Dem. xxII 52, Lyc. I 61.

118 Wade-Gery (1958), 279, n. 2; Avery (1963). Aeschin. I 173 insists that Critias' connection with Socrates had a large part in Socrates' condemnation; Critias is 'one of the Thirty who put down the democracy'. Cf. Dem. xxIV 90, where Critias epitomizes the autocratic tyrant.

119 E.g. Lys. xxvI 1f., 'when the city was subject to the Lacedaemonians'; Isoc. *Areop.* 64f.; Aeschin. II 77 and 176. Cf. also Xen. *Hell.* II 3.13ff., the oligarchs' request for a Spartan garrison; and II 4.28ff., the oligarchs, hard pressed by Thrasyboulos and his men, send to Sparta for help, and both Lysander and Pausanias intervene in Athens. Oligarchic betrayal to Sparta is common to both the oligarchic periods, and the fortification of Eëtioneia was offering that possibility.

120 E.g. Aeschin. II 76; cf. Thuc. vI 93.

Thrasyboulos and 'the party from the Piraeus'.[121] It is also used, by extension, of the fall of the tyranny and 'restoration' of democracy in the late sixth century (see Ch. 5.2). An audience familiar with the patriotic recollections of the end of the Thirty will naturally have taken the phrase to refer to the restoration of democracy in 403. The exile of the demos that it implies was appropriate for the rule of the Thirty, but not for the period of the Four Hundred and Five Thousand. Aristocrates' descendant can only have meant the return of democracy after the Thirty.

The family tradition, then, associated Aristocrates' razing of Eëtioneia with certain notorious elements of the second oligarchy as remembered in polis tradition: Critias, the *epiteichisma*, and the return of the demos from exile. Aristocrates' role at Eëtioneia has been remembered, but to our astonishment telescoped with the more decisive stage of oligarchic revolution whose significance in Athenian democratic tradition obscured memory of the first oligarchy.[122] Aristocrates was recorded by his family tradition as one of the heroes of the return of democracy after the fall of the Thirty. Thus the tradition seems to have been much influenced by the patriotic polis traditions which dwelt on the later, more brutal oligarchy.

But there is more to it than that. Let us return to Thucydides' version. He tells us that Aristocrates was actually a member of the earlier, extreme oligarchy of the Four Hundred and held office under the regime (VIII 89.2, 92.2, 92.4). He joined with the 'moderate' oligarch Theramenes and, like him, turned against the Four Hundred, urging that the 'Five Thousand' citizens, who had not even been assembled yet, should be allowed to participate in government and thus form a mild oligarchy in place of the Four Hundred (§89.2). According to Thucydides, the extreme oligarchs pressed on with the wall at Eëtioneia while trying to make peace with the enemy Sparta and the Peloponnesians. Theramenes believed that the wall was in fact to let in the enemy (§90). The approach of Peloponnesian ships, in fact come to aid Eëtioneia and the oligarchs, brought matters to a head and the plot against the Four Hundred was developed (§§91–2). Thucydides tells us incidentally (§92.4) that Aristocrates, taxiarch for the Four Hundred, was already in Eëtioneia building the wall ('the hoplites . . . among whom was Aristocrates, taxiarch (i.e. colonel) and commander of his own tribe') and that the hoplites turned on Alexikles, the general, and imprisoned him. When Theramenes arrived, pretending to be on the extreme oligarchic side, he agreed with the hoplites to pull the wall down. It was at this point, on the eve of the

---

[121] Whereas *kataluo* and *katalusis* are used for the end of the Four Hundred in *Ath. Pol.* 33 and 34.1: here *katalusis* seems to be the accepted term for the transition from the Four Hundred to the Five Thousand effected by Theramenes and Aristocrates.

[122] Cf. the version of the Persian Wars given by the dicasts in Ar. *Wasps* (1071ff.), amalgamating the two stages into one: see p. 226, below.

assembly to discuss the institution of the Five Thousand, that the Peloponnesian ships arrived. There was panic and the assembly voted to depose the Four Hundred and institute the Five Thousand, a mild oligarchy (§§96–7).

Aristocrates was thus working quite unambiguously for the oligarchs as a member of the Four Hundred. In Thucydides' narrative he initiated the destruction of Eëtioneia which was a decisive stage in the final establishment of the Five Thousand. Thucydides told us earlier (§89) that he was one of those who believed they should actually institute the Five Thousand. But in the narrative of the destruction of Eëtioneia Aristocrates is presented simply as the taxiarch amongst the hoplites who takes the initiative and imprisons Alexikles.[123] It is Theramenes' arrival which finally accomplishes the destruction.

The only feature common both to Thucydides and the family tradition, then, is the actual destruction of Eëtioneia. The family conveniently omitted and forgot Aristocrates' membership of the Four Hundred and the fact that his action was decisive only for the end of the Four Hundred, not the return of democracy.

Other evidence fills out the picture, still leaving his political position blurred. He was well-known enough to be subject of a joke in comedy which may suggest oligarchic inclinations, and his respect for wealth was mentioned by Plato.[124] He was certainly general at least once (Ar. fr. 591, lines 70–1 K.–A.) and may have been the Aristocrates named without a patronymic who swore to the Peace of Nicias and the treaty (Thuc. v 192, 24.1) and who was general in 412 (viii 9.2). An Aristocrates was general in 410/9 (ML 85), which would be consistent with the recent achievements at Eëtioneia. An Aristocrates is also general in 407 and in 406, when Alcibiades is deposed, fights at Arginusae and is executed.[125] These need not all be the same,[126] but if our Aristocrates held one generalship, it is likely he held more. It is very probable that all these generals with the same name in the same decade were the son of Scelias.[127] If so, he was able to serve under both democratic and

---

[123] Andrewes, *HCT* on viii 92.4.

[124] Citing the dedication for a choregic victory, *Gorg.* 472a (Ch. 2, n. 115), in the early fourth century: Socrates produces witnesses apparently from different political camps, Nicias, Aristocrates and the house of Pericles. Ar. *Birds* 126 (414 B.C.) mentions him scornfully as an 'aristocrat', which may simply be a pun on his name (Wilamowitz (1893), vol. I, 100 n. 3 warns against the political interpretation). Even if not aristocratic, the family had been prominent for several generations (*APF* 1904).

[125] 407: Xen. *Hell.* I 4.21 (with Alcibiades); 406: Xen. *Hell.* I 6.29 and 7.2; Philoch. *FGH* 328 F142.

[126] At least two other officials were called Aristocrates in the late fifth century, but they are known definitely only as *hellenotamiae* (in 421/0 and 415/14): Andrewes and Lewis (1957), 179, Andrewes, *HCT* v. 295f.

[127] *APF* 1904, p. 57.

oligarchic regimes and was either 'a trusted soldier with no strong political feelings'[128] or simply a time-server. Though associated with Theramenes in the overthrow of the Four Hundred, he need not have failed, like Theramenes, to gain the full trust of the restored democracy. He was less deeply implicated in oligarchy. We thus have a picture of a man who held repeated generalships and retained popularity despite his brush with Theramenes and the Four Hundred.

Thucydides' version may not have been the only one current at the time. There are slight indications that Aristocrates' part was magnified in popular and patriotic tradition for a short time after the event – or was actually greater than Thucydides suggests. We cannot discount the possibility that Thucydides was deliberately suppressing a popular and exaggerated version as he did with the Megarian decree. The vitriolic attack on Theramenes in Lysias' *Against Eratosthenes* (XII 62ff.) declares that Theramenes followed Aristocrates and did so only out of fear and jealousy (§66): 'Then he joined Aristocrates because of his jealousy of them [other members of the Four Hundred] and his fear of you [the people].' The speech must have been delivered shortly after 403. Lysias is trying, it is true, to denigrate Theramenes who was important in his opponent's defence, yet he still suggests that Theramenes and Aristocrates (in whichever order) were thought mainly responsible for the dissolution of the Four Hundred. Aristotle expresses the same view in *Ath. Pol.* 33.2 where he states quite baldly that 'Aristocrates and Theramenes were most responsible for the "dissolution" (*katalusis*) of the Four Hundred' and where Aristocrates' name is placed first. Even Thucydides (§89.2) names those of the Four Hundred who opposed the extremists as 'Theramenes and Aristocrates and others'.[129] Thus, there is a hint that whatever Aristocrates actually achieved, a popular tradition paired and perhaps even contrasted him with Theramenes as one of those most responsible for ending the oligarchy. His generalships in the next few years confirmed and enhanced his status as a democratic hero.[130]

Clearly the family tradition has real memory only of its ancestor's action at Eëtioneia, exaggerated in the course of transmission. The razing of Eëtioneia is no longer remembered in its true context, but has somehow become associated with the more glorious overthrow of the Thirty. But family tradition was more astute than this confusion implies. Aristocrates' association with the Four Hundred (and Theramenes) has

---

128 Andrewes, *HCT* v, 295.
129 Cf. Diod. XIII 38.2, who names Theramenes as the one who advised Alcibiades' return.
130 The discredit thrown on Theramenes may also have enhanced Aristocrates' position. Theramenes also served as general after 410 (ML 84, l.35) but not after Alcibiades' return, as Aristocrates probably did in 407/6 and 406/5. The further controversies about Theramenes' own political views concern us less here: see Harding (1974).

been lost: not only omitted but denied by implication through the association of Eëtioneia with the later oligarchy. This shift to the later period is the more striking if Aristocrates was in fact one of the generals executed after Arginusae (some time, therefore, before the Thirty). The family tradition preserved the core of his achievement longer than others would. But its shift to the later period betrays the strong influence of the polis traditions which concentrated on the later, more terrible period of oligarchy. A similar shift and alteration of the original events occurs in Andocides' tradition.

How consciously or cynically had the family changed the content of these traditions? It need not have been an entirely deliberate attempt to whitewash the family ancestor. The process of change in a tradition and the results of failure of memory can be very gradual.[131] If Aristocrates was regarded soon after 410 as responsible for the downfall of the Four Hundred, a great democratic hero, that could have been enough to start the process. After the rule of the Thirty, it was that latter period of oligarchy which understandably had a far deeper place in Athenian consciousness and popular tradition. With the passing of time it was all the easier to confuse the two oligarchies and suppose that Aristocrates' great action at Eëtioneia had been part of the final restoration of democracy in 403 after the Thirty.[132] This late restoration had been more decisive in its results and less ambiguous than the transition from oligachy to mild oligarchy in 411 in which Aristocrates had participated. So we find the telescoping of events around that latter, more glorious restoration. The ancestor becomes a full democratic hero attached clearly to those events most important to the Athenian democracy. His less democratic past is lost. Without Thucydides this passage would be important evidence for Aristocrates and the role of Eëtioneia under the Thirty. Family tradition has, it is true, recorded something which would have dropped out of general memory sixty or seventy years later. But this kind of deformation we should expect, or at least suspect, of family tradition. The tradition has dealt with the embarrassing aspects of the ancestor's career, in effect, by transferring the events to the later and less ambiguous period, omitting unsuitable details. One does *not* receive an elaborate defence or apology of the ancestor's actions in their original setting. Memory and tradition deal with them far more effectively. They are shifted and amalgamated with the period more suitable for the democratic actions they declare.

---

[131] Vansina (1980) and introduction above.

[132] Nouhaud (1982), 253, notes the confusion, but not that Aristocrates was one of the Four Hundred, and therefore misses the full force of the alteration. His excuse – that it is easy to confuse the two periods of oligarchy (!) – totally misses the possible significance of such an error.

2.4.2 Andocides

Andocides' family tradition offers a close parallel to this kind of partial preservation and partial transposition of a genuine memory. I discussed Andocides' account of Athenian history in its relation to his ancestors' roles (Ch. 2.2). Here I concentrate on the specific achievements he claims for his ancestors in the 'family defence' made shortly after 410 (And. II) and again in 399 (And. I).

Andocides claims that Leogoras and Charias were generals when the people defeated the tyrants 'at Pallenion' (I 106) (i.e. end of sixth century). He then identifies them rather vaguely with those Athenians who fought in the Persian Wars and who contributed to the settlement and amnesty (I 107f.). At II 26 he again mentions his ancestors who fought against the tyrants. His maternal uncle, Epilykos, was on the embassy which organized the truce with the Persian king (III 29); and he died in Sicily (I 117).

Most important is the passage at I 106 which I quote in full:

> For when evil times had fallen on the city, when the tyrants ruled it and the demos were in exile, your ancestors (*pateres*) fought and overcame the tyrants at Pallenion. Their generals were Leogoras, my own great-grandfather, and Charias, whose daughter married Leogoras and bore my grandfather. They returned from exile to their homeland; and some of their enemies they put to death, some they exiled, and some they allowed to remain in the city without citizen rights.

Andocides is talking about the period at the end of the tyranny and the 'return of the demos from exile' as popular tradition expresses the complex events which ended the tyranny and instituted the Cleisthenic democracy (roughly from 514 to 508/7).[133] Thus he presents his two ancestors as the leaders of the democratic victory: this implies that only one democratic victory was necessary and that these two men were the only important commanders. Indeed they were 'generals', an embellishment of oral tradition which I discussed above (Ch. 2.2). Similar claims were made by the Alcmaeonid family defence and the speaker of Lysias XXVI. This was the conventional assertion of the required democratic action.

But Andocides puts the victory 'at Pallenion', and there is little doubt that this is the same battle by which the tyrant Peisistratus gained power

---

[133] See Ch. 5 for discussion of this vision of the period, its near monopoly of the tradition by the fourth century and the certain influence of the two periods of oligarchy on the tradition.

in about 545 and which both Herodotus and Aristotle mention.[134] Suggestions to the contrary assume that Andocides and family traditions could tell only the historical truth, which is clearly not so. We have just seen what Aristocrates' descendant said of Aristocrates, against the contemporary account of Thucydides. If such distortion and dislocation could occur in the course of sixty or seventy years, how much more likely is it after one hundred and fifty.

Unlike some family traditions, Andocides is quite specific about detail here. He cites the names of his ancestors, his relations to them and the name of the battle. Thus, we cannot doubt that this represents some kind of genuine family memory. But it has been displaced. As with Aristocrates' family tradition, we must distinguish carefully between what actually happened and what the speaker is conveying to his audience. Some traces remain in what he says which point to the original historical 'facts', here Pallene. But these traces may be construed in an entirely different manner and amalgamated into a quite different picture. They stand out because they do not fit the new context. These 'anomalous' elements help to indicate the different layers of a tradition. Hence the importance of starting first with the alleged place of the battle at Pallene. The tradition must indeed represent actual participation in the battle of *c.* 545, but the family tradition has transferred this memory to a much later period.

Once we have accepted that the battle in question heralded another period of Peisistratos' power, the political standpoint of Andocides' ancestors can probably never be known.[135] Andocides says his ancestors won a victory against the tyrants at Pallenion. Is the family more likely to remember accurately the fact that these two men were on the winning side – in which case they must have been in Peisistratos' party? Or would they remember that they were fighting against Peisistratos – in which case they were in fact on the losing side? The statement as it stands is self-contradictory. This needs stressing since the very contradiction is seldom even noticed, and Andocides' statement is often taken as straightforward historical evidence, regardless both of its part in family defence and of the manner of transmission through the family for over a

---

134 Hdt. 1 62.3 (ἐπὶ Παλληνίδος Ἀθηναίης ἱρὸν), Arist. *Ath.Pol.* 15.3 and 17.4 (ἐπὶ Παλληνίδι) taken from Herodotus. Pallene is usually taken to be the same as Andocides' Pallenion (Blass, Kirchner and others), surely rightly. MacDowell postulates another, completely unknown battle in the expulsion of Hippias ((1962), app. O), Raubitschek (1955) in the expulsion of Isagoras in 508/7: mainly because of the slight difference in name and the chronology (but on chronology see below Ch. 2, nn. 138 and 140), assuming Andocides' placing is right. But MacDowell's comment, 'I do not think that §106 contains any historical inaccuracy' is strange of an orator who can produce the extraordinary version of recent Athenian history in III 3ff.

135 The period was one of factions struggling for power, in any case: Hdt. 1 59ff.; D. M. Lewis (1963).

century and a half.[136] Other oral traditions suggest that defeats tended to turn into victories for the Athenian democracy.[137] But equally, family tradition was capable of reversing the dubious roles of the ancestors to produce a fine democratic past. Andocides' family tradition tells us more about the processes of family memory than the family's real past.

The period of the end of the tyranny stands at the very limit of family memory by the early fourth century (Ch. 2.3 above), and even the surviving family traditions are coloured by the superficially similar period of the Thirty (see further Ch. 5.2). Andocides' tradition in I 106 forms a clear example where faint memories from an even earlier period have been telescoped with the later period of Peisistratid tyranny which was still important in the general polis traditions. The latter period in this tradition was more coherent and unambiguous, a clear triumph for the 'people' after exile and return. It seems to have attracted the faint memories of Andocides' family to form a far better democratic defence, just as Aristocrates' achievement was telescoped in his family tradition into the later, less ambiguous triumph of democracy in 403, in which the ancestor could be presented in unalloyed opposition to the tyrants. Details and interpretation can be altered by later, contemporary events. Chronology may be upset by the simple process of telescoping. If such telescoping is characteristic of family tradition, arguments of chronology must be offered with care, if at all.[138] Indeed this applies to all oral tradition (see further, Ch. 3). Certain similarities in different family traditions are not necessarily proof of exactly similar family history.[139] They may be explained by the processes of oral transmission and memory and the influence of the polis traditions.

In his second speech Andocides offers further elaboration of his ancestors' position under the tyrants. On an unprejudiced reading

---

[136] E.g. Raubitschek (1955); MacDowell (1962), repositioning the battle: mainly because, 'Andocides' great-grandfather can hardly have been old enough to be a general about 545'. But *was* he actually a general, along with his father-in-law, or is this another elaboration of oral tradition? Davies aptly sums up the problem, *APF*, p. 27, on Andocides (I): 'He may . . . have initiated a family tradition of hostility to the tyrants . . . which was later to be valuable for forensic purposes to Andocides (IV) and for which the orator's confused *obiter dicta* are the only evidence.' D. M. Lewis ((1963), 23) is even more cautious.

[137] E.g. Leipsydrion, Lys. II 48ff., Plato *Menex.* 242a, Aeschin. II 75; see Ch. 4 for the background in the epitaphic tradition.

[138] Cf. Jacoby's attempt to support some chronological data in oral tradition, *Atthis* 188f. Rightly more sceptical, Heidbüchel (1957) questions Jacoby's view: he analyses Peisistratid chronology and decides that the Atthidographers in fact used no other evidence than Herodotus (possibly through Hellanicus).

[139] As Raubitschek (1955) assumes, comparing Isoc. XVI on the Alcmaeonids (but both are highly simplified and conventional versions of complex events).

the passage refers plainly to the same events, the same democratic standpoint upheld by his ancestors and the same Leogoras (II 26).[140]

> The great-grandfather of my father, Leogoras, led a faction against the tyrants on behalf of the people; though he could have set aside his hostility, married into the tyrants' house and ruled the polis with them, he chose rather to go into exile with the people and suffer hardships in exile rather than be a traitor to them.

Here he insists that Leogoras engaged in stasis or faction against the tyrants on behalf of the demos. He could have allied with them in marriage and shared their rule, but he preferred exile with the demos. So again he stresses his ancestor's democratic actions and participation in the demos' exile. At I 106 he said in effect that Leogoras and Charias returned from exile with the demos and inflicted the great defeat on the tyrants. Here Leogoras' democratic zeal is intensified by the information that he could have ruled with the Peisistratid house. Again, is this an interesting and isolated family memory of a possible marriage alliance, perhaps encouraged by the family's uneasy awareness of its high status? Or is it a sign of the tyrants' appeasement of their opponents? It is at any rate incorporated into the family defence so as to render it neutral and unobjectionable. The theme of rejected opportunity actually enhances Leogoras' democratic stance. The same rhetorical point was made of the Alcmaeonids in the same period (Isoc. XVI 26); they were kindred to the Peisistratids, yet still went into exile. In the Alcmaeonid case, we know there was actually an alliance to conceal (see Ch. 2.4.3), but the same rhetorical trick manages to subsume this awkward fact into a seamless family defence. Here, we see the formation of family tradition in the same pattern, transforming a genuine but embarrassing memory into a fine democratic past.

Andocides may also be in doubt about the relationship he bears to Leogoras. The texts of II 26 and I 106 give different relationships, and one is usually emended. But it is possible that Andocides was himself unsure and could have hazarded both possibilities (see Ch. 2.3, p. 130 above). The telescoping of oral tradition renders absolute chronology

---

[140] The texts are usually taken to refer to the same Leogoras, though he is great-grand-father (*propappos*) of Andocides at I 106 and great-grandfather of Andocides' father (*patros propappos*) at II 26; and they are emended to eliminate the extra generation of the second. From strict calculations of chronology the extra generation might be necessary for the mid-sixth century battle of Pallene (see *APF*). But one doubts if strict calculations have much meaning here, since Andocides is trying to refer to the late, not the mid-sixth century, and the telescoping of oral tradition here plays havoc with chronology. Arguments such as Raubitschek's (1955) (who thinks that there are two men called Leogoras here, one of the mid- and one of the late sixth century) simply misunderstand how the tradition has changed.

meaningless here, and the shift from the original battle at Pallene to what Andocides thought happened implies strongly that the generations were extremely muddled in the tradition. Surely Andocides did not really know for certain how many generations back Leogoras was.

Finally, Andocides boasts of his uncle Epilykos who was 'on the embassy to arrange a truce with the Persian king' (III 29). As we have seen (Ch. 2.2), the family tradition has preserved here record of a treaty otherwise unmentioned by the popular tradition or by historians. Though comparatively insignificant, it was a source of pride to the family itself.

Andocides' family tradition exhibits a remarkable length of memory. Though displaced and isolated, the battle of Pallene is still recorded a hundred and fifty years later. The polis traditions presented a more simplistic picture by now, concentrating on the end of the sixth century. So we must recognize the ability of family tradition to preserve genuine memories, particularly ones which did not conform to, or which actually contradicted, the patriotic tenor of the polis traditions – 'anomalous' memories which might otherwise have been forgotten. As with Epilykos' embassy, the family alone had the interest to retain these traditions.

But these memories may become displaced and isolated from their original context. Indeed, without detailed historical knowledge, how could they not? The memories are then subject to telescoping both of events and chronology. They are amalgamated into a later, more memorable and decisive series of events. In the examples so far, the telescoping results in a perfect, fully democratic pose for the ancestor. Moreover, different family traditions share characteristics which seem related to the needs of family defence and the changes of oral tradition. Ancestral generalships, or the opportunity to ally with the tyrants, are not necessarily signs of identical family history, but rather of the similar ways in which family traditions may develop. Both Aristocrates and Andocides' ancestors are transferred to the two great 'liberations' of Athenian history. But the traditions reveal the shift because they have still retained anomalous elements that do not belong to the later period. Andocides' ancestor of a hundred and fifty years before has been transposed forty years forward to a wholly 'democratic' role, and we can no longer tell what his position was in 545. Aristocrates' activities have been transposed less than ten years forward, his main achievement has become part of a far less ambiguous fight for democracy, and any trace of his involvement with the Four Hundred has disappeared. Here the slide was perhaps encouraged by popular acclaim, but the necessities of a democratic family tradition exaggerated this tendency. Such telescoping makes a mockery of chronology. It is no longer possible, once one has seen what is happening, to make literal calculations of chronology from a tradition equipped with telescoping and anachronisms.

Telescoping is a familiar phenomenon in oral tradition. But how does one explain it? In both the examples above we can discern the influence of the polis traditions which seem to have attracted the individual family memories. But influence, a vague term, needs closer definition, and the question here involves the complex processes of memory and oral transmission.

An Athenian may deliberately try to suggest that his ancestors took part in the main landmarks of the polis tradition without having any genuine memories to go on (e.g. Lys. XXVI: above, p. 129). This may itself *create* family tradition. The more interesting effect of polis tradition lies in the complex and unconscious sphere of memory. The dominating polis traditions of crucial events (e.g. the battle of Marathon) form and reinforce most Athenians' knowledge of their city's past (Ch. 4.1). They reinforce memories peculiar to certain people or families. Therefore it is understandable that, with the lapse of time, isolated memories will tend to become amalgamated with those more prominent periods much celebrated by the city. To make sense of them, they are set in the context provided by the wider traditions. Each stage in transmission, each mistake, would add to the character of the tradition.[141] The process may be helped by wishful thinking on the part of the family ('of course one's ancestors fought for the democracy') and by successive needs for family defence. But as the polis tradition also constantly stressed the triumphs of the Athenian demos, the two influences could only converge to the same result. Family tradition tends not to offer a detailed apology or explanation for the family's past. Defence is effected, however unconsciously, by altering the traditions completely and omitting awkward details. This also helps in the rapid transformation of tradition. At the same time recent events also have some influence. For instance, the rule of the Thirty actually produced changes in most traditions about the end of the Peisistratid tyranny (Ch. 5.2). The same influence extended to family traditions about that period.

2.4.3 The Alcmaeonids

Isocrates' early forensic speech (XVII *De bigis* 25–7, *c.* 397 B.C.) on behalf of the younger Alcibiades claims to prove that the family's friendship to the demos is 'ancient and genuine' (παλαιὰν καὶ γνησίαν) (§28). What makes it particularly interesting is that Isocrates elaborates

---

[141] For Andocides' tradition, its shortcomings will have been created gradually in the course of transmission; if Andocides makes a mistake in the transmission, that is yet another stage. He may indeed not be guilty of deliberate falsification (*APF*, p. 28): the transposition and confusion here are recognizable characteristics of oral transmission.

on the ancestry of Alcibiades (III) on the female side, that is, the ancestry of the aristocratic Alcmaeonid family whose most famous member was Pericles himself. Another member was Cleisthenes who founded the democracy in 508/7 after the fall of the tyranny. This is the nearest one can come to evidence of what the 'Alcmaeonid tradition', so prominent in theories of ancient historiography, actually contained. I shall concentrate here as strictly as possible on the passage of Isocrates itself and its similarities to other family traditions. I postpone till later a detailed treatment of the intricate controversies about the Alcmaeonid tradition as it has been discussed in connection with Herodotus' sources, the tyrannicide 'myth' and the wider polis traditions (Ch. 5). This passage has been curiously neglected, hence the value of a detailed comparison with other similar traditions. Here, too, we will see how the family tradition forgets or transposes awkward elements in its past to a more admirable context.

Isocrates begins by claiming that the older Alcibiades (III, the famous fifth-century general) was on the male side a Eupatrid, on the female side an Alcmaeonid. Thus Alcibiades' family boasts of belonging to the ruling aristocracy of Athens before Solon.[142] Yet, this distant aristocratic ancestry can probably be questioned. Isocrates does not mention any members of the Alcibiades family until the Alcibiades (I) who helped Cleisthenes restore the democracy. Alcibiades (I) was an historical character attested elsewhere in a Delphic dedication.[143] But he is also the first known member of the family, so it is doubtful that the family was important enough to have been Eupatrid in the seventh century.[144] However, the Alcmaeonid side *was* Eupatrid, since the Alcmaeonid Megacles was archon during the notorious Cylonian conspiracy (this episode in the late seventh century brought a curse on the family which dogged it throughout its history: Megacles had been held responsible for murdering the conspirators who were suppliants at an altar. This was an impious act which brought pollution on both city and family.) Yet this the family tradition does not say. Surely their omission is connected with the evasion of the family curse which we will find repeatedly in the family tradition.

On the female side they are descended from the Alcmaeonids (§25), 'who left a glorious memorial of their wealth, for Alcmaeon was the first

---

[142] They surely do mean the Eupatrid aristocracy, not (as Wilamowitz and Toeffer thought) the Eupatrid genos: Wade-Gery (1958), 106ff., APF 600, pp. 10–12. The Eupatrid genos is not attested until the Hellenistic period.

[143] *BCH* 46 (1922), 439f. (= *IG* I² p. 272.90); probably last quarter of sixth century.

[144] Kleinias, friend of Solon, supposedly implicated in the Chreokopidai scandal (Plut. *Sol.* xv 7) is generally taken to be an invention of the later Peloponnesian War aimed at contemporary figures including Alcibiades and cannot be used as evidence of a Kleinias at that time (*APF* 600 III).

Athenian citizen to win at Olympia with a team of horses'. This is Alcmaeon (1) (*APF* 9688) whom we meet in Herodotus as the founder of the family's wealth (VI 125). Alcmaeon was probably the eponymous ancestor of the family for several reasons. It was with him that the family was said to have become distinguished (Hdt. VI 125.1), and the very fact that the family seems not to have had its own cult or association with one suggests that their position in Athens was rather different from the very old families who did have such religious control. The Alcmaeonids were simply an *oikia* (i.e. 'house', 'family'). As Wade-Gery pointed out, there are no known 'Alcmaeonids' who cannot be traced back to Alcmaeon 1,[145] and the earlier Megacles I is not called an Alcmaeonid, though the family must have been Eupatrid for him to be archon. Both the tradition in Isocrates and Herodotus' outline of the family's past (VI 125) – who knows elsewhere of Megacles – start with Alcmaeon I. This, then, is the tradition about the eponymous ancestor. Again the notorious earlier ancestor, Megacles, though still remembered in the fifth century, is evaded. Surely Alcmaeon was the eponymous ancestor precisely so that the family could distance itself from Megacles and the curse.

Herodotus also mentioned Alcmaeon's Olympic victory, apparently only adding the tale about his visit to Croesus, king of Lydia. Yet in his presentation the connection between victory and wealth differs. The chariot victory – the first Athenian one according to the family – is not itself doubted, and later Alcmaeonids continued the tradition of victories dramatically.[146] But Herodotus tells the story about Alcmaeon's undignified visit to Croesus and says in effect that it was because of this that Alcmaeon was able to win the victory on his return (VI 125.5): 'So this house became extremely wealthy, and Alcmaeon was thus able to keep a four-horse chariot and was victor at Olympia.' Isocrates' version says nothing of how the wealth was gained and implies that it was ancient, not recently acquired and certainly not from an eastern potentate. The family's emphasis on ancient and reputable wealth sets Herodotus' tale in a rather different light. In fact, the tale of the visit to Croesus may belong to a type of popular tale often invented to explain the origin of an individual's or family's wealth. It has been assumed to be the Alcmaeonid version mainly because Herodotus' whole excursus (VI 125ff.) is believed to repeat 'Alcmaeonid tradition'. This, too, is questionable (Ch. 5.5). For the time being, it is enough to stress that the family

---

[145] Wade-Gery (1958), 106f. For the late and very dubious traditions about pre-Solonian Alcmaeonids, see Wade-Gery (1958), 107f., *APF*, pp. 369f. (Paus. II 18.9, that they came from Pylos; Kastor *FGH* 250 F4 for occurrence of an Alcmaeon and a Megacles in the Athenian king-list; Suda and Hesychius for an 'Alcmaeon in the time of Theseus').

[146] Pind. *Pyth.* VII 10ff. celebrates the family victories. See Ch. 2, n. 112 for dating of Alcmaeon's. His chariot victory is also appropriate in a speech about a yoke of horses.

tradition implied ancestral wealth and omitted any mention of reliance on an eastern ruler.

Family tradition continues with proof of the family's goodwill to the demos, 'that goodwill which they had towards the people they displayed in the time of the tyranny'. There follows the family defence concerning the period of the tyranny, the claim that the family was in stasis against the tyrants which we have met in Andocides, Lysias (XXVI 22) and Antiphon (fr. 1). I quote it in full up to the restoration of democracy with the return of Alcibiades and Cleisthenes (25f.):

> For they were kinsmen (*syngeneis*) of Peisistratos and closest to him of all the citizens before he came to power, but they refused to share his tyranny and chose rather to go into exile than see the citizens being enslaved. In the forty years of civil strife, the Alcmaeonids were hated by the tyrants so much more than the other Athenians that whenever the tyrants had the upper hand, they not only destroyed their houses but even dug up their tombs. And so well were they trusted by their fellow exiles that they continued to be leaders of the people during that whole time.

This presents the fiction of the Alcmaeonid 'tyrant-haters' complete. Though kinsmen of Peisistratos and the closest to him of all the citizens before Peisistratos came to power, they could not bear to share his tyranny and so preferred exile rather than see the citizens enslaved. During forty years of stasis they were most hated by the tyrants who, whenever they had the upper hand, destroyed the Alcmaeonid houses and tombs. The Alcmaeonids continued (in exile, it is implied) to lead the demos during the whole period.

We have heard something like this before (Ch. 2.4.2), the democratic principles behind the actions and the return from exile with the demos. But as with Andocides' family tradition, some elements retain hints of a more complicated version. Despite the continuous exile asserted by the Alcmaeonids, the tyrants destroyed houses and tombs 'whenever they had the upper hand'. This at least implies something of the stasis and upheaval of the period, the different periods of Peisistratos' power, and perhaps even the fact that the Alcmaeonids were not always in disfavour.

Then there is the Alcmaeonid claim of kinship (*syngeneis*). We cannot help being reminded of the marriage alliance of Megacles and Peisistratos (Hdt. 1 61). Is this a faint memory of the alliance? If it is, it is changed almost beyond recognition. For the family asserts actual kinship, not a relationship through marriage,[147] and it is hard to believe that this has

---

[147] *Syngeneis* can also denote relations by marriage. If its use is ambiguous (as here) it would be more likely to be understood to denote kinship. There is little question of actual kinship. The occurrence of the name Hippokrates in both families is explained by

any truth. But its effect on the Alcmaeonid claim of being tyrant-haters is highly favourable and must surely explain why the family defence can remind the audience of 'kinship' with tyrants. Kinship was something one could not help, a marriage alliance was clearly deliberate. The family can thus both assert the kinship and repudiate its implications – enhancing their democratic stance. The claim of democratic sacrifice of power occurred in Andocides' tradition and similarly for the period of the oligarchy.[148] Its recurrence should warn us against trusting either its factual content or the political interpretation of the rejection. The Alcmaeonid tradition has converted a difficult and disreputable alliance into a simple matter of repudiated kinship. If these elements do represent memories of the original factions, they are interwoven into family tradition in such a way as to neutralize their implications and present a seamless democratic picture.

We are given to understand that when the Alcmaeonids repudiated their 'kinship', they retired into exile for forty years and remained there until they returned in the final glorious overthrow of the tyranny. This is implied by the sequence of Isocrates' account, the mention of 'fellow exiles' and their 'continual leadership of the demos' in this period.

This useful tradition of Alcmaeonid exile throughout the tyranny suffered a fatal blow from the new evidence of the inscribed archon list. This showed clearly that the Alcmaeonid Cleisthenes was archon in Athens in 525/4, a year after the tyrant Hippias himself. Were there, then, different periods of exile during the tyranny? For instance, Meritt suggested an expulsion of the family by Peisistratos and their return and reconciliation with Hippias, then another expulsion after the murder of Hipparchus in time for them to return for the fortification of Leipsydrion.[149] (This, in fact, ignores two more attested exiles connected with the curse.) But if the continuous exile was a crucial element of the Alcmaeonid anti-tyrant stance, how carefully need we preserve the remaining fragments of the long exile? Why should we still accept its 'forty-year' length and suggest small sections of exile on either side of Cleisthenes' archonship in order to preserve the implied chronological span?

Here, it is useful to balance family tradition against all the external evidence. If we re-examine all the possible Alcmaeonid exiles, their rough dating and circumstances, a very different picture emerges – with interesting implications. The family tradition, then, of forty years of exile

---

Raubitschek ((1949), 339) who suggests that Hippokrates, son of Megacles (II) (and father the Megacles (IV) of Hdt. VI 131.2), was named after Peisistratos' father.

[148] Lys. XVIII 5, the father preferred to die for the safety of the demos, though he could have become one of the Thirty; similarly of Nikeratos, §6.

[149] Meritt (1939), 59–65 on archon list; Eliot and McGregor (1960); Andrewes (1982), 406.

must itself refer to the years of continuous tyranny from Peisistratos' third return, which Herodotus gives as thirty-six years (v 65.3).[150]

Herodotus repeats a tradition that the family went into exile after the battle of Pallene, that is, at the start of Peisistratos' third period of power (I 64.3, some Athenians fell in battle, 'some of them fled the country with the Alcmaeonids'). They are still in exile during the harsher period of Hippias' rule (from 528/7) and the fortification of Leipsydrion. Indeed, the Alcmaeonids are introduced as 'the family in exile': 'The Alcmaeonids, an Athenian family driven into exile by the Peisistratids (γένος ἐόντες Ἀθηναῖοι καὶ φεύγοντες Πεισιστρατίδας), tried with the help of the other Athenian exiles . . . to liberate Athens' (v 62.2) (and cf. VI 123.1 on the Alcmaeonids, 'who were in exile throughout the period of the tyranny'. This is akin to the family's tradition. Similarly in Thucydides, Hippias' rule is said to have been ended by the Spartans and 'the Alcmaeonids in exile' (VI 59.4). So Herodotus, at least, believed that they were exiled throughout the tyranny. This, we know, is untrue. There may even be signs of immediate conciliation by Peisistratos after Pallene.[151] Since Herodotus produces the claim as a sign that the family were 'tyrant-haters', clearly it could have been a defence useful to the family in the fifth century as well as the fourth. Its crucial importance in the family defence should throw doubt on its historical truth.[152]

There may have been a period of exile in the harsher years of Hippias' rule, as Meritt suggested[153] (though I do not see that actual exile was necessary for the Alcmaeonids to secure their influence at Delphi). There may have been some 'return from exile' at the time of the expulsion of the tyrants by Sparta, as our sources insist. But there was also another clearly attested exile and 'return' later: the Spartan king Cleomenes and Isagoras forced the Alcmaeonids to go into exile *after* the tyrants had been expelled. That exile was enforced because of the curse, which meant the family was polluted and could be expelled from the city. As Thucydides said (I 126.12), the family was driven from Athens at the time of the original atrocity (see Ch. 5.5) and again by

---

[150] Now mostly accepted in a notoriously tricky area of chronology: Rhodes (1976), supporting Herodotus' calculation; Andrewes (1982), 399.

[151] Hdt. I 63.2, Andrewes (1982), 406; also Arist. *Ath.Pol.* 16 on the whole reign, esp. 16.9, ταῖς ὁμιλίαις ('friendly dealings').

[152] Cf. *APF*, p. 372, rightly sceptical about the importance of the Herodotean evidence, 'possibly another [period of exile] between Pallene and 525/4 if Herodotus' credit is to be saved at all'. Hdt. VI 121ff. is discussed further in Chs. 5.1 and 5.5.

[153] (1939), 59ff., and Gomme, *HCT* on I 126.12. The offerings at the Ptoion often seen as a sign of exile need be nothing of the sort, as Bicknell points out (1970), additional note – for there is also a dedication there by the tyrant's brother Hipparchus! He shows refreshing scepticism about the Alcmaeonid exile, pointing out its importance as propaganda, but he still does not go far enough.

Cleomenes:[154] 'Cleomenes, the Spartan, and the Athenians in faction also drove them out later; they drove out the living and took up the bones of the dead, and thus cast them out.' Herodotus narrates in more detail how Isagoras persuaded Cleomenes to expel the accursed Alcmaeonids, which involved seven hundred families, then how they were brought back by the Athenians (v 70–3). They were expelled *after* the tyranny had been ended with Spartan help. So there was another Alcmaeonid exile in the late sixth century which was not referred to by the family's tradition of exile, and it was explicitly connected with the family curse.

It is particularly interesting, however, that the family version retains the results of the curse but not its causes. The speaker stresses that whenever the tyrants had the upper hand they razed Alcmaeonid houses and even dug up their tombs (§26). Such extreme action could only be connected with some feeling of religious pollution. It is very close to Thucydides' statement (I 126.12, see above) that the bones are cast out at the time of the family's expulsion by Cleomenes. Surely the family is referring to this.[155] But like the 'anomalous' memories we saw in other traditions, the family retains a genuine memory of the destruction of tombs, but it has changed its timing and significance. The exile enforced by Cleomenes because of the curse is omitted, but lengthy exile of political and not religious significance is asserted for the whole period of tyranny. The destruction of the tombs is also transferred back to the 'exile during the tyranny', so that it can be presented neatly as a sign of the intense hatred of the Peisistratids for the family.[156] The transposition was clearly very useful for the family.

What, then, of the great Alcmaeonid exile which all the sources record? Surely that great exile did not actually happen, but the germ of the tradition was the huge exile of seven hundred families enforced because of the curse and attested by Herodotus. For that exile is the most dramatic and best attested exile of that confused period. Surely that was the great exile that heralded the 'return of the democracy' in the traditions. It also involved a large enough number of families to have provided the germ of the later popular traditions of the 'exile of the demos' under the tyrants: and those traditions were then elaborated on analogy with the overthrow of the Thirty (see Ch. 5.2). (Reading these simple versions, we may well forget how complex the events surrounding

---

154 The role of the curse in Alcmaeonid exile is missed even by Bicknell (see my preceding note).

155 As Raubitschek (1955), 260. But he uses Isocrates to support his theory that Andocides' ancestors were involved in the casting out of Isagoras. On the expulsion of bones, see Williams (1951), n. 35 (who, however, misses the wider significance of this transposition) and Gomme, *HCT* on I 126.12.

156 For a fourth-century audience, the destruction of tombs might fit aptly with the later conventional views of typical tyrannical acts of hubris.

the end of tyranny had been.) This enabled the Alcmaeonids to claim later that they were 'in exile with the demos' (Isoc. XVI) just as Andocides' ancestors were, and so they could present a picture of far more united opposition to the tyrants then there had in fact been. Moreover, the curse which separated the family from the rest of the Athenians[157] is thus removed from the family tradition. Its effects, the destruction of the tombs and the exile, are transposed to the period of the tyranny itself. The exile becomes a lengthy and entirely 'ideological' one sustained with the demos for democratic reasons.[158] Similarly the family tradition had managed to eclipse Megacles' marriage alliance (which failed because of the curse) and enhance their democratic stature. The curse and its consequences are steadfastly avoided.

Finally, the family tradition continues with the return from exile itself (Isoc. XVI 26): 'At last, Alcibiades and Cleisthenes, the former my great-grandfather on my father's side, the latter my father's maternal great-grandfather, as generals of the exiles led back the demos and expelled the tyrants, and set up the democracy . . . ' This is the tale of 'the expulsion of the tyrants', by now familiar. Since I discussed the theme in relation to both Andocides' and Aristocrates' family traditions, I need only stress the presence of all the conventional elements: the return of the demos, leadership by the family ancestors, the expulsion of the tyrants. It is perhaps unnecessary to emphasize that the sequence envisaged is one in which the family returns and immediately expels the tyrants – with the demos, but without the Spartans who are not mentioned (see further Ch. 5). And, of course, in this simple version there is no question of the additional later exile prompted by the curse.

The younger Alcibiades was careful to claim the participation of members of both sides of the older Alcibiades' family. Alcibiades (I) is attested in a dedication at Delphi (see n. 143, above), but this passage in Isocrates is our only evidence that he took part in the establishment of the Cleisthenic democracy.[159] The genealogical relationship itself is doubtful. Isocrates says that this Alcibiades was great-grandfather of Alcibiades III (the famous Alcibiades). Vanderpool's study of the genealogy in the light of the new evidence of ostraka[160] suggests that Alcibiades (I) should, in fact, be one generation further away, the

---

157 And with which Athenians seem to have concurred: Thuc. I 126.12 says 'they' dug up the bones, which could denote either the Athenians or Cleomenes' Athenian supporters.

158 Exile *with* other Athenians in Hdt. I 64.3 (after Pallene), V 62.2 (before Leipsydrion) and Thuc. I 126.12 (driven out with other Athenians because of the curse); discussed above, p. 149.

159 Not the Alcibiades who was ostracized in the early fifth century, omitted by the family tradition but stressed by opponents, Lys. XIV 39, [And.] IV 34.

160 Vanderpool (1952), 1–8 and n. 9 on Isoc. XVI 26.

great-great-grandfather of the famous Alcibiades. So once again we find
that family tradition has remembered the family genealogy wrongly – just
as Andocides was probably unsure of the precise relationship he bore to
Leogoras. Is this the point at which genealogical accuracy as well as other
family tradition begins to fail? (I return to the question of Greek
genealogies in Ch. 3.)

More serious is the assertion that Cleisthenes was also a grandfather of
the famous Alcibiades on his mother's side. This is simply not true. The
great Alcibiades' mother was Deinomache, an Alcmaeonid certainly,
daughter of Megacles IV. But the great-grandfather on the female side
was Hippokrates (I), son of the Megacles (II), who allied with Peisistratos for a short time.[161] The statement Isocrates makes is either a piece of
wishful thinking or a deliberate lie based on real Alcmaeonid descent in
the female line. Yet this is the only family tradition recounting participation of the expulsion which actually mentions Cleisthenes at all. So much
for the precise claims of direct ancestors' participation.

What were the processes behind this transformation? The similarities
of the tradition in Isocrates with other family traditions of the time help
reinforce our suspicions. Here, too, we find traces of genuine memories
which record something of the original events. At the same time such
transformation has taken place that those memories become almost
unrecognizable. Other features are clearly much influenced by the
prevailing polis traditions which help impose a further stereotyped
picture on the fading memories. The Alcmaeonid tradition, however, is
considerably more complex than the others and certainly involves more
conscious manipulation. Their tradition, like the others, dealt with
awkward parts of their history by omitting them or transferring them to
other periods where democratic implications could be stressed. But the
family had more of such awkward aspects to conceal – not least the curse
itself – and its importance in Athenian history means that its tradition
was inextricably bound up with the general history of Athens.

The Alcmaeonid curse was by no means forgotten in the fifth century
by family or polis, and it is also hard to believe it was forgotten by the
family in the early fourth century. So, when we find that the restructuring
of the family tradition involved the eclipse of all parts of the family
history related to the curse, this is surely deliberate manipulation. The
process may have been a long one, but the steady development of the
myth of the Alcmaeonid tyrant-haters (*misotyrannoi*) and their continuous exile throughout the tyranny will have helped gradually to eclipse
the elements of their history which involved the curse.

---

[161] *APF* 600 I, 9688 x: we cannot automatically take Isocrates seriously for the genealogy
(as does W. E. Thompson (1970)).

By the processes of transposition and telescoping with which we are by now familiar, Alcmaeonid family tradition developed their 'continuous exile' throughout the tyranny, apparently telescoping together the exiles in the later stages of the tyranny and that prompted by Cleomenes. All our sources are proved wrong about the long exile by the archon list, and they are clearly prey to the family myth of continuous exile throughout the tyranny. But the long exile has obscured more than an archonship. The final result that we see in the tradition repeated by Isocrates has a neat and compact quality which obviously made it easy to propagate in Athens.

The tradition of continuous exile during the tyranny was particularly useful for the family. But the germ of this tradition seems in fact to be the exile imposed because of the curse after the expulsion of the tyrants. It may also have helped to crystallize the tradition of 'the exile of the demos' and so provide the family with a full democratic exile in company with the demos. Some of the transposition and telescoping may have been the result of memory and oral transmission, but not all. Elements which do not conform to the democratic leanings asserted are either simply omitted or transposed in a process of 'telescoping' so that they form part of a neat and continuous democratic narrative. We are not presented with a cunning detailed 'reinterpretation' of the offending elements. In later tradition they are disposed of more simply, and the process of forgetting eventually does the rest. Here both the family tradition and the polis traditions were also influenced by the recent events of the late fifth century, which had included an 'exile of the demos', too. The supposed parallel seems to have been responsible for the further crystallization of the exile and return. In fact, the Alcmaeonids had very much more to hide. Both they and the polis traditions succeeded in producing a seamless and simplistic version of the end of the tyranny which bore little relation to the complex narrative of Herodotus (Ch. 5). There is a combination of original memories and 'events', astute manipulation by the family, and the subtle influence of the prevailing democratic polis traditions on individual family memories. As with Andocides' family memories, the Alcmaeonid family tradition gradually becomes worn down into stereotyped and irreproachable democratic action against the tyrants.

*

These Athenian family traditions have introduced certain crucial features of oral tradition in general and methods of approaching it. In the comparatively simple sphere of family tradition, we have seen how the manner and opportunity for transmission are essential. They are very closely related to the detail and calibre of the traditions, and when trying to assess the accuracy of any tradition, one must first determine the type of transmission. The fluidity of family transmission in Athens partly explains the short life span and dramatic changes of its family traditions. This is a foretaste of the wider oral traditions of Athens and probably the rest of Greece. We need also to consider the motives and ideals which encouraged, selected and eventually transformed memories. For instance, the Athenian democracy encouraged family tradition from the recent past and stressed certain elements of that. At the same time, the traditions alert us to contemporary ideals: these traditions suggest some surprising beliefs about what was admirable even in the democracy.

As contemporary interests select and alter tradition, so we find layers of memories or traditions. Traditions may retain some genuine memory of an original event, but as we see clearly in the lengthier family traditions, they can be transformed beyond recognition. One way of determining the layers is to look for 'anomalous' elements which do not fit either what is claimed of them or other external evidence. Or else a comparison with other oral traditions may bring to light similarities which spring from the needs of family tradition or the processes of memory rather than identical past history. The unconscious processes of memory themselves are essential in understanding how such transformations take place. This is not to overlook deliberate distortion. But it is important to stress first that such distortion will itself affect the oral traditions and eventually become indistinguishable from them; secondly, that many of the distortions envisaged by modern scholars are more sophisticated than they need be, for a family could deal with the awkward elements of its past by merely omitting and forgetting them. Much of the resulting telescoping and transforming can be explained by the processes of remembering and forgetting in the incredibly unstable and shifting world of oral tradition. The general polis traditions – to which I return later – exert particular pressure on individual memories which they attract and distort. They help produce the stereotyped family traditions of anti-tyrannical achievement of the early fourth century.

Yet what we have seen of oral tradition so far does suggest that family tradition had a crucial role in remembering individuals, incidents and details which were forgotten or elided by the polis. It was especially valuable in Athens where certain democratic ideals tended to play down individuals and individual achievements altogether.

3

GENEALOGY AND FAMILY TRADITION: THE INTRUSION OF WRITING

Greek genealogy is an area where both oral tradition and writing are involved. It is not pure oral tradition untouched by writing but the product both of written coordination and oral tradition. Genealogy and the part of family tradition that recorded legendary and heroic ancestors raise questions rather different from the oral traditions of family history of the last chapter. As shall be argued, it attracted a certain amount of written or literate study. It therefore introduces crucial and particularly interesting problems concerning the influence of writing and written study on oral tradition. More specifically, it bears also on the formation of a written 'history' and chronology for early Greece.

With genealogy we are largely shifting our attention back to a more archaic period and set of interests than those dealt with so far and to the very beginnings of written study of the past. Up till now we have been concerned mainly with the late fifth and fourth centuries, the high classical period of Athens and its full radical democracy. But genealogies and their study are redolent of an earlier Greece, that of Pindar, Herodotus and indeed of the earliest prose writers of Greece, the writers of *Genealogies* (the first, Hecataeus, flourished *c.* 500 B.C.). This genre of writing appears first in the very late sixth century and was still practised in the late fifth century. The genealogists' writings seem to belong to a world of predominantly aristocratic values, of legendary heroes and Homeric ancestors. They take us back to the very dawn of historiography.

Genealogy, therefore, introduces some fascinating questions about oral tradition, writing and the interaction between the two. First, what was the character of the oral traditions that concerned genealogy? Then, what is the effect, if any, of writing on oral tradition? Does the writing down of oral tradition affect its content or its general nature? What is the possible effect of early written scholarship? More specifically, what were the roles of the early genealogists in coordinating and to some extent creating a 'history' (mostly legendary) and indeed the very chronological framework for early Greece? We can now consider this kind of family tradition against the background of oral transmission we have been discussing (Ch. 2), the surprising omissions in family traditions, and its short memory for ancestors and genealogical relationships. In many societies genealogy is notorious for being one of the most complex kinds of oral tradition: genealogy above all reflects a family's image of its own past and provides prestige and status. We will begin to see what kind of problems oral transmission produces for any reconstruction of chronology. The background of oral transmission also sets in perspective the few examples of full genealogies that go back to a hero in a continuous line. Here it is possible to discern the influence of writing and literate study on the oral traditions. The same factors probably apply to other lists that were written early. In the methods of the genealogists we can see the application of writing and written methods of organizing information to fluid and changeable oral tradition. This may give us some insight into other areas where the use of the written word or written record was being extended.

Here we return to writing from a rather different angle. In Chapter 1 it was argued that writing and the 'effects' of writing must vary greatly with the society using it and that we should turn our attention away from 'literacy' to the uses made of writing. Writing obviously does have certain advantages over and differences from oral communication (for example, it may preserve information more easily and accurately than memory). But whether these differences are made use of still depends on who is using the writing – its potentials may not necessarily be seen at all. In this chapter I shall be looking at areas where writing may organize and preserve information in a manner very different from oral communication. In the sphere of genealogies the very use of writing by early Greek prose writers may have had far-reaching effects on the oral traditions they were dealing with. The precise way writing was adapted was not predictable, but once used it could have startling effects. The ways writing may affect or even change certain elements of oral tradition are fundamental to our understanding of historiography based on oral tradition. The early Greek genealogists lie at the very beginning of this development when the Greek past was still preserved – if at all – only in poetry, legends and oral tradition.

It is often loosely assumed that Greek aristocratic families had long genealogies that reached back to a suitable heroic ancestor. The writer Hecataeus (*c.* 500 B.C.) is often quoted: he told the Egyptian priests that his family tree reached back to a god in the sixteenth generation (Hdt. II 143). The famous tombstone of Heropythos of Chios, probably from the mid-fifth century, simply lists his ancestors through fourteen generations.[1] These examples seem to indicate long, impressive family traditions recording family pedigrees.

---

[1] *SGDI* 5656, but see Wade-Gery (1952), fig. 8 (p. 8) for photograph and correct text with a further generation missed out of *SGDI*.

But from the start this inference confuses two aspects of family tradition that should remain separate: legendary ancestry and full genealogy. (By 'full genealogy' I mean a continuous series of names from the original ancestor to the historical period, apparently complete.)[2] Put simply, does a Greek aristocrat know the names of the intervening ancestors down to his own day when he cites his heroic ancestry? Not necessarily. Anthropological studies have provided impressive examples of lengthy genealogies remembered in oral societies (see below, p. 187). They show that such memory is possible without writing (though further study may show that writing has, in fact, played a part in the elaboration of some of them – see Ch. 3.2). The Greek evidence, however, must be examined on its own terms. What we have already seen of family tradition in Greece indicates a concentration upon the heroic and legendary period, that, in the circumstances of oral transmission within the Greek family, would usually have led to considerable telescoping of the period between the heroic age and the very recent past. Full genealogies were probably very rare.

Greek aristocrats seem to have been far prouder of their legendary, and especially Homeric, ancestors than their more recent historical ones.[3] Indeed, the legendary period was often used for argument and proof for present-day claims. This will have produced a corresponding imbalance in family traditions. Legendary ancestries were remembered because they were ancient and crucial to the prestige and position of a family. The recent past was remembered simply because it was recent. It was only under the Athenian democracy that this emphasis was reversed. Under such conditions a man had to prove his democratic antecedents and thus remember the achievements of his recent ancestors – though even under the democracy legendary ancestries were still remembered (Ch. 2.1, p. 108).

So we often find that there is apparently a sharp jump in a tradition from the very recent members of the family to the heroic ancestors. An excellent example occurs in Isocrates' eulogy of Evagoras (*Evag.* 12ff.) where Isocrates moves from the excellence of Evagoras and his father straight to Teucer, their Homeric ancestor. In this and other cases, should one suppose that there was any family tradition about the intervening period? In most cases there was not. For in most of these

---

[2] The terms 'pedigree' and 'genealogy' are often used by modern scholars to mean the full records of ancestors available to modern aristocrats (see Ch. 3, n. 87 for useful distinction). This imports modern expectations which may partly be encouraged by literate methods of recording family tradition (e.g. Jacoby, commentary on *FGH* 323a F24, the 'pedigree' of the Kerykes). So the presence of an heroic ancestor is thought to imply knowledge of the whole line. For the crucial difference between memory for individual ancestors and of ancestors in an amorphous group see Ch. 2.1, p. 100.

[3] Ch. 2.1 and Bethe (1935).

citations of heroic ancestry the crucial point is that the family's prestige rests upon the heroic ancestry itself, not on the linking generations in between. At the other end of the spectrum, we have already seen how family memory fades very rapidly after the third or fourth generation back. Even within that short time span, the precise relationships of family members become falsified (Ch. 2.3).

The general implications are clear. We are seeing here the well-documented phenomenon of 'telescoping' which is so frequent in oral societies. This phenomenon occurs when a group remembers only the recent past and the 'time of origins'. The intermediate period after 'the origins' is barely remembered at all. This dramatic scarcity of information for a period which anthropologists often most want to understand has been described vividly as 'the hour-glass effect' (expressing the great increase of traditions at either end). The result is that periods drop out of the traditions completely and the remaining periods (very remote and recent) draw closer together. Hence the term 'telescoping'. One should thus expect to find telescoping in Greek family tradition, as indeed we have already in non-genealogical instances.

But there is a further element in the phenomenon of 'telescoping' hinted at in some criticisms of the term. It has been pointed out that the description of the phenomenon as 'telescoping' is misleading as it implies a fixed chronological model or time-scale to be telescoped. One can only speak of telescoping as the impression received by an outsider who has a fixed chronological time-scale. Most oral societies where this appears to happen would not, of course, perceive the phenomenon thus.[4] In fact, it seems a useful and graphic description of what is, in effect, happening to past history, past periods and events, as large areas of the past 'drop out' of peoples' memories – and I shall continue to use it. If the people concerned could perceive the phenomenon, after all, it would not occur. But one can go further and emphasize what may be implicit in this criticism. For we perceive the process as telescoping because we do have a fixed idea of a chronological time-scale and we are able to bring all the disparate material together to compare it in a way that would be hard for a totally oral society. Both are made possible or made easier by the use of writing. The telescoping of a king-list or a genealogy becomes clear when it is written down and compared with other evidence.

Does this idea of the significance of writing help our examination of Greek genealogy? I think it does, for study of the full genealogies we have and of the activity of the genealogists themselves suggest that full genealogies are very rare and that when they occur they have been

---

[4] J. C. Miller, *APS* 17; Vansina, *OTH* 168f. on the 'floating gap' and 176ff. on the way memory organizes sequences. See further Ch. 3.2.

elaborated with the help of the literary genealogists – that is, with the use of writing. (It should be stressed at this point that the so-called 'genealogists' were not full-time or professional genealogists who, as nowadays, spent their time tracing genealogies; but they were writers or proto-historians who wrote works, among others, called 'Genealogies'.)

We have much evidence, then, for descent from some heroic ancestor but almost none for full genealogy. Most aristocratic traditions probably knew only of the recent generations of the family and the distant legendary generations. For instance, we are told that Hellanicus said Andocides was descended from Odysseus and Telemachus and therefore from Hermes (Hell. *FGH* 323a, F24), but it is improbable that Hellanicus gave a full genealogy from Telemachus down to Andocides.[5] We have full genealogies only for the Philaid family (Pherecydes *FGH* 3 F2), for Heropythos of Chios, and for Hippokrates, the famous physician (Pherecydes *FGH* 3 F59).[6] This is a tiny number considering how often we know of a legendary ancestor claimed by a family.[7] But this very paucity of full genealogies may be significant. They alone contradict the otherwise overwhelming impression that Greek family traditions normally knew little between the legendary and recent past – hence their importance, though the evidence is so sparse.[8]

But there is a further point here. Of these full genealogies, only the genealogy of Heropythos does not go back to a legendary or heroic ancestor.[9] Nor is it connected with any of the genealogists. But the full genealogies of the Philaids and of Hippokrates (traced back to Askle-

---

[5] Jacoby, commentary on Hell. *FGH* 323a F24.

[6] Jacoby, commentary on Pher. *FGH* 3 F59, insists Pherecydes could not have taken the genealogy down as far as Hippokrates, but surely Hippokrates himself was the reason for the genealogy in the first place, and dating should proceed from there.

[7] Alcibiades was descended from Eurysakes and therefore from Zeus, as he says, Plato, *Alcib.* I 121a: the descent from Eurysakes may show that his family were Salaminioi (Davies, *APF* pp. 12f.). Plato was descended from Solon and Codrus (Diogenes Laertius III 1, Plut. *Sol.* I 2); for Kerykes' legendary ancestors, see Androtion *FGH* 324 F1 – with commentary for the several variants; Bethe (1935), 54ff. gives non-Athenian examples. For Homeridae, see Wade-Gery (1952).

[8] Sparse, yet still extensively used for modern chronological theories (Ch. 3.2 below).

[9] Kyprios is the first ancestor (probably not an adjective, as Wade-Gery points out), Eldios the next. So far as we know, neither are legendary or divine, but nor can Kyprios simply be an ordinary person (as Masson (1964)), for he is their original ancestor.

The interesting, long genealogy of Klearchos from Cyrene, going back eight generations to a Battos (*SGDI* 4859) is much later (first or second century A.D.) than those here, though some of my points may still apply: the first ancestor, a Battos, must in Cyrene surely imply one of the kings, especially when the line carefully leads back to him. Nor can the chronology be calculated literally (as does Masson (1974)). Note also the list's arrangement on the stone with each patronymic (in the genitive) on a different line, surely to give the impression of a longer stemma. In a second-century B.C. epigram at Dodona, Agathon of Zakynthos boasts of his descent from Cassandra, adding that his family had been proxenoi for 30 generations since the Trojan War (Robert, *REG* 73 (1960), 184 and Davreux (1942), 85–7).

pios, as befitted a doctor) occur in the genealogists Pherecydes and Hellanicus. Andocides' descent from Odysseus was mentioned by Hellanicus. As for Hecataeus' famous descent from a god in the sixteenth generation – Hecataeus is himself a genealogist. It seems hardly a coincidence that most of these lines of descent which give the impression of accurate knowledge (i.e. either specify all the names or the number of generations) actually occur in the work of the prose genealogists. It is difficult to evade the conclusion that these impressively long genealogies are in part the work of the genealogists themselves: thus of written analysis and codification of legend and of chronological calculations made possible by written methods. Wade-Gery has presented a table of the known, full genealogies set out in tabular form by generation.[10] Unintentionally this arrangement helps emphasize the concentration of this material in the genealogists' work and stresses that it requires written coordination and methods.

Our evidence for both ancient genealogy and the genealogists is fragmentary and inconclusive. Many interesting questions one can only attempt to answer generally against the background of oral family tradition. We saw in Chapter 2 some examples where genealogical information was only remembered with gross inaccuracies. We have seen the rarity of full genealogy in Greek family traditions and its possible connection with the genealogists' activity. It is now time to look in detail at the one example of a full genealogy which is counterbalanced by much external evidence, that of the Philaids (Ch. 3.1, below). This illustrates more precisely the functions of legendary genealogy and the historical limitations of a genealogy; and it suggests some of the reasons for the extraordinary distortions we find in the recent historical generations. These include both the need to glorify the family through the genealogy and the very formation of a written genealogy from oral tradition. It is to be stressed that since this is the only example where we do have a chance to check the information in the genealogy, we must take all the more seriously any conclusions we can draw from it.

Chapter 3.2 is then devoted to a more general discussion of genealogy and the work of the genealogists. This partly builds on the detailed discussion of the Philaid tradition and the two sections should complement and confirm each other. The non-historical significance of genealogy (especially legendary genealogy) is discussed, the way it provided proof or explanation for the present. Despite interesting work

---

[10] He takes the genealogies to be correct enough to count the generations and date the Dark Age Ionian migration (assumed to have occurred at the very beginning of Heropythos' genealogy); followed by M. Miller (1970), 153f. and 210ff., and Snodgrass (1971). The following discussion will make it clear why I do not think they can provide accurate records either of names or of chronology.

on some aspects of genealogy,[11] the general and most important points about Greek genealogy have not been gathered together, so far as I know, and therefore their wider significance has been neglected. We may then return to the effect of oral transmission on genealogical memory and thence to the part that genealogists and written methods may have played in the organization and crystallization of full genealogies.

3.1 The Philaid genealogy

The Philaid clan was a famous and distinguished one in Athens. In the fifth century it produced Miltiades, the great general of the Persian Wars, and Cimon, equally prominent in the next generation and the early years of the Athenian empire. During the Peisistratid tyranny in the sixth century, eminent Philaids founded, and then ruled, the important Athenian colony in the Chersonese.

The genealogy given for the Philaid line[12] (Marc. *Vit. Thuc.* 3) is a rare – in fact unique – example for us of a full genealogy that extends from a legendary ancestor down into the historical period. Moreover, we do have external evidence in Herodotus against which to judge the genealogy itself. Quoted by Marcellinus for Thucydides' ancestry, the genealogy derives from the fifth-century genealogist Pherecydes (and Hellanicus), through Marcellinus' source Didymus (Pher. *FGH* 3 F2). So it is possible to compare Herodotus' account of the family with Pherecydes' genealogy. Where they overlap, there are gross discrepancies – in fact the differences are extraordinary. It is probably impossible to be certain about some of the relationships in the family tree. But without dwelling at inordinate length on problems that are insoluble, I shall examine the genealogy as a specific illustration of a genealogy's character, the functions it may fulfil, the 'distortions' in content and chronology that it may represent, and thus some of the peculiarities of genealogy that make it historically the least trustworthy part of family tradition. We may go further and see it also as the written construction of a genealogist from the oral family traditions.[13]

---

[11] Nilsson (1951), esp. 65ff., has interesting remarks on the importance of legendary ancestors and eponyms; van Groningen (1953), ch. 5 on genealogy and its aetiological function; Bethe (1935) similarly; Fränkel (1975), 96ff. discusses genealogy as a way of organizing information.

[12] Wade-Gery (1951) suggested the use of 'Cimonid' for the side branch prominent after Miltiades, the oikist. The name 'Philaid' is apparently unattested in ancient literature. However, it was a Cleisthenic deme name: Plato, *Hipp.* 228b, saying Peisistratos' family was 'of the Philaidai', is usually taken to denote the deme (i.e. Brauron), Whitehead (1986), 11 and 24.

[13] Main works, all concerned with the *actual* family tree of Miltiades rather than the character of the genealogy and family tradition: Berve (1937), 1–6; Wade-Gery (1952),

First a little about Pherecydes and the context of the genealogy. Since Pherecydes and the other fifth-century genealogists concentrate overwhelmingly upon the legendary period, the genealogy probably came in a legendary context (see Ch. 3.2). There is little reason to assume that it went further down than Miltiades III, the founder of the colony in the Chersonese, with whom Marcellinus' text stops, since Didymus, who quoted it, evidently thought that this Miltiades was a direct ancestor of the fifth-century Cimon and therefore of Thucydides, the historian.[14] Nor can we date it with much exactitude. Pherecydes can only be placed in the first half of the fifth century. Despite Jacoby's more precise dating, we can merely say that Pherecydes was a generation before Herodotus, if that.[15]

The emended genealogy runs as follows:

> Philaios, son of Ajax, lived in Athens. Philaios begat Daiklos, and he begat Epilykos, and he begat Akestor, and he begat Agenor, and he begat Oulios, and he begat Polykles, and he begat Autophon, and he begat Philaios, and he begat Agamestor, and he begat Teisander, and he begat Miltiades, and he begat Hippokleides who was archon when the Panathenaic festival was established, and he begat Miltiades who founded the colony of the Chersonese.[16]

The genealogy as Pherecydes gives it starts with Philaios, son of the hero Ajax. It runs for thirteen more generations of successive fathers and sons. The last generation he mentions is that of Miltiades (III) who founded the colony in the Chersonese. Added to the bare bones are three comments about Philaios, Hippokleides and Militiades, the oikist or colonizer. The text is very corrupt and I have included some emendations above (with n. 16). But one must specify *how* corrupt. Some of the

esp. 88–94; Bradeen (1963), 193 and 206f.; Davies, *APF* 8429; Schachermayr (1938), 2113f.; Toepffer (1889), 269ff.

[14] Didymus quoted it to show how Thucydides was descended from Philaios. But he makes the same mistake elsewhere, and this is only problematic if one believes Didymus must have been right: D. M. Lewis (1963), n. 39, Davies, *APF*, p. 294. One may suspect that the 'Cimonids', too, liked to think they were descended directly from Philaios.

[15] Jacoby ((1947), 13ff.) puts the date of the genealogy before 476/5 because the line would have extended to Cimon if it could (i.e. if Cimon were alive) – clearly an unsound argument. Wade-Gery (1952, 94) thinks Pherecydes was contemporary with Cimon.

[16] Φιλαῖος (Steph. Φιλαίας codd.) δὲ ὁ Αἴαντος οἰκεῖ ἐν Ἀθήναις. ἐκ τούτου δὲ γίγνεται Δάικλος, τοῦ δὲ Ἐπίλυκος (Göller: Ἐπίδυκος codd.), τοῦ δὲ Ἀκέστωρ, τοῦ δὲ Ἀγήνωρ, τοῦ δὲ Οὔλιος (Köhler: Ὄλιος codd.), τοῦ δὲ Πολυκλῆς (Wade-Gery: Λύκης codd.), τοῦ δὲ Αὐτοφῶν (Wade-Gery: Ἰοφῶν Gervinus: Τόφων codd.), τοῦ δὲ Φιλαῖος (Wade-Gery: Λάιος codd.), τοῦ δὲ Ἀγαμήστωρ, τοῦ δὲ Τίσανδρος [ἐφ᾽ οὗ ἄρχοντος ἐν Ἀθήναις secl. Rutgers], τοῦ δὲ Μιλτιάδης, τοῦ δὲ Ἱπποκλείδης, ἐφ᾽ οὗ ἄρχοντος Παναθήναια ἐτέθη, τοῦ δὲ Μιλτιάδης, ὃς ᾤκισε Χερρόνησον.

names, particularly the unusual ones, have been corrupted during the textual transmission; they have been convincingly restored by Wade-Gery from recurring family names in later generations.[17] But how much further can the genealogy be 'emended'? We clearly cannot assume that such a genealogy – or any family tradition – must be correct and so alter it until it fits with Herodotus. One certainly cannot change the form of the genealogy and make it branch out, as Wade-Gery does. For linear genealogies by their nature tend to ignore such branching (see below, p. 191). I shall thus examine the genealogy with the emended names but without alteration of the actual structure.[18]

We may presume that the genealogy derives from the traditions of the family (I use the word 'derive' deliberately). It is inconceivable that any other group in Athens should have had the interest to remember so long a genealogy. But we cannot rule out the possibility that the genealogy in this form was not exactly as the family knew it, for our knowledge so far of Greek family tradition suggests forcefully that the professional genealogists themselves may have played some part in the elaboration of the written form. We must at least bear this possibility in mind as we look at the stemma in more detail.

In the early and legendary part of the list, most of the figures are only names to us and any legendary associations they may have had are unknown. But we know something of the significance of Philaios and Oulios.

Philaios was crucial not only as the eponymous ancestor of the genos (see n. 12), but also for Athens' claims to the island of Salamis. Solon was said to have claimed that Philaios and Eurysakes had granted Salamis to Athens and then settled in Attica (Plut. *Sol.* 10). They were non-Athenian, but the presence of the Philaids in Attica confirmed that this grant had taken place. The opening comment in Pherecydes, that Philaios lived in Athens, is thus programmatic. Herodotus has a similar story, rather expanded (vi 35) (speaking of the house of Miltiades, the oikist): 'The family . . . was by origin descended from Aeacus and Aigina, but further down the line it was Athenian, from the time of Philaios, son of Ajax, who was the first member of this house to be an Athenian citizen.' But what about Eurysakes? For Solon, Eurysakes was as responsible for the gift of Salamis as Ajax. Indeed, Pausanias (i 35.2) made Philaios the son of Eurysakes and grandson of Ajax. These

---

[17] Wade-Gery (1952), 88f.; cf. Davies *APF*, pp. 294ff.
[18] Wade-Gery changed round generations, omitted a Miltiades and introduced a double line at the end, changing the genealogy's character. Note also that the names are corrupt only in the middle part of the genealogy, well before that part for which we have overlapping external evidence. So it really only affects a few names of which we know nothing.

supposed relationships were, of course, fluid and changeable according to their context.[19] But one can point out, as Ferguson has done (1938), that Philaid glory would be enhanced if they could omit Eurysakes and say that Philaios alone granted the island to Attica.

There was more manipulation of cult and legend connected with Athens' claim to Salamis. The only Cleisthenic tribe not named after an Attic hero was named after Ajax himself (Hdt. v 66). This was probably just after the final acquisition of Salamis by arbitration.[20] Eurysakes also had a cult in Attica and it was tended by the Salaminioi. The Salaminioi seem to have been a genos (or pseudo-genos) formed quite late from an actual group of Salaminians who settled in Attica. Again their name was programmatic.[21] They were connected with certain cults which were moved over from Salamis – thus incorporating it in Attica – and their care of other Attic cults shows their immense significance to Athens.[22] Salamis was thus attached to Attica, and this link was reflected in both legend and cult.

Athens' struggle for Salamis continued through most of the sixth century at least (see n. 20). It must then have been in this period that the legends about Philaios, Salamis and Ajax were crystallized. The new significance of Philaios and the Philaids living in Attica will have prompted new elaborations or explanations to be drawn from the eponymous ancestor.[23] This familiar example thus illustrates how crucial the original ancestor was – far more important than the later ones – and how it is the relationships of the early ancestors which hold most significance, rather than the others who link the early heroes to the later generations.

The name Oulios later in the list may also have been connected to some further 'propaganda' – and propaganda, at that, which suggests that the list was being perfected in the early fifth century. This extraordinarily rare name is first attested in the early fifth century and it belongs to a son of Cimon (*APF* 8429 xiii). It may be more than a coincidence that it occurs about the time of Pherecydes' publication or just after. Moreover, it was connected – or made to connect by

---

[19] E.g. in Sophocles' *Ajax* (530ff.), Eurysakes is the only son of Ajax.

[20] If the name of one of the arbitrators, Cleomenes, is that of the Spartan king. Plut. (*Sol.* 10) puts the acquisition in Solon's time, but the name Cleomenes is revealing. The despatch of the Athenian cleruchy also occurs in the late sixth century (see Nilsson (1951), 28ff. and Ferguson (1938), 17). This may be another example where the figure of Solon exerts a magnetic attraction on extraneous events: cf. p. 280 below.

[21] Bourriot (1976), 13f.; Ferguson (1938), though he seems not to think the Salaminioi were actually from Salamis.

[22] Ferguson (1938); Nilsson (1951), 28ff.; on the Oschophoria, Jacoby, *FGH* iiib (suppl.), vol. ii, 205ff. and 295ff.

[23] The second Philaios in the genealogy, just before the sixth-century names attested elsewhere, may be relevant for this claim.

Pherecydes – with the tale of the early migration from Athens to Ionia which Pherecydes was the first to articulate. The legendary migration was a partial justification for Athens' expansion of power in the fifth century.[24]

The connections are now nebulous, of course, and we cannot know whether Cimon's son's name was a response to Pherecydes' genealogy or if the influence was the other way round. But the point remains that an obscure name which seems to have had important legendary significance occurs attached to an attested historical figure about the time of Pherecydes' genealogy. The genealogy manipulates that legendary and political significance, probably incorporating it in genealogical form. Pherecydes may have been responsible for crystallizing it in a consistent written genealogy.

So the early part of the genealogy embodies figures which were the basis of important political claims. This reminds us that certain family ancestors *became* more important (or were even invented) as political needs changed, therefore that the family genealogical tradition must itself have been changing, even in the early fifth century. Pherecydes may have been instrumental in this process, even if he was also merely voicing the contemporary claims made by the family, as he incorporated them into a coherent and consistent genealogy.

The latter part of the genealogy, from the first independently attested figure, Teisander, compounds our suspicions. Much of it overlaps with Herodotus' account of the family, but the two versions are irreconcilable. Thus we find Pherecydes' genealogy wrong, or at least disquieting, in just that part of it which approaches the better known historical period for which we have external evidence.[25] Yet if the only names for which we do have external evidence are questioned by that evidence, then presumably the whole genealogy is doubtful. Whatever the precise relation of Pherecydes' genealogy to the family tradition, the genealogy illustrates the uncertainty of family tradition over genealogical matters a few generations back, while producing a stemma enhancing the family's position. It also shows some of the ways in which written genealogy itself oversimplifies, crystallizes or elaborates oral tradition to produce a distorted and elongated stemma.

[24] See Davies, *APF* 8429 XIII (B), for more detail, including the importance of Agenor, father of Oulios, in the genealogy. Agenor is a Neleid name in late sixth-century Miletus, that is, one of the Neleid aristocracy who claimed to have come from Pylos in the early Ionian migration. On migration stories, remodelled in the sixth century, but really important and established after the beginning of the Delian League, see Nilsson (1951), 59ff. and Sakellariou (1958).

[25] The Agemestor, father of Teisander, in the genealogy has been accepted as correct for want of alternative evidence. He is also one of the life-archons according to Kastor,

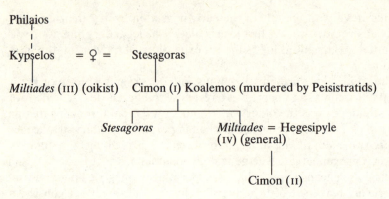

Figure 1

I shall outline the elements of disagreement between Pherecydes and Herodotus.

Pherecydes has a straight line of descent from father to son from Teisander (the first independently attested figure) to Miltiades who founded the colony, the oikist. It runs: Teisander, Miltiades, Hippokleides (in whose archonship the Panathenaia was established), Miltiades, the oikist (see stemma on p. 167).

Herodotus concentrates primarily upon the Miltiades, who colonized the Chersonese, and the later members of that family, Cimon (1), Stesagoras and Miltiades IV, the great general.[26] Thus, he is dealing with family members mostly later than those in Pherecydes' list and, since Miltiades, the oikist, died childless, with a branch of the family which was not in the direct line of descent from Teisander. Herodotus is, however, extremely careful to explain the rather complex relationships between the various rulers of the Chersonese – Miltiades, the oikist, was, as he says, the half-brother of Cimon by the same mother. Moreover, the stemma his account implies is completely consistent, though complex. One should therefore trust Herodotus against a schematized genealogy.[27]

Figure 1 is the accepted stemma from Herodotus' account (the rulers of the colony are italicized).

Thus for Herodotus, Miltiades, the oikist, was the son of Kypselos (VI 35, 38.1); and he is careful to distinguish this Miltiades from the later Miltiades, son of Cimon. This Kypselos is usually thought to be the

FGH 250 F4 no. 28 (see Jacoby, commentary to Hell. *FGH* 323a F23 with n. 72 on list of life-archons).

[26] Hdt. VI 34–41, rule of the Chersonese and eventual flight of Miltiades, the general; VI 103, repeated victories of Cimon (1) (Koalemos).

[27] Supposed inconsistency: Hammond (1956), who created three men called Miltiades, refuted by Bradeen (1963).

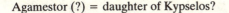

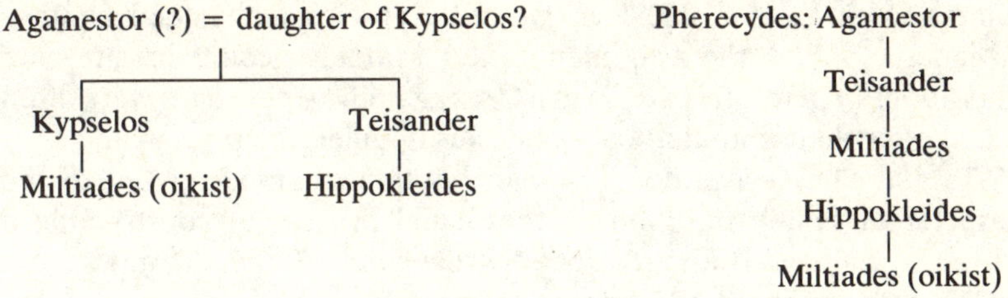

Agamestor (?) = daughter of Kypselos?

Kypselos   Teisander

Miltiades (oikist)   Hippokleides

Pherecydes: Agamestor

Teisander

Miltiades

Hippokleides

Miltiades (oikist)

Figure 2

grandson of Kypselos, the tyrant of Corinth. Herodotus also said of Hippokleides that he was favoured as suitor by Cleisthenes of Sicyon because he was 'related by descent' (τὸ ἀνέκαθεν προσήκων) to the Kypselids of Corinth (VI 128.2). The family connection seems clear.[28] Pherecydes, however, makes Miltiades (the oikist) son of Hippokleides, and he has a previous Miltiades, son of Teisander.

Herodotus also says that Hippokleides was son of Teisander (VI 128.2). Hippokleides is mostly familiar from Herodotus' tale, so redolent of archaic Greece, of the wooing of Agariste, daughter of Cleisthenes of Sicyon, in which Hippokleides 'danced away his marriage'. Pherecydes has a Hippokleides and a Teisander, but they are separated by a son called Miltiades, so that they span three generations not two (see Figure 2). Between the two versions we have three possible individuals called Miltiades: a Miltiades, son of Kypselos, a son of Hippokleides, or a son of Teisander.

We simply do not know how Kypselos and Teisander were related. It is most likely that they were brothers, both sons of the same father, Agamestor, but we cannot tell which one was older.[29] Figure 2 sets out clearly the stemma that is most probable and agrees with Herodotus (Agamestor is taken from Pherecydes, perhaps unwisely, in lieu of any other evidence) and next to it that of Pherecydes.

In graphic form it is fairly clear that what Pherecydes has done is to

[28] A suggestion of Ed. Meyer, accepted by Berve (1937), 3, Davies, *APF*, p. 295, Wade-Gery, first edition of *CAH* III, 570. This also accounts for the incorporation of the Lapith Koronos into the Philaid genealogy, through the mother of Philaios, daughter of Koronos: see Hdt. v 92 β1, and Toepffer (1889), 276f. for references. (This would confirm that Kypselos was in the main branch.)

[29] An old theory identified them (e.g. Toepffer (1889): see Davies, *APF*, pp. 295f., Bradeen (1963), 193, for arguments against this, partly because it was based on Marcellinus' text which is corrupt (though – as I shall argue – genealogical trees like this are by their nature misrepresentations); an alternative view – that *Hippokleides* and Kypselos were brothers – is more difficult chronologically and Kypselos appears on the archon list for 597/6, which would make him too young.

string out contemporary generations as successive ones, making two generations into four. He has omitted Kypselos and added another Miltiades, so that the two men called Miltiades come in alternate generations (a plausible pattern in a Greek family, where sons were often named after their grandfathers), and thus doubled the time span.

Why did Pherecydes do this? Can his treatment be related to the character of family tradition or the actual process of constructing a written genealogy? Both are probably relevant, and they illuminate the genealogists' work considerably.

One area of explanation involves chronology. Pherecydes created four generations out of two. Was this to produce a longer family tree? Perhaps he was aware that the line reached back to the son of Ajax with two few generations and so engaged in the manipulation of generations that was part of the genealogists' method (see Ch. 3.2). The duplication of the name Miltiades was perhaps to right the generations, a method used by Hellanicus.

Alternatively, there may be less sophisticated reasons. Perhaps it was assumed that the given names belonged to a father–son succession in a linear line. Hippokleides and Teisander may have been known by name and recognized as important family ancestors, but their precise relationship to the other branch forgotten. This would not be exceptional in Greek family tradition. It would be easy to assume that they all belonged to the main line in a linear sequence and to insert them in good faith. A linear genealogy encourages exactly this kind of distortion and simplification. It is a well-known mistake in king-lists and genealogies and it lengthens a line considerably, whether that is the aim or not.[30] The establishment of a *written* genealogy – which I return to in a moment – may have exacerbated or crystallized this tendency.

The genealogy also achieves the glorification of the family. This would particularly explain Hippokleides' presence. The genealogy does present the family well. Eurysakes was excluded from the earlier stages, and the three comments attached to the genealogy further the glorification. The first, about Philaios' residence in Attica, has already been discussed. The other two concern very recent family members: it was in the archonship of Hippokleides that the great Athenian festival of the Panathenaia was established, and Miltiades' colonization of the Chersonese is mentioned at the end. If Hippokleides was a figure the family was proud of, as this shows, he might have been included in the linear genealogy because the family wanted to show him off and because they assumed he must have been in the direct line. Similarly with the omission of Kypselos. Was he omitted (or simply forgotten) because his very name had obvious

---

[30] Henige (1974); cf. Miller, *APS* 18f. and below, Ch. 3.2 and n. 87.

tyrannical connections? Those connections had to be played down in the period after the end of the tyranny at Athens. Miltiades, the general, was tried on a charge of tyranny in the Chersonese, and most discussions of Herodotus' sources for the family make use of 'stories produced' at Miltiades' trial. It was probably simply too much to have an ancestor named Kypselos: he was 'forgotten' and Pherecydes crystallized the omission.[31]

Thus the genealogy does not simply enhance Philaid glory. It presents a family line that had served Athens well – in acquisition of territory for Attica, overseas colonization and civic cult. It also omits elements of the family past that could be disreputable. The tyrannical hints in the person of Kypselos were not the only ones to be smoothed over: the archonship of Miltiades under the tyrant Hippias (which the stone archon list has revealed) is also unmentioned, though that of Hippokleides can be included. This reminds us of the Alcmaeonid evasion of *their* tyrannical connections (Ch. 2.4.3 and Ch. 5). The genealogy also presents the Philaids as free from entanglement with the Peisistratids. It could be a political statement which had some weight in the first half of the fifth century.

These possibilities may be confirmed by wider considerations: first by what we know of the range of family memory, particularly for genealogical detail; secondly by consideration of the effect of a written genealogy on these family traditions.

We know that aristocratic traditions might extend a little further than the more usual three or four generations (Ch. 2.3). But those traditions recorded more than purely names. Might family tradition be better able to remember genealogy, the memory of names and relationships alone?[32] After all, the genealogies of the Philaids and of Heropythos include many unknown names which cannot all have been invented. We should take it that several names could perhaps be remembered and that names of ancestors would be reinforced by repetition later on in the family. But this supposition should be heavily qualified. It is quite possible for the names of ancestors to be known, even something of their deeds, but for their precise genealogical position to be extremely vague. Our direct evidence shows that even where there is an impressive family tradition a descendant is by no means sure of the exact relationship he bears to some of the ancestors he cites. Sometimes he is certainly wrong. In short, the traditions may record names without necessarily recording

---

[31] As Davies points out (*APF*, pp. 299f.), the Philaids were more at loggerheads with the Peisistratids from the 540s than the Alcmaeonids were. However, the Philaids, too, had things to conceal.

[32] Vansina, *OTH* 24 stresses how different the transmission of genealogies is from that of many other accounts, because they are used for the present.

their place in the family tree. We have seen how the younger Alcibiades cites his relationship to the Alcmaeonids in grossly simplified form (p. 151).[33] Andocides and Plato confused their family trees of only a few generations back.[34]

Plato's family tradition is particularly interesting, since the genealogy he gives of his ancestors reveals the same process of telescoping we have been discussing and the same process of constructing a written genealogy. For his family tradition remembered the ancestors who were contemporaries of Solon and who were mentioned in his poetry – indeed that was surely why they were remembered at all. But they seem to have been remembered in isolation, simply connected to Solon. It will be helpful to look at the tradition here.

In the *Critias* and *Timaeus* Plato constructs the genealogy of his uncle Critias' family in order to explain in some detail how the story of Atlantis was passed down through the family (*Tim.* 20d–21). But his construction crystallizes a linear succession which omits two generations that we can be pretty sure did exist. Five generations are thus compressed into three. The resulting genealogy, constructed from ill-organized family memories, has drastically telescoped the chronology. It has provoked modern confusion and controversy, but it is easily explicable in terms of oral family tradition. The remote ancestors, Dropides (II) and Critias (II), seven generations and over two hundred years from Plato, were surely remembered because of their connection with Solon. Plato's more recent family was remembered because it was recent. The two generations who lived in the latter half of the sixth and the early fifth centuries were forgotten. It was only when a precise genealogy was constructed by Plato to explain oral transmission within the family that the incomplete family memories were crystallized in a linear form that omitted the two forgotten generations. The formulation of a coherent genealogy by Plato thus fixed the telescoping process which was implied by the confused family memories. It is particularly striking that this was a genealogy meant to go back only so far as Solon (i.e. early sixth century): the double process was occurring with ancestors who were well within the so-called 'historical period'.[35]

---

[33] This may have been cynical distortion or wishful thinking. But in either case the simplification was effected.

[34] If need be, this very confusion would be enough to show that Greek aristocratic families did not keep records of their family trees as they went along.

[35] *Tim.* 20c–26c and *Crit.* esp. 108d–113b, present the Platonic myth of Atlantis (on which see R. Weil (1959) and C. Gill (1977)). The oral transmission is said to proceed from Solon to Dropides' son Critias (the 'older Critias'), then from Critias to his grandson Critias 'the younger' who tells the tale in the dialogue. Apparently describing a simple transmission over three generations to a small boy of ten, this account plays havoc with calculations of chronology. Without signs to the contrary, the obvious assumption is that the Critias of the dialogue is Critias the oligarch, and there are simply not enough

This brings us back to the establishment of a written genealogy. Surely it was this that made Hippokleides' position a problem. It cannot have been easy without more formal means to remember the genealogical relationships of ancestors no longer alive, even of direct ancestors in linear succession, and most families seem not to have done so. It is hardly surprising, then, if Hippokleides' relationship to Teisander and Miltiades was not clearly known in the early fifth century. Hippokleides was probably remembered in family tradition for his connection with the establishment of the Panathenaia, but his precise position was left vague (not even Herodotus tells us how he was connected).[36] He was known as an illustrious figure of the family, but perhaps in isolation. The genealogy brought him in, but in its assumption of a linear succession of fathers and sons it incorporated this rather misty figure in the only possible way and succeeded in producing a longer and more impressive line of descent.[37] This stabilized the supposed relationships in what was essentially an artificial construction developed from a family tradition which did not record its ancestors in that way. Chronological calculation perhaps also encouraged the ordering of the line. I see this partly as illustrating the effect of writing and written formulation upon oral traditions which were differently organized. We shall return to this in Chapter 3.2.

Finally, however, how do we account for Herodotus' information? Is he not also using family sources for what seems to be a far more reliable account?

It is widely held, certainly, that Herodotus had access to Philaid family tradition.[38] He is in fact rather better informed in some ways about

generations to reach the dramatic date of the dialogue. Extra epigraphic evidence reinforces the suspicion that two generations have dropped out. A 'Critias, son of Leaides' known from ostraka seems to provide the two missing names (Davies, *APF* 8792, pp. 322ff., and E. Vanderpool (ed.), *Hesperia*, Suppl. 8 (1949), 399 no. 12). Otherwise one must argue that the Critias of the dialogue was not the oligarch, but his grandfather, a very old man: but this is implausible (see, e.g., Rosenmeyer (1949)), and it also assumes that family tradition was correct, which is yet to be established. The family tradition thus omitted two obscure generations of the late sixth and early fifth centuries. The two earliest ancestors' connection with Solon is stressed with pride, *Tim.* 20e and *Charm.* 157e. This connection helped the family's memory of them. This pattern of memory and faulty knowledge is characteristic of oral family tradition, not of Plato's carelessness (*pace* Rosenmeyer).

[36] If we can take this as family tradition, it is interesting as a rare example recording an archonship (cf. Ch. 2.2). Perhaps this was because (i) it was an archonship not apportioned by lot and so more exclusive, and (ii) it is the establishment of the Panathenaia rather than the office alone which gives weight to the family memory.

[37] For the sake of simplicity, I have been assuming that Kypselos was the older brother, Teisander the younger, and so that Miltiades belonged to the older branch (perhaps confirmed by the Lapith ancestor, see Ch. 3, n. 28 above). If the other way round, however, the argument would still stand, for the point about incorporating Hippokleides into the main tree would then apply to Miltiades, the oikist.

[38] Primarily by Jacoby (1913).

Miltiades' family in the sixth century than about the sixth-century Alcmaeonids. However, it is enough in a discussion about genealogy to notice that Herodotus is dealing mainly with the minor 'Cimonid' branch of the family (descended from Cimon Koalemos) and with members of it who were prominent after Miltiades, the oikist – that is, a period after the end of Pherecydes' genealogy (roughly late sixth century). There would have been more information still known about these comparatively recent figures. In addition, Herodotus is not dealing just with a family, but with a dynasty – with the Cimonids as rulers of the Chersonese. The focus is largely upon the succession to that position. Miltiades, the oikist, would have been remembered, with patronymic, as founder of the colony, and as such he had a cult (Hdt. VI 38). The successors would be remembered as part of the colony's history. They were Miltiades' successors as well as related members of the same family. These are two important reasons for a higher quality of oral tradition than is common in the ordinary family, and there is no reason why Herodotus should not have derived information from the colony itself. Miltiades, son of Kypselos, would have been the focus of such traditions.[39]

The character of the Philaid genealogy is extraordinary. It departs dramatically from the actual genealogy of the family even in the very recent past. Miltiades, the oikist, was barely two generations from Pherecydes, if that, yet Miltiades' father is represented wrongly. It does suggest some interesting conclusions about genealogical family tradition and the genealogists. The genealogy given by Pherecydes apparently becomes doubtful at just the point where we begin to have external evidence about the family. One should extend one's obvious scepticism about the early, legendary part to the later part also. The legendary generations illustrate what anthropologists know already about the importance of genealogies as 'charters'; furthermore they remind us that the names in those generations were still fluid or being reformulated as late as the early fifth century. Some of the recognized genealogical methods for producing consistency in the heroic legends seem to have been used, too, for the later part of the genealogy. One can see how the genealogy has distorted and lengthened the stemma. This may be explained variously: by the poor family memory for purely genealogical information, by the desire to glorify the family wishing to include its most famous members in the genealogy, and finally by the actual process of

---

[39] Cf. also Herodotus' account of the dynasty of Cyrene from founder legend down through Battos' successors to the Persian conquest. The coherence and detail here may be related to the fact that the information was centred round a dynasty and partly transmitted through it. Compare the interesting remarks of Murray (1987) on the tendency of royal traditions to involve the status of the institution itself and the people as a whole.

constructing a written genealogy within some kind of chronological framework from oral sources. Pherecydes' genealogy is in part an artificial written construction ordering family members who were not all remembered in that schematized way. The linear genealogy crystallized incohate or confused oral tradition into a deceptive and much lengthened line of father–son succession, which yet included those ancestors of whom the family was most proud. The family's impressive service to Athens is incorporated and hints of its tyrannical connections omitted, in what is clearly a political statement as well as family tradition. The genealogy provides a coherent crystallization in writing at one particular time of one particular view of the Philaid family.

The construction of a genealogy from an Homeric hero to the recent day was not simply a matter of writing down the oral traditions as they were remembered, nor even a matter of synthesis. It involved manipulation, adding new generations, filling in gaps in the family tradition, incorporating ancestors who were remembered in a vacuum. The family also had to be presented in a flattering guise. Moreover, if genealogical knowledge could begin to fade as early as the sixth century, there was an extremely wide span of time to be bridged to connect the recent generations to those of the Trojan War.

3.2 Genealogy and the genealogists

Greek legendary genealogy may exert little attraction. We would not regard it as a form of entertainment, and if we look at it as historians, it seems to offer little in comparison with other materials. So it is neglected. But it is crucial to recognize how popular at least legendary genealogy was in Greece and how it was thought to provide proof or explanation for the present. These beliefs have a fundamental bearing on oral tradition, since memory and, therefore, oral tradition are formed and re-formed by prevailing attitudes: it is the beliefs about legendary genealogy (for instance) which mould family tradition. It is also against this background that one must see the activity of the genealogists. The role of the prose genealogists – and therefore of written methods – in coordinating and perhaps rewriting the oral family traditions into consistent and lengthy genealogies requires more precise attention. It is now time to return to the wider context of Greek genealogy.

Legendary genealogy was certainly popular. Polybius (IX 1.4) distinguishes the various kinds of history and attaches a certain kind of reader to each one. Somewhat to our surprise, genealogy is linked with the man who just likes listening (τὸν . . φιλήκοον), as opposed to the curious and those with antiquarian interests (τὸν . . . πολυπράγμονα καὶ περιττὸν) and the statesman (τὸν πολιτικὸν). Genealogy is just entertainment. Plato tells us (*Hipp. Mai.* 285d) that Hippias of Elis found the Spartans delighted most in the genealogies of men and heroes, the ancient founding of cities, 'and, to put it briefly, all forms of antiquarian knowledge (*archaiologia*)'.

Hippias contrasts these subjects with others, such as music and maths, which the Spartans did not want to hear. It is implied that enthusiasm for genealogy was rather old-fashioned – or rather that the Spartans did not share the advanced tastes that the sophists expected from their audiences in the late fifth century. Legendary genealogy was the subject of much poetry, of which Hesiod's *Theogony* and the *Catalogue of Women* are the best surviving examples.[40] The heroes of Homer cite their genealogies before engaging in conflict.[41] Clearly, genealogies were not the dull lists we tend to imagine. Interspersed with some elaboration for one or two of the figures, as in Glaucos' genealogy, they form the bare bones of a story or narrative. This is seldom appreciated.[42] Against this background the prose genealogists cannot be regarded simply as antiquarians.

The few criticisms of genealogy that occur serve rather to highlight its evidently widespread popularity. Polybius' remark implied a certain contempt for genealogy as truthful history. Another Hellenistic writer, Asclepiades of Myrlea, a grammarian (*c.* 100 B.C.), seems to have gone further (Sext. Empir. *Adv. gramm.* 1 252). He regarded genealogy as even more false than comedy and mime which were only 'seeming true'. But since he was speaking in the rhetorical terminology of Hellenistic grammarians, the value of this scepticism is unclear.[43] He does at least imply that there was a lot of 'false history' around. Indeed, genealogy continued to thrive. More revealing is the criticism made by Plato in the *Theaetetus* (174e–175b), sometimes quoted without much comment as a solitary stand against the habit of boasting of one's genealogy. He makes fun of those who boast of their ancestors (τὰ . . . γένη ὑμνούντων), citing seven rich *pappoi*; and he mocks the man who 'proudly cites descent through twenty-five ancestors back to Herakles' (175a). This is the most articulate and straightforward criticism of the custom – which

---

[40] See M. L. West (1985), ch. 1.

[41] Most impressive are those of Glaukos, *Il.* VI 145–211, which extends to six generations, and that of Aeneas, *Il.* XX 200–41 (eight generations). Others are a great deal shorter: Achilles, *Il.* XXI 188f. (two generations to a god), Idomeneus, *Il.* XIII 448–53; Krethon and Orsilochos, *Il.* V 541–9 (two generations from R. Alpheios); Telemachus, *Od.* XVI 117–20; Theoclymenos, XV 225–56, and Diomedes, *Il.* XIV 113–27 (four generations).

[42] M. L. West (1985) explains enjoyment in genealogy by simple 'delight' in factual knowledge for its own sake, which may also have an element of truth. But again, genealogy is more than facts.

[43] See Gabba (1981). On Asclepiades, see Slater (1972); however, Fornara ((1983), 10f.) points out the rhetorical background to Asclepiades' statement and interprets 'genealogical story' rather differently.

may have been common by Plato's day.[44] The grounds on which Plato argues his point are therefore very significant. If one looks more closely at what he says, one sees that he does not argue on the grounds of historical truth: he does not say that these lengthy genealogies cannot possibly be true. He only points out that amongst all those myriads of ancestors some will be kings, some beggars. Though a man may cite his descent from Herakles through twenty-five generations, it is in fact entirely a matter of chance what kind of man he will be. This criticism leaves intact the assumption that these genealogies are true. The claimed descent is accepted. It is only the inference drawn from the descent that Plato questions.

If genealogies, then, were mostly regarded as 'true' in antiquity, in what sense were they true?

Genealogy is often an explanation or expression of a relationship that is non-historical. For instance, in Plato's *Theaetetus* (155d) we find the following remark: 'He who said Iris [messenger of heaven] was the daughter of *Thaumas* [wonder] made a good genealogy' (οὐ κακῶς γενεαλογεῖν). That is, one of the ways of expressing a relationship or similarity between two things or two concepts is to put it in genealogical terms. Plato was in fact referring to Hesiod's *Theogony* where this device is used repeatedly.[45] The genealogical relationship seems to be merely conceptual or metaphoric, yet it is expressing something that is also 'true'. In another example from Plato (*Symp.* 178a–b) genealogy is used in a different way: Eros, it is said, must be the oldest of the gods because we do not know his father.[46]

This readiness to express ideas and related concepts in genealogical terms is paralleled by the Greek use of genealogy to explain links between human groups. Friendship between cities may be explained or justified on the grounds that their respective eponymous ancestors were related. Present circumstances are often supposed to correspond to the legendary past.[47] This could effect a circular process and one which

---

[44] The passage may suggest that by the time of this late dialogue, it was more common for people to have worked out their line of ancestors back to a hero. Perhaps the development of historiography, chronological awareness and increased application of written methods encouraged families to ensure the links were there. But this may be taking too literally Plato's exaggerated picture leading up to his more serious criticism of the custom's premise.

[45] Examples in *Theogony* 211ff. and 383ff.; Fränkel (1975), 96ff.; M. L. West (1985).

[46] In general, see Haedicke (1936), introduction; Philippson (1944); van Groningen (1953). Such symbolic relationships are hardly absent from the modern world: cf. the 'marriage' recently celebrated in New York between the Statue of Liberty and Christopher Columbus to symbolize the links between New York and Spain (*The Times*, 13 October 1986).

[47] Cf. Bickerman (1952); Nilsson (1951) collects numerous examples in which cult or legend are changed for 'political propaganda' in order to express in legend what is felt should be the case in the present.

recurs with other kinds of oral tradition. For if legendary ancestry corresponds to the present, that correspondence would apparently confirm that the legendary past had relevance for the present.[48]

Tribes and cities had eponymous ancestors who were often extracted from the name of the tribe or city. The importance of the eponymous ancestor was so great that original ancestors were made as back formations from the names of tribes.[49] For instance, Doros and Ion were the eponymous heroes of the Dorians and Ionians and they were connected genealogically to Hellen, the eponym of the Hellenes. The old Ionian tribes clearly did not derive from heroes' names (e.g. Hopletes, Geleontes), but by the time of Herodotus (v 66) they had acquired eponymous heroes whose names (Hoples, Geleon) were again back formations from the tribal name. They were said to be the sons of Ion. Legendary genealogy thus clearly expressed the contemporary divisions of society. This may not have been regarded as a literal statement of blood relationship, yet that is how it is expressed and it is hard to see how the idea of a merely metaphorical ancestor could be maintained for long – there surely can have been no distinction made. By their nature eponymous ancestors had to correspond to the number of present-day tribes (or whatever group they represented). Thus, they could also change as the situation changed.

In an interesting and stimulating study van Groningen has drawn some of these phenomena together to stress how Greek ways of thought were based upon the past and how often present reality is explained by the past.[50] In some sense this must obviously be true. But as he himself shows, the 'past' is influential in a rather restricted way. Often it is the 'beginning' which is regarded as significant, rather than the past in a wider sense, implying the whole of past history and perhaps some sense

---

[48] Cf. Vansina's examples (*OTH* 157 and 187) of oral traditions connected to monuments or other visible remains: stories grow up to explain the monuments or geographical formations, then the stories are said to be confirmed by those material objects – the monuments are in fact cited as proof. Gabba (1981) and Wiseman (1986) have interesting discussions of the often similar role of monuments in the 'traditions' of early Rome.

[49] Nilsson (1951), esp. 65ff., on eponymous ancestors and later examples. The heroes of the new Cleisthenic tribes at Athens do not seem to be regarded as ancestors. But the language of Demosthenes' *Epitaphios* (§§28ff.) comes very close to treating them as ancestors of each tribe, as he finds in each eponymous hero a particular source of inspiration for his tribe. Cf. especially the use of *syngenē* (§28) and *archēgos* of Oineus, Kekrops and Hippothios (§30, §31), though Erechtheus is called only eponym (§27). *Archēgos* surely carries a strong implication of first origins or original ancestry. Cf. Ch. 4.2 on the demos' acquisition of legendary ancestry. Numerous anthropological examples of legendary ancestors who correspond to divisions of tribes or regions and which change when the divisions are reduced in Goody and Watt (1968); M. L. West (1985) collects others.

[50] (1953), esp. ch. 5.

of historical change. In the case of genealogy it is less misleading to talk instead about the influence of the model of the family and of inheritance from the original family ancestor. It is not the past as such that seems to be the basis of these expressions I have been discussing – that seems to import implications of historical awareness that are perhaps out of place. The emphasis lies rather upon the idea of inheritance and the importance of family relationships – particularly those of the legendary period. This seems to be the basis of the genealogical linking of concepts that we see in Plato and Hesiod. Such links were naturally explained in terms of family links or genealogy.[51]

This same assumption seems to lie behind certain statements of ancient writers about historical figures, statements we regard as non-historical. For instance, it is often pointed out what reckless assumptions ancient biographers make about the kinship links of those whose lives they describe. Ancient writers who wrote in a similar genre often appear in the ancient biographies as related in some way. Not all these links can be historical.[52] But the assumption behind this cavalier treatment (which we see merely as invention) is an interesting one, however contemptuous one may be of the biographers' lack of historical sense. For here again similarity in outlook and in writing is made to connect with, or reflect, kinship. (It may also reflect the fact that profession was often inherited from father to son.)[53] One biographer, Hermippus, even thought Thucydides was descended from Peisistratos. Why? Because of Thucydides' treatment of the period of the tyranny and the tyrannicides, which to Hermippos could only suggest family relationship and descent (*Vit. Marcell.* 18).

Genealogy supplied proof of status and prestige. It seems hardly necessary to stress that the importance attached to ancestry by Greek aristocrats means that it was likely to be changed and falsified. But this was compounded by the fact that it was legendary ancestry which was regarded as the significant ancestry, not recent genealogy of historical times. Legendary ancestry was beyond the range of reasonable memory, so it could not be disproved.[54] But more important are the beliefs I have just been discussing that legendary ancestry should correspond to present-day circumstances.

---

[51] See further Haedicke (1936). It is questionable whether the elaborate genealogies in the *Theogony* imply that Hesiod's contemporaries had similar genealogies.

[52] See Fairweather (1974), who argues the case to its limits.

[53] E.g. in families of seers like the Iamids or Melampodids (*Od.* xv 225–55); Haedicke (1936), 32f. When Socrates says he is descended from Daidalos (Plato, *Alcib.* I 121a) this must be explained by the fact that his father was a stone mason – the expression of paternal profession in legendary terms.

[54] What constitutes 'proof', however, in an oral context, is an interesting question. See Ch. 1.2 for the slow acceptance of writing as proof, and see also below, p. 179: membership of a fratry or genos would be important.

The significance of legendary ancestry I have stressed repeatedly, and most of the discussion above confirms it. So here I shall only add that legendary ancestry was important because it was the beginning of the family which was thought to characterize it later. A fragment of Aristotle, surprisingly, expresses precisely that idea (*On Nobility* (*Peri eugeneia*), fr. 94 Rose³): 'But not even those descended from good (*agathoi*) ancestors are noble (*eugenes*), only those who have among those ancestors originators who are good (*agathoi*).' (*οὐ μὴν ἀλλ' οὐδ' οἱ ἐκ προγόνων ἀγαθῶν εὐγενεῖς πάντως, ἀλλ' ὅσοις τυγχάνουσιν ἀρχηγοὶ τῶν προγόνων ὄντες ⟨ἀγαθοί⟩.*) The ancestors in between were comparatively insignificant.[55] Prestige through birth is an essentially aristocratic value.[56] But for the Greek aristocrat it is not so much the long line of ancestors, each named in succession – the 'pedigree' – that is prestigious, as the original ancestor.

The corollary to the idea that legendary ancestry reflected the present circumstances of the family in some way was that the ancestry could change in what we would take to be a wholly ahistorical manner. One of the clearest and most interesting examples is that of the Iamids. When the Iamid seer Teisamenos was given an exceptional grant of Spartan citizenship (Hdt. IX 33), a Spartan element was incorporated into the legend surrounding the Iamid eponymous ancestor, the seer Iamos. This took the form of the woman Pitane, who is inserted into the legendary genealogical tree in Pindar's ode for an Iamid descendant, *Olympian* VI.[57] Thus, legendary genealogies do not always remain stable but may change with the later fortunes of the family.[58] While the incorporation of further elements has no basis in actual historical genealogy, it has clear enough basis in the feeling that the beginning of the family sets its character. Confusion could obviously result.

---

[55] Bethe (1935), ch. 8; Haedicke (1936), 13f.; van Groningen (1953), stressing the beginning or *archē* in Greek thought.

[56] Loenen (1926) has an interesting discussion of other aspects of 'nobility'. Much later, Dionysius of Halicarnassus (first century A.D.) remarks on the ignoble, 'he cannot even trace his family back to the third ancestor' (Ant. IV 47, p. 759): perhaps a commonplace about having no heroic ancestor or no ancestors beyond the grandfather; or implying a later concern in the Roman period with tracing back ancestors step by step.

[57] On this, see p. 107. Another example is the Philaids' addition of the Lapith Koronos to their genealogy (Ch. 3, n. 28 above). For a similar alteration to a king-list (Argead), see Greenwalt (1985). Cf. the genealogy of Hippokrates which goes back to the healing god Asklepios, though Asklepios was only worshipped in Cos from 400 B.C.

[58] Cf. the extreme example of fluid genealogy, which exactly reflects present-day organization, among the Tiv of Nigeria: Bohannan (1952). Van Baaren (1972), however, gives an example of a genealogy which was officially unchanged, but when a change of ruler necessitated alteration to the 'traditional' genealogy, the priests slowly and almost imperceptibly changed it until it 'fitted' the new ruler. Other studies of genealogy:

Legendary genealogy by itself could be of intense interest to the audiences of both genealogical poets and prose writers. In fact, it has contemporary relevance without any explicit reference to present-day descendants and thus without continuation of the genealogy down into the historical period. The legends could not help being significant to later audiences, and alterations which we might take to be only of antiquarian interest may have had important political implications.[59] If aristocratic pride concentrated on legendary forebears, explicit continuation down into the historical period was simply not necessary. Therefore, oral traditions were unlikely to record continuing genealogies to make that link, for that kind of memory was not necessary to reinforce the main functions of the legendary ancestors. So, in the case of Athens' claim to Salamis, the argument rested upon the notional event in the legendary period combined with the vague continuity assumed between the original hero Philaios and his descendants later resident in Attica. Plato and Solon were said to be descended from Codrus, though there was some doubt about the identity of a crucial link, Solon's father.[60] The original ancestor could be known and believed in, even if intervening links were not.

At this point we might see our modern insistence on the intervening links as one made possible or necessary by a highly literate society and a highly developed sense of written proof. *We* wish to know how a family could prove its heroic ancestry to satisfy others. But such proof as was necessary probably lay in the fact that everyone 'knew' of the heroic ancestor; alternatively, the legendary hero might be enshrined in cult or confirmed by a descendant's membership of genos or fratry and the way the hero corresponded to present-day circumstances. If an aristocrat belonged to a descent group centred on a fratry or a genos, his ancestry would be confirmed by his very membership of that group and therefore his descent from whatever hero was involved. We see descent and genealogy as representative of the historical 'truth', but Greek genealogy expresses more than that: it was not necessary to cite the intervening links back to the Trojan War for legendary ancestry to have its full force. We must simply accept that family tradition could accommodate a void between the great legendary forebears and the recent, more prosaic past, while we demand historical verification of each genealogical link. The modern aristocrat might revel in the immensely complicated web of a

Vansina, *OTH* 160f. and 182ff.; Person (1972); I. M. Lewis (1962); W. de Mahieu (1979).

[59] M. L. West ((1985), ch. 1) also stresses contemporary relevance.

[60] Plut. *Sol.* 12; D.L. III 1: Plato's mother was descended from Solon, Solon from Neleus and Poseidon, Solon's father from Codrus. Plutarch gives the alternative identity of Solon's father.

written family tree; the Greek aristocrat would tend to think of his heroic ancestor and thus of his ultimate descent from a god. The difference is partly connected with the use of writing, as well as beliefs about the first ancestor. For it is possible to trace the elaborate ramifications of genealogy, and indeed to demand proof of each link, in a highly literate society with complex written records.

Here we must return to the question of full genealogy. It is sometimes recognized that the Greeks saw great significance in the legendary origins of a family at the expense of their recent past. But the background of oral transmission, less often appreciated, considerably alters the way we see these traditions and the whole subject of ancient genealogy.

Legendary ancestors may have become enshrined in poetry, and so their memory was not entirely left to the vagaries of the most fluid type of oral transmission, that without a verse text. But even this poetry was meant to be heard and was not until the late sixth century made the subject of detailed enquiry and comparison. So inconsistencies and illogicalities could continue to exist in the great mass of poetry that dealt with legendary genealogy. Oral poetry and oral tradition can accommodate inconsistencies far more easily than a written text which is meant to be read. Legendary origins could change, as we have seen. But they could be altered the more readily because the traditions were transmitted in an essentially oral manner.[61]

This concentration on legendary origins has many parallels in other oral traditions and societies. As we saw, we should expect to find telescoping in such family tradition. Greece did not have the incentives or actual mechanisms for remembering without writing immensely complex genealogies down to the present that anthropologists sometimes find. In any case, the legendary ancestor was most important in Greece. Where we can check, memory of ancestors more than four generations back is very shaky, if it exists at all.[62] Even Plato's family tree had lost two generations of the sixth and early fifth centuries, and the sixth-century figures at the end of the Philaid genealogy were extremely doubtful. Neither length nor accuracy can be expected. We should assume that most families with legendary ancestors probably had genealogical information only about the legendary period surrounding the ancestor and about the recent past – and in exceptional cases perhaps some muddled knowledge of ancestors between the recent and legendary

---

[61] When literacy was introduced among the Somali, an unfortunate result was that it became harder for them to alter genealogies to suit the present: I. M. Lewis (1968).

[62] Contrast Wade-Gery's optimism ((1952), 92): 'A distinguished family would know its own pedigree, as we see from Pindar often, from Herodotus VI 125, 131 (Alcmaeonidai)' and (he adds) in the cases of Heropythos, Hecataeus and Hippokrates. This confuses pedigree, and thus *full* genealogy, with legendary ancestry. Pearson (1942), 9f., is more cautious but still over-optimistic.

periods: but not necessarily a full genealogy from the present day to the legendary period.

How, then, do we regard the activities of the prose genealogists? It will be clear by now that I believe their work must be seen as the application of literate methods of study to poetic and essentially oral material that could be contradictory by its very nature. The full genealogies that we occasionally find are, I think, to be connected closely to the activity of these genealogists: they are largely the product of recognizable methods of sorting out conflicting genealogies to fit them into a coherent and chronologically plausible framework of generations. The apparent elaboration of genealogy (especially by the prose genealogists) in the late sixth and early fifth centuries has, of course, been noted before. But the only attempt to explain the phenomenon in terms of family tradition sees it as the product of a narrowing circle of aristocratic families who, therefore, needed more urgently to prove their legendary ancestry. Erudition was called in to provide the continuous stemmata – erudition in the form of the genealogists.[63] It is certainly right to emphasize that genealogists' work was of great importance to their contemporaries, as we have seen. But their activities, particularly their provision of full genealogy down to the present day, must also be seen as an application of written methods to a mass of oral traditions which were neither factually nor chronologically stable.

I shall first briefly outline what little we know about the activity of the prose genealogists.[64] The five main ones are Hecataeus (*FGH* 1), Akousilaos of Argos (*FGH* 2), Pherecydes of Athens (*FGH* 3), Hellanicus (*FGH* 4, *FGH* 323a), and Damastes of Sigeum (*FGH* 5). Of these, Hecataeus was the earliest we know of (late sixth century) and he apparently set the pattern that the later ones followed, proclaiming his distinction in his preface (F1). Their interests are primarily in the legendary and mythical past, as the fragments and testimonia show. They concentrated upon tracing the genealogies of certain heroic families, for instance the Aiakids, the Heraklids or the Deucalionids. Their overwhelming concern seems to be in tracing legendary genealogy, not in reaching down to the present day.[65] Indeed, it is its subject-matter which

---

[63] Bethe (1935), 57f. and 69, followed by Haedicke.

[64] They have attracted little discussion, and what there is, is sometimes partial and confusing. Most important are the fragments themselves and Jacoby's commentary; also Jacoby (1956), 16–64 and (1947) on Pherecydes; Fornara (1983), 4–12 (mostly concerned with the separation of the legendary past from the 'historical period').

[65] Fornara (1983), 4–5 is confusing: 'For it is a reasonable inference that Hecataeus drew a boundary between "heroic times" and "historical times" – the point at which the genealogical approach could be replaced by the exercise of historical memory.' But as the full genealogies show, legendary genealogy could be joined to 'historical' genealogy. Murray's scepticism (1987) as to how much Herodotus (or others) explicitly distinguished *logos* from *mythos* is also relevant here.

makes it likely that genealogy was one of the earliest kinds of prose literature in Greece.[66]

While we have only fragments of their works, which might therefore not be representative, ancient testimony confirms that they were primarily dealing with the legendary genealogies of poetry. Clement of Alexandria (*FGH* 2 T5) objected that Eumelus of Corinth and Akousilaos simply turned Hesiod's poetry into prose and published it as if the contents were their own. Josephus (*Contra Apionem* 1 16) notes the divergences: 'It would be superfluous for me to instruct those who know better than I do how often Hellanicus disagrees with Akousilaos about the genealogies and how often Akousilaos corrects Hesiod.' The subject-matter was that of the genealogical and epic poets. But the task involved putting into order a great mass of often confused and contradictory material. As I have already said, different areas or groups produced differing 'versions' of the legends or legends about the same characters with different implications. These reflected the various claims made through the legends, as well as actual changes made in these genealogies to reflect later circumstances. The genealogists collected together this information and produced in a systematic manner a version that was at least consistent with itself (see below, p. 184), a stupendous task.[67]

This information was naturally of great interest to contemporaries: though legendary, such genealogy could not help being relevant. One must therefore regard the prose genealogists not simply as antiquarians or as forerunners of the chronographers, mainly interested in chronology (see below, p. 185). Their subject had an intrinsic interest for those groups who believed themselves descended from any of the heroes included. One must therefore also expect them to produce versions of genealogies which favour the claims of their own city and other groups: this is why they disagree with each other (e.g. Akousilaos *FGH* 2, F5–6), continuing in the same tradition of using legendary genealogy for contemporary claims. We have already seen an example of this in the legendary Philaid genealogy.

One wonders, then, how the full genealogies or *any* references to later history actually fitted into their work. And did they often continue legendary genealogies to the present day? We can only answer this last question by repeating the overwhelming emphasis in the fragments on the legendary period – which had contemporary relevance by themselves. But we simply cannot know the position of the very few genealogies that did continue. Jacoby put Hellanicus' mention of Ando-cides' ancestry in his *Atthis* (history of Athens), not his genealogical

---

[66] Jacoby (1947), Fornara (1983).
[67] M. L. West (1985) gives genealogical tables at the back; cf. Ch. 3, 71.

works (*FGH* 4 F170=*FGH* 323a F24), and thought it improbable that he gave all the intervening links: it thus came in retrospectively, introduced via an historical person, Andocides' grandfather. The Philaid genealogy of Pherecydes (*FGH* 3 F2) was probably introduced into a mythical history of Greece via Ajax or Philaios.[68] Legendary interest is still predominant. Indeed, one suspects in reading these fragments that what people really wanted to hear was not a continuation down to the prosaic present generation but continuation *back* from the hero to a god. In several proud citations of genealogy (e.g. Hecataeus') that is the emphasis – Alcibiades (Plato *Alcib.* I 121a) says he is descended from Eurysakes and therefore from Zeus.

The genealogists' methods demand the use of writing. It is barely appreciated, if at all, that their methods are essentially literate ones and that the genealogists' work must represent new uses of writing and literacy.

Hecataeus in his famous preface to his *Genealogies* (*FGH* I F1) declared that 'the tales of the Greeks are many and absurd'. The usual interpretation is that Hecataeus intended to rationalize the absurdities of legend,[69] but Fornara has recently pointed out that he also criticizes the plurality of tales: genealogies were numerous and contradictory and this Hecataeus intended to rectify.[70] Whether this is the correct interpretation of Hecataeus or not, the vast number of competing and conflicting legendary genealogies confirm that such plurality was a major problem for any genealogist. It would be interesting if Hecataeus had himself commented upon it. But one must add to this picture that the original genealogies were products either of pure oral tradition or of poetry which was orally delivered;[71] such diversity, plurality and contradiction could exist, in part, precisely because the genealogies were orally delivered or transmitted. The correction of their inconsistencies and chronological implausibilities by the genealogists needed written study. Inconsistent relationships can be voiced and believed in different poems (or areas),

---

[68] As Jacoby (1947), n. 48: Pherecydes is primarily interested in the prehistory of the clan. F146 is the only other contemporary allusion in extant Pherecydes apart from the Philaid genealogy. On Andocides' 'genealogy', Jacoby, commentary on Hell. *FGH* 323a F24 – he is not connected with the Kerykes (against Toepffer (1889)).

[69] E.g. K. von Fritz (1967), vol. I, 71.

[70] Fornara (1983), 6: 'The preface may be explained as a criticism of the inconsequence of the genealogical tradition in the strict sense of the word.'

[71] Even if there was a written text, it was not approached and studied in that form (and cf. Ch. 1.2, p. 48, for uses of a written text which might involve *oral* transmission from the text). This applies to the immensely complicated *Catalogue of Women*, whose author synthesized disparate traditions: M. L. West (1985), 166 thinks the tradition in which local genealogies of the eighth century evolved into the sixth-century *Catalogue* was not likely to have been an exclusively oral one. This is surely true – though he gives no argument for it – for the reasons I am discussing.

especially if they each correspond to some contemporary situation or belief. Oral tradition can accommodate contradictions comparatively readily and each version can be regarded separately as 'true'. The plurality Hecataeus complains of is that of oral tradition, as are the inconsistencies he implies. Such inconsistencies can only become glaring and worrying when traditions are brought together and compared – which is easier in writing – and when one definitive version is attempted (again, a 'definitive' version is very much easier to obtain by means of writing). Akousilaos himself seems to have been aware of this new significance of writing. He seems to have claimed that he composed his *Genealogies* from bronze tablets which his father dug up in the garden.[72] It is an interesting attempt to claim written and documentary sources for an early work of coordination. Against the background we have been describing, it seems to indicate some awareness of new uses of writing in treating the old legendary material of poetry (cf. Ch. 1.2 for other extensions of writing in the fourth century).

The mass of genealogical relationships for the legendary period produced glaring problems of synchronization. Figures who were supposed to be contemporaries during the Trojan War might turn out to be in different generations. Various authors tried to explain Theseus' supposed rape of Helen of Troy, which implied particularly absurd chronology.[73] Genealogists had to solve these problems. One solution used by Hellanicus[74] was to suppose that there had been two people of the same name and (presumably) that the more famous one had ousted the other from memory. This method (not unknown in modern scholarship) also levelled out the generations and, by adding extra ones, produced a coherent and plausible schema for the legendary period. The very idea of synchronizing generations like this requires written methods and probably a written mode of study. For writing made it easier – perhaps even possible – for the different relationships expressed in different poems to be brought together. The generations could be worked out, counted and synchronized; the chronology had to be plausible. In a completely oral context it is doubtful if the need for synchronization would even be felt, still less fulfilled. Synchronization revealed confusion. The coordination of the disparate material requires written and graphic forms.[75]

---

[72] *FGH* 2, TI (Suidas).

[73] It could be calculated that Theseus was fifty, Helen still a child: Hell. *FGH* 4 F168a = Plut. *Thes.* 31.

[74] Pearson (1942), 9ff.

[75] We do not know precisely how the genealogists coordinated the material. Pherecydes' genealogy is couched in continuous prose though it is essentially a list. Heropythos' genealogy is written out as a bare list, as is Klearchos' (Ch. 3, n. 9). See further on the list, Ch. 3, p. 189, below.

Though a crude method, such synchronization also formed incipient chronology. The genealogists' chronological interests may be over-stressed, particularly since modern historians are interested in the beginnings of Greek chronology, related to early historiography. The genealogists' predominant interests were in 'correcting' the legendary genealogies so relevant to their contemporaries. This tends to be ignored.[76] However, their writings did obviously have chronological implications which they surely realized. Calculations of chronology would use the same written methods of synchronization. In fact, chronological complications may have been revealed by the attempts to make the legends cohere. There are other problems with the chronological emphasis which one should mention here, if only briefly. Genealogical telescoping would make accurate dating from genealogy impossible. Could the genealogists have tried to use genealogy to work out chronology back to the Trojan War, as is sometimes thought? This seems unlikely, too. By the time of Herodotus (II 145.4) the Trojan War was dated to the thirteenth century, yet it is notorious that neither the full genealogies nor the Spartan king-lists could be made to extend much beyond the tenth century B.C., whether they were calculated with a thirty- or forty-year generation. The Philaids, for example, had twelve ancestors back to the Trojan War. Thus, dating of the Trojan War could hardly have been derived by calculations from the genealogies, though they did purport to go back to a generation contemporary with the Trojan War or earlier.[77] On the contrary, it would seem that the dating of the Trojan War would be a reason to stretch and lengthen the genealogies, perhaps even to exaggerate the length of a single generation. Its dating must have been based on some other kind of calculation.[78] Whatever that basis, however, we begin to discern how the genealogists'

---

[76] E.g. Pearson (1942), 9f., 'The only way of establishing a chronological basis for mythology was to construct parallel family trees for the various families beginning with the divine ancestor of each one', implying that chronology was the dominant interest.

[77] Thus Snodgrass (1971), 10ff. He suggests 'some kind of barrier to this type of recollection in the region of the tenth century B.C.'. I would say it was not so much a barrier to recollection as a process of forgetting, telescoping and reconstructing that, when calculated, happened to result in a span of 400 or 500 years. We can hardly use these telescoped genealogies purporting to go back to the Trojan War to date the Ionian migration (as Wade-Gery does, followed by Snodgrass). More literally, Burn used them to date the fall of Troy to c. 1010 B.C. ((1935), 131 and 146), which highlights the difficulties!

[78] Snodgrass ((1971), 12f.) suggests another source, perhaps oriental (but nothing specific): 'The forty-year generation would then be a by-product, not a cause of the dating of the Heroic Age'. Herodotus' preoccupation with the Greek time-scale compared to the Egyptian in Book II (e.g. §§142–6) suggests how worrying fifth-century thinkers found their chronology. Herodotus suggests (§146.2) that the 'births' of the Greek gods were in fact calculated only from the time when the Greeks first heard about them from Egypt. On generation calculations in historiography, see Mitchel (1956) (with my next note), Prakken (1943), Strasburger (1956).

work could raise suggestions and problems concerning chronology which others could take up, even if the genealogists themselves were not primarily interested in those aspects.

The other element I would stress in the genealogists' method is that it is not merely a matter of synthesis; it is creative in the most literal sense. The genealogists do not simply take the lineages from the poets and put them together. The method I have outlined above actually infers new generations, in effect inventing new figures.[79] That is, the organization of consistent genealogy may involve manipulation and addition, even if the basic material is preserved in poetry. The process of setting out a stemma in written form may entail apparently logical but invented additions.

We recognize that this occurs in the genealogists' treatment of the legendary period, but less readily that it must apply just as well to their treatment of the historical period. If one accepts their (necessary) manipulation of legendary genealogy, it is in principle likely that they should use similar methods for any genealogies that continued into the historical period. But one may go further. To produce a full genealogy down to the historical period they had to use family tradition. This was even more fluid than the poetic sources they used for the legendary period, and it is unlikely that much of it can have been preserved in poetic form. It is clear that there must have been large gaps in knowledge of any one family line and figures in the tradition who were known of but not clearly connected to the family stemma in family memories. Still worse, they had to be connected somehow to an Homeric hero over a wide span of time, which in most cases was far longer than our conventional 'Dark Ages' – since, as we have seen, genealogical memory actually falters in many cases as early as the sixth-century ancestors of a family.[80] The genealogist's task in ordering such oral family traditions was even more 'creative' than his treatment of the purely legendary genealogies from the poets. In the Philaid genealogy of Pherecydes we see one such artificial construction which has ordered the family memories into an impressive linear genealogy from Philaios to Miltiades.

This brings us back to the question of the precise effect a written genealogy may have had upon oral family traditions. Recent anthropological studies have provided interesting confirmation of the role of writing in the formation of many genealogies and other kinds of list, and it will

---

[79] Cf. Mitchel (1956), 49, 'the genealogists were only recorders of what they uncovered in traditional materials' (my point is that oral tradition probably would not provide it in the right form). Later he explains the deteriorating chronological schema of Herodotus for the centuries before the Persian Wars, as a matter merely of perspective and interest. Contrast Jeffery (1976), 34–6.

[80] Herodotus puts the Trojan War over 800 years before his time (*c.* 1250?); so even by fifth-century time-reckoning there was a wide gap.

be illuminating to consider these first, before we reach final conclusions about the Greek genealogies.

Henige (1974) has made an extensive study of certain kinds of oral tradition that imply the measurement of time, particularly king-lists and genealogies. This study examines many of the ways in which oral tradition distorts chronology – it achieves, for instance, telescoping and artificial lengthening by treating contemporary rulers as successive ones or by imputing very long reigns. A drawback of this approach is that many of the most impressive examples of these lists occur in societies which are (or were) not entirely illiterate when the lists were first written down.[81] It is often very difficult to determine how far they are actually products of *purely* oral tradition, yet for a long time it has been assumed that they are simply written versions repeating faithfully long-lived 'oral traditions' transmitted (orally) for generations or centuries. So Henige's study often leaves it unclear whether these king-lists or genealogies might have been elaborated with literate methods or at least after the society ceased to be entirely illiterate. But for certain types of example he does point out the effects of literacy. For instance, he stresses that 'the extensive manipulation of genealogies for synchronistic symmetry . . . could not have been carried out in an oral society. Indeed, its need would not have been perceived . . . much of the genealogical oral traditions available from Africa are the products of an era of at least restricted literacy.'[82] (This quotation encapsulates the confusion produced by calling genealogies elaborated through writing 'oral traditions'.) Genealogical data were also often produced in response to the British colonial administration,[83] again at a period when literate methods were beginning to be used more widely.

Since then, there has been more careful study of the role of writing (or lack of writing) in genealogical tradition. Of course, there are impressive examples of careful transmission and recitation of genealogies, particularly in Polynesia.[84] But these are not found in all societies. Genealogical information is often merely general knowledge and not recited in isolation for its own sake. There is a crucial difference between 'genealogical information' which has been collected together from various snippets of information and 'a genealogy' recited or regarded as such. If

[81] An extreme example is the twelfth-century (A.D.) chronicle of Kashmir (see Henige (1974), 49), which has very long reigns, or any of the other Indian examples.

[82] Henige (1974), 26. He also mentions (*ibid.*, 23) the Greek historians of the sixth and fifth centuries and their use of the 'grid effect' (i.e. synchronization of generations).

[83] Henige (1974), 12. But he also explains artificial lengthening (*ibid.* 39ff.) as either unconscious or because of 'the universal propensity to revere antiquity for its own sake'.

[84] Vansina (1973), 32, stressing the importance of social mechanisms in preservation; *OTH* 95f. and 182ff., is more cautious. An instance is known from Polynesia of recitation involving over 700 names and thirty-four generations (Smith (1921), 16ff.).

one speaks of distortion or change in a genealogy, one is in a sense speaking from a modern literate standpoint, assuming that there is an 'original text', as it were, from which there are deviations. But if genealogy in a certain society is always tied to a practical issue, as it often is, and not recorded separately, then it is misleading to speak as if there were a whole genealogy which could be thought of in isolation from the practical application of the relationships.[85] It is therefore important to remember that when field anthropologists produce complex genealogies, they are often constructing artificially a genealogy which, pieced together from isolated information, may not correspond to the way in which their informants see their family and ancestral relationships.[86] Here I would particularly stress the effect of a written and graphic form on these oral traditions (rather than emphasizing simply the difference in outlook of researcher and informant).[87] Behind all these observations lies the problem that the process of forming a written genealogy from oral tradition may involve the ordering of information not necessarily remembered in that precise form and the recording in a 'definitive version' ('definitive' because it is in writing) of information that was not stable. The actual form of the written genealogy may alter the form of the oral traditions. (One need only think of the conventions of modern genealogical tables which stress descent in the male line.) In addition, the collection of varying pieces of information perhaps not seen as connected

---

[85] Finnegan (1970b), 198, a point akin to that made about telescoping above. This applies to the classic case of shifting genealogy (or 'structural amnesia') according to present-day reality, that of the Tiv (Ch. 3, n. 58 above). Finnegan's point is that changes are not dependent on lapses of memory or distortions, precisely because the genealogical knowledge is always tied to a practical issue. In many societies genealogies are never recited as a whole all at once: those parts which are relevant may be discussed and reconstructed by consensus, Vansina, *OTH* 95f. and 182ff. Cf. also Vansina's experience with Kuba traditions (*ibid.* 95). He says he misjudged the coherence of the royal 'annals', for the Kuba do not give a full performance of their whole dynastic history at any one time – much of it consists of anecdotes of kings told in various circumstances.

[86] Miller, *APS* 18f. But rather uneasily, he takes genealogy to be merely a cliché, a way of expressing a certain element in a genealogical metaphor: the oral narrators could understand the true meaning behind the metaphor (i.e. they could translate it), and only modern historians misunderstand. But I find it very hard to believe that the narrators could keep separate in their own minds the historical reality and a metaphor very close to a possible reality. Cf. Vansina, *OTH* 44f. and 137ff., on interpreting clichés: some can be meant literally.

[87] Cf. Barnes (1967), esp. 118–21: he distinguishes genealogies – the actual family trees – from pedigrees, the accounts of their genealogy which an individual or family would give. But with unconscious irony he points out *both* (i) the genealogy of the ethnographer may misrepresent the relations as conceived by the informants (e.g. as patrilineal when they are not) *and* (ii) how there are various ways of setting out genealogical charts (which give rather different emphases through their graphic form). Though he does not say so, this seems to be an excellent illustration of the fact that genealogical charts are essentially written and graphic formulations of relationships which were not necessarily conceived like that, and in particular that they may impute merely through their form a western and literate idea of a 'family tree'.

by the informants actually highlights omissions and shows inconsistencies which had happily existed in oral form – and these must then be eliminated.

Goody has done stimulating work on early uses of literacy and the list which draws together some of these ideas, relating his observations to the overall development and effect of literacy.[88] He has pointed out that lists, whether genealogical lists or king-lists, are essentially a written phenomenon; simple lists, which are non-syntactic, do not occur much in a completely oral society and they are not a 'natural analytical category' by themselves.[89] Genealogy is the most likely type of list in such a society, but since it would thus exist in an oral form alone, it could not be finite, with a definite form in the way that a written list is. It would not have the independent existence that a written list could have. Oral lists would not be very long.[90]

Such suggestions have prompted re-examination of certain king-lists which were once taken to be pure products or oral tradition. For instance, Henige himself returned to the Ganda and Nyoro king-lists to suggest that they were in fact 'oral' only in the sense that they were collected in spoken form.[91] Originally they may even have been a product in some way of early Arabic literacy.[92] It is striking that the Ganda king-list grows in length dramatically from the first written record made of it by a European in 1865. The first list was short, but it developed as time passed, acquiring a great many new names, until by 1901 it was much augmented. That its contents agreed with another king-list had seemed to guarantee its authenticity. But in retrospect this consistency was a suspicious sign that both lists were products of similar environments where writing was becoming increasingly common. As Henige says, 'literacy was actually having its greatest impact at precisely the moment that remembrances of the past were undergoing their final mutations'. These augmented king-lists were perhaps not based on oral

---

[88] Goody (1977), esp. 108; followed by Miller, *APS* and Vansina, *OTH* 179–81. Here Goody moves away from the strict 'autonomous' model of literacy presented in his 'Consequences of Literacy' (1968): Ch. 1.1 above. Goody (1986), 67, explores further the potential of writing or rather, as he sees it, 'the nature of writing' which 'means that each activity is transformed in significant ways by its introduction'.

[89] Oral lists are kept when they have social meaning, but they are never very long, except when there has been some feedback from writing, Vansina, *OTH* 179ff. Cf. also Goody (1986), 54 and (1987), 114ff.

[90] For length, cf. the genealogical list of Heropythos: one name out of fifteen was left out by the first scholar who recorded it, and that was even with the help of writing.

[91] *APS* on 'The Disease of Writing', 240ff.

[92] Literacy and the resulting 'harm' to indigenous oral traditions are mostly associated simply with the European colonial presence, and contact much earlier with the Arabs' literate culture in large parts of Africa is often grossly underestimated. Cf. Finnegan (1977), who stresses how very few (if any) 'oral societies' now studied have actually had no contact with literacy at all; also Henige (1982), 80–7; Goody (1987), ch. 5.

tradition at all; certainly their increasing length was made possible by the presence of writing.[93] The flowering of the list was contemporary with European presence and growing literacy, not a final relic of oral tradition shortly to be stunted by the coming of literacy.[94]

Much research remains to be done on this whole subject, especially on the precise rather than the overall, effect of writing in this sphere (and see Ch. 1.1, for provisos).[95] However, it is clear that writing itself may help order information which in its oral context may not be remembered in that form; that the list as we think of it is almost always a literate phenomenon, one particularly associated with early literacy; that such lists may grow dramatically in length from their oral origins under the conditions of early literacy; and that while writing encourages the accretion of names on a list, it also shows up gaps and inconsistencies.

If we return to the Greek genealogies, these studies confirm what we suspected of their formation. The very process of constructing a written genealogy from family tradition must often have involved the ordering of disparate information, some in genealogical form, some remembered without context. Production of a stable genealogy obviously prompted the inclusion of figures whose position in the family tree was unclear or unknown. We saw an example of this in the Philaid genealogy. Moreover, the other, more complex elements in producing a genealogy – such as chronological or generational calculation, appropriate lengthening of the line and inclusion of duplicated figures of the same name – are the product of applied written methods, that is, written study beyond the simple recording in writing itself. Greek family traditions did not remember such genealogies unaided. Especially problematic was the gap – which we must assume was usual – between the legendary Homeric ancestors and the recent, historical members of the family. The necessity to bridge the gap in a plausible number of generations called most urgently for the help of genealogists. Here Heropythos' genealogy seems to be exceptional, but we must judge it against the cumulative evidence and inferences from other family traditions or genealogies. It did not extend to an Homeric ancestor, nor is it explicitly associated with the

---

93 It is not always clear how the names were added and where they came from. Henige is vague on this (though the overall pattern is clear) except for the use made of royal and semi-royal tombs to augment the list.

94 Another example of this combination in Oliver ((1955), 111–17), who shows that the oral traditions reached a peak only in the twentieth century, particularly with the publication of Ganda oral traditions; cf. remarks in Goody (1987), chs. 3 and 4.

95 Cf. recent work on early medieval king-lists and genealogies. Dumville (1977) examines the roles of ideology and learning in the construction of genealogical schemes and king-lists. Bede, *HE* III 1 (cited p. 81) comments that those who count the length of kings' reigns have agreed to delete the reigns of Edwin's apostate successors.

genealogists (though we have no way of knowing otherwise). So, at least the chronological inconsistencies produced by an Homeric hero were not present. The original ancestor, Kyprios, must have had special importance to the family. But since we have no external evidence whatsoever of Heropythos' family, we should suppose that in his case, too, the same processes of memory, telescoping and forgetting would have occurred, if his family tradition was transmitted in a similar way to all the others we have examined.[96] Even his genealogy only 'extends' as far back as the tenth century. The full genealogies (or instances of numbered generations) back to a god or hero were in part a product of the applied literate methods of the professional genealogists.

A further distortion is introduced by the linear form of a genealogy, since in its extreme simplification it allows only a list of fathers and sons.[97] Genealogical information in linear form would be misleading even in oral tradition; when a linear genealogy is constructed in writing the problem is exacerbated. The elongation of the line I mentioned above is partly encouraged by the linear form – so that collateral members might be included.

But there is a further element of distortion in the linear genealogy. Not only may a linear genealogy be formed by including members not of the direct line: a list that represents some kind of succession to office may also be interpreted or assumed to be one of father–son succession. Henige produces numerous examples where king-lists purport to show a continuous line of fathers and sons over a long period of time, whereas other evidence shows that brothers sometimes succeeded. So the process is similar to the one by which brothers become included in a linear genealogy. This has the effect of lengthening the chronological time span, since successive generations are thus indicated by the line. Yet, where lines of succession can be checked (e.g. in the British royal family) it is extremely rare to find continuous father–son succession for many generations. The holders of office unvariably have to include others.[98] Thus, in Greece, for example, the Spartan king-lists purported to represent fathers and sons in succession, at least for the period about

---

96 Wade-Gery took Eldios as a semitic name, and other names in the list may not be Greek: in which case one may wonder if the genealogy belongs to a different tradition which encourages the preservation of genealogies (in writing?) from an early period – cf. Momigliano's remarks ((1966c), 19f.) on the Jewish imperative to remember their past. Even so, what I have said about the significance of genealogy for status and family character and the formation of a written list would still hold.

97 Such linearity implies that the lateral links of the family and ancestors were not considered socially important: if they were, perhaps we should expect appropriate family memories.

98 Henige (1974), esp. 42ff., and ch. 2.

which little was known (Hdt. VII 204). Each was presented both as a king-list and a linear genealogy of the appropriate house.[99]

I suspect a similar background to the list of priests of Poseidon Erechtheus from the genos (clan) of the Eteoboutadai.[100] Pseudo-Plutarch tells us (*Vit. X Orat.* 843e–f) that the genos was descended from Boutes and Erechtheus, son of Gē and Hephaistos, and 'most recently from Lycomedes and Lycurgus' (fifth- to fourth-century figures):

> And this genealogy (*katagogē*) of the family of the priests of Poseidon exists on a complete tablet (*pinax*) which lies in the Erechtheum . . . and there are wooden statues of Lycurgus, the orator, and his sons . . . His son Habron dedicated the tablet, who received the priesthood from the genos (λαχὼν ἐκ τοῦ γένους) and handed it over to his brother Lycophron.

By his use of *katagogē* ('bringing down', i.e. 'pedigree', 'genealogy'), the author shows that the *pinax* represented *both* a list of the priests and a genealogy of the family from Boutes and Erechtheus down through Lycomedes to Lycurgus, the orator: the implication is that the whole list was interpreted as a linear genealogy of father–son succession.[101]

The way in which genos priesthoods were handed down is unclear,[102]

---

[99] Also Hdt. VIII 131. Huxley (1962), 117–19 and (more sophisticated) Cartledge (1979), app. 3 attempt in various ways to sort out the genealogy/king-lists. The line of each is satisfyingly linear only for the early kings about whom least is known. They then branch out in the latest generations, forming an interesting parallel to the Philaid genealogy. The early Eurypontid line includes suspicious names, Eunomos and Prytanis. Herodotus does not say the list of VIII 131 was a king-list for the recent generations, but Pausanias (III 7.2) called the Agiad list a king-list of fathers and sons. He does the same of his Eurypontid list which is rather different from that of Herodotus. The King Soos is again suspicious and there seems to have been some attempt to even up the generations of the two houses. Henige (1974), App. c has an interesting discussion of the problem.

[100] On the family of Lycurgus, see Davies, *APF* 9251.

[101] Lists of priests might be particularly prone to this kind of distortion if the priesthood was held by a genos. *Syll.*³ 1020, the first century B.C. list of priests of Poseidon at Halicarnassus, purports to list the priests going back to the foundation by the legendary Telamon. It says (lines 1–2) that it was copied from an ancient stele. Cf. the later decree from Eleusis honouring the daduch Themistocles (20/19 B.C.; Clinton (1974), 5off.): it gives his predecessors, his father and eight other ancestors. What is interesting is that it then says: 'And before all these, Hermotimus and Hierocleides were daduchs before the registering (*anagraphē*) of the Kerykes on the tablet.' So the contemporary record presents an extremely complex family tree, in which successors do not form a linear line; but for daduchs before the written record (i.e. end of third century) all is very vague. See *Atthis* 280, n. 39 and 358, n. 26. In general, on lists in shrines, see *LSAG* 59ff., Jeffery (1976), 34–7, and *Atthis* 58.

[102] At least occasionally apportioned by lot rather than inheritance: Dem. LVII 47. But it is unknown how common this was. The phrase used above seems in the context to imply the lot here, too. It is still uncertain whether Habron or Lycophron was the eldest son of Lycurgus (see Davies, *APF*, pp. 351f.): either way the priesthood was passed by one brother to another, and probably the only candidates were Lycurgus' sons (Humphreys (1985c)).

but it is certain that the list of priests, taken to be a genealogy, was very misleading. Pseudo-Plutarch gives us evidence in the same paragraph of precisely the kind of non-linear succession which was obscured in the list of priests and turned into a linear genealogy – and obviously, if it happened once, it had done so before. For he says (see extract, above) that Habron who set up the tablet ceded the priesthood which he had received to his brother Lycophron. So the succession is not the simple linear one implied by the rest of the list; and the assumption that the list represents the linear descent from Boutes is clearly incorrect.[103] A similar observation and explanation may be made of the famous line of Egyptian priests whose statues Herodotus said he was shown in Thebes (II 143). The statues represented three hundred and forty-five priests who, it was insisted, had succeeded each other in continuous father–son succession from the earliest period. Thus, both the creation of linear genealogy and the assumption of linear genealogy from lists of succession form gross distortions which stem in part from their creation in written form in the first place.[104]

These, then, are some of the ways in which written genealogy may have affected the original oral traditions. In the first place, the mere collection in writing may increase the amount of information that is thought relevant. This may result in an impressive accretion to the genealogy of names of people who were not clearly remembered themselves or whose genealogical position was not clearly recalled. The form of the genealogy also has an effect. A linear genealogy in its simple form may exaggerate the tendencies of lengthening and addition of extraneous figures – as we saw in the Philaid genealogy. It may also be confused with lists of offices, so that a list of priests may be taken to represent both a list of 'office-holders' and a linear genealogy: this we saw in the case of the priests of Poseidon Erechtheus. Beyond this, the use of writing may encourage – indeed make possible – the comparison of different genealogies, the counting of generations and the construction of a plausible sequence of generations. These methods we know the genealogists used at least for the legendary period. But one may extend it

---

103 Cf. again the complex line of daduchs at Eleusis (n. 101). We do not know the provenance or reliability of the list itself. It may have derived from an earlier list of priests or from a list partly reconstructed artificially (Plutarch implies the first, like the statues). Since the list was regarded as the family genealogy, it represents family tradition (and manipulation?). But more complicated, it is also an official list of priests of the sanctuary, perhaps kept by the sanctuary.

104 This obviously bears on other early Greek lists, e.g. the list of priestesses at Argos, the Olympic victor list or the Athenian archon list. Were they remembered for a long time before being written down (as Jeffery (1976), 35f., citing the role of *mnēmones*)? When were they written down, and were the early reaches partly reconstructed from memory and speculation? This needs much further examination. I outline some preliminary points in the appendix.

to the case of the full genealogies down to the historical period. For a Greek aristocratic family it was extremely rare to have a full genealogy back to legendary times. And genealogical information certainly began to be very inaccurate four or five generations back from the present day. Where such genealogy occurs, we may suspect that information in it has been gathered together from the family's oral traditions, ordered and improved to produce a coherent and plausible stemma. The genealogies we find are thus the product both of written record itself and of the organization that comes – or may come – from literate study of that material.

*

I have tried to build up a picture of Greek genealogy of the sixth and fifth centuries, the one form of family tradition that seems to have extended over an extraordinarily long period of time. Such genealogy has interesting implications for the possible effect of the written word on the oral traditions and for the activities of the early proto-historians of Greece in constructing a written framework for the past. The direct evidence is sparse, but for that reason it is important to look the more closely at what there is. My argument has necessarily been a cumulative one, supported by detailed examination of particularly illuminating examples.

Genealogical information was both popular and important for the Greeks, but it was genealogy primarily of the legendary period. Genealogy was seen as an explanation of observed relations which was far removed from historical 'fact'; and legendary genealogy was believed to explain or to correspond in some way to the later descendants, whether tribe, city or family. Thus it was liable to change as circumstances changed. Similarly, one should expect in the conditions of oral transmission that the great concentration upon the legendary period would produce a vast gap of forgotten history or generations between the legendary period and the recent past, with telescoping of the two extremes. This is what we find, and it seems most striking in the case of family tradition, since we are well used, from our standpoint, to lengthy and complex genealogies that reach back over centuries. But full genealogy, a list of ancestors purporting to be complete from the legendary hero, seems to have been exceedingly rare in Greek family tradition. Indeed, much evidence suggests that there was knowledge of the legendary and recent ancestors, but a dim period of ignorance between which was not bridged and did not need to be: the heroic ancestor was enough, and there was no need to know or prove the intervening links.

But there were some full genealogies, and they prompt interesting and far-reaching suggestions about the role of writing and written coordination in elaborating and crystallizing the oral traditions. The genealogists themselves concentrated mostly upon legendary genealogy – the same preoccupation with the heroic period. This was of intense relevance to their contemporaries and could reflect contemporary 'propaganda' and argument. Again, there was no necessity to continue the genealogies down to the present day explicitly. However, it is no coincidence that the few examples of full genealogies occur in the work of the genealogists (except, apparently, for Heropythos' genealogy). I have therefore suggested that such genealogies are essentially constructions of the genealogists and their written and graphic methods. They collected and organized oral family tradition which was often disparate, remembered in non-genealogical form, illogical or contradictory. They used the essentially written methods of generation counting and synchronization to produce lengthy and impressive genealogies. Plato's construction of his family's recent genealogy shows a similar process on a smaller scale. The application of written methods to family tradition showed up its gaps and illogicalities. I have examined in detail some of the possible effects of both writing and written study on this kind of material in Greek family tradition. The Philaid genealogy both illustrates this process and suggests some reasons for it. Pherecydes crystallized in writing a genealogy that encapsulated both legendary propaganda and later historical figures who enhanced the family's glory. Both parts were peculiarly appropriate to the early fifth century, and the written genealogy preserved in definitive form the family's view of its past at one particular time. It also contains evidence of literate manipulation of generations, partly for chronological reasons, a process that often occurs when oral tradition is transferred into written genealogy.

The full Greek genealogy is therefore essentially a written and artificial construction of the genealogists: it crystallizes the claims made through genealogy in that period and orders and elaborates the material with methods that are literate and graphic ones. The genealogists' activities represent an extension and new application of writing and writing study to the oral traditions – albeit in one limited sphere. Though not themselves interested primarily in chronology, the genealogists highlight the extreme problems of reckoning any chronology from such oral traditions and indeed producing any chronological framework for Greek history. They offer a foretaste of the problems of early historiography derived from oral tradition.

4

OFFICIAL TRADITION? POLIS TRADITION AND THE EPITAPHIOS

We can now turn to the more general traditions of the whole community or city-state, the polis traditions of the fifth and fourth centuries. Compared to family tradition and its transmission, the general polis traditions are exceedingly complex. Yet, these are the traditions which must have formed the usual view or memory of the past, the Greek equivalent of 'national' history. How did a city-state remember or create a picture of its own past from oral tradition alone? Were there official traditions and official 'memory men' such as we meet in anthropological studies? How were any general traditions transmitted at all and by what groups of people?

In fact, as with family tradition, the wider oral traditions in Athens seem particularly fluid also, and it is questionable how far it had an 'official tradition' at all. The same is probably true of many other Greek city-states. Against the complexity of the general polis traditions and of any general oral traditions, to which I shall return in the next chapter, I concentrate here on the Athenian epitaphios or public funeral speech, which comes nearest to an 'official tradition'. It forms an extreme example of Athenian polis tradition and is most illuminating for oral tradition and the way it is formed. As for the complicated web of popular tradition, individuals' knowledge and the polis traditions of the assembly, Chapter 4.1 discusses some of the general problems, introducing certain important characteristics of these polis traditions, mainly as a background to the official tradition; and briefly discusses the form and character of the epitaphios. The ideals expressed in the epitaphios are then analysed (Ch. 4.2) and the 'official tradition' of Athens' past presented there (Ch. 4.3). For, as oral tradition is moulded by prevalent beliefs, the ideals themselves help to select, form and influence the image of the past that goes with them.

It is the public funeral oration over the war dead, the epitaphios, that seems closest to Athens' official tradition. For this presents a coherent vision of its past regularly transmitted and crystallized in strict form. Usually studied simply as a rhetorical genre, it must have influenced, and even created, tradition. Indeed, if it is seen in the living context of fifth- and fourth-century Athenian society, its content and rhetorical commonplaces make sense as expressions of ideals and values that played an important part in the creation of an official and patriotic tradition. For the ideals expressed are very closely related to the image of Athens' past found there (see Ch. 4.2 below). Moreover, this public funeral ceremony seems to be the counterpart of the aristocratic funerals curbed by legislation. The whole ceremony was started shortly after the Persian Wars at the latest, thus after the establishment of the Cleisthenic democracy and in the early years of Athenian naval expansion and empire. It was probably an expression of polis confidence and patriotic unity and a deliberate replacement of individual aristocratic ostentation. Thus, the Athenian demos is glorified in noble terms as if it were an aristocratic family. Indeed, the ideals and beliefs render much of Athens' history irrelevant, encourage a kind of anonymous democratic history, and concentrate heavily on the legendary origins of Athens. So we see here how oral tradition is in part formed by such ideals. They help explain many of the features of Athenian oral traditions elsewhere.

Let us first return, however, to the wider polis traditions, the nature of their transmission and their extreme fluidity.

4.1 Polis tradition and the assembly

The very term 'polis tradition' is a vague one, but it expresses a vague and diffuse concept. Are we talking about popular tradition, official tradition, democratic polis tradition, or simply what everyone knows? How, for instance, were the polis traditions about the fall of the tyranny actually transmitted?

It is increasingly recognized how complex such general traditions in any society must be.[1] There is no single line of transmission: that is very rare even with esoteric traditions. One must rather think of many different informants passing on information simultaneously. People will have varying degrees and varying areas of knowledge. Different 'informants' may be able to add different, sometimes contradictory elements to the same body of tradition. Vansina has recently argued that there is a corpus or common pool of information. Out of that, different members of the society know different things, and though individuals will have varying knowledge, even variant versions, their testimony will be backed up by the 'collective memory' of the group which is most responsible for knowing the tradition.[2] The concept of a 'collective memory' is a difficult one. For it implies some homogeneous, unified memory or a severely functional corpus of tradition. Moreover it oversimplifies the intricate

---

[1] Most recently, Vansina, *OTH* 148ff.   [2] *OTH* 152–4.

multiplicity of traditions. The processes of memory also complicate the picture. Individuals' memories are reinforced by other people's reminiscences, memories of any group they belong to, and wider traditions.[3] Some traditions last longer than others, some will be referred to only in certain contexts, others will be more widely known. Clearly the web of transmission, diffusion and knowledge must be immensely complex. We cannot easily separate and identify the general traditions of a community by a well-delineated type or area of transmission as one may with certain other oral traditions.

This is true in the case of classical Athens whose polis traditions were particularly diffuse. However, did Athens have any official tradition? And if it had any, who transmitted it and how carefully? Anthropological studies treat official traditions extensively. Oral tradition has even been divided up sharply between official and private tradition.[4] Kings, dynasties, official dynastic 'historians' and special mnemonic aids enable us to pin-point official tradition definitely. But ancient Greece is notable for its lack of official 'remembrancers',[5] and the continuous institution of kingship was hardly common in the archaic and classical city-state.[6] The types of traditions found in a society are linked extremely closely to its institutions or social structure.[7] What would constitute official tradition – or official transmission – in the Athenian democracy? Its magistrates and politicians changed rapidly, and it had no official institution for preserving tradition.

The organs of the democracy – the assembly, council and lawcourts – are the nearest one finds to institutions which could propagate official tradition and democratic history. The orators included in their speeches to the assembly allusions to the Athenian past which seem to constitute patriotic polis tradition.[8] The end of the Peisistratid tyranny, the Persian Wars, the greatness of the Athenian empire, and the fall of the Thirty were favourite topics. They amount in some sense to the official (democratic) version of Athenian history. Other types of example they used had an obvious democratic function. One common example con-

---

[3] Halbwachs (1980), Baddeley (1976), Lieury (1975), and introduction to this book.

[4] E.g. Vansina, *OTH* 98ff.

[5] Murray (1987); Simondon (1982), appendix. The *mnēmones* we hear of seem to be responsible for judicial decisions rather than the past. Their role can be exaggerated: e.g. Evans ((1982), 148ff.) thinks Herodotus found specialist keepers of tradition, *mnēmones*, in various cities.

[6] Cf. the coherence of tradition apparently attached to the dynasty at Cyrene, described reign by reign by Herodotus, above, Ch. 3, n. 48.

[7] Vansina, *OTH* 114. This would suggest that in a period of aristocratic faction, as in sixth-century Athens and much of Greece, there would be no official tradition at all.

[8] Democratic and patriotic characteristics vary in emphasis and overlap: see below, p. 234, for the difficulty in assuming that official tradition was necessarily overtly democratic.

cerned the punishment of some famous politician: despite his services to
the city he was not let off and his misdemeanour was punished heavily.
The type is so common that it forms a rhetorical topos.[9] It reminded the
demos of its ultimate authority and was particularly apt in a political
system where such service was actually expected to benefit those who
gave it (Ch. 2.2). This is democratic polis tradition: its character was
encouraged, partly because it was expressed before the demos and partly
because it was tied to the democratic institutions.

Much knowledge of Athens' past was transmitted through the
repeated references of orators in the assembly. But the references are
scattered and depend on the various orators, on the needs of rhetoric and
persuasion. There was no fixed method of transmitting this kind of
tradition, no fixed body of officials to do so. This is obvious but needs
stressing. When we look closely at the body of traditions about the
ending of the tyranny (Ch. 5), it becomes clear how misleading it is to
talk simply of 'official traditions' without qualification. Democratic
tradition, though particularly tied to democratic institutions, was
dependent for its most energetic propounders on a fluid, ever changing
group of politicians and the sheer force of convention and context for
continuity between them.

But the democratic polis traditions of the assembly went side by side
with any other gossip, rumour, anecdote or historical example that
orators also chose to use. For example, stories about certain families'
wealth were clearly common knowledge, widely disseminated through
the assembly and through gossip and rumour (Ch. 2.2, p. 109). The
orators were fond of stressing the type of tradition that 'everyone knows'
(see below, n. 14). There are hints of stories attached to a building, a
monument or a name – not necessarily with much historical accuracy.[10]
Traditions without particular democratic tenor but widely known by the
demos might be better described as 'popular tradition': popular tradition
was also transmitted through the assembly and obviously overlapped
considerably with the democratic polis traditions. And what about those
interesting popular memories of the past which contradicted the democratic polis traditions – such as the popular tradition of a 'Golden Age'

---

[9] Said of numerous men: [And.] IV 33 and Dem. XXIII 205 of Cimon; Dem. XXIII 205
of Themistocles; Plato, *Gorg.* 516d (and cf. [Dem.] XXV 6) of Miltiades; Dem. XIX
273 of Callias; Dem. XIX 280 adds Epicrates, Thrasyboulos and a descendant of
Harmodius.

[10] E.g. Aeschin. I 182, the house named after the horse and the girl. It is not clear that
monuments necessarily reinforce accurate memory: cf. the statues of Harmodius and
Aristogeiton and the complex traditions which still continued despite them, Ch. 5, or
the monuments connected with Cimon's victories, p. 203 below. Monuments can
actually encourage the invention of tradition, which then seems to be confirmed by the
existence of the monument, p. 176, n. 48.

under the tyrant Peisistratos, which is occasionally hinted at?[11] Some
of these popular traditions were to be heard in the assembly alongside
the patriotic references to Marathon and the end of the tyranny – for
instance popular gossip about people's wealth. Far from being
esoteric, both kinds of tradition were 'what everyone knew', hardly
confined to a particular institution or family. Again, the web of
knowledge and diffusion for such general traditions was extremely
intricate.

In contrast to this fluidity of transmission, the epitaphios, the great
funeral oration over the war dead which was peculiar to Athens, had
much stricter transmission. The Athenians brought back the bones of
their dead for state burial in the Kerameikos.[12] They were buried in great
ceremony there in the presence of citizens, women and aliens. An orator
chosen by the state gave an oration in their honour, praising them and
glorifying Athens. The epitaphios was exceedingly conventional in form
and content, in its praise and its review of Athenian history. It was more
coherent by its very form than the isolated historical traditions used
elsewhere by oratory, and the 'transmission' of its conventional contents
was frequent. So it comes closest in Athens to what one might term an
expression of 'official tradition'. It still had no official guardian, no set
text, no set form except in its use of the conventions of the genre.
Individual orators could select, omit and add details to introduce a
semblance of originality. But the underlying principles and ideals
remained constant: the epitaphios forms a coherent expression of
Athenian official 'ideology'. The same beliefs, ideals, justifications and
examples from Athenian history recur elsewhere in much classical
Athenian literature, particularly tragedy.[13] And it is the ideals which
determine the overall pattern of history celebrated. The occasion was in
a sense a great funeral celebration in the aristocratic mould, but for the
Athenian people.

What was the role, then, of oratory and the democratic institutions in
forming oral tradition? Orators' allusions had to be familiar to persuade
the demos the more easily. So they must largely represent the image of
Athenian history that was generally accepted and known. At the same
time, the orators continued to transmit the tradition, no doubt altering
them gradually as they were passed on. The assumption of oral tradition

---

[11] Arist. *Ath.Pol.* 16.7; [Plato], *Hipparchus* 229b.
[12] Other Greek states seem to have buried their dead where they died: cf. Thuc. II 34.
Pritchett (1985) collects the evidence.
[13] See esp. Strasburger (1958) for recurrent pattern of political ideas and justification;
Schroeder (1914); Loraux (1981a); Kierdorf (1966). For the themes in tragedy, cf.
Aeschylus, *Eleusinioi* (Schmid (1933), 258); Sophocles, *Triptolemos* (Schmid (1933),
313f.); Euripides' *Heraklids*, *Erechtheus*, *Herakles*, *Suppliants*.

and oral transmission is ubiquitous in oratory: people knew about the past from oral tradition 'from their elders'.[14] In extant oratory there is no hint that someone would – or should – know of the past from books. Much was transmitted through the assembly and its continual reiteration of certain themes, the achievements in the Persian Wars, the empire and the end of the oligarchy. Though some knowledge was passed on through the theatre and tragedy,[15] it mostly concerned the Athenian legends rather than the 'historical' period. There are hints of a body of information which was apparently well known through the assembly alone.[16] We must remember that history was not taught in its own right. If transmission was affected by rhetorical needs and by the patriotic desire for admirable *exempla*, then the oral traditions were selected and transformed in that direction, like any other oral traditions.

Much attention has been devoted to these historical allusions in terms of rhetorical style and *topoi* alone.[17] Obviously they have a wider historical significance and represent the kind of historical knowledge expected of the audience, the demos.[18] But we cannot absolve the orators from the ignorance displayed, assuming that they, being more educated, would have a better knowledge of history. We have seen numerous examples of the 'inaccuracy' of oral tradition, including Andocides' own version of Athens' past (Ch. 2.2). There is simply little reason to think that orators deliberately and consciously distanced themselves from the 'Thucydidean' version of their history, as it were,

---

[14] From many references, sometimes contrasting younger citizens with older, [Dem.] LVIII 62; Dem. XX 52 (modestly!); Dem. XX 77; Isoc. XVI 4; Dem. XVIII 50; Din. I 25; Ant. *Herod.* 69. Isoc. *Panath.* 149 imagines an objection to his remarks about the ancestral constitution being handed down from Theseus – that Isocrates was not there at the time. His answer is that more truth is gained through *akoē* ('hearing', 'oral tradition') than *opsis* ('seeing'). The stories of Demeter (*Paneg.* 30) and of the Amazons and Thracians (*Paneg.* 69) are true, he says, because they are old and they have often been told and heard. Assumption of common knowledge ('everyone knows') for recent events: [Dem.] LVIII 28; [Dem.] XL 11; Dem. XXI 78; Is. XI 48. Less recent: Cleophon, Lys. XIX 48; Themistocles' fortification of Athens, Dem. XX 73; Glauketes, the first to desert to Decelea, Dem. XXIV 128; Miltiades, general at Marathon, Aeschin. III 186; Tyrtaeus, sent as general by Athens to Sparta, Lyc. I 106; treatment of Callias, Dem. XIX 273; Aeschin. I 25, on Solon's statue, reminds us that it could be a persuasive rhetorical topos. There seem to be fewer notorious examples or stories drawn from the more recent fourth century: those from the fifth are more anecdotal, moralizing and 'exemplary'.

[15] Isoc. *Panath.* 168, referring to the fortunes of Adrastus in the theatre. Later, Pausanias (I 3.3) criticized people's false belief in whatever they have heard in choruses and tragedies, esp. the common view that Theseus established the democracy.

[16] P. 84; note especially the Theban decree, 'so often read out to you', Din. I 25.

[17] Jost (1936); Schmitz-Kahlman (1939); most recently, Nouhaud (1982) is more imaginative, but it still has a highly rhetorical slant and strange misunderstandings.

[18] Pearson (1941); Crosby (1936) gives a brief run-through of Athenian ignorance about their past.

and descended to an alien level of historical ignorance purely for the gratification of their audience – as we would otherwise have to suppose. There is hardly any sign that orators used an historian for historical knowledge, and their knowledge is so vague and inaccurate that they did not need to.[19] When orators object to the use of an historical example, they do so on completely ahistorical grounds, betraying a striking lack of historical sense.[20] The vision of Athenian history presented in oratory must express what orators and demos know.

On the other hand, orators' use of history shows the ideas, attitudes and opinions of fourth-century Athenians on the past.[21] In fact, the two strands combine in the single phenomenon of oral tradition. Attitudes or ideas about the past alter the actual image held of it. The historical allusions of oratory help to form, and in turn transmit, traditions which belong as much to the orators' picture of the past as to that of their audience. Changes are all the easier because the traditions are oral.

The picture of Athenian history that emerges from these allusions is extraordinary. As well as indicating oral tradition, its character is crucial for our understanding of the role of oratory in its transmission. The overall simplicity and omissions are astonishing and easily overlooked when couched in rhetorical prose. The picture of the Athenian empire is patriotic, nostalgic and exceedingly simple.[22] Very few of the great

[19] There are only two clear examples where an orator uses a passage from an historian: Lys. II 48ff., discussed below, and Dem. LIX 94ff. on Plateia which, interestingly, is taken not from narrative but from a speech in Thuc. III 53ff. Orators use Thucydides only when he suits their purpose (Strasburger (1958), 24, n. 5). Other attempts to trace the influence of historiography rely on scanty and unconvincing 'echoes', e.g. Bodin (1932); cf. Nouhaud (1982) who, however, omits both the striking examples above. Aeschin. II 172 went to Andocides for a résumé of fifth-century history. Isocrates seems better read, but his originality lay in his use of well-known aspects of the past in unexpected ways, and he contradicts himself when necessary: Baynes (1955) stresses his sophistic background.

[20] The only extant example where an orator queries an opponent's *historical* arguments is Demosthenes' attack on Aeschines' use of the statue of Solon at Salamis (XIX 251, Aeschin. I 25); he is more at home when attacking Aeschines' use of poetry: XIX 25 and Perlman (1964). Lyc. I 68 corrects his opponent's use of the ancestors' retreat to Salamis, but he corrects interpretation, not fact, and that rather naively. Isocrates imagines an objection to his remarks about Theseus (see Ch. 4, n. 14): simply that Isocrates was not there, so could not know; the defeats of Amazons and Thracians were very great because the *logoi* have lasted so long (*Paneg.* 59). Lyc. I 68 imagines an objection to his citation of the Trojan Wars and Athenian tyranny: merely that they were not the deeds of one man alone. In fact, the orators' history is very similar to some of the Atthis in its patriotic bias, both apparently 'respecting' the ignorance and prejudice of the audience. (Pearson (1941) uneasily realizes the parallel but avoids the implications.)

[21] Perlman (1961), though I disagree with details of interpretation: he overstresses the extent to which examples are changed for precise political argument.

[22] The length of hegemony was often cited: Dem. IX 23; And. III 38; Isoc. *Paneg.* 103ff.; Lys. II 55; cf. Dem. *Ol.* III 25. Atrocities are cited by Isocrates in special arguments

generals of the Pentekontaëtia (the fifty-year period after the Persian Wars) or the Peloponnesian War are noted.[23] There is a tendency for defeats to be remembered as victories (see below). There is much confusion and ignorance over some of the most important and most memorable episodes of the Pentekontaëtia,[24] even about certain outstanding politicians of the fifth century. Callias was remembered primarily for his wealth (p. 109) rather than his politics – despite the Peace of Callias. In fact, he makes a good moral example of punishment by the demos (Dem. xix 273: see above, n. 9). Ephialtes seems almost to have disappeared: though largely responsible for introducing the radical democracy, he is mentioned only once and that is for the mystery surrounding his murder, cited comparatively early by Antiphon.[25] Perhaps more significant, he is very far from being an important democratic hero.[26]

Cimon, too, has almost disappeared. He is an apt illustration of the

against empire: *Paneg.* 100, *Panath.* 63, and disasters, *Peace* 86. The general picture is most vivid in Andocides: And. i 130 and see Ch. 2.1, p. 119 on And. iii 3ff.; the reduction of Samos is simply remembered as expensive: Isoc. *Antid.* 111. Lyc. i 72f. sums up the period we call the Pentekontaëtia as a catalogue of successes against the Persians culminating in the Peace of Callias. Dem. xxiii 13 could argue simply that Athens' prosperity coincided with the time when it had the most triremes, so it must build more. For Lycurgus (*ibid.*) and Din. i 37, the period is a vague and glorious part of history; it generally brought prosperity (Lys. ii 56) and silver to the Acropolis (e.g. Dem. *Ol.* iii 24). Detailed knowledge of the administration of empire is extremely sparse: Isoc. *Panath.* 63 mentions opponents' criticism. The Hellenotamiae officials are only referred to by Ant. *Herod.* 69 and And. iii 38, both early.

23 Xanthippos and Leocrates (Thuc. i 105.2) do not occur in extant oratory. Myronides occurs once, but in Lys. ii, a passage based on Thucydides (below, p. 227): yet he was remembered as a great figure in comedy, Ar. *Lys.* 801ff., *Eccles.* 303 (early fourth century), where his time is regarded as a better one (also Eupolis, *Demoi*; cf. Plut. *Per.* 16.3 and Diod. xi 82.4). Aeschines mentioned an exploit of Tolmides with great admiration (ii 75): apparently a garbled memory and amalgamation of stories preserved by Thuc. i 108.5, 113.1 (Koroneia) and Diod. xi 84, and perhaps avoiding having to mention the defeat at Koroneia.

24 See Ch. 4, n. 2, above; and the bland use of imperial acquisitions by Lycurgus (fr. 58 Blass): Pericles, 'who took Samos, Euboia and Aigina, who built the Propylaia . . .'. Campaigns in the eastern Mediterranean are barely mentioned: Isoc. *Peace* 86 lists disasters for his particular argument. Cf. Lyc. i 72f., a catalogue of successes against the Persians which includes the only extant mention of Eurymedon. There is considerable confusion here, explained by Meyer (1899), 9ff.: the epigram given by Diod. xi 62.3 actually belonged to the later battle in Cyprus, *c.* 449, but was taken by Ephorus and Lycurgus to refer to the double battle at Eurymedon and a description derived from it.

25 Ant. *Herod.* 68: Ephialtes is called 'your fellow citizen' (τὸν ὑμέτερον πολίτην) (cf. Arist. *Ath.Pol.* 25.4, by which time the murderer is named, Plut. *Per.* 10).

26 Or even a scapegoat. Isocrates' criticisms of the reform of the Areopagus (*Areop.* 50) sedulously avoid names; cf. his diatribes against *poneroi*, lit. 'those who toil' (*Peace* 79), or the 'licence' (*akolasia*) (*Peace* 77 and 126–8), which he hints was present before Pericles. But it is all infuriatingly vague. I doubt if we can assume enough historical knowledge on his part to paraphrase in our terms (as Perlman (1961), 156).

problem, especially compared to the earlier tradition of his family, the Philaids (Ch. 3.1). Allusions to him are muddled, and it is clear that he was sometimes even confused with his father Miltiades, even though Miltiades was the great general of the Persian Wars, and Cimon was prominent just afterwards in the early expansion of empire. One cannot necessarily blame this entirely on a supposed 'democratic tradition',[27] simply because there is confusion as well as omission. How could the aristocrat Andocides recollect in the late 390s that Athens recalled 'Cimon's son Miltiades, who was ostracized and living in the Chersonese, to negotiate the Fifty Years Peace, as he was *proxenos* of the Spartans' (III 3)?[28] Later in the mid-fourth century it is said (Dem. XXIII 205) that Cimon narrowly escaped with his life and was fined fifty talents for trying to change the 'ancestral constitution' (*patrios politeia*) – presumably some kind of allusion to the reforms of Ephialtes in the 460s. This seems to have amalgamated Cimon's trial with his ostracism.[29] But it is also similar to the trial of his father Miltiades after Miltiades' Parian expedition. The expedition had been a fiasco, it led to Miltiades' trial and he was fined 50 talents, which his son had to pay (Hdt. VI 136).[30] There are many stories in the literary tradition about how Cimon managed to pay this fine, but Demosthenes' comment is the only evidence for Cimon's own fine. The tradition in Demosthenes has simply amalgamated Miltiades' trial, conviction and fine with Cimon's ostracism. Andocides inverted Cimon and Miltiades for both embassy and ostracism (above), and Pseudo-Andocides IV paired them together.[31] We are seeing an

---

[27] Fuks (1953), 28, n. 37; Perlman (1961) and Nouhaud (1982) blame the 'disappearance' on the anti-democratic bias of a speaker. Cf. Connor (1968), 126, who attributes the disappearance of minor figures generally to the literary tradition.

[28] Apparently referring to the five years of truce of Thuc. I 112 before the great second expedition to Cyprus led by Cimon (Meiggs (1972), 111 and endnote 9 for evidence of Cimon's recall, incl. Theopompus, *FGH* 115 F88). [And.] IV 33 believes Cimon to have been ostracized for his relations with his sister, though he and his father were Olympic victors: this is surely popular tradition (*pace* Perlman). The scandal was said to be initiated by Eupolis, *Poleis* (Schol. Aristeides III 515 Dind., Plut. *Cim.* XV 3). There is also confusion with the sixth-century Cimon, an Olympic victor, who was buried with his horses (Hdt. VI 103; cf. Plut. *Cim.* 19.4.).

[29] According to Plutarch he was prosecuted on his return from Thasos (*Cim.* 14.3–5). Later, after Ephialtes' reforms, he was ostracized, accused of Spartan sympathies and of irregular relations with his sister (*Cim.* 15). He was probably acquitted in his trial: Demosthenes is the only evidence for actual conviction.

[30] Confusion with Miltiades' trial noted by Meyer (1899), 25. Cf. the variant but absurd reading in Dem. XXIII 205, of Παρίων for πάτριον. Plato *Gorg.* 516d also has a (presumably) popular tradition that Miltiades was thrown into a pit but was saved by the prytanis. Meyer discusses later variations. Cf. Dem. XIX 273: Callias (II) was nearly executed and fined 50 talents for taking bribes.

[31] Dem. XXIII implies that Cimon did succeed in overthrowing the 'ancestral constitution' (ὅτι τὴν πάτριον μετεκίνησε πολιτείαν) which here seems to mean the democracy.

extraordinary fusion of Cimon with Miltiades, two individuals whom one might expect to be remembered in their own right. Some of Cimon's achievements were remembered. Aeschines cited the Eion victory from the Hermae epigrams (III 186) and Athenians gloried in the ravaging of the Asian coast which occurred after the Persian defeat of 479.[32] But Cimon is not associated with these exploits by name, and Aeschines does not seem to know the name of the general so modestly omitted from the epigrams.[33]

Perhaps Cimon's ambiguous position contributed to his eclipse. But he was instrumental in the early expansion of the Athenian empire, and he brought back the bones of Athens' hero Theseus.[34] Moreover, the most unsuitable elements of Athens' past could be used for exempla and the modern apportioning of 'biases' does not always reflect the way such examples are used.[35] We must look beyond to the character and processes of oral tradition. Two factors are crucial. First, the confusion with Miltiades: Cimon was closely associated with his father, and his position may originally have depended a great deal on Miltiades' achievement. The Painted Stoa singled out Miltiades, and the statues sent to Delphi in the 450s celebrated Miltiades (who was set apart with the gods), Theseus and probably Philaios, founder of the clan to which Miltiades and Cimon belonged.[36] Held in such reverence, Miltiades perhaps engulfed his son, just as a 'culture hero' attracts achievements originally associated with someone else. Secondly, the official democratic tradition tends to celebrate the demos rather than the achievements of individual generals (Ch. 4.2 below). This would also blur Cimon's role in the exploits of the Pentekontaëtia which were remembered as those of the demos as a whole. I can only leave these as suggestions for a notably surprising gap in the polis traditions which contrast aptly with the Philaid family tradition.

Most of the assembly's 'history' is exceedingly simple and sparse,

---

Perhaps this further confusion was encouraged by the events of the late fifth century when the democracy was overthrown (cf. Ch. 5.2 for similar effect on other traditions).

[32] Lyc. I 72f. (see Ch. 4, n. 24), Ar. *Wasps* 1092, but there is more emphasis on the permanent – as opposed to temporary – gains of empire.

[33] Epigrams also mentioned, Dem. xx 112. Yet in Ar. *Lys.* 1143ff. (411 B.C.), Cimon is said to have saved Sparta. His use of his wealth is mentioned by Gorgias (Plut. *Cim.* x 5) and by a character in Cratinus' *Archilochi* (*Cim.* x 4) who wishes he had dined with Cimon before he died (cf. Arist. *Ath.Pol.* 27.2–3); for his judgement in the theatre, *Cim.* VII 7–8, and Ch. 4, n. 34 for Theseus' bones. For more general treatment of literary traditions, see Meyer (1899), 1ff.; Connor (1963); Barns (1954).

[34] Apparently popular for this, Plut. *Cim.* VIII. For Cimon's association with Theseus and use of the legend, Connor (1970), 143–74.

[35] E.g. Athens' help to Sparta against the Messenians, quoted by Ar. *Lys.* 1143f. and useful in diplomacy, was remembered amidst hostility to Sparta, precisely because Athens and Sparta were at war.

[36] Paus. x 10.1: the name is corrupt. See Connor (1970), 143ff.

peopled by few individuals and generally self-congratulatory. It is supplemented by certain more detailed anecdotes and much financial gossip (p. 109). References to more recent events (say, ten or twenty years earlier) have a different calibre to those for the exemplary past. In the late fifth century, Antiphon could use a precise example of miscarriage of justice in the administration of the empire which one cannot imagine in a later fourth-century speech (*Herod.* 69). By the later period, the empire belonged to the glorious past. A small core of historical 'facts' was enough to provide the basis for vastly differing arguments.[37] Historical detail and complicated historical arguments based on differing information were not necessary for rhetorical arguments of widely differing aims. Clearly the Athenians and their orators were content with a very narrow range of their city's past.

Let us return to the epitaphios. Like the rest of oratory, it represents more than rhetorical clichés. The same ideals, justifications and examples recur elsewhere and are more than mere propaganda. It seems that most Athenians believed in them passionately.[38] If we see the peculiarities of epitaphic history only in terms of propaganda,[39] we miss much of its significance for Athenian beliefs and attitudes – which themselves affected the image of the past. As Socrates said in the *Menexenus* (see p. 210 below), one feels proud and dignified after hearing a funeral speech. He also said that it was easy to praise Athenians amongst Athenians. Athenians wanted to hear and believe what they were told in the funeral oration, even if the resulting exaltation wore off eventually. The same expressions were still being offered at the other end of the epitaphic tradition by Aelius Aristides in the second century A.D.[40]

---

[37] Some actions which could be presented in criticism of Athens are simply quoted as admirable achievements: Lycurgus (fr. 58 Blass) boasts how Pericles took Samos, Euboia and Aigina. Democratic oratory likes examples where politicians are punished severely by the demos (above, Ch. 4, n. 9): yet Plato uses the same ones to show how fickle the demos is (*Gorg.* 516d). Isoc. *Paneg.* 154 actually argues thus: Themistocles defeated the Persians at Salamis, yet they thought him worthy of the greatest gifts; this proves that the Persians reward their opponents and not their friends, therefore Athens should oppose them. There seems no limit to which unsuitable 'facts' could be turned! Such flexibility in the use of the same core of 'facts' is important, since it is often assumed that different interpretations, arguments and biases will be reflected in use of different historical information.

[38] As Strasburger (1958).

[39] As implied by Loraux (1981a): things non-Athenian disliked (e.g. democracy) were omitted, partly to present Athens so that others would approve. The term 'propaganda' is misleading because it implies (i) systematic dissemination and (ii) that the disseminators know their propaganda to be untrue. In the context of oral transmission, both orators and audience had little means of distinguishing mere propaganda from Athenian history. They may have had no other point of reference.

[40] See Day (1980), esp. 175f. and introduction. He stresses continuity but does not clearly distinguish a living *rhetorical* tradition, partly nourished by literary sources, and a

The 'ancestral custom' of public burial – the *patrios nomos* – itself began even earlier than the speech, as Thucydides believed (II 34.1)[41] and the evidence of Pausanias confirms (I 29.7).[42] Attributed in antiquity to Theseus or Solon,[43] it can best be assigned to the Cleisthenic democracy, perhaps a little before the Persian Wars. It is very probable that the public burial was a direct replacement of the aristocratic family burials that Cleisthenes may have tried to curb.[44]

The epitaphios probably originated just after the end of the Persian Wars, an expression of polis confidence and cohesion after the victory against the Persians and in the early days of Athenian expansion and power. Diodorus (XI 33.3) placed it straight after the Persian Wars, Dionysius of Halicarnassus either after the battles of Artemisium, Salamis and Plateia or after Marathon (V 17.4). Its most conventional elements confirm the close connection with the Persian Wars. For the ancestral achievements in the epitaphios included five main topics, four from the legendary period: Athens' defeat of the Amazons, its expulsion of the Thracian Eumolpus from Attica, its expulsion of Eurystheus which saved the Heraklids, and its acceptance of the Argives' request to bury their dead after the attack of the 'Seven' against Thebes. The fifth great topic was Athens' contribution to the Persian Wars. Since this list of achievements always recurs, we can look at its examples for indications of the period at which their formalization would have been most appropriate, as Kierdorf (1966, 93ff.) has done.

The Amazon invasion, repelled by Athens alone, was an obvious legendary parallel to the battle of Marathon. Both were later portrayed

genuinely popular tradition. The continuing popularity of the epitaphic version of history implies that most people by then thought it was historically true.

[41] If speech and burial began at different times, some confusion is resolved: e.g. Ziolkowski (1981), 13ff.; Bradeen (1969).

[42] This disposes of Jacoby's arguments (1949) for origin in 465 (after Drabeskos), using one phrase from Pausanias. But Pausanias also cites the earlier monument from the Aiginetan Wars (I 29.7). See Gomme, *HCT, ad loc.*; Bradeen (1969), app. I, 154ff., and (1964), 57f. and n. 105, on intrusions of later casualty lists amongst the fifth-century ones.

[43] Dionysius of Halicarnassus, V 17.4: the custom established by Theseus, the epitaphios during the Persian Wars.

[44] Stupperich (1977), 220ff.: perhaps first for the citizens who fell in 506 in defence of the new constitution. The epitaphios must rest on familiar elements. For possible predecessors in the grave elegy, Aly (1929), 35f.; Stupperich (1977), 225. Erection of the casualty list should not be underestimated as part of the ceremony, though Thucydides omits it. But it may have grown up quite late (Gomme, *HCT* II p. 97, n. 3), perhaps after Eurymedon or in 465. Perhaps so few fragments have survived from earlier monuments (cf. Clairmont (1983)) because there were none. See Bradeen (1967), 324f. for fragments possibly pre-464. Bradeen (1969), 155, believes the inscribed lists could not begin later than the speech. But I doubt if this is true in a society where written record was not used for all the purposes we would expect. We cannot read back the custom indefinitely, assuming numerous earlier lists have been lost.

in the Stoa Poikile (*Paus.* I 15). The defeat of the Thracians offered a similar analogy. In the other two episodes Athens receives suppliants. Already in 467, in Aeschylus' *Eleusinioi*, we find Adrastus' request and the burial of the dead at Eleusis. In both legends Athens' role is essentially a combination of champion (*prostatēs*) and leader (*hegemon*). This may point to Athens' acceptance of the hegemony of allies partly prompted by the hubris of Pausanias. These legendary examples are particularly suited to the justification of Athens' role as *hegemon* (which partly led to the Athenian empire), both by its outstanding contribution to the Persian Wars and by its 'ancestral' role as champion.[45] This suggests an origin in the early years of the Athenian hegemony after the Persian Wars.[46] That was the point, in other words, at which Athens acquired a formal occasion to celebrate official polis tradition and patriotism.

When we turn to the character of the epitaphios, its form and conventions are very strange to our eyes, stilted and highly artificial, as well as excruciatingly smug and congratulatory. The best known is the Periclean funeral speech in Thucydides, but it is uncharacteristic and by far the most approachable for the modern reader. It will help to outline the main elements of the epitaphios in general and of the examples we have. For we shall be dealing with a complex combination of conventions and a parody of those conventions. Different orators bring out different tendencies of the official tradition. (References from now on will be to the epitaphioi of each orator unless otherwise indicated.)

The epitaphios' general tenor and conception, which determine the form of commemoration, were established within a few years of its origin, well before our first extant examples;[47] the themes are already dismissed as very well known in Thucydides (I 73.2; II 36.4).[48] After the proemium (introduction) there is the section of praise (*epainos*). This started with the ancestry of the deceased, that is, the deeds of the Athenian ancestors (labelled the *genos* by later rhetorical theory). Here Athens' past was treated, the legendary period, the Persian Wars and possibly its later achievements down to the present day; also the praise of

---

[45] As Kierdorf (1966), 93f. Less reliable are abstract criteria like the degree of imperial or democratic emphasis used by Loraux (who accordingly dates the origin to the time of Ephialtes). It is notoriously difficult to date anything in the Pentekontaëtia by the degree of 'imperialism' implied.

[46] Closer dating is impossible: Kierdorf supposed 478; Hauvette (1898) a connection with the return of Theseus' bones, Aeschylus' *Eleusinians* and Cimon; cf. Landmann (1974), Clairmont (1983).

[47] Ziolkowski (1981) treats the most conventional elements of praise; see also Clavaud (1980).

[48] See Strasburger (1958).

the deceased and of their fatherland, often indistinguishable from that of their ancestors.[49] This might include treatment of the constitution (*politeia*) and upbringing (*paideia*) of the deceased; but both, in fact, are treated as equally applicable to the ancestors. Then, there followed the consolation, encouraging emulation of the dead. Finally the epilogue. Within these conventions some variation and innovation were possible. The repetitious topoi of praise that recur in the preserved examples have often seemed uncharacteristic of the authors they are ascribed to (except Hypereides'). But the demands of the genre explain this. Each example, however, has some departure from the epitaphic conventions, preserving some originality within the much repeated topoi.

We do not know much of Pericles' Samian oration,[50] nor of Gorgias' epitaphios (*c.* 420), which apparently praised Athens' victories over the Medes but declared that victories over Greeks called for dirges.[51] The Periclean epitaphios in Thucydides (II 35ff.) is the best known of the genre, but it is not actually typical. Hardly a direct and accurate representation of what was said at the time,[52] it is crucial to Thucydides' own analysis of Periclean Athens and the changes it undergoes during the war.[53] But it is still a literary representation of a funeral speech, and it includes many of the conventions.[54] The most interesting departure from convention is the deliberate omission of Athens' past achievements. Pericles glances at the ancestors, their freedom and autochthony (36.1); but he declares that in fact 'our fathers' are more worthy of praise than the ancestors: for they added to the empire and passed it on (36.2), and, what is more, most of it has been increased by the present generation itself. So he leaves out ancestral achievement and discusses instead how Athens became great and by what efforts (*epitēdeusis*), constitution (*politeia*) and character (*tropoi*) the Athenians achieved their power

---

[49] Termed *praxis* later, but misleadingly, as the epitaphios praised only their glory in war. Cf. Ziolkowski (1981), esp. ch. 3, on later rhetorical theorists, whose scheme for the funeral oration differs greatly from the classical one.

[50] Arist. *Rhet.* I 7.34, III 10.7, III 4.3.

[51] Fr. 5b; other fragments can be found in Diels *Vorsokr.* (6th edn.), F5a–6; Cf. Kennedy (1963), 156; Vollgraff (1952). For dating, Vollgraff (1952), 16; Blass (1887), I 66. As a foreigner, he could not have delivered it himself.

[52] As with other speeches, it is enough to examine correspondences not only between pairs of consecutive speeches but across books, which play a special part in presenting Thucydides' analysis of Athenian power (see, e.g., Macleod (1983)).

[53] Most recently, Landmann (1974), largely against Flashar (1969): combining the epitaphios with III 82 on the deterioration of *gnomai* ('judgement') in war, Flashar sees the epitaphios as the ideal of Athens before the war and how Athens reached its power, but the ideal was not quite reached and fell away rapidly once the war began. Cf. also Diller (1962).

[54] Ziolkowski (1981).

(36.4). This is a bold reversal of the usual exaggerated reverence for the ancestors.[55]

Lysias' epitaphios (II) from the Corinthian War (394–387)[56] is remarkable for its lengthy section surveying fifth-century history. It includes one of the two passages in oratory where verbal similarity is close enough for us to be sure that the material was taken from an historian, here Thucydides. So we see very clearly how unscrupulously an epitaphios deals with an historian's account. Demosthenes' epitaphios (LX)[57] was delivered over the dead of Chaeronea (338 B.C.). The allusions to Athenian history are peculiarly vague, and its original feature is its enumeration of the eponymous heroes of the Athenian tribes who each provide some special reason for their tribe members to show bravery. In Hypereides' speech over the dead of the Lamian War (323), the conventions of praise are tediously well represented. But he deliberately leaves aside the deeds of Athens in the past (§§4–6) and concentrates on the general Leosthenes and the campaign in which the men died. Similarly, his attempt to outline the campaign may be explained by the special character of the Lamian War, seen as Athens' last struggle for freedom.[58]

Plato's funeral oration in the *Menexenus* needs more discussion. It was supposedly delivered by Pericles' mistress Aspasia shortly after the King's Peace (386 B.C.) and recited by Socrates to Menexenus after a conversation about epitaphioi in general. Ancient criticism concentrated on the funeral speech itself; regarded as the epitaphios par excellence, it was recited yearly in Athens during the Hellenistic period (incidentally proving Socrates' initial points about the genre).[59] In the dialogue, Menexenus also took it as a straightforward epitaphios. But there are clear signs that Socrates or Plato meant it as a parody. No interpretation can be valid if it ignores the introductory conversation between Socrates and Menexenus about funeral orations.[60] Here Socrates' views about the falsity of the genre are made clear, so we are alerted immediately to the possibility of irony and satire. The following epitaphios may be plausibly interpreted only as a satirical parody of the

---

55 Strasburger ((1958), 24) stresses its unique subject-matter; it ignores Athens' service to the rest of Greece, in favour of Athens' own internal circumstances, the freedom and quality of life the Athenians provide (only) for themselves. Contrast the Athenians at Thuc. I 73, rather tired of bringing up the Persian Wars continually; in the Melian dialogue (Thuc. v 89), the past and justice are dismissed alike by the Athenians as irrelevant. Cf. Hdt. IX 27.4, questioning the relevance of past exploits.

56 Now usually accepted as Lysias' own work: Walz (1936), Dover (1968), 54ff. and 61ff. (against Blass (1887–98), Jebb (1893), and Pohlenz (1948)).

57 Proved genuine by Sykutris (1928); Clavaud (1980) and others. The absence of the usual Demosthenic spirit is explained by the genre.

58 Colin (1938); Hess (1938).   59 Cic. *Orat.* 151, apparently at the Epitaphia festival.

60 As does Kahn (1963), 226, 'an almost Demosthenic appeal' for patriotism.

funeral oration as a genre.[61] For instance, in the opening conversation
Socrates points out (234c) how death in battle is a glorious thing: even if
you are poor and worthless you get a splendid funeral, with praise by a
wise man who has long since prepared his speech – praise both for what
you have and have not done. This cuts through the extravagant praise of
the excellence (aretē) of the deceased and the pretence that the orator
has written his speech for those specific circumstances: praise is transfer-
able. Socrates points out (235a) how he is always enchanted when he
hears the orator's words; he thinks he is a greater and better man than
before, and foreigners treat him with more respect. The feeling of
solemnity (semnotēs) lasts over three days. Only then does he remember
that he does not live in the Islands of the Blest: so clever are the orators.
He points out twice how easy it is to praise Athenians amongst Athenians
(235d, 236a). There follows the speech itself. This includes, amongst
others, the boast that Athens was (after 386) continuing its struggle for
freedom and 'had freed the king of Persia and expelled the Lacedaemonians from the sea' (246a),[62] the exact reversal of its crucial boast of
freeing Greece from the Persians. Plato unmasks the conventions and
pretences of the epitaphios and illustrates Socrates' earlier mocking
criticism of the genre.[63] This satire by its very exaggeration brings out
many characteristics or latent elements in the epitaphic tradition.

Yet, far from being merely empty rhetorical convention, the broad
epitaphic tradition of Athens' past recurs wherever defence, praise or
emulation of the ancestors was called for, and it gives the impression of
being an automatic and conventional response. So, in Herodotus'
account of the debate before Plateia (479 B.C.), obviously anachronistic,
the Athenians assert their superiority with the examples of the epitaphios
(IX 27): the legendary Athenian help to Adrastus and to the Heraklids,
its defeat of the Amazons. Somewhat vaguely the Athenians add their
participation in the Trojan War (27.4), but turn decisively from that to
the recent and therefore more important achievement of Marathon. A
Phliasian speaker in Xenophon (Hell. VI 5.38ff., esp. 46f.) tries to
persuade the Athenians to help the Spartans and Peloponnesians against

---

[61] See especially Wendland (1890); Henderson (1975); Méridier (1931); Löwenclau
(1961), Clavaud (1980).

[62] Cf. the horror expressed at their enemies in the Peloponnesian War who allied with the
Persian king (243a–b).

[63] See Henderson (1975), Clavaud (1980). It is a commonplace to say that one cannot do
justice to the deeds of the ancestors for lack of time and because of their very greatness:
but Plato says that their ancestors' deeds, especially those in the Persian Wars, have not
been worthily dealt with by the poets and still lie buried in oblivion (cf. Lys. II 1–2, Dem.
LX 9). Finally, Plato says absurdly (Menex. 246a) that the deeds which have been
omitted are both far more numerous and more glorious. This becomes meaningless,
especially after so detailed an account.

Thebes. He cites Athens' help to Adrastus and the Heraklids. These examples recur in a scene reported by Xenophon (*Mem.* III 5.8ff.). In a conversation with Socrates, Pericles wonders how to improve the standards of the sailors and, indeed, of all Athenians. Socrates suggests they be shown that virtue (*aretē*) belonged to their oldest ancestors. Pericles cites the judgement of the gods made by Kekrops; Socrates adds the birth of Erechtheus and the war he waged with Athens' neighbours, the war on behalf of the Heraklids and those in the time of Theseus (which must refer both to the Amazon and Theban episodes). If he likes, Socrates continues, Pericles may add their descendants who defeated all Asia (a hyperbolic reference to the battle of Marathon) and other victories with the Peloponnesians by land and sea (rest of Persian Wars). Finally, indigenous origin, autochthony, is added (5.12). By imitating these ancestral deeds they will recover *aretē*. Aristotle (*Rhet.* II 22.4–6) discusses the need to know the elements of the question in hand and asks rhetorically, how anyone could praise Athens if we did not know of the sea battle at Salamis or the battle of Marathon or what the Athenians did for the Heraklids – and so on. 'For men always base their praise on what are, or are thought to be, glorious deeds.'

These examples are strikingly similar in tenor, and they appear to be set responses. The examples of ancestral achievement concern the Amazons, the Heraklids, the Theban contempt of the Argive corpses and Athens' contribution to the Persian Wars. Autochthony is also essential. Athens' part in the Trojan War is a poor and rather weak addition. Perhaps it was much used before the Persian Wars but became redundant after they provided a more telling example. The function varies – from persuasion of non-Athenians to encouragement or simple praise for Athenians. This reminds us how the same, relatively tiny selection of examples could serve a multitude of purposes. But behind all is the fundamental idea of Athenian *aretē* which is present in Athens' struggle for freedom and justice against enslavement. They are stereotyped examples for Athens' praise.

The same chronological spread of achievements occurs in the epitaphios; the mythological examples are followed by the 'next' instance, the Persian Wars, and the catalogue stops there. The themes of the epitaphios, its historical examples and sentiments were not only propagated through the epitaphios (above, Ch. 4, n. 13). Indeed, the legendary tales reappeared in tragedy. But the epitaphios brought together these legendary tales and crystallized them in a set form that remained remarkably firm right into the second half of the fourth century and beyond, transmitted in conventional and repetitive form every year when the war dead were commemorated. As Demosthenes said (*Epit.* 6), it was worth recalling them even for those who were familiar with them. The 'catalogue' of deeds probably originated in the period after the Persian Wars and was adapted about the same time for the funeral oration (Kierdorf (1966)). But the epitaphios itself confirmed certain ancestral deeds as the conventional ones for defence or example and established them as a series which was seldom varied. The instances above show that the series was almost automatic in any situation where Athens was to be praised. They also suggest that for most Athenians Athens' past history was the past they heard about in the epitaphioi. The epitaphios that showed the ancestral *aretē* of the Athenians did actually form official oral tradition and thus most people's knowledge of their past. Moreover, its ideals cannot be overemphasized, not only because they affect oral tradition, but because the influence of the epitaphioi on Athens' oral traditions has been much underestimated. The epitaphios has been discussed extensively as a rhetorical genre and a collection of topoi. Occasionally it has been studied, though considerably less, as an expression of propaganda or ideology.[64] It has been recognized as part of Athenian military and ephebic education,[65] but not as a direct propagator of oral tradition about the past.

4.2 The nobility of the demos

The ideals and values of the official epitaphios are clearly reflected in its choice of subject-matter, indeed they determined the vision of the past found there.[66] They influenced individuals' memories and what they thought worth commemorating. We find a curious combination of values which seem primarily aristocratic. But they are applied to the democracy and the demos itself. Nobility, *aretē* ('excellence' or 'virtue'), and the stress on heroic death in battle create an aristocratic vision of the Athenians. But they are accompanied by values which are more obviously democratic in implication. For instance, individuals were not to be glorified, only Athens as a whole. This was clearly meant to glorify the democracy.[67] Similarly, Aeschines cited the fifth-century Hermae epigrams approvingly because they commemorated the Strymon victory without naming the general (III 183). So, while the demos acquires its

---

[64] Most recently by Loraux (1981a): she is unusual in recognizing that the epitaphios formed people's attitudes and (though less emphasized) their knowledge of the past.

[65] Loraux (1981a), 144f., talking of oral ('ephebic') education in the fifth century.

[66] On influence of ideals and beliefs in general, see Vansina, *OTH passim*, esp. chs. 4 and 5.

[67] Not an attempt to hide it, as argued by Loraux (1981a), ch. 4: she has mistaken throughout the use of 'aristocratic' words like *eugeneia* and *aretē* as a sign that the democracy was not itself being praised. This misunderstands the democracy's appropriation of terms previously used of aristocrats and maintains a far too rigid distinction in meaning (below, p. 218). The ideal was perhaps originally a hoplite one (as in Tyrtaeus), strengthened by the archaic avoidance of hubris: cf. Murray (1987), Jaeger (1932).

own aristocratic ancestry in Athens' autochthony, the overall effect becomes one of anonymity and bareness. This contradicts the common assertion that oral tradition concentrates on individuals. The official ideals rendered individual achievement and much of the past irrelevant.[68]

Thus the deceased were not commemorated by name. Neither commanders nor other individuals should be singled out for special praise. The ideal extended to any commemoration of Athenian victory. It perhaps contrasted with the customs of some other cities, though Sparta seems to have had the same egalitarian ideal. An apt comparison has been made between the Athenian and Samian commemorations of the campaign in Egypt of 460/59: the Samian inscription commemorates a named individual who may have been their general,[69] the Athenians erected a casualty list for all the dead and presumably delivered a funeral oration.

Praise of the deceased is exaggeratedly generous, but it is praise of the Athenians as a whole and couched in extreme generality. Pericles (Thuc. II 42) extravagantly praises the heroism of the deceased, who chose 'to die resisting rather than live submitting'. They are unnamed, the battle of their death is unmentioned, and Pericles treats them almost as one with the Athenians in general whom he has just been celebrating. Lysias (II 67ff.) says only a little of the war in which the deceased fought, how they dared 'to die for the freedom of their enemy' (Corinth) against the allies of Sparta. Plato's parody (*Menex.* 246a–b) follows upon his 'praise' of the deceased for fighting at Corinth to free the king of Persia: most of the deeds of these men and of others who have died for their city have not been mentioned at all, even the best of them, for there has been no time.[70] Demosthenes had to deal with a resounding defeat – that of Athens by Philip of Macedon at Chaeronea. He praises the deceased for their excellence and their realization of 'the danger that affected all Greece' (LX 16–18). One side must always suffer defeat: those who do die in battle remain conquerors in spirit (§19). This extremely allusive passage refers in fact to the battle which signalled the end of Greek freedom from Macedonia.[71]

Thus the deceased are both glorified anonymously and identified completely with Athens, its policy, and even its ancestors. No details are given of the campaigns or battles in which they died. They are one with

---

[68] Cf. the 'immortal memory' promised, Thuc. II 43.3; Lys. 79; Dem. 32.
[69] Clairmont (1983), 5; the inscription: *LSAG* 331, no. 21, ML 34; Peek (1939).
[70] The striking similarity of Lysias and Plato here suggests that Plato was parodying Lysias especially.
[71] Demosthenes probably said something of the circumstances because of his own strong espousal of that policy, which ended in defeat.

the rest of Athens and its policy of fighting for freedom.[72] Their identity with the Athenian demos is repeatedly implied (Thuc. 11 42; cf. Dem. 18 above). The later orator Hyperides knew that his eulogy of the general Leosthenes went against the convention. Even he, in 323, still felt he had to offer an apology or excuse for overturning the democratic ideal. He dismisses the past ancestral deeds and the ancestry and education of the deceased (*Epit.* 4–8) to tell of their courage and, most important, to eulogize their general. The following encomium (10ff.) contrasts astonishingly with other epitaphioi and other Athenian commemorations. Perhaps this was the tendency Aeschines and his contemporaries noticed in the mid-fourth century towards more adulation of individuals. The epitaphic section of the *genos*, which used to refer to ancestors of Athens as a whole, is now made to denote individual ancestry.[73] Yet, Hyperides takes care to reassure his audience that 'praise of Leosthenes is tribute to the rest' (§15), apparently lip-service to the old convention.[74] These hyperbolic departures from convention throw into relief the ideals that are overturned.

The democratic anonymity of this memorial must have affected oral tradition. If the official tradition does not remember individual generals or acts of bravery, how long will they be remembered at all? The 'immortal memory' promised the deceased is of a limited kind, for though their names went on the casualty lists, they were celebrated as a mass. Similarly with the details of the battles. At the time of the public funeral everyone would know who the commanders were, and would know something about the campaign or battle. Such memories could live on for a while but not necessarily for long. Once immediate reminiscences died, it would be the official traditions or memorials which helped to prolong certain memories. Habits of commemoration and recall may have a cumulative effect upon the character of the traditions, even those memories preserved by private individuals or families. In short, official tradition by itself encouraged anonymous collective history of Athens. It was left to individuals or their families to preserve memory of participation, death or particular bravery in war, even narrative detail about particular campaigns or battles. Such memories were not reinforced by the official commemorations. These tendencies are related to the underlying conception of the continuity of Athenian *aretē* which we shall return to in a moment.

---

[72] There is little mention of past generals in the sections on the ancestors: Lysias mentions Themistocles and Myronides, but the *Menexenus* cites Tanagra, Oinophyta, Eurymedon, Cyprus, Egypt and the Peloponnesian War without a single commander.

[73] Loraux (1981a), 111–13. Hyperides even describes Leosthenes' arrival in Hades.

[74] He also describes the campaign in which they fought, departing again from convention, but with exaggeration and falsification: Braccesi (1970).

We can sometimes see the effects of this. When Aeschines cites the epigrams of the Stoa of the Hermae (III 183), he even quotes the epigrams. He points out with admiration that the general is not named. But he does not tell us who he was, as he does for his other example, the commemoration of Marathon in the Stoa Poikile. Does he even know? Probably neither he nor others knew that the general was Cimon. The victory was remembered ultimately because of the written epigrams which survived purely oral tradition. But the 'modesty' of the general was too effective and his memory disappeared. This tendency is almost certainly one reason for the fading in the traditions of most of the great fifth-century generals, particularly Cimon (above, Ch. 4.1). Compare the reticence of epigrams whose occasions are often not identifiable.[75] The written commemoration was only a reminder of what everyone knew at the time of celebration, a reminder of oral tradition (while it existed), not a duplication of it. Even the written memorial was less and less useful in preserving information as memory faded.

The deceased are also praised as heroes. Death in battle for your country is an heroic deed.[76] It also has a timeless quality which is connected to the idea that such a death is part of the continuous line of Athenian achievement and *aretē* from earliest times. So again, the individual details and context are irrelevant. As Demosthenes said of those who died at Chaeronea, the dead were not really defeated, they were conquerors in spirit. If official commemoration glorified them as heroes in this way, why need individuals remember much more? As Socrates said cynically (234c), death in battle is a glorious thing, for you get a fine funeral and praise, even if you are poor and not good for much, and the orator will have his praise prepared already. In fact, death in battle would blot out any previous misdemeanours and merit a funeral fit for a hero. As Pericles said (Thuc. II 42.3), 'it is true that the good action [here, death in battle] may blot out the bad, that his merits as a citizen outweighed his demerits as an individual': the deceased died at the summit of their fortune.

So, official commemoration ignored historical context to concentrate on the victory. This is why epitaphic history consists of a string of victories (below, p. 231). Similarly with private family traditions. It seemed surprising at first that so many family traditions simply stressed that members had died in battle (Ch. 2.2). The death was a glorious and

---

[75] Especially the notorious 'Marathon epigrams': see ML 26 and, e.g., W. C. West (1970), Gomme, *HCT* II 98f.

[76] E.g. *Menex.* 246ff.; Dem. 32ff., esp. 34, the deceased must now be seated beside the gods below with the same honours as the brave men who preceded them in the Islands of the Blest; Lys. 79–81 (in fact *passim.*). Loraux (1981a), 137f. and 147ff. discusses the presentation of the deceased and past Athenians as equally heroic.

timeless heroic deed without historical context. There was a distinctly aristocratic flavour to the kind of traditions remembered. The background lies in the official commemoration and its details. The epitaphioi encouraged the memory of death in battle as an heroic achievement with no immediate context. Even the casualty list reflected this: the places where the deceased met their death are given and the lists of names by tribe, sometimes an epigram – but nothing more and, above all, no date.[77] Of course, individuals told of their experiences in war, as Cimon did in the anecdotes of Ion of Chios or as we read at the beginning of Plato's *Laches*. But these were casual reminiscences and would suffer the fate of such reminiscences, to have a fairly short life-span. The official traditions and ideals did not encourage or preserve such details.

This brings us to the themes of ancestral *aretē* and the nobility of the Athenians which lie behind so much of the epitaphic tradition. The nobility or *eugeneia* of the Athenians is derived from their originating from their own land, their 'autochthony'. Both are closely linked with the sense of innate Athenian justice thought to have existed from legendary times and with the idea, which we find occasionally, that Athens had democracy in the legendary period. Thus, Athenian *aretē* may be regarded as continuous from legendary times to the present, enabling orators to treat the deceased as in some way the same as the ancestors (e.g. Thuc. II 42.2). First origins and ancestry determine or reflect the later character of the Athenian demos just as they do for the individual aristocrat (see Ch. 3.2). The Athenian polis thus acquires a noble ancestry which appropriates the language and ideals of aristocracy to exalt the democracy.[78]

Autochthony was crucial and a conventional element of the epitaphios: this origin from their own land, they claimed, was unique.[79] It was 'just' because the Athenians did not have to replace others (Lys. 17; *Menex.* 237a–b), and with it began Athenian justice. So Athenian *aretē* is also associated with this unique origin which made the Athenians 'noble' both in the legendary and the historical period.[80] As Socrates said

---

[77] See Bradeen (1969) for characteristics of the lists.
[78] Loraux has an interesting discussion ((1981a), ch. I v, esp. 183ff.) of autochthony and 'aristocratic' terminology (but see Ch. 4, n. 67 above); Gomme, *HCT* on Thuc. II 41, p. 126; Loraux (1981b).
[79] Thuc. II 36.1: the ancestors always dwelt in their own land; they have handed it down free through their *aretē*; Lys. 17, our ancestors fought battles of justice since the very beginning of their life were just, they were autochthonous. *Menex.* 237a–238d, somewhat far-fetched; Hyp. 7; cf. Xen. *Mem.* III 5.12.
[80] Loraux ((1981a), 337) explains the importance of autochthony by a belief that Athens is incapable of change. But this ignores the importance of origins in Greek thought, especially legendary origins (Ch. 3). As Menander of Laodicea (third century A.D.) said on the epitaphios (§290), one should begin with ancestry (*genos*) for it is the source of all things.

(*Menex.* 237a), the deceased were *agathoi* ('good') because they were descended from *agathoi*, and this *aretē* was loosely associated with their noble birth (it is particularly important to bear in mind here that *agathos* ('good') and *aretē* ('virtue', 'excellence') had strong aristocratic overtones). This has interesting implications. One is that the demos may be glorified in noble terms. Another is that there is a further tendency to what I have called democratic anonymity. Since the whole demos is said to be descended from the same stock, it can be treated as a whole, and the length of Athenian history can be seen as expressive of this single origin in the distant legendary period.

The nobility (*eugeneia*) of the Athenians is expounded most clearly by Demosthenes (3ff.) and carried to its furthest extreme by Plato. Demosthenes praises their nobility: the deceased were not just brave, he says (§3), but 'they were nobly born, strictly brought up and lived with *philotimia* ('love of honour') (γεγενῆσθαι καλῶς καὶ πεπαιδεῦσθαι σωφρόνως καὶ βεβιωκέναι φιλοτίμως) so that they were good men (σπουδαῖοι). He will begin with the origin of their race (*genos*):[81] their nobility has long been acknowledged (§4). 'For it is possible for them and for each of their remote ancestors to trace back their nature (*physis*) not only to a father, but also to this land of theirs as a whole which they have in common and of which they are agreed to be the indigenous offspring (*autochthones*).' Each could not only trace back his nature to an ordinary father; they might also trace back their ancestry to their fatherland, since they were autochthonous: the land of Attica was the mother of their ancestors (§5). He then describes (§6) the courage and *aretē* of the ancestors, before coming to the conventional achievements which were proof of this excellence.

So the Athenians were noble because they were sprung from the earth itself. The democracy had its own rival ancestor and therefore could challenge the ancestry of individual aristocratic families.[82]

The nobility of the Athenians is often mentioned elsewhere. For instance in Euripides' *Ion* (1060), the Athenians are referred to as 'noble Erechtheids'. Or in *Oed. Col.* (728), Creon addresses the Athenians as 'noble inhabitants' (*eugeneis*).[83] The gradual adaptation of terms that were once applied to aristocrats or denoted aristocratic virtues can be

---

[81] The same three themes recur in *Menex.* 237a–b; nobility of birth, upbringing and education, and exploits.

[82] The autochthony myth must therefore have been partly adapted at least in the fifth century for this democratic application. See Ermatinger (1897); Loraux (1981a), 150ff.

[83] Loenen (1926) and Schroeder (1914), 5ff. give other references. E.g. Eurip. *Heraklid.* 69 and 826; Hdt. VII 161.3, 'the only Greeks who have never changed their abode' (μοῦνοι δὲ ἐόντες οὐ μετανάσται Ἑλλήνων). Arist. *Rhet.* 1 1360b defined *eugeneia* for a city as meaning its members are autochthonous or ancient or that its first members were famous.

traced through the fifth century.[84] In a sense, the public funeral speech can be seen as a democratic equivalent of the old aristocratic funerals and funeral feasts, following the model of the family and the aristocratic significance attached to the family ancestry.[85]

Plato produces an exaggerated parody of this liking of the democracy for 'aristocratic' origin (*Menex.* 237a–238c). Often misunderstood, the passage brings out interesting features of the official tradition. He introduces the topos of *eugeneia* (237a) by saying that the deceased were *agathoi* because they were sprung from *agathoi* – using the term which he had used to denote the aristocrat. And he praises their autochthonous origin, which explains why they are *agathoi* and noble. The land which bore their ancestors is likened to a woman and mother, described as dear to the gods (*theophilēs*) (237d–238b). We then come to the topic of upbringing (*trophē*) (238b–239a), which he declares to be the *politeia* or constitution ('for a *politeia* is the nurture of man', 238b–c). And he moves to what is perhaps the most astonishing statement in the epitaphios: Athens' *politeia* is and was an aristocracy: καλεῖ δὲ ὁ μὲν αὐτὴν δημοκρατίαν, ὁ δὲ ἄλλο, ᾧ ἂν χαίρῃ, ἔστι δὲ τῇ ἀληθείᾳ μετ᾽ εὐδοξίας πλήθους ἀριστοκρατία. 'One person calls it a democracy, another something else, as he pleases, but it is in truth an aristocracy, a government of the best with the approval of many.' This is proved by the fact that Athens has always had *basileis*; now they are elected. Athenians give office to those who seem to be the best (*aristoi*), rejecting none for weakness, poverty or obscurity of family, unlike other cities which have unequal (*anōmalos*) governments like tyrannies. They are all born of one mother, so they have no desire to be slaves or masters of each other. In fact *isogonia* ('equality of birth' – an extraordinary coinage) brings *isonomia* ('equality in law').

The description has perplexed commentators, particularly as there seems to be an echo of Thucydides' verdict on Periclean democracy as, in reality, a rule by one man (II 65.9).[86] But there is a wider context, too, which is what Plato is parodying. It was a rhetorical catchphrase to say that a democracy was really an aristocracy, meaning 'aristocracy' in its literal form as 'government by the best'.[87] In a passage claiming that the Athenians were *agathoi* or *aristoi*, the theme clearly forms part of that exaggerated epitaphic praise of the Athenians which appropriated noble terms. Moreover, Plato does in fact include features that are recognizably democratic alongside more ridiculous ones, such as the conceit about

---

[84] See, esp. Loenen (1926), 216f.   [85] Van Groningen (1953), 56–8.

[86] E.g. Kahn (1963) – not parody, only 'tendentious protreptic'. Loraux thinks Plato is mainly attacking the Thucydidean epitaphios and Pericles.

[87] Isoc. *Panath.* 131, 153; cf. Gomme, *HCT* II, p. 109. For other variations or inversions, cf. Isocrates' claim (*Areop.* 61) that Sparta was democratic.

the 'kings'. He is clearly talking of the humble members of the demos. But he is being satirical about their 'aristocratic' pretensions at the same time.[88] He is simply exaggerating conventional claims and extending them to the constitution, with a result that was actually presented in all seriousness by Isocrates.

Plato surely intended irony and satire to expose the hollowness of the claim.[89] But the idea so aptly parodied was crucial to the epitaphic tradition and to Athenians' image of themselves. Their nobility was connected closely with Athenian *aretē*, justice and equality (as in the *Menexenus* above), and liberty follows loosely. In the passage above (239a), there is a slide in ideas from the noble origin of the Athenians to their freedom, implying that one led to the other ('And so, having been brought up in perfect freedom . . . '). The implicit connection recurs elsewhere.[90] Nobility derived from the mythical origins thus lies behind the virtues of past and present Athens which the official tradition praised most warmly: *aretē*, equality and freedom.

This noble birth of the Athenians thus reinforces communal origin and communal virtue. It provided an aristocratic origin for the demos as a whole which was surely self-consciously rivalling aristocratic legendary ancestors. It implied that there was no longer any need for individual ancestry and reinforced the anonymous character of the Athenian demos. As Hyperides put it (§7), he did not need to give the ancestry of each one of the deceased. This would be necessary for the citizens of other cities. But in speaking of Athenians, born of their own country and sharing a lineage of unrivalled purity, it was unnecessary to present a eulogy of the descent of each one. Democratic moves to reduce the relevance of ancestry and opportunities to boast of it were hardly successful. In fact, it became useful to cite ancestral service to the

---

[88] Thus Henderson ((1975), 38, n. 55) points out that Plato claims this constitution caused the goodness even of the dead (238c): later it is clear the dead do not deserve this praise, which sheds irony on the remarks about the constitution. He also points out the latent absurdity in οὔτε ἀσθενείᾳ οὔτε πενίᾳ οὔτ᾽ ἀγνωσίᾳ πατέρων ἀπελήλαται οὐδείς, 'neither is any man rejected from weakness or poverty or obscurity of fathers': the last item could well be an insult, especially as you could not be a citizen if your father was unknown. 'Weakness' has no parallel in Thucydides (cf. Thuc. II 37.1 on openness of political office).

[89] As is even clearer from the sentence directly after the praise of constitution: thus reared in liberty, Athenians could think it right to fight both against Greeks for Greeks on behalf of freedom and with barbarians for the whole of Greece (note the order!). Cf. also the statement (246a–b) that they fought to free the king of Persia: the *eugeneia* is therefore revealed as fraudulent, as such an alliance was declared wicked earlier (243a–b).

[90] Loenen (1926), 220. See Raaflaub's interesting discussion on the importance of 'freedom' in democratic political theory (1983) and (1985), ch. 6. The dependence of Athenian freedom on its empire seems also to have been realized (Raaflaub (1984)), in which case Plato (see previous note) is surely exposing and satirizing the connection.

democracy (Ch. 2). But the official ideal was that there was no need for individual ancestry.

The ideal also lies behind the sense of the continuity of Athenian *aretē* that we see in the funeral speech. Each victory, each heroic death in battle, is a further example of Athenian excellence that originated with their autochthony. The salient characteristics of Athens' excellence are read back to the legendary past and linked closely to Athens' origins. This is a powerful disincentive to remember, or even recognize, historical change or detail. It has peculiar effects on the memory of 'democratic' history. We see the result of this in the official epitaphic image of the Athenian past.

4.3 Official tradition

The Persian Wars were essential to the catalogue of the epitaphios, parallel and exactly complementary to the legendary wars against the Amazons or Eurystheus. They all had the same heroic stature. As Demosthenes said of the legendary victories, they provide such becoming themes that our poets and many historians have made them their subjects (§9). Yet he will also mention more recent deeds, not inferior, but which, because they were closer in time, 'have not yet been elevated to legend nor exalted to epic rank' (οὔπω μεμυθολόγηται οὐδ᾽ εἰς τὴν ἡρωϊκὴν ἐπανῆκται τάξιν). And he exalts their achievement over that of the Greeks who fought at Troy (§10), a comparison often made.[91] Nothing could illustrate more clearly the continuity in deeds and *aretē* felt between the legendary past and the Persian Wars (with nothing in between). The differences were mainly those of time – an interesting comment. The Persian Wars had only failed to have heroic rank because they were more recent. What, then, was the further significance of the Persian Wars, and particularly of their first stage, the battle of Marathon in 490?[92]

Athens' proud boast was that it alone of all the Greeks defended Greece against the barbarians at Marathon (Lys. 20f.; *Menex.* 240c; Dem. 10). The help given by the Plateians was forgotten, as is well known.[93] Thus, Marathon was the only victory in the Persian Wars won without Peloponnesian help. The superfluous elaborations of Plato's

---

[91] Isoc. *Paneg.* 83; Hyp. 35; cf. Thucydides' Archaeologia (1 2ff.) which sets the Trojan War in its place against later conflicts.

[92] There has been much discussion of the Persian Wars, especially Marathon, most recently by Loraux (1981a), 157ff. The views about the Persian Wars in the epitaphios pervade all rhetoric, and I shall give few references.

[93] Cf. Hdt. VI; so, omission of Plateians is probably not satire. An interesting counterclaim occurs in [Dem.] LIX 94ff., where the Plateians' part in the Persian Wars is boasted of: the passage is taken from the Plateians' speech in Thuc. III (see Ch. 4, n. 19).

pastiche bring this out (*Menex.* 240c): there the Athenians were leaders and 'teachers' of Greece who showed the rest that Persia could be beaten. So the victory was also the 'first', an example to the rest.[94] Lysias' version is hardly more moderate (20ff.). He claims that the Persians attacked Athens first because Athens would help any others if the Persians started elsewhere. Athens did not wait for her 'allies' (this disguises the Spartans) and announced to Greece both the Persian arrival and the Persian defeat at the same time (§23). He stresses Athens' superior position and the rapidity of victory: Sparta did not even try to help. This rapidity of events, contradicted by Herodotus' account, was a rhetorical cliché, possibly encouraged by fifth-century Athenians' conception of their own character.[95] But it also stresses an essential factor, that the victory was solely Athenian and won before the rest of Greece even knew there was an invasion.[96] The point of the chauvinistic Athenian version is that their immediate self-sacrifice for the common good saved Greece.

That is why the history of the Persian Wars, and indeed all history, begins with Marathon in the epitaphios. Here, there is no mention of Persian attacks on Thrace, Naxos and Eretria narrated by Herodotus; the Persians head straight for Athens. Athenian achievement is further exalted.[97] Most Athenians cannot even have known that there were campaigns before Marathon. Concentration on Marathon as the epitome of Athenian *aretē* and self-sacrifice simply erased from memory anything which contradicted that impression. Plato understands and exaggerates the tendencies of this treatment. His version is so interesting that it is worth looking at in detail. After the rhetorical platitudes, he reminds us of what we are missing.

His approach is unique. He does not plunge into the historical section with the conventional glorification of Marathon. Rather, he sets the picture against a brief outline of the growth of the Persian empire (*Menex.* 239c–240b). Cyrus had freed the Persians and enslaved the Medes and ruled the rest of Asia; his son ruled Egypt and Libya; the third king was Darius who ruled as far as the Scythians by land and sea. Darius quarrelled with Athens and Eretrians (240a) and sent Datis. Datis sailed against the Eretrians, reputed to be amongst the most famous in war, and netted Eretria. Then he went on to Marathon (240c).

---

[94] Plato may also parody Pericles' famous claim (Thuc. II 41) that Athens was the educator of Greece.

[95] E.g. Ar. *Knights* 565ff.; Pericles at Thuc. II 40; Aesch. *Eumenides* 916–20 and 996–1000; Plato, *Crito* 50c; cf. Hdt. VI 113.

[96] It is misspent ingenuity to look for elements of genuine haste in the historical tradition, as does Pritchett (1960), 173. There was considerable delay before the Athenians set off for Marathon: Gomme (1962).

[97] This cannot simply be explained by a characteristic desire of the epitaphios to hurry over events, as Loraux (1981a), 159f.

This remarkable picture of the Persian empire has been convincingly interpreted as an attempt by Plato to point out that freedom for some results in slavery for others.[98] We might further suggest that he is pointing out similarities between the Persian empire and the Athenian and their similar development from the initial act of liberation. Plato often satirizes Athens' claim to liberate various states of Greece. The speech ends with Athens 'liberating' the king of Persia himself and expelling the Spartans from the sea. The coupling of Athens and Eretria as equal recipients of Darius' irritation is just as striking. After detailed description,[99] Plato overturns the cliché that no one helped Athens in its lonely struggle and declares (240c) that 'none of the Greeks came to help either the Eretrians or the Athenians'. This repeated pairing of Eretria with Athens surely parodies the commonplace of Athenian sole achievement at Marathon.[100] One can see by contrast the point of the official tradition's isolation of Marathon.

It could even be claimed that Athens was entirely responsible for Persian defeat in the rest of the war ten years later (480–479). Lysias was comparatively realistic (27ff.), including Thermopylae with the other engagements. He claimed only that Athens helped most towards Greek freedom (§42) – Salamis was the climax of achievement (though he continues with the events leading up to Plateia). For Plato's orator, Salamis complemented Marathon as an educative example (and Thermopylae is omitted). But Demosthenes managed to suggest that Athens alone was responsible for saving Greece (9f.). Without naming any battles, he claims that the Athenian ancestors alone repulsed the expedition from the whole of Asia – twice – and saved all Greece: this can only refer to both halves of the Persian Wars: 'Those men single-handed twice repulsed, both by land and sea, the expedition which came from the whole of Asia' (ἐκεῖνοι τὸν ἐξ ἁπάσης τῆς Ἀσίας στόλον ἐλθόντα μόνοι δὶς ἠμύνατο καὶ κατὰ γῆν καὶ κατὰ θάλατταν). Greek achievement in the Trojan War was much inferior.

We possibly see here the gradual triumph of Athens' view of the Persian Wars, a triumph perhaps largely effected through continual repetition in the epitaphioi.[101] But hints of the exaggeration can be found

---

98 Henderson (1975), 35.
99 The Eretrians are even described as 'most famous' (*eudokimōtatoi*) (240b); the netting of the island, not in fact correct (Henderson (1975), 37f.), is described in detail, and Datis intended to do the same to Athens.
100 When Plato reverses another commonplace in saying that 'other deeds still lie in oblivion' (239c) he may seriously refer to those important episodes which the epitaphios omitted and which would correct the distorted image there.
101 See Starr (1962), 328ff.: there is slight evidence for people who did not accept Athens' action as decisive: Thuc. I 69.5, the Corinthians; Diod. XI 11.5 on the dead of Thermopylae.

far earlier than the late fourth century, and it may be connected with characteristics of oral tradition that we have encountered elsewhere. For the speech made by the Athenian envoys at Camarina in Thucydides (VI 82f.) implies the claim, 'we make no fine professions of having a right to rule because we overthrew the barbarian single handed (μόνοι καθελόν-τες . . .) or because we took those risks for the freedom of their subjects' (83.2). In the context, they imply the boast was normal.[102] It also occurs in Isocrates.[103] Demosthenes' exaggeration was not unique.

What is happening here? The essential claims are of a solely Athenian victory at Marathon and that Athens deserved hegemony because of its outstanding contribution to the Persian Wars.[104] These are amalgamated into a boast that Athens defeated the Persians alone. Thus, the idea of Marathon and the reasons for its importance have been extended to the rest of the Persian Wars: Marathon came to epitomize Athenian achieve-ment and it gradually became difficult – at least in oral tradition and propaganda – to distinguish it from the other episodes (e.g. Salamis and Thermopylae) ten years later. Oral tradition telescopes the complemen-tary events together. This seems to be confirmed by the nostalgic appeals to 'the days of Marathon' in late fifth-century comedy. There are even hints that oral tradition could amalgamate the campaigns into one.

The stress on Marathon at the expense of Salamis has often been seen as a political one: Marathon was a hoplite victory symbolizing the bravery of the citizen soldier of earlier times, Salamis a naval one connected unpleasantly with mere sailors, the radical democracy, Themistocles and empire. Men of different political opinions would stress one or the other. Cimon has even been credited with the 'cover-up' of Salamis.[105] The idea has superficial plausibility,[106] but one runs into difficulties on closer examination. For instance, the denigration of a commander, Themistocles, must be separated from that of a victory. In the epitaphic tradition the Athenians are praised as a whole, and generals are almost never named. The glorification of Athenian *aretē* concerns all. As for Cimon's politics and propaganda, of which we know so little, it is equally possible that he extolled Salamis. For it established

---

[102] Cf. earlier Athenian claim, Thuc. I 73, very close to that of Lysias. Strasburger (1958) discusses how far Thucydides' speeches repeat the types of claims made by contempo-raries.

[103] XVI 27: the democracy trained citizens to such bravery that they defeated single-handed the barbarians who came to enslave all Greece.

[104] E.g. Lys. II 47, on granting of hegemony.

[105] Most recently, Loraux (1981a), 162ff. But what if Cimon originated the tradition of the epitaphios, as has been thought? Fornara (1966) has the opposite plan and cites the 'implicit' denigration of Themistocles in the epigram of Eion (Gomme (1948))!

[106] For instance, Athenians worried by the radical democracy in the late fifth century harked back to the days of Marathon as the 'good old days'.

the naval hegemony and empire which he promoted so successfully himself.[107]

The Aristophanic comedies are especially telling, for they abound with patriotic references to the great *Marathonomachai* or 'Marathon-fighters' and the victory of Marathon.[108] Marathon is regarded with nostalgia as typical of the good old days. Or it is used as a political goad by the demagogues (*Kn.* 781–5). Stress on Marathon is undeniable, but surely it is stressed as the epitome of the whole of the Persian War and not because it is a hoplite battle as opposed to a naval victory. Thus, the sausage-seller (*Kn.* 781ff.) woos the demos with reminders of its achievements both at Marathon and Salamis. The chorus of jurymen in the *Wasps* (1071ff.) produce their notoriously muddled reminiscence of the Persian Wars which rolls together salient features from both halves of the war and concentrates them into a single episode around the battle of Marathon. They turn from this to memories of sailing over to Asia and taking many cities from the Medes (1092). When the demos is stewed and rejuvenated in the *Knights*, it is said to be worthy of the city and the trophy at Marathon (1334); a little later it is compared favourably to the bad old demos (i.e. of the late fifth century) who preferred salaries to building ships. Nostalgia for the Athens of the days of Marathon is inextricably linked with naval power and the beginnings of the empire. There is no significant distinction of Marathon as a hoplite victory unassociated with naval power and empire, even in these nostalgic reminiscences. Perhaps most revealing, Marathon can even be connected by itself with the delights of empire.[109] The main burden of these allusions to Marathon is a nostalgia for the great days of the Persian Wars, for the time when the demos fought bravely for its country uncorrupted by flattery and pay, when it was winning victories against the Medes and spreading its sea-power over the Aegean.

These allusions must voice popular and widespread views. Perhaps some Athenians resented Salamis as forerunner of 'mob rule', but if Marathon can be so easily regarded as the epitome of the Persian Wars and Athenian imperial power, we cannot read into the allusions any political opinions other than general approval of that Athenian achievement. We must question the easy identification of different battles of that era as dear to one political 'party' or another.[110]

---

[107] Cf. Ch. 4, n. 105 above for contradictory arguments.

[108] *Marathonomachai*: *Acharnians* 179ff. and 692ff.; *Knights* 1334; *Clouds* 985; *Wasps* 711, 1060ff.; Ar. frag. 429 K.–A. Marathon victory: e.g. *Acharnians* 699; *Wasps* 682ff.; *Knights* 781ff.

[109] Cf. *Wasps* 682ff. and 711, addressed to jurymen, urges them to enjoy the fruits of empire, worthy of the trophy at Marathon.

[110] Cf. Lys. II 47f., they were judged worthy by all to lead Greece, both as foot-soldiers and sailors, and war broke out because of the jealousy of others. Athens contributed most

When they reminisce, the old men in the *Wasps* roll the two parts into one continuous campaign centring on Marathon. The barbarians, they say (1079ff.), burn the city (surely the second part of the war), but the Athenians rush out and engage them in battle (Marathon, presumably). You could not see the sky for arrows (cf. Hdt. VII 226, said of Thermopylae). They pushed the Persians back towards evening, for there had been an owl omen before the battle (an owl omen was said to precede Salamis).[111] The salient and picturesque elements have been brought together into an image of events which revolves around Marathon. This muddled account may be intended as a joke. Yet, joke or not, the confusion confirms the exaggerated concentration on the battle of Marathon we find elsewhere. And it suggests that this concentration might actually help oral tradition to amalgamate the two separate stages into one overall episode.

Marathon began the catalogue of recent Athenian deeds so that the Persian expedition seemed to be against Athens alone. Athens won the only victory which could be claimed as solely Athenian (and that wrongly). So Marathon was the most apt continuation of the legendary exploits of Athens, a further example of its championship of Greece as both benefactor and saviour. The battle both reflected legendary heroism and began the *aretē* of the historical period.[112] It was already crucial as the beginning of the Persian Wars. The epitaphios made it the beginning of Athens' recent history. Hence Marathon came to epitomize Athenian success in the Persian Wars. It expressed the triumph of Athens' chauvinistic version of history, which least of all celebrated the battle of Plateia, so obviously a communal effort with the other Greeks. The epitaphios with its overt patriotism must have been extremely influential in reinforcing this picture, affecting the general oral traditions of the city. Athenian claims about Marathon were extended to the whole of the Persian Wars.[113] Nostalgia for the days of Marathon represented nostalgia for the early days of patriotism and empire as well. Marathon came to epitomize the whole.

---

to the defence against the Persians and most ships to Salamis. Cf. And. III 3ff., who is quite happy to cite the strengthening of the navy as one of the advantages of peace. Cf. Ruschenbusch (1979) who questions the extent of 'democratic' principles in fifth-century politics.

[111] Austin (1973), 134 insists it represents Marathon. They go on to boast of how they subdued the Persians 'when we sailed over there with triremes' – i.e. the battle of Mycale and other campaigns straight after Plateia, in which they 'took many cities from the Medes'.

[112] Loraux (1981a), 166.

[113] Cf. W. C. West (1970) on 'panhellenic' claims made by Athens, but rather muddled. Pindar's dithyrambs for Athens (which he omits) change the picture: fr. 76 Sn. calls Athens: Ἑλλάδος ἔρεισμα ('bulwark of Greece'), and fr. 77 apparently for Artemi-

By convention the epithaphios moved down through Athenian history after the Persian Wars. Only Lysias and Plato give detailed accounts, and those are obviously highly selective. The scantier treatments of Demosthenes and Thucydides illustrate the general tenor of the epitaphic version more neatly. Demosthenes sums up the period (§11): Athens continued to check acts of arrogance (*pleonexia*), to enforce justice and to bear the brunt of all dangers until the present generation, one hundred and fifty years later. Pericles comments only that their own fathers, and they themselves even more, created and augmented the empire: the omitted history is that of the increasing empire, and the patriotic message is clear. The general tenor of the later history is that Athens continued in the course already set in the Persian Wars and before – defending the wronged, checking arrogance or injustice, champion and benefactor of Greece; its hegemony, well deserved, was extended by the same principles. Its later history as well as its legendary past is created in the image of the epitaphic version of the Persian Wars.

This is what Lysias implies. There was war in Greece, he says (§48), because of envy (*zēlos*) and jealousy (*phthonos*). He describes the sea-battle between Athens and Aigina in which Athens took seventy ships (i.e. First Peloponnesian War). He, too, avoids describing the Second Peloponnesian War but sums it up thus (55f.): they made Greece free, showed their own country to be great, ruled the sea for seventy years, prevented stasis among their allies, forcing equality (*to ison*) on all, prevented enslavement, made their allies strong and showed their own power to be so great that the Persian king could no longer desire other peoples' land . . . So Athens alone was champion and leader of the cities.[114] Here again is Athens' innate justice, defence against slavery, championship of Greek freedom and well-being exemplified in its defence of Greece against the barbarians throughout the period.

What of the specific instances of such *aretē*? Lysias' passage based on a section of Thucydides, shows how epitaphic conventions deliberately distort the historical events. He concentrates on two episodes from the early 450s (II 48–53), taken from Thucydides I 105. Both deal with the siege of Aigina, then the campaign in the Megarid under Myronides in which the very young and old Athenians had to fight. The information Thucydides gives about the sea-battle with Aigina and the siege (I 105.2) is reproduced fact by fact by Lysias. He omits only the name of the

---

sium: ὅθι παῖδες Ἀθηναίων ἐβάλοντο φαεννάν κρηπῖδ' ἐλευθερίας ('where the Athenians laid the radiant foundations of liberty').

[114] Cf. another typical example of distortion of history from Aelius Aristides (Strasburger (1958), 25f.): Athens stands alone against barbarians, and its policy is the only one which can stand for the whole of Greece.

general, as appropriate for an epitaphios. Seventy Aiginetan ships were taken. This is an episode of Athenian history worthy of the epitaphios.

His treatment of the next episode is more interesting. Corinth seized Geraneia when both Aigina and Egypt were being besieged by Athens and its fighting men were away. Athens decided not to call away soldiers from the siege of Aigina (Thuc. 1 105.4) but to send the young and old under Myronides.[115] This is embroidered into Lysianic rhetoric about the greatness of the young and old who volunteered of their own accord, when Athens was considering not sending anyone at all (!) 'trusting in their own spirit and despising the invaders . . . ' (§50). They demanded that they take on the danger alone. Myronides, he continues (§52), defeated the entire enemy force in the Megarid with his unusual army, 'and they set up a trophy of an achievement most glorious for them but most shameful for their enemy' (§53). For the epitaphios it was an overwhelming victory and a moral one, too, since it was won by Athenians who were not even of military age.

But in Thucydides the sober account ends in an evenly matched battle and worse follows. Athens had the advantage and set up a trophy (105.6), but a little later the Corinthians tried to erect one. The Athenians sallied out from Megara, killed those erecting a trophy and defeated the rest. A large portion of the Corinthians got cut off on a piece of private land surrounded by a deep ditch. The Athenians surrounded them with the hoplites in front and stoned to death all who were in the area. It was a severe blow to the Corinthians. So, Lysias has done more than transform a drawn battle into an outright victory. He has omitted the quarrelling over trophies and above all the overwhelming calamity (*pathos*) Corinth suffered at the fight over the trophy and the stoning to death by the Athenians. It is hard to know how Thucydides meant this episode to be taken or how Athenians would react to the stoning of a marooned enemy.[116] It should at least alter someone's opinion of the victorious force: we see this exceptional army of the inexperienced or elderly only just managing to win a standard battle, then encircling a part of the enemy which had got stuck behind a ditch and stoning it to death. This is not the Athenian *aretē* that the epitaphic tradition boasts of, and one may well see it as the shameful resort of the weak and enfeebled.

It appears – precisely because Lysias omitted this episode – that he was aware of it, and the official tradition covered it up. Lysias described two glorious victories in which the Athenian spirit even in the very young and

---

[115] Beloch, in fact, suggested Myronides had left with the main force, and the young and old were sent to reinforce him ((1905), 364, n. 2).

[116] Connor (1984), 200, n. 40 points out a recurrence of scenes of encirclement with cumulative terror through the Histories, beginning with 1 106; in Book VII it is the Athenians and Demosthenes who become trapped and encircled in Sicily.

very old triumphed over their enemies. Thucydides must have written his account of the Pentekontaëtia against an epitaphic tradition of this kind. Was he deliberately presenting an account of the bare facts, well researched, in order to counteract the oral traditions encouraged by the epitaphioi?[117] I have dwelt at length on this example as it shows so well how the epitaphios distorts even when the historical facts are known. The tendencies of the official tradition are all the clearer.

Plato's parody brings out the epitaphic transformation of history. The *Menexenus* also concentrates upon one episode of Athenian glory in the Pentekontaëtia, the battles of Tanagra and Oinophyta (242a–b). Again we can compare Thucydides (I 108). Having just praised Athenian success in saving Greece from the Persians at Eurymedon, Cyprus and Egypt (as if they were all successes!), Plato says that war with the Greeks started now, because of their envy (*zēlos*) and jealousy (*phthonos*).[118] The Athenians, he adds, fought the Spartans at Tanagra on behalf of Boiotian liberty. The result was undecided and they left, but on the third day they were victorious at Oinophyta (242b): 'These men were the first since the Persian Wars who fought in aid of Greeks against Greeks for the sake of liberty, brave men who freed those they helped.'

This is another parody and exposure of Athenian claims to fight for the freedom of others – which culminated in their defending the freedom of the Persian king. It is also a more blatant falsification of history than Lysias'. Tanagra was a great defeat of Athens which involved much slaughter on both sides (Thuc. I 108.1). The battle of Oinophyta was sixty-two days later; Athens defeated the Boiotians and so gained control over Boiotia and Phocis.[119] Plato's version has not only changed a defeat to a draw. It has cancelled out even that humiliation by putting Oinophyta almost immediately after. Similarly, he has just implied wrongly that the Egyptian expedition was a success, and we forget the eventual failure of Athenian interference in central Greece with the ignominious defeat at Koroneia (Thuc. I 113).

If Plato's distortion seems extreme, the fourth-century historian Ephorus provides a parallel one (Diod. XI 80.2–82): Ephorus also states that the battle at Tanagra was undecided, and he inserts another Athenian victory between Tanagra and Oinophyta which is otherwise quite unknown. He says himself – rather suspiciously – that, though this battle is well-known, no historian has described the way it was fought or the disposition of troops (82.4). He praises it extravagantly. It is very

---

[117] Strasburger (1958) argues that he was deliberately counteracting the official versions, which could include the epitaphios.
[118] Possibly a dig at Lysias who used the same excuse, but more blandly.
[119] Problems about the Boiotians' role in the Tanagra campaign (Meiggs (1972), 417f.) make no difference to the falsity of Plato's claim.

probable that his source was an epitaphios which had substituted a more honourable result for Tanagra.[120] This needs little further comment. Clearly, the official tradition about Tanagra was that it was undecided.[121]

As a final illustrative commentary on the presentation of Athens' past in the epitaphios, I shall simply paraphrase briefly Plato's account of the Peloponnesian War, a war so little mentioned in the other epitaphioi and a clear and resounding defeat for Athens:

Then there was a great war in which they devastated our country. But we won a sea-battle at Sphagia (presumably Sphacteria), took their leaders prisoner and though we could have killed them, we made peace for the good of Greece, thinking it right to destroy barbarians only (242c–d) . . . (more on the superiority of Athens):

Then there was a third war which was terrible and in which many men died fighting in Sicily for the freedom of Leontinoi (242e–243a), bound by their oaths (more on why the Athenians were so unfortunate). Then there was the battle in the Hellespont in which the Athenians took all the enemies' ships in a single day, 'having defeated many others'.[122] But our enemies allied with the king of Persia, uniting all Greece with him against us, the worst act of the war (243b). However, though our ships were blockaded at Mytilene, our citizens embarked and conquered the enemy, winning both the sea-battle and the rest of the war. (This must be the battle of Arginusae, Xen. *Hell.* I 6.26–33, hence the remark that the dead could not be buried in Athens.) This showed Athens was invincible. Then Plato continues immediately with Athens' own war (*oikeios*) that it waged with itself (that is, the civil strife of 404). Even this was conducted with mildness and there was joyful reconciliation at the end.

The orator ends the 'narrative' of the great war straight after the Athenian victory at Arginusae: Athens won this war. The resounding defeat of Athens at Aigospotamoi, in which they lost almost all their ships, is simply omitted.[123] There follows only some internal dissension within Athens, isolated from the circumstances of the war; Athens could only be defeated by itself (243d). That was how to deal with a crushing and unambiguous defeat by Sparta which left Athens humiliated. Athens' reputation for freedom and justice and victory remains perfectly unscathed!

[120] Strasburger (1958), 25, n. 3. Meiggs (1972), 12 and *HCT* I, p. 317 prefer to attribute the duplication to Diodorus. It is quite possible that Ephorus concocted the three battles because of the *Menexenus* – which shows how difficult it would be to form an accurate picture of Athenian history if epitaphioi were one's main source.

[121] Cf. Koroneia: the official version in the epigram attributed defeat to a demigod, *HCT* I, p. 339; Cameron (1940).

[122] Perhaps intentional ambiguity, since the 'battle in the Hellespont' usually meant the disaster at Aigospotamoi.

[123] Cf. Lys. II 58: *aretē* even in adversity, when the ships were captured in the Hellespont.

There emerges an image of Athenian *aretē* from earliest times. The legendary achievements and the Persian Wars are the essential elements. Complementing each other, they present Athens as defender of justice, champion of Greece, saviour and liberator of the oppressed or enslaved, natural and superior leader of Greece. The past is strictly selected to reveal only the Athenian *aretē* born of autochthony, Athenian success and support of the liberty of others. This reflects the role of the epitaphios to provide an encomium of Athens and exempla from the past to encourage the present generation to emulate their ancestors.[124]

One of the most obvious results is that defeats are forgotten. Athens' past is transformed by selection and alteration so that it consists of a series of victories – moral victories if necessary. What chance was there of defeats being remembered, then, at least in the next generation? The heroic commemoration of the deceased would also encourage this process (Ch. 4.2 above). Such distortion of defeat is not, of course, confined to Athens or indeed to what is primarily oral tradition, but the epitaphic tradition was one of the most important channels of transmission for Athenian history. After the participants had died, there was little except memory to preserve the record.[125] Moreover, if few defeats are remembered, then the superiority of Athens, a crucial tenet of the epitaphios, would seem to be confirmed.

There are other important characteristics of the epitaphic treatment of history. First, it tends to present a fragmentary and timeless catalogue of achievements, despite the roughly chronological structure. This is hardly surprising as its purpose was to praise the ancestors and illustrate Athenian *aretē*. But we must not miss the more intangible features of the history so transmitted. As far as we can tell from the extant examples, Athenian exploits are indeed presented as a list of achievements: the German term *Tatenkatalog* is an apt one. We find a monotonous enumeration of wars: for instance, Lys. 48, Ὑστέρῳ δὲ χρόνῳ Ἑλληνικοῦ πολέμου καταστάντος διὰ ζῆλον ('At a later time there was a Greek war which arose out of envy . . . ') or Plato, *Menex.* 242a, μετὰ δὲ τοῦτο γενομένου πολέμου . . . ('After this, there was a war . . . '); 242e, τρίτος δὲ πόλεμος μετὰ ταύτην τὴν εἰρήνην ἀνέλπιστος . . . ἐγένετο

---

[124] As Socrates' remarks in the *Menexenus* illustrate. Cf. the third-century writer of 'On Figurative Expressions' (*Peri eschēmatismenon*) VIII 9 (Ziolkowski (1981), 35f.) on its role of exhorting one's audience to war.

[125] Unless an historian committed their accounts to writing. It is striking how useless the casualty lists are for such information beyond the places of conflict and extent of casualties. Occasionally they are accompanied by an epigram (e.g. *IG* I² 943 or 946): but these often assume the reader or hearer knows the background, for instance the occasion of the epigram of *IG* I² 946, possibly of 431 B.C., cannot be identified certainly (*HCT* II, p. 101). That of I² 943 is put around 440/39: it only mentions the Hellespont.

('After this peace, there was a third war which was unexpected . . . ').
Rhetorical commonplaces are interspersed about Athenian superiority,
its opponents' jealousy, and other variations on Athenian virtue.[126]
Sometimes specific battles are mentioned, but with very little explanation (cf. *Menex.* 241d–e). The connecting links are not those of
historical development or change: they are the underlying and ever
present Athenian *aretē* and its accompaniment, military success.[127] Since
the engagements may be commemorated by themselves, they have a
somewhat timeless and heroic quality. Again, that is complemented and
encouraged by the very idea that death in battle is by itself a heroic deed
(see Ch. 4.2).

The implications for Athenian oral tradition are clear. The official
tradition not only discouraged memory of defeats. It preserved memory
of individual, often isolated victories which, though in roughly chronological order, were not set in more precise chronological or historical
relationship to each other – a catalogue of Athenian successes rather
than campaigns. Nor is detailed narrative encouraged, despite Lysias'
unusual account.[128] It must be stressed that while commemoration might
well take the form of detailed narrative, it did not do so in Athenian
official tradition. The quality of a timeless catalogue of heroic deeds
likewise influences the knowledge of the Athenians of their city's past
and their own ancestors (Ch. 4.2).

The epitaphic traditions are almost exclusively about Athens' external
relations with other Greeks or barbarians: in fact its military achievement and expansion. One may disagree about the degree to which the
'democracy' is conventionally praised in the funeral oration (see below,
p. 234). But it is beyond doubt that the epitaphic history pays no regard
to the internal history of the city. It gives no catalogue of episodes in the
growth and development of the democracy. The sole exception is the
return of the democracy after the oligarchy of the Thirty in 403,
mentioned twice (*Menex.* 243d–e; Lys. 61). Lysias praises the democratic
Piraeus party (who helped restore the democracy) fulsomely, as imitating their ancestors' support of liberty; but Plato brings in the civil strife
only as an explanation of Athens' failure to win the war.[129] The

---

126 Andocides' version of the Pentekontaëtia (III 3ff.) has a similar character, perhaps
influenced by this way of presenting history.

127 Contrast Loraux's explanation of the 'gaps' in the epitaphic vision of the past ((1981a),
135). Oral tradition can accommodate gaps.

128 Taken, in any case, from Thucydides as one marvellous example of Athenian bravery.
Nor is there narrative of the campaign in which the deceased died.

129 Loraux ((1981a), 201ff.) has interesting remarks on the absence of stasis, which she
explains by the epitaphic emphasis on the unity of the city and denial of political
disagreement; cf. the unease at using terms and honours for victims of stasis in the late

concentration on external and military history cannot be overstressed when so much modern interest lies elsewhere.

Thus the official tradition of Athens did not commemorate the great episodes in the history of the democracy, neither the establishment of the radical democracy nor even the fall of the tyranny widely cited in other contexts; still less any of the more detailed constitutional enactments. The lack of a theory of democracy has been remarked upon.[130] Just as interesting is the lack of 'democratic history' in what is the nearest Athens has to an official tradition. Some of these episodes might be known. But they needed other channels to be preserved. What the official tradition did transmit were traditions about Athens' legendary past, its victories in the fifth century and, probably most important, the overall themes of Athenian superiority, *aretē* and championship of the enslaved, which could all be traced back to the distant, legendary past. This was appropriate to the commemoration of the war dead. The official view of the past influenced family traditions which remembered deaths in battle more than civic virtue. Similarly, this emphasis may explain the paucity of knowledge about Athens' internal and constitutional history by the fourth century which could only be supplemented by written documents. Official emphasis simply lay elsewhere than on the details of democratic history.

The underlying ideals and values of the epitaphic tradition seem to lie behind this treatment.[131] The role of the epitaphios was the sheer glorification of Athens' superiority. That superiority involved military success and above all its part in the Persian Wars. The democracy was praised in general terms, but it was seen as the background to Athens' glory, not the principal subject-matter of such glorification. Chauvinistic Athenian history required military history.

Moreover, the democracy of the classical period is often not distinguished from the legendary past in the epitaphios. This brings us back to the underlying conception of Athenian *aretē* from the very earliest of times (p. 217). Athenian *aretē*, freedom and defence of freedom are conceived to have existed from legendary times. They were closely linked with Athenian autochthony and inherent nobility. The victories of Athens in the fifth century continue the legendary bravery. The tendency to see Athenian *aretē* and its accompaniments as a continuum from

---

fifth century which were usually used for victims (or heroes) of war. Certainly unity and harmony in the city is important, but all internal history is absent, not just stasis.

[130] Jones (1957), esp. ch. 3; Finley (1962). In fact, there are signs of democratic theory (e.g. Eurip. *Suppl.*), but they do not amount to what the modern historian would expect.

[131] One can hardly see the stress on military achievement simply as an archaic survival, expressive of the origins of the epitaphios after the Persian Wars.

Theseus onwards obviously reduces the significance of recent change. Moreover, if recent change, such as Athenian championship of Greece in the Persian Wars, is read back into the legendary past, there is a circular process. The importance of origins in Greek thinking combined with the belief in continuity to render the intervening period comparatively free of historical and dramatic change.[132]

We can therefore begin to understand the extraordinary treatment of the democracy and 'democratic history'. Just as Athenian military prowess and *eugeneia* continue from legendary times, there are hints that the democracy was regarded in the same way. Much of the epitaphic praise of Athenian democracy is indistinguishable from that of the remote ancestors who were autochthonous and reared in freedom – in fact, one can overemphasize the degree to which the classical democracy is treated at all. So, by the extension of the present to the legendary past, the legendary ancestors are also thought to have established the democracy. Demosthenes (§28) called Theseus the founder of *isēgoria* ('equal right of speech', 'equality'). So did Isocrates.[133] Lysias, too, seems to put the establishment of democracy, so named, in the distant period (§18). In a eulogy of Athenian pursuit of liberty and justice, he says that 'at that time' Athens was the first to drive out 'the aristocratic masters (*dynasteias*) amongst them' and establish democracy. As he has just been talking about Athens' autochthonous origins (§17), this can only refer to the mists of legendary time. For him, too, democracy was pushed back to the earliest period.

In fact it is the logical and necessary corollary of the autochthony and noble birth (*eugeneia*) of the Athenian demos. Athenian *eugeneia* (of the classical period) is claimed to arise from their special origins: freedom, *aretē* and the characteristics of the democracy are associated with it, as we have seen. If these qualities are inherent in the nobility of autochthony, then obviously Athens had a democracy in the legendary period also. Against this conception there was clearly no need in the epitaphic tradition to deal with the recent history of the democracy.[134] What need was there to remember the comparatively recent develop-

---

[132] Cf. Loraux (1981a), 195 rather differently on linking democracy with autochthony.

[133] Isoc. *Panath.* 127ff. The relation of the epitaphic tradition to the debate about the 'ancestral constitution' is complex. See Ruschenbusch (1958) for the *patrios politeia* in historiography: but he assumes all rhetorical allusions are responses to historians' publications and contemporary propaganda and presents far too rigid a scheme (see also Finley's criticisms (1975), 38 and n. 10). The ideal of *eugeneia* suggests that some of the debate was less propagandist or partisan than often thought.

[134] An omission only perplexing if we expect an official tradition to consist of a kind of 'Athenian Constitution', a description once actually applied to the Periclean epitaphios (Oppenheimer (1933), 12).

ments of the radical democracy, when it could be established that democracy or its essential components existed in legendary times?

Finally, however, despite its ahistorical tendencies, the chronological span of the epitaphic tradition has some significance for Athenian oral tradition. It may have helped preserve a very broad schema of Athenian history. The epitaphios presented the only opportunity for most Athenians to hear an account of Athenian history set out in roughly chronological sequence from its earliest times, and this could be crucial. We have seen several examples of private traditions and individual memories which are chronologically very vague or simply exist in an historical vacuum. Both context and chronological position might be provided by the general or official traditions which presented a broad span, however simplified, of those episodes most important to the whole city. Family memories of events which were not part of the polis traditions gradually became approximated to those that were (Ch. 2.4), changing chronological place and factual content. Or individual ancestors might be remembered by their association with a more famous Athenian, as were Plato's (p. 170). Chronological implications had to be inferred by synchronizing the ancestors with another figure or event and so attaching the esoteric family traditions to the wider spread of Athenian history. Individual traditions gain their place in wider polis history by being attached to polis traditions.

This would partly be a matter of memory. Even memories of recent events could be influenced by the prevalent official traditions, propaganda and celebration in the assembly. They might also help deliberate reconstruction of the past. Herodotus and Thucydides collected information mostly from oral tradition and personal reminiscences, highly simplified general traditions and detailed individual memories. The epitaphioi, however selective, could provide the broad framework of Athenian history. Since there was no teaching of history in its own right, this framework could be more useful than we would expect. A detailed résumé of events since the Persian Wars (as in Lysias and Plato) could transmit and reinforce the sequence of Athenian history – while the period was still within living memory. Even Thucydides' dating for episodes in the Pentekontaëtia is inaccurate or vague, though he must have been able to consult people who had taken part. The period was presumably reinforced – and adjusted – in people's memories by the epitaphioi. Lysias' epitaphic treatment of Myronides' campaign suggests that Thucydides was partly writing against the distorted epitaphic version of Athenian *aretē*.

The span of official tradition extended widely from legendary times to the present. But it contained huge gaps. There was nothing of the vast stretch of time between the legends and the battle of Marathon. There was no official tradition recording the broad sequence of Athenian history in the sixth century. Neither the Peisistratids nor even Solon were included. The traditions available to Herodotus for the sixth century were neither helped nor distorted by official tradition; they may have been exceedingly blurred before Herodotus collected them (see further Ch. 5). For the official tradition, recent history began with Marathon. We may suppose that concentration on legendary history and the post-Marathon period encouraged rapid loss of memories and therefore the 'telescoping' of that period in between. It may have helped to preserve the sequence of fifth-century history. But the official tradition encouraged knowledge of Athens' past only at its extreme ends.

*

The funeral speeches propagated both the official traditions of Athens and a powerful group of ideals about Athens which determined the picture of history found there. Thus they form an outstandingly clear example of the way beliefs, values and 'ideology' help form and transform oral tradition.

Certain values with democratic overtones actually rendered much of the past irrelevant. Much of Athens' history is anonymous, celebrating the Athenian demos certainly, but not individuals and individuals' achievements. Individual ancestry is also irrelevant. Though many of the values seem essentially aristocratic in tone, their democratic application produces a bare and anonymous past. The innate superiority of Athens, which in the epitaphios is essentially military and heroic, pervades the whole.

Certain other tendencies which we might see rather as aristocratic served to render Athens' recent history comparatively unimportant, a mere reflection of its legendary past. For the Athenian demos acquired an official tradition on the model of an aristocratic family tradition. It acquired a noble, legendary ancestry which was crucial for later character and repeated those characteristics which had existed since earliest times – virtue, justice, nobility. There was little need to distinguish individuals, different campaigns, differing historical contexts, if the whole of Athenian history was seen as a manifestation of heroic Athenian virtue present from the start. The pattern of emphasis and memory in aristocratic tradition is repeated: there is an immense gap of ignorance between the legendary origins and the recent events which may themselves reflect the legendary origins. The implications of this for memory or tradition of the recent historical period are far-reaching, and it is worth wondering how far these ideals are reflected in the treatment of Athenian history by its historians, especially the Atthidographers. Against these ideals even the democracy could be read back into the legendary period. Certainly there was little pressing need to chart its recent developments. The interest of the official tradition simply lay elsewhere.

The fact that Athens' official tradition was encouraged and propagated at the public celebration of its war-dead deserves reflection. It was the achievements of war, rather than more civic achievements at home, which provided the best occasion for official commemoration of the polis' identity and past. Along with the complacent clichés of excellence, the overwhelming patriotism expressed throughout the epitaphioi cannot be overemphasized. Athens' superiority, which is primarily military, is fundamental, and we must adjust our view of classical Athens accordingly.

Similarly with the official tradition of its past and its relation to Greek historiography. Some of the peculiar features of epitaphic history are linked not with political bias, but simply with the ideas behind the official celebration (especially Athens' innate superiority). Thucydides was probably writing against the gross distortions of Athens' recent past that the official tradition encouraged. It is easy to discern these distortions, but we should not see them merely as predictable propaganda and leave it at that. For they point to some interesting characteristics and problems of oral transmission against the written word. First, without certain kinds of written documents there would be little check on the content of oral tradition except other people's memories. Of course, official history may distort and select equally in a modern society equipped with numerous newspapers and historical accounts to contradict it. But when oral transmission is dominant and knowledge of the past not gleaned from contemporary documents or written histories, there might be almost no checks at all on such distortion, whether it be deliberately misleading 'propaganda' or wishful thinking based on faulty memory. So, the memories of individuals and their families would here be an important, if fallible, counterbalance.

But secondly, the 'distortion' would be encouraged or reinforced by certain ideals, and again the line between deliberately misleading propaganda and wishful thinking might be blurred. Compare, for instance, the ideal that death in battle was itself a glorious and heroic deed regardless of the outcome. This ideal was even reflected in the written records of the dead, the casualty lists, which named only the place of death. Given that, it was all the easier to forget the actual outcome and assume, once immediate memories had faded, that it must have been another Athenian victory. The processes of forgetting and of memory, which – unlike the written word – is not preserved by accident, could achieve considerable distortion by themselves.

5

THE LIBERATION OF ATHENS AND THE 'ALCMAEONID TRADITION'

The traditions of Athens' 'liberation' from the Peisistratid tyranny in the late sixth century are perhaps the best known, indeed most notorious, of her oral traditions. We have already touched on them from the perspective of family tradition (Ch.. 2.4.2 and 2.4.3). In this chapter, I shall re-examine the whole complex of traditions in various sectors of Athens and over the course of two hundred years. They may be treated as a case study for the character, development and processes of oral tradition in Athens.

So far we have concentrated on a single type of tradition at a time, yet as we have seen also, traditions and memories affect each other: no memory is totally independent. Different types of tradition may complement, reinforce or contradict each other. What, then, was the overall picture provided by the various traditions? What kind of complexity were Thucydides or Herodotus faced with when trying to enquire about the past? If we are to understand the overall character, mechanisms and development of oral tradition, rather than individual examples or groups, we must confront a whole body of related traditions and their gradual changes – in short, the fluid and ever-shifting spectrum of memories which made up Athens' images of its past.

The 'expulsion of the tyrants' in the late sixth century was an important part of family tradition and defence. It was also crucial to the polis as a whole: the 'liberation of Athens' which supposedly brought back the democracy was one of the most admired parts of Athens' history. Harmodius and Aristogeiton, the tyrannicides, had killed Hipparchus, brother of the reigning tyrant Hippias and son of Peisistratos, in 514, four years before the tyranny was finally brought to an end. They received statues and an official cult glorifying their deed. It was Cleisthenes who, some years later in 508/7, was mainly responsible for establishing the democracy itself. He was a member of the prominent Alcmaeonid family which we have already encountered (Ch. 2.4.3). So the Alcmaeonid family tradition recurs again. It later claimed that their ancestor had been responsible for the end of the tyranny and the establishment of democracy. And since Cleisthenes was so crucial a figure in the new democracy, we may expect him to recur in the general polis traditions, too. We may thus compare family and polis traditions, popular tradition and official tradition. We can analyse the different versions or character of each, the influence and interaction of different memories, and the process of change over the course of time (roughly from the time of the original events to the late fourth century B.C.). We may see how knowledge or memories about a certain period built up, developed, became simplified and eventually broke down over a long period and amongst several sectors of Athens. Closely linked to these problems are the traditions and origins of the traditions about the Alcmaeonid family itself. This illuminates not only the processes of memory and oral tradition, but the opportunities and problems of the ancient historians in reconstructing the past. Herodotus, for instance, is widely believed to have depended heavily on an 'Alcmaeonid source'[1] – which bulks large in modern discussions – and his historiographical methods are judged accordingly. But closer analysis of the sources with more sophisticated understanding of oral tradition shows that this is unconvincing, and we may adjust our evaluation of Herodotus' achievement. We cannot judge ancient historiography adequately without some understanding of the historians' problems in gathering information.

There is a further advantage in examining this particular group of traditions. Since the expulsion of the Athenian tyrants provides perhaps the best known examples of oral tradition, it has tended to form most people's ideas of Greek oral tradition; Thucydides commented in a famous passage on Athenian misconceptions about the tyrannicides and the themes recur frequently in comedy. Propounded most forcefully by Jacoby, it has become a commonplace that the people of Athens and the official tradition held that Athens had been liberated by the tyrannicides and their murder of Hipparchus, whereas the Alcmaeonid family, remembering Cleisthenes and his establishment of the democracy, claimed it was *they* who had done so. We know from the detailed accounts of Herodotus and Thucydides, however, that the tyranny continued for four years after the tyrannicides' act and that the final expulsion of Hippias involved 'the Alcmaeonids in exile', the Spartan army and confused and lengthy military activity before the democracy was eventually established by Cleisthenes in 508/7. So, apparently confirmed by Thucydides' remarks on the people's mistaken beliefs, the whole case provides a classic and notorious example of 'oral tradition', its limitations, simplistic nature and general inaccuracy. How, one wonders, could Herodotus have managed to find out anything at all?

But this picture, too, is misleading and simplistic. In particular, it misunderstands the nature of oral tradition and the ways in which it

---

[1] Most influentially argued by Jacoby, *Atthis* 161 and (1913), 413f. For others, see Ch. 5.5 and n. 72 there.

develops and changes. The extensive discussions on the subject present, on the whole, a simple picture of two parallel and unchanging traditions – the Alcmaeonid tradition and the popular tradition – which vary only in the extent to which their proponents used them. The role of crucial elements like the Alcmaeonid curse is barely considered, and the supposed Alcmaeonid tradition has a much exaggerated part. Evidence outside the historians, such as other family or polis traditions, has received little attention. Re-examination of the evidence for the oral traditions shows that there was no dichotomy between two versions of the liberation, and the traditions were much more complex and interesting than the accepted picture. Since this case has seemed so typical of oral tradition in general, I hope to show how complicated and resilient oral tradition could be and what were the reasons behind its changes in content. In the process, the methods and difficulties of the historians, from Herodotus to the fourth-century writers, are clarified: in other words, we return to the relation between oral tradition and the historians themselves with their written accounts. The traditions of 'the liberation' can be taken as a test-case.

First, it is helpful to run briefly through Herodotus' narrative of the 'liberation' (v 62ff.) to emphasize the complexity in his account of the original course of events. This complexity is reduced to the utmost simplicity by the traditions we shall be examining and often overlooked by modern discussion: After the murder of Hipparchus by the tyrannicides, the tyranny became harsher under Hippias, and the Alcmaeonids in exile tried and failed to fortify Leipsydrion. Then they gained the contract for rebuilding the temple at Delphi. The Athenians add (§63.1) that while there they bribed the Delphic prophetess, the Pythia, who therefore repeatedly told Sparta to free Athens, instead of delivering the genuine words of the god Apollo. After initial failure, the Spartans tried again and succeeded in besieging the Peisistratids and capturing their children. Thus Athens was freed (§65.5). Then Herodotus tells of the rivalry for power between Cleisthenes and Isagoras (§§66ff.) and how Cleisthenes took the demos into partnership and rearranged the tribes. Isagoras retaliated by persuading the Spartan king Cleomenes to expel Cleisthenes and many other Athenians on the grounds that they were accursed. (The Alcmaeonids were accursed because of their irreligious murder of those taking part in the seventh-century conspiracy of Cylon (Hdt. v 71). The murder of suppliants was a crime against the gods, for which the Alcmaeonids needed purification to remain in the city.) This involved the exile of seven hundred families. Cleomenes and Isagoras took the Acropolis, but the rest of the Athenians besieged and defeated them. The Athenians were able to recall Cleisthenes and the seven hundred families (§73.1). Shortly afterwards Athens defeated the Boiotians and Chalcidians. The sequence of events is complex but clear.

If we return to modern ideas about the traditions, we must start from Jacoby's influential schema and its implications for oral tradition which subsequent criticism or refinements have not really tackled. The 'Alcmaeonid tradition's' salient feature in its modern guise is its opposition to the 'official tyrannicide tradition' forcefully presented by Jacoby.[2] According to Jacoby (*Atthis* 162), the 'Alcmaeonid tradition' (of the fifth century) consisted mainly of their claim that it was they who liberated Athens, with the help of Sparta and Delphi; this was opposed by the 'official' and popular belief that the tyrannicides were responsible, and that was reinforced by their statues and cult. The second notion had won by the fifth century because of the Alcmaeonids' ambiguous policy between 510 and 490 B.C. Later discussions and even criticisms have been on the lines laid out by Jacoby, without complete re-examination of the evidence or allowance for the oral character of the traditions.[3]

But the actual content of the 'tyrannicide version' is not clear. Jacoby seems to assume that most Athenians believed the tyrannicides were literally the liberators: that liberation occurred without the intervention of Sparta or Cleisthenes, which were part of his 'Alcmaeonid version'.[4] There is more serious confusion in Jacoby and later discussions between emphasis or 'notions' and actual 'traditions' which imply a coherent narrative. Jacoby insists that 'there is no variation of any importance as to the facts'; the disagreement centred on who had the merit of liberating Athens.[5] However, the debate is not actually couched in those terms,[6] nor should it be. We cannot talk of 'emphasis' in oral tradition without implying variation in the tradition's content. Difference in judgement is expressed by exaggeration and omission, and that forms a 'tradition'. Omissions are eventually forgotten. There were, in fact, extremely significant variations in the traditions' accounts of the 'facts' which have barely been noticed.

Far from a straight division between the 'Alcmaeonid version' and the 'official tradition', the evidence actually shows a considerably more

---

[2] There is an extensive earlier literature, e.g. Hirsch (1926) who stresses the folktale aspect.

[3] Podlecki (1966) with variations or correction of Jacoby; Ehrenberg (1950) and (1956); Fornara (1968a) and (1968b), then modified substantially in (1970). Cf. also Forrest (1969); Fitzgerald (1957), who imports the idea of oligarchic/conservative views to Jacoby's theory; Lang (1954–5). Vlastos' article 'Isonomia' (1953) has a brief but extremely clear-headed discussion of the whole controversy.

[4] As taken by e.g. Forrest (1969). Fornara (1970), esp. 167f., is more complex.

[5] *Atthis* 153; for the slide from the term 'notions' to 'tradition', see *Atthis* 162.

[6] Compare even Fornara (1970), who allows that the dichotomy between Alcmaeonid and popular tradition comes to the fore later on.

complicated web of oral traditions for the latter half of the fifth century and even later. We must be particularly aware that the oral traditions change with the passage of time and analyse them accordingly. There is a tendency to envisage them as remaining much the same from the late sixth century into even the fourth (if the passage of time is considered at all). But oral traditions can develop rapidly, and the traditions of 'liberation' were still alive in the fourth century. Moreover, the character and changes of later versions may sometimes explain the earlier ones, since in the continuous development of tradition certain elements become exaggerated or submerged (this will be clearer with examples below).

I shall use the term 'Alcmaeonid tradition' in inverted commas to denote Jacoby's idea of the contents of their tradition. In Jacoby's schema that tradition was the one which remembered the military side of the expulsion (i.e. with Cleisthenes and Spartan help), as opposed to the simple killing of the tyrant. But I shall need to refer to versions that presupposed military action and not simply tyrannicide and which do not correspond to Jacoby's schema.

I will look first at the traditions of the liberation that existed in the fifth and fourth centuries, from our earliest dateable evidence (Herodotus) to the less familiar evidence of comedy and of oratory (Ch. 5.1 and 5.2). This will reveal the changes in traditions and suggest that the prevalent habit of seeing the historians as representative of the 'Alcmaeonid tradition' is very misleading. These later traditions, for which there is much evidence, show how complex traditions still were beyond living memory. We can return to the accounts of the late sixth and early fifth centuries with more realistic expectations of memories so soon after the expulsion (Ch. 5.3); then to the Alcmaeonid family tradition itself (Ch. 5.4); and finally to the remaining information about the family from Herodotus' 'Alcmaeonid excursus', and to the traditions concerning the origins of the Alcmaeonid curse (Ch. 5.5).

5.1 The fifth-century traditions

Popular tradition in the fifth century did not simply hold that the tyrannicides liberated Athens. It was quite well aware of the military events (though much simplified) surrounding the establishment of the Cleisthenic democracy which formed Jacoby's picture of the 'Alcmaeonid tradition'. This is even clearer in fourth-century tradition, and it disproves Jacoby's schema conclusively.

I shall start with Thucydides. His notorious criticism of the ignorance of the Athenian people has often been taken to show that the fifth-century demos believed the tyranny was ended by the tyrannicides alone and thus knew nothing of the Alcmaeonids' part and the military intervention of Sparta.[7]

But this misunderstands what Thucydides actually says (I 20 and VI 53ff.). He is not complaining that most people (*to plēthos*) think Harmodius and Aristogeiton ended the tyranny, but that first (I 20.1), 'most of the Athenians think Hipparchus was the tyrant when he was murdered by Harmodius and Aristogeiton', and secondly, they did not know that Hippias was the older and the ruler. (Harmodius and Aristogeiton, he continues, realized they had been discovered and instead of attacking Hippias, turned on Hipparchus, so as not to lose their lives for nothing.)[8] The belief that Hipparchus was the tyrant recurs in [Plato] *Hipparchus* (228b), and, as Thucydides acknowledges, it is easy to see why the mistake, if it was a mistake,[9] arose.

Thucydides returns to the ending of the tyranny in Book VI (53–9), in the midst of his narrative of the mutilation of the Hermae and the Sicilian expedition of 415. The digression is not merely an expansion of I 20, as is often thought. Introduced in the manner it is (§53.3), it may prompt us to consider the similarities of circumstances after the mutilation of the Hermae and in 514 when Hipparchus was murdered and so the possibilities of tyranny in 415.[10] There is factual coherence as well as artistic unity. The passage adds much to our picture of fifth-century oral traditions.

The digression is introduced thus (§53.3):

> For the people (*demos*) knew from oral tradition (*akoē*) that the tyranny of Peisistratos and his sons had been very harsh in its later stages and further that it had been brought to an end not by

[7] Jacoby suggests that he is also attacking Hellanicus. Fornara (1968b) and (1970), 168 discusses in detail the 'vulgate' which he believes Thucydides to be criticizing and which is Jacoby's 'official tradition' with some extra details.

[8] I shall not be discussing fully the details surrounding the actual murder itself. Even in Thucydides' narrative, the assassination has some political motivation, despite the love affair that initiated it: the conspirators originally intended to murder Hippias and end the tyranny, and they have accomplices. On the discrepancy between Thucydides and Aristotle here, see Fornara (1968b), Lang (1954–5) and Dover and Andrewes *HCT* on VI 54ff.

[9] Cf. Dover and Andrewes, *HCT* on VI 54ff. Thucydides and modern scholars are perhaps pedantic to stress the 'constitutional' primacy of Hippias. Hipparchus may have been regarded in his life as a 'tyrant', hence the title of 'tyrannicides' may reflect popular nomenclature, later misunderstood (see Fornara (1970)). [Plato] *Hipp.* 228b–229d has everything: Hipparchus is the oldest, *and* the tyranny gets worse after the murder.

[10] Curiously, most discussions detach what they call the digression (§§54–9) from the sentence introducing it (§53.3) and regard that as contradicting the tenor of §54–9 (*Atthis* esp. 338, n. 51), though it is improbable that a sentence written to introduce a 'digression' should contradict it (cf. Dover and Andrewes, *HCT* on VI 54ff.). On the direct bearing of the digression: Schadewalt (1929), 89ff. For interpretations of Thucydides' aim, see Momigliano (1971a), Pearson (1949), Hunter (1974), Taylor (1981); Dover, *HCT* against similarities between the situations in 415 and 514.

themselves and Harmodius, but by the Spartans. So they were constantly afraid and took everything suspiciously.

Thucydides is telling us explicitly that the people knew by oral tradition (*akoē*, repeated in §60.1) that the ending of tyranny was difficult and accomplished not by themselves and Harmodius the tyrannicide, but by the Spartans. That is, it was popularly known that the tyranny was ended by the military events which might approximate to Jacoby's 'Alcmaeonid tradition'.[11]

In fact, Thucydides is contrasting not the Alcmaeonids' part and the tyrannicides', but the tyrannicides and the knowledge that it was Athens' main rival Sparta which ended the tyranny. He may imply that some said the liberation was an entirely Athenian affair. This emphasis recurs elsewhere (see below, p. 246). Was this, then, the more important conflict of tradition in the fifth century – between memories of Sparta's help and attempts to recall the expulsion as a purely Athenian achievement? There were obvious incentives for the latter, but memories of Spartan help had not yet died.[12]

Thucydides continues with the lengthy digression on the actions of Harmodius and Aristogeiton and the continuation of tyranny after the murder. But the corrections he makes do not contradict his previous remarks. His complaint here (§54.1) should be taken in its literal and vague sense: he does not say that Athenians have a totally mistaken view of the ending of the tyranny, but simply that their beliefs about the tyrants are very inaccurate (ἀκριβὲς οὐδὲν λέγοντας, 'they say nothing accurate'). He implies he is criticizing a grossly simplified or incorrect conception of the murder and following tyranny. As he says, the Athenians and 'others' (probably Hellanicus)[13] have no accurate knowledge of the tyranny's end. He argues against a view that Hipparchus was tyrant when murdered and that the plot was conceived in entirely altruistic and democratic spirit. He may imply more. For instance, the belief that Hipparchus was the tyrant may have engendered an idea that his murder ended the tyranny. But even so, Thucydides' other remarks (§53.3) show clearly that that belief left room for military force as well, Athenian or Spartan or both. In fact, the last tyrant, Hippias, was popularly known, often mentioned in comedy,[14] and remembered pre-

---

[11] Dismissed curiously by Jacoby (*Atthis*) as telling us nothing about popular traditions: he thinks Thucydides' statements about the knowledge of the demos are relevant only to his own research, i.e. VI 53.3 criticizes what the demos does not know.

[12] Dover, *HCT* 329, suggests that there might have been a recent warning before 415, but that is not what Thucydides says, and the *Lysistrata* presupposes the same knowledge. Theories that Thucydides refers to recent historians (Fitzgerald (1957), Taylor (1981)) overestimate historians' influence on the demos.

[13] *Atthis* 159, though Jacoby thinks he simply produced the 'official' tyrannicide version.

[14] Ar. *Wasps* 500–2 (pun on name); *Knights* 447ff.

cisely because his expulsion had ended the tyranny. Though they might have been confused, Athenians were aware that Spartan intervention had been necessary.

It is striking, then, that this Spartan help is also stressed in another source very close to popular tradition and opinion. In Aristophanes' comedy *Lysistrata* (411 B.C.), Lysistrata tries to show the futility of the war. She cites both Athens' help to Sparta against the helots in the mid-fifth century and Sparta's help to Athens in expelling her tyrants. This reference, omitted from most discussions of the traditions,[15] confirms what Thucydides tells us: the Athenians knew that the end of the tyranny involved military intervention, and Spartan intervention at that (*Lys.* 1150ff.):

> Do you not know how the Spartans came in force when you were dressed in sheep skins and slaughtered many Thessalian men, many of the friends and allies of Hippias, how they fought together with you alone on that day. And they freed you, and instead of the sheep skins, they clothed you, the demos, in the civic cloak again.[16]

So no credit is given to the tyrannicides, nor in fact to Cleisthenes. The Spartans alone are responsible (*monoi*, 1154). This same stress on the Spartans can only be representative of popular knowledge gained and transmitted in the theatre, though its emphasis may be rather different from public statements in the assembly.[17]

Other allusions in the *Lysistrata* to Sparta and the expulsion make the picture more complicated. The chorus of old men hint grimly that this women's plot may involve tyranny and Spartan soldiers (619ff.).[18] They will stand firm against any attempt at tyranny, near the statue of the tyrannicide Aristogeiton (625ff.). They associate tyranny and Sparta, attempts to impose tyranny and Spartan help – as is understandable

---

[15] Noted, however, by Fornara (1970), 168f.

[16] οὐκ ἴσθ᾽ ὅθ᾽ ὑμᾶς οἱ Λάκωνες αὖθις αὖ / κατωνάκας φοροῦντας ἐλθόντες δορὶ / πολλοὺς μὲν ἄνδρας Θετταλῶν ἀπώλεσαν, / πολλοὺς δ᾽ ἑταίρους Ἱππίου καὶ ξυμμάχους, / ξυνεκμαχοῦντες τῇ τόθ᾽ ἡμέρᾳ μόνοι, / κἠλευθέρωσαν κἀντὶ τῆς κατωνάκης / τὸν δῆμον ὑμῶν χλαῖναν ἠμπέσχον πάλιν;

[17] Ch. 5.2, below. It is interesting that the *chlaina* here is used in contrast to sheep skin to signify the urban demos as opposed to the rural, and the urban image is associated with political institutions.

[18] καὶ μάλιστ᾽ ὀσφραίνομαι τῆς Ἱππίου τυραννίδος / καὶ πάνυ δέδοικα μὴ τῶν Λακώνων τινὲς / δεῦρο συνεληλυθότες ἄνδρες ἐς Κλεισθένους / τὰς θεοῖς ἐχθρὰς γυναῖκας ἐξεπαίρωσιν δόλῳ / καταλαβεῖν τὰ χρήμαθ᾽ ἡμῶν τόν τε μισθόν, . . . 'I can smell the tyranny of Hippias. I'm very much afraid some Spartans have met together here at the house of Cleisthenes [late fifth-century contemporary] and have incited these impious women to take our money and pay by stealth.' See Hopper (1960) on their description of themselves as 'white-footed' (665–70) and associations.

during the Peloponnesian War. They then recall their stand at Leipsydrion (665–70). It is interesting that they call on Leipsydrion as if it had
been a victory, an inversion of defeat to democratic victory that recurs in
Athens' oral traditions (Ch. 4, p. 231). But its relation to the tyranny's
overthrow is quite unclear. As a final surprise we also find the old men
recalling the Spartan king Cleomenes' seizure of the Acropolis (274ff.)
and how they besieged him there (281–2). This refers to the Spartan
attempt, *after* the actual expulsion, to unite with Isagoras, and, reversing
their previous action, expel the Alcmaeonids and bring back the tyranny
(as in Hdt. v). The association of ideas which prompts this reminiscence
is between the seizure of the Acropolis by Lysistrata and by Cleomenes
('who occupied it first', 274), which introduces into the chorus' muddled
minds and historical knowledge the ideas of betrayal to Sparta, treason
and tyranny.

Clearly these reminiscences contradict Jacoby's ideas of the 'popular
tyrannicide tradition'. Patriotic reminiscences of the military events
accompany proud reference to the tyrannicides. But these old men did
not think the tyrannicides ended the tyranny; they did that themselves.
Moreover, their picture of the military events is complex, if muddled.
Leipsydrion, usually taken to be an aristocratic affair, the great stand of
the Alcmaeonids in exile and other nobles,[19] has become important in
popular tradition. The 'Marathon-fighters' (*Marathonomachoi*) of
Aristophanes' choruses can recall it with pride and nostalgia. There is
little room for the Alcmaeonids, and the men say nothing of the
expulsion itself, recalling only their own siege of Cleomenes. This siege
thus seems to be the other salient element in their conception of the
expulsion. The Spartan occupation of the Acropolis perhaps obscured
the genuine help Sparta gave, and, given its association with tyranny,
helped to amalgamate the tyranny's end and the siege of the Acropolis.
The old men apparently envisage a liberation effected by their resistance
at Leipsydrion against tyrants and Spartans, then the siege by the demos
of the Spartan Cleomenes on the Acropolis (without the Alcmaeonids).
The logical inference is that the 'liberation' was finally achieved when the
demos defeated Cleomenes.

In other words, the tyrannicides are part of the patriotic call, but
marginal symbols of the kind of resistance one must make against
tyranny (631ff.).[20] They are not incompatible with a popular tradition
recording the original events in some complexity. The Alcmaeonids are
absent from both the old men's picture and Lysistrata's, but with

---

[19] Hdt. v 62.2, Arist. *Ath. Pol.* 19.3; cf. Bowra (1936), 383f. on the Leipsydrion skolion
and its allusion to the Eupatridai, 'the only poem in the collection which can be referred
with some confidence to the Alcmaeonids'. But it does not mention them.

[20] So the Aristophanic allusions to the Harmodius song cannot be taken in isolation either.

different results. For Lysistrata, Sparta simply liberated Athens; according to the old men's chorus, the Athenian demos did (cf. Thuc. VI 53.3).
In some version representative of popular tradition, the liberation was a
wholly Athenian affair achieved by the great Athenian demos, encouraged by the tyrannicides, and finished off by the expulsion of Cleomenes
from the Acropolis. I suspect that this patriotic and chauvinistic vision
was encouraged by the democratic rhetoric of the assembly (cf. Ch. 4 on
the patriotic tendencies of official tradition). The fifth-century conflicts
between oligarchic Sparta and democratic Athens would help reinterpret
events. Fourth-century rhetoric later elevates it to a democratic and
Athenian struggle (below, Ch. 5.2). The more important distortions in
the oral traditions were not connected with the rival 'tyrannicide' or
'Alcmaeonid' versions but with the role of Sparta. Sparta's prominent
part in this great landmark of the democratic tradition was wholly
unwelcome. In fact, that Sparta had freed Athens was still popular
knowledge in the late fifth century. It is hard to imagine how this survived
if not because the events were only just beyond living memory.[21] But that
very survival brings into relief the omission of Sparta's help from the
more patriotic traditions. Such distortions were prompted by the narrow
needs of Athenian patriotism.

What then of Herodotus? It is only in his history that we find explicit
sign of controversy about who liberated Athens, the tyrannicides or the
Alcmaeonids.[22] For after his narrative of the battle of Marathon, he
discusses the accusation that the Alcmaeonids tried to betray Athens to
the Persians and Hippias. He explicitly defends them (VI 121–4) and then
relates their earlier family history (125–30). Jacoby and others have
thought he was simply reproducing Alcmaeonid tradition.

He declares (VI 121) that it is extraordinary to him that the Alcmaeonids should have raised the shield at Marathon, for they were 'tyrant-
haters' (*misotyrannoi*). He elaborates on his reasons: 'For they were in
exile for the whole time the tyranny lasted, and it was through a trick
(μηχανή) of theirs that the Peisistratids lost the tyranny' (VI 123.1). 'And
thus it was they who freed Athens far more than Harmodius and
Aristogeiton, as I believe' (123.2).

Comparison between the tyrannicides and Alcmaeonids is explicit.
Certainly it is a matter of emphasis only, and so should not imply a severe
division between two traditions.[23] But more significant, he is making a

---

[21] Perhaps brought up as a reason for helping the Spartans against the helots, the parallel
example Lysistrata uses. The same two examples are cited by Spartan ambassadors in a
Xenophon speech (370 B.C.), *Hell.* VI 5.33.

[22] On the tyrannicide skolia, thought to support Herodotus, see Ch. 5.3 below.

[23] As I said, discussions have not been couched in terms of emphasis alone, but of separate
traditions.

rather different contrast from that hinted at in Thucydides and the *Lysistrata*. Bereft of Thucydides' support, the view that Herodotus' 'Alcmaeonid excursus' represents the Alcmaeonid tradition needs closer scrutiny.

Most important is the basic assumption that Herodotus is voicing an 'Alcmaeonid source' for this whole section on the family – partly because he seems to defend them, partly because he describes their past history. But the excursus has several curious elements which contradict this theory. Here I concentrate on the first half (returning later to the other half on earlier Alcmaeonid history, which seems to represent neither the family version, nor a straightforward 'defence' of the family). The first part itself (VI 121–4) explicitly defends the Alcmaeonids against the charge of treason at Marathon, for the family were 'tyrant-haters' and in continuous exile during the tyranny (121 and 123.1). These are two genuine family arguments for they occur in Isoc. XVI as well (Ch. 5.4, below), but one should not be misled into taking the whole passage as indicative of the Alcmaeonid defence and tradition. For Herodotus uses other, very unsuitable arguments for the family defence; indeed, he gives a non-family source for them.

Herodotus gives other reasons against Alcmaeonid treason: that the tyranny continued after the murder of Hipparchus and the Alcmaeonids really liberated Athens, 'if in fact it was they who persuaded the Delphic priestess to instruct the Spartans to free Athens, as I have shown already' (VI 123.2). Thus, Herodotus is stressing the Alcmaeonid bribery of Delphi to utter false and non-divine advice as the crucial factor in their liberation of Athens.[24] He told us this before and repeats it (V 63.1, 66.1, 90.1, 91.2), and in the actual narrative of the liberation (V 63.1) he adds that this is something 'the Athenians say'. I see no reason to disbelieve this source citation,[25] and Herodotus certainly accepts its information as true.[26] If we look at the excursus without preconceptions about an Alcmaeonid source, Herodotus seems deliberately to be adding

---

[24] See Bornitz (1968), 30ff, for Herodotus' stress on the Alcmaeonid 'trick' or *mēchanē*. As Fornara admits (1970), 63, n. 39), this emphasis makes his own interpretation difficult.

[25] The text was once even emended to read 'the Lacedaemonians' (Schweighäuser), accepted by Forrest (1969): this implied that Herodotus was using a different Spartan account. Against the emendation, Kinzl (1975), esp. 194f., n. 8. As for the beginning of the sentence (ὡς ὦν δὴ οἱ Ἀθηναῖοι λέγουσιν), ὦν δὴ is normally 'resumptive after a digression' (Powell, *Herodotus Lexicon* s.v.), which further tells against the idea that an alternative story is being added.

[26] Argued away on the grounds that Herodotus is simply following 'the Alcmaeonid source' or that Athenians only knew about the tyrannicides' liberation, Forrest (1969).

awkward and non-Alcmaeonid confirmation of the Alcmaeonid claim to have liberated Athens.[27]

So we return to the bribery of the Pythia and the intrusion of Spartan help. Who remembered these, and can they possibly have been part of an Alcmaeonid defence? There can be little doubt that for the fifth century and even more for the participants themselves, bribing the Delphic Pythia, the prophetic mouthpiece of Apollo, to give false utterances was not something to boast of, but a most shameful thing. In Herodotus' narrative, the Spartans are most incensed when they discover they have been tricked (v 90.1, 91.2).[28] For Herodotus' own view, we may compare his shocked opinion of Cleomenes, who also tried to corrupt the Pythia, or his treatment of oracles in general.[29] Nor can we assume that most Athenians even in the second half of the fifth century would have had little objection.[30] One might recall here Plutarch's disapproval of Herodotus, for though he wrote so much later, his reaction is surely closer to that of classical Athens than ours. For him, Herodotus' stress on the importance of the bribery is yet another sign of Herodotus' '*malignitas*' (*De malig.* 23): he 'attaches an accusation of such impiety and villany to so noble and just a deed' (καλλίστῳ μὲν ἔργῳ καὶ δικαιοτάτῳ προσάπτων ἀσεβήματος διαβολὴν τηλικούτου καὶ ῥᾳδιουργήματος).

The general attitudes to such corruption are crucial in considering an Alcmaeonid 'defence', their justification of their magnificent part in the expulsion. For the 'liberation' was regarded as perhaps the greatest landmark in Athenian democratic history. Both the polis traditions propounded through the democratic organs and the Alcmaeonid family tradition had reasons to avoid, and therefore eventually forget, undesirable aspects of this achievement. The Alcmaeonids also had the embarrassment of the family curse which played an important part in events (see Chs. 2.4.3 and 5.5). Could they afford to boast of a 'liberation' in terms admitting that they had also bribed the Pythia? Here

---

[27] Hence vi 123.2, 'As I think . . . as I have already shown', stressing his own opinion (not merely an Alcmaeonid's) and its basis on the fact of bribery which he attributed before to the Athenians.

[28] §90.1: 'For the Spartans had learned of the tricks (τὰ μεμαχανημένα) played on the Pythia by the Alcmaeonids and those of the Pythia against themselves and the Peisistratids, and so they suffered a double misfortune.' Cf. §91.2 in their speech to Hippias, 'misled by treacherous oracles'.

[29] Herodotus says (vi 75.3) many Greeks thought Cleomenes was punished (by going mad) for his corruption of the Pythia; Paus. iii 4.6 thought he was the only man to have tried anything so impious; Hdt. vi 86 (Glaucus) and Diod. xiv 13 (Lysander).

[30] The scepticism of the Sophists may not have extended much further than the circle of their pupils. The *Clouds* makes fun of the Sophists' 'irreligion', among other things. Cf. the uproar over the mutilation of the Hermae and parody of the Mysteries. Propaganda and rhetorical defence had to rely on *popular* ideas of morality and religion (Dover (1974), ch. 1).

public opinion and family tradition would tend to converge. The suspicion that neither wanted to recall the role of Delphi is confirmed by the treatment of the story in fourth-century traditions (Ch. 5.2 below). Delphi is eventually eased out of the liberation, the bribery and the willing help of Sparta which so closely went with it are smoothed down to produce a democratic and almost wholly Athenian achievement. These tendencies may already have been present in the fifth century before genuine memories had died. We have seen an unwillingness to acknowledge Sparta's help in some of the popular fifth-century traditions, and the roles of Delphi and Sparta are so closely linked that if one is omitted the other loses its causal connection.

But these tendencies would act gradually on the traditions, not obliterating the offending elements completely until the fourth century when memories were fading. Some of Herodotus' contemporaries still knew that the Alcmaeonids had corrupted the Pythia – and Herodotus chose to stress that. Surely this must be information remembered against the Alcmaeonids, perhaps anti-Alcmaeonid gossip, not an aspect that the family tradition would stress. If not actually libel, it can only have been damaging to the family.

In other words, in the late fifth and early fourth centuries, it was known even by the demos that it was not the tyrannicides alone who freed Athens. But in the memories of the complicated military events, there are already signs of a willingness to make the liberation an entirely Athenian achievement. Neither the Alcmaeonids nor the patriotic, democratic traditions stressed the ambiguous or unwelcome role of Delphi and Sparta. Yet, it was still known by Athenians, and Herodotus managed to find it out. The conflicts behind the changing traditions centre around far more realistic issues than Alcmaeonid propaganda.

Why, then, did Herodotus imply a comparison between the relative contributions of the Alcmaeonids and the tyrannicides when oral tradition seems happily to have acknowledged the two different achievements together? The implicit comparison may have arisen, I think, from the fact that Herodotus was writing down the oral traditions about the end of the tyranny for the first time. Oral tradition can accommodate different tales or versions with contradictory implications. They can be remembered or told in isolation from each other and so that the inherent contradictions are not striking.[31] No one need put them together and weigh their implications, carefully reckoning the relative merits and contributions of different parties. One family thought they were the

---

[31] As Schadewalt realized (1929), 86ff., popular traditions could digest inconsistency. Cf. the isolated memories of individual ancestors not necessarily remembered as part of a family tree, Ch. 3.2 p. 171, Vansina, *OTH* 95, Firth (1961).

decisive leaders, another family thought *their* ancestors were, everyone knew something of the armed intervention whether they thought it was Spartan or Athenian. Some aspects got omitted. Meanwhile, there was a state cult of the tyrannicides and extensive public honours for them. But this was not felt at all incompatible with the traditions of a military expulsion and even a belief that it was the glorious demos who expelled the tyrants. Herodotus brought together the traditions and wrote them down, and the inherent contradictions between excessive public honours to the tyrannicides and recognition of military expulsion became a glaring one. Having researched carefully into the original events, he felt he had to reassert the decisive part that the Alcmaeonids played – though he did this with details which were known to the Athenians themselves. This seems to be a striking – and notorious – instance where the actual collection and writing down of oral traditions revealed the inherent contradictions or illogicality of their literal interpretation.

5.2 The fourth-century traditions

The fourth-century traditions confirm our impressions gained from the fifth-century ones. They are also still developing under the pressure of fourth-century preoccupations, and the relation between the oral family traditions and the polis traditions of oratory becomes clearer.

First the family traditions. We have met those presented by Andocides and the younger Alcibiades (Ch. 2.4), by the speaker of Lys. xxvi (p. 129), and by Antiphon, who was accused of having an ancestor who was a partisan (*stasiōtēs*) and even bodyguard of the Peisistratids (Ant. fr. 1).[32] No doubt other traditions of opposition to the Peisistratids were produced after the oligarchic revolutions. Family defence before the demos must have been acceptable and familiar to the audience. It is striking that they all presuppose the military events of the expulsion and make no attempt to attach themselves to the tyrannicides. No allusion in the brief résumés of events in family defence is made either to the tyrannicides[33] or to the Alcmaeonids (except, of course, in the defence by an Alcmaeonid himself). Thus, traditions presupposing a return from exile and military expulsion of the tyrants were current in the early fourth century in both family and polis traditions of oratory. There is no

---

[32] Note the ease, however, with which Antiphon uses non-historical and logical points to discount the historical 'fact', indicating how to circumvent arguments from ancestral merit without historical knowledge. Cf. also Is. v 46, where the opponent is descended from Harmodius and Aristogeiton; or Dem. xxiv 127 (punishment is even more necessary if the father was virtuous).

[33] Only Is. v 46 brings in the tyrannicides, but to demolish possible arguments from the opponent who was descended from them.

dichotomy between 'official tyrannicide tradition' and 'Alcmaeonid tradition'. In fact, family traditions , whatever the family, claimed that it was *their* ancestors who played the most prominent role alongside the demos. Andocides claims of his ancestors what the Alcmaeonids claimed of theirs and makes no mention of Cleisthenes. This has its amusing side, since the name of the decisive battle he gives (Pallenion) was actually 40 years before the expulsion, and family tradition has transferred it to the later period (p. 139). Can this be representative of the aristocratic family traditions of early fourth-century Athens? Some perhaps attached them-selves to the returning demos as did the speaker of Lys. xxvi 21, but others were clearly less realistic.

So, there were still independent family traditions strong enough to maintain claims for over a hundred years without having to merge completely with the polis traditions.[34] They could be as resilient and dogmatic as the 'Alcmaeonid tradition' was supposed to be. In fact, such family traditions probably helped preserve memories of military inter-vention, for they had to stress that side of the story (as opposed to the simple act of the tyrannicides alone), in order to boast of their demo-cratic achievements.

But these family traditions were beginning to fail by the early fourth century and to lose the individual or 'anomalous' details that showed they preserved genuine memories (Ch. 2.3). Becoming more and more assimilated to the conventional polis traditions about the expulsion, they were approximating to a simple and stereotyped narrative bearing little relation to the actual events.[35] There is a highly complex relationship between family traditions and the more general conceptions of the polis traditions. We deduce from the family traditions that the polis traditions still entertained the version of military expulsion. But at the same time family traditions are themselves influenced by the prevailing conceptions of the polis traditions. Fading memories are reinforced by these general traditions and the family 'memories' eventually reduced to simple stereotypes.

Here the oligarchy of the Thirty (404 B.C.) played a crucial part. It served to rejuvenate memories about the earlier period by analogy, especially the 'exile of the demos' under the tyrants. We can thus see one of the ways in which traditions become simple stereotypes: past events are re-formed according to later perceptions and on analogy with later events which seem to be similar (I have touched on this already in Ch. 2.4). The end of the Peisistratid tyranny was cited as an analogy to a

---

[34] Ch. 2.4. The only other family tradition Jacoby and others consider is that of the tyrannicides, the Gephyraioi.

[35] Assimilation could have begun earlier, but we can only discern that influenced by the Thirty.

speaker's democratic behaviour during the rule of the Thirty. The same phrases are used of both periods of tyranny. Most significant are the variations on the phrase denoting the 'return of the demos from exile' – e.g. Isoc. XVI 26, 'As generals of the exiles, they led back the people (στρατηγήσαντες τῆς φυγῆς κατήγαγον τὸν δῆμον ...) and expelled the tyrants' – which is also used of the return of the democratic party from the Piraeus after the Thirty (e.g. Dem. XIX 277, 'those who led back the people from the Piraeus', τῶν ἐκ Πειραιῶς καταγαγόντων τὸν δῆμον).[36] This small catchphrase – κατήγαγον τὸν δῆμον – signifies a substantial change in the actual content of family and polis traditions of the liberation. In effect, it transfers what everyone knew to be a salient feature of the end of the Thirty to the earlier period.

How have the traditions of this exile developed? We do not know if an 'exile of the demos' appeared at all in fifth-century traditions. There seems no trace of such mass exile – or any exile – in the popular traditions of the Lysistrata. The patriotic reminiscences of the old men about their siege presuppose a more complex series of events and make no reference to return from exile. In fact, according to Herodotus it was after the siege that the seven hundred exiles were recalled, precisely because of the Athenians' victory over Cleomenes. That particular 'return' from exile was irrelevant to the demos' own resistance to the enemy and therefore to their memories. In Herodotus and Thucydides the main exiles are the Alcmaeonids, said sometimes to be with 'other Athenians'. In Herodotus' detailed narrative the only numerous group exiled are the seven hundred families expelled because of the Alcmaeonid curse. Can the 'exile of the demos' be a relic of that? As I argued earlier (Ch. 2.4.3), the Alcmaeonid tradition of their own continuous exile during the tyranny is largely a fabrication, developed partly to avoid mention of the curse. Their exile became an exile self-enforced for purely 'ideological' reasons. Has a similar transformation begun to seep into the polis traditions, starting from the exile of seven hundred families and crystallized by the 'exile' of the Piraeus party at the end of the fifth century? Clearly, the later return of the democratic party from exile under the Thirty serves to clarify and exaggerate the traditions about the earlier liberation. The later conditions and perceptions of the early fourth century alter people's memories and interpretations of the earlier period, and the traditions' content changes. Family traditions are also being influenced by the period of the Thirty as it was presented in the polis traditions. They are

---

[36] Also used of the end of Peisistratid tyranny by And. I 106 and II 26 (exile of the demos), Isoc. Antid. 232; Dem. XXI 144 only has 'in faction on behalf of the demos', ὑπὲρ τοῦ δήμου στασιάζοντας. In the defences against misodēmia (i.e. 'hating the people') under the Thirty, only the Peisistratid tyranny is an appropriate parallel: nothing else similar is cited from the period in-between.

still living oral traditions which undergo constant transformation, and for reasons far more complex than Alcmaeonid or anti-Alcmaeonid feeling.

We should bear in mind shifting relevance as well as memory. The need for democratic defence after the oligarchy stimulated memories which were fading fast. Ancestral help in the expulsion of Hippias was dragged out over one hundred years later and the parallel was strengthened by similar catchphrases. Thereafter, however, there is a shift in emphasis and memory as the Peisistratid expulsion ceases to be the touchstone of democratic sympathy, and the period of the Thirty takes its place as an element of the family defence. The family tradition of Aristocrates' descendants ([Dem.] LVIII 66f.) was transformed by the magnetism of the Thirty.[37] The same process is occurring for the later 'tyranny' as for the earlier one. Actual memories were fading in any case. All these factors will have contributed to the demise of living oral traditions about the earlier liberation. It is only in the late fourth century that we begin to find the most glowing and uncritical allusions to Harmodius and Aristogeiton. It is possible that 'the Athenians' really began to think only then that the tyrannicides alone liberated Athens.[38]

It is also interesting to trace the roles of Delphi and Sparta in these later traditions. The polis traditions of oratory show how the tale of liberation was being altered to decrease both.

Delphi is twice mentioned by the orators, and in terms bearing no relation to the fifth-century traditions. In Isocrates (*Antid.* 232), Cleisthenes 'persuades' the Delphians by eloquence (λόγῳ πείσας) to lend him money from Apollo's treasury. The addition of 'eloquence' is Isocrates'.[39] What is important is that Delphi is only a money-lender here. Sparta's role is gone and so, of course, is its cause, the Delphic oracles to Sparta.[40] In Demosthenes, too (XXI 144, 347 B.C.), the

---

[37] Ch. 2.4.1. Other examples (less important): Lys. XVIII 6 and X 4f., shortly after. Not in family tradition: Dem. XIX 277 and 280, on 'those who led back the demos from the Piraeus', Epikrates and Thrasyboulos.

[38] In theory Jacoby's dichotomy was now possible. The only well-known inscription the orators cite is that honouring the tyrannicides (Dem. XXI 170: see Ch. 1.2). Dem. XX 70 says Conon's bronze statue is the first of such honours since then; cf. Dem. XX 18 and 127; Isoc. *Peace* 143, Dem. XIX 280 (the greatest of Athens' benefactors), And. I 98 (decree of Demophantos); Lyc. I 51; Is. V 46f. Later hyperbole: Din. I 100; Hyp. *Epit.* 39 imagines Leosthenes meeting the tyrannicides in Hades and eulogizes them. He also mentions (IV *Ag. Philipp.* 3) a law passed by the demos forbidding anyone to speak ill or sing disparaging songs of them. Other references in Taylor (1981). The later concentration on statues and honours suggests that by then it was the tyrannicides who were mostly remembered.

[39] Isocrates is arguing the advantages of eloquence, but his method, used next for Themistocles, is to take a well-known historical example and insert the emphasis he wants.

[40] *Antid.* 232: μετὰ δὲ ταῦτα Κλεισθένης ἐκπεσὼν ἐκ τῆς πόλεως ὑπὸ τῶν τυράννων, λόγῳ πείσας τοὺς Ἀμφικτύονας δανεῖσαι τῶν τοῦ θεοῦ χρημάτων αὑτῷ, τόν τε

Alcmaeonids borrow money from Delphi;[41] 'and having borrowed money from Delphi, they freed the city and expelled the sons of Peisistratos' (καὶ δανεισαμένους χρήματ᾽ ἐκ Δελφῶν ἐλευθερῶσαι τὴν πόλιν καὶ τοὺς Πεισιστράτου παῖδας ἐκβαλεῖν. If this version occurs twice in extant oratory, it cannot have been unfamiliar to the Athenians, and it must represent some kind of polis tradition.[42] Bribery of Delphi has disappeared, as has the possibly unscrupulous use of the temple-building.[43] So has Sparta. None of these omissions is surprising in the patriotic polis traditions. Where the Alcmaeonids are remembered in any detail as the liberators of Athens, their relations with Delphi have been softened to a perfectly legitimate financial transaction.

The fourth-century historians and scholia are more concerned with the practical financial details. Again the focus is on the precise way Cleisthenes managed the expulsion. Essentially products of speculation and fourth-century preoccupation with money and mercenaries, they all omit the bribery and therefore the connection between Alcmaeonid activities in Delphi and Sparta's part in the expulsion.[44]

Most striking is the narrative of Aristotle's *Athenaion Politeia* (19.4). We know from the details and even wording that much of this was taken from Herodotus.[45] It combines the contract for the temple and the story of the Pythia telling Sparta to free Athens, both of which are in

δῆμον κατήγαγε καὶ τοὺς τυράννους ἐξέβαλε καὶ τὴν δημοκρατίαν ἐκείνην κατέστησε. 'After this, Cleisthenes was expelled from the city by the tyrants and persuaded the Amphictyonic League [who administered Delphi] by his eloquence to lend him money from the treasury of Apollo. So he led back the demos from exile, expelled the tyrants and set up the democracy.'

41 He stresses the services of the Alcmaeonids, Alcibiades' ancestors, as an example for the common topos that Athens punishes those who insult it despite their services (Ch. 4.1).

42 It is less important here to analyse the different literary versions with their sources, since the general picture is clear. I shall look at them briefly only for the effect of their alterations on the tradition and what this tells us about the needs of patriotic Athenian history. See Ch. 5, n. 44 below.

43 Difficulties of chronology and details of Alcmaeonid activity at Delphi tend to obscure some basic points: (i) Exile was not necessary for their influence at Delphi (as for the offerings at the Ptoion – taken as another sign of their exile – Bicknell (1970) points out there are Peisistratid offerings there too). (ii) The temple was burnt down c. 548/7, and subscriptions were being collected from far around (e.g. Amasis, Hdt. II 180). But in Herodotus' narrative the Alcmaeonids do not begin their contract till after their defeat at Leipsydrion (i.e. 514), and the fine building of the temple is after that. So there is a long gap before rebuilding, and it is unclear why. Archaeological evidence confirms that the temple was completed after the Peisistratid expulsion (Homolle (1902), 612ff.).

44 Detailed discussion in Jacoby, *Atthis* and commentary on Philochorus, *FGH* 328 F 115; Forrest (1969), Rhodes on Arist. *Ath. Pol.* 19.4. Cf. Kinzl (1974). E.g. Forrest attributes the orators' versions to Kleidemus, the first scholion to Androtion, but he still relies on the basic idea of pro- or anti-Alcmaeonid versions. The Atthidographers' independence and use of new sources can be overestimated: Heidbüchel (1957) with Ch. 2 above, n. 138.

45 See Rhodes' commentary *ad loc.*

Herodotus. Yet it says nothing of the bribery, so there is no reason for the Pythia to tell Sparta that frequently to free Athens. Moreover, Aristotle takes the contract as the source of Alcmaeonid funds, and it is these funds which provide Spartan help – in the form of mercenaries (19.4, ὅθεν εὐπόρησαν χρημάτων πρὸς τὴν τῶν Λακώνων βοήθειαν, 'from which they acquired ample money to enlist Spartan help', can only mean this). The *Ath. Pol.* has therefore deliberately omitted the bribery on which Herodotus lays so much stress.[46] Philochorus presented an even more complicated version, apparently reconciling Herodotus with fourth-century chronology. The Alcmaeonids took the contract and hired mercenaries. When they had succeeded, they finished the temple more extravagantly to fulfil a vow. There are other hints of different fourth-century versions with variants on the use or misuse of Delphic funds.[47]

There is a considerable manipulation of 'facts' here, which tends to become submerged by chronological problems, the Atthidographers' attempts to clarify them, and the supposed pro- and anti-Alcmaeonid bias. The variations on Cleisthenes' acquisition and use of the money are clearly fourth-century speculations arising from contemporary concerns. This very emphasis reveals how single-mindedly these accounts avoided the fundamental elements of Herodotus' narrative, where there had been no need for great financial resources. Fourth-century accounts all omit the bribery, and if they mention Delphi, it only provides Cleisthenes with money. The way the dubious elements in Delphi's part are, as it were, defused, suggests deliberate avoidance of the bribery Herodotus stressed. All produce a liberation achieved without corruption.[48]

These transformations are clearly related to the patriotic demands of the democratic polis traditions. The Alcmaeonids are comparatively irrelevant. The polis traditions of oratory present, instead, a mild, anaemic tale of borrowing money from Delphi. Sparta's role also disappears. One can understand why. As in some fifth-century popular traditions, the 'liberation' remains an entirely Athenian achievement,

---

[46] Jacoby also disregards the bribery story of Herodotus as a variant detail added to the 'Alcmaeonid source' (*Atthis* 155 and 335, n. 27) or talks of 'persuasion' (339, n. 53), though it is crucial to Herodotus' argument. Cf. Aristotle who keeps the oracles and Spartan help but without explaining the oracles; and Isocrates who has the persuasion of eloquence. Bribery, though omitted, is the essential link behind all these versions. Forrest (1969), 277 assumed that the mercenaries in the Atthis (meaning the two orators and their 'sources') were Spartan, but the point is that they say nothing of Spartans.

[47] Philochorus *FGH* 328 F 115, and schol. on Dem. XXI 144, 622.27 and 623.14 Dindorf. See Jacoby on Philochorus.

[48] Except the first scholion on Dem. XXI 144 (622.27), which has misappropriation of the building funds, not bribery of the Pythia.

and Athens has the monopoly of anti-tyrant idealism. Sparta's later occupation of the Acropolis may also have helped. The relations of the Atthidographers to fourth-century oral traditions are obscure, but they apparently continue the tone and preoccupations of the polis traditions, too. Their speculative reworking of the narrative produces a similarly patriotic tale favourable above all to Athens and its democracy.[49] The Alcmaeonids had their own reasons for wishing to forget the Pythia's corruption. But the polis traditions also preferred to see the achievement in a more suitable and admirable light, and patriotic motives were far stronger than any partisan manipulation.

5.3 The earlier stages

So, later fifth- and fourth-century traditions show resilience and flexibility, and, even then, there is little sign that anyone thought the tyrannicides simply liberated Athens, despite their honours. We can now return to the earlier traditions of the late sixth and early fifth centuries with a more realistic idea of what memories would still exist. So soon after the actual events they could be complex and reasonably accurate.[50] Everyone in Athens in the late sixth century knew how the tyranny had really ended. Yet, that was when the 'tyrannicide' statues were set up. Why were the tyrannicides honoured in the first place? Why did the official honours, statues and cult not create the 'official' and popular tradition that Jacoby envisaged? There seems to have been no incompatibility between reverence for the tyrannicides and recognition of the military side of events. Immensely complicated discussions have revolved round the drinking songs or skolia which mention the tyrannicides (nos. 10–12; *Poetae Melici Graeci* nos. 893–6), the term *isonomia* (literally 'equality in law') and speculative reconstruction of rival contemporary groups. For Jacoby, for instance, the tyrannicides were originally glorified by the nobility hostile to the Alcmaeonids; they sang the skolia in honour of Harmodius and Aristogeiton, thus the conflicting traditions of Alcmaeonids and the others began quite early.[51] But the emphasis of the later traditions suggests a rather simpler explanation for the continued glorification of the tyrannicides.

First it is important to stress that the tyrannicides were honoured officially fairly soon after the end of the tyranny. The famous statues of

---

[49] It may often be more profitable to examine the *effect* of these changes on the projected image of Athens' history (including the Atthis) than to trace literary traditions from lost historiography; and to see the mainly lost Atthidographers in the light of earlier sources, not the other way round.

[50] Fornara (1970) particularly stresses the importance of the early stages.

[51] 'After the overthrow of Cleisthenes', *Atthis* 162; cf. 160.

the tyrannicides by Antenor were removed by the Persians and replaced in 477. Pliny's early date of 510/9 for them (*N.H.* 34.16–7) is supported by the evidence of vase painting and the dates of Antenor's attested activity.[52] In 510 everyone knew how Athens had been liberated. Perhaps in 510 the tyrannicides could be perceived as performing the decisive action leading to the liberation and the title 'tyrannicide' had some factual basis – but no one regarded them literally as liberators since they clearly were not.[53] However, this explanation ignores the events themselves and misunderstands the nature of political symbols. For otherwise, why were they honoured alone and, so far as we know, none of the participants in the later expulsion were?[54] After all, the storming of the Bastille had little immediate practical effect in the French Revolution.

Much has been argued from the skolia themselves – of which three mention the tyrannicides – and the *isonomia* mentioned in one of them. The tenth skolion cites Harmodius and Aristogeiton as having brought *isonomia* to Athens:

> ἐν μύρτου κλαδὶ τὸ ξίφος φορήσω
> ὥσπερ Ἁρμόδιος καὶ Ἀριστογείτων
> ὅτε τὸν τύραννον κτανέτην
> ἰσονόμους τ' Ἀθήνας ἐποιησάτην.

In a branch of myrtle I'll carry my sword like Harmodius and Aristogeiton when they killed the tyrant and made Athens free (*isonomous*).

Is the *isonomia* here a purely aristocratic ideal opposed to Cleisthenes' measures or a catchword Cleisthenes used himself? Interpretation has been much influenced by Jacoby's schema.[55] But clearly it is unwise to interpret either the skolion or *isonomia* as it is used here through arguments about pro- and anti-Alcmaeonid traditions. Moreover, we are dealing at best with a term whose meaning changed. For later in the fifth century (e.g. Hdt. III 80.6), *isonomia* was synonymous with democracy. Vlastos analysed all references to *isonomia*, its possible derivations and

---

[52] Fornara (1970), 157 and references supporting the early date (rejected by Ehrenberg and Podlecki). Vases representing the early statues confirm it. As Cromey points out ((1979), 140f.) Antenor was even supposed to have carved or supervised the Alcmaeonid pediments at Delphi.

[53] Fornara (1970), 165ff.; Hipparchus had wielded power (Hdt. VII 6.3) and could be considered a tyrant too; this was only misunderstood in the later fifth century.

[54] Herodotus does not mention the tomb of Anchimolios, the Spartan who led the first unsuccessful expedition against the Peisistratids (v 63.4), but it is in Alopeke, rather than a place associated with public honour. It may have helped preserve the memory of Spartan help.

[55] E.g. Ehrenberg (1950), 531.

the whole controversy. He concluded that everywhere the term refers essentially to institutions which are in some sense democratic.[56] The only exception is the tyrannicide song itself, but only if it is (as is usual) interpreted as anti-Cleisthenic according to Jacoby's schema.[57] That leads easily to a circular argument, since so much depends on the one, undated skolion. So *isonomia* must remain essentially democratic. Ehrenberg accepted Vlastos' argument, reversed his previous view and redated the skolia. He thus argued that Cleisthenes himself made use of the tyrannicides and made *isonomia* the catchword of democracy. The skolia were no longer a sign of aristocrats opposed to Cleisthenes, and he saw no. 10 (above) as 'das Triumphlied der Demokratie'.[58]

At this point one begins to wonder about the skolion's validity for that kind of argument. Skolia are drinking songs, not legal documents, as Vlastos pointed out. Nor are they vehicles of political propaganda, at least in their original context where they are improvised songs performed at aristocratic symposia.[59] By their nature, it should be impossible to date them precisely or assume a set text.[60] In any case, the two aspects of the liberation, the tyrannicides and the military expulsion, were not seen as incompatible: the skolion's claim does not necessarily exclude the Alcmaeonids. Moreover, if *isonomia* had any democratic nuances at all, the main evidence disappears for the rival claims of a nobility who tried to glorify the tyrannicides at Cleisthenes' expense.[61] *Isonomia* might at first have had primarily aristocratic nuances and relevance, particularly since it is sometimes used vaguely, as opposed to tyranny. But if so, its meaning changed. It might even be argued that Cleisthenes took over the slogan and slightly altered its implications.[62] The undated skolion above is the main evidence for rival aristocrats with a rival slogan.[63] The suspicion arises that Cleisthenes himself either coined the

---

[56] Vlastos (1953); confirmed by Ostwald (1969) and Griffith (1966). Pleket (1972) has a more complex examination of the different usages of *isonomia*.

[57] As Vlastos points out, (1953), 341f.

[58] (1956), adjusting his old theory (1950). He puts no. 12 before 507 when all aristocrats are united with Cleisthenes.

[59] By the time of Aristophanes, though, the 'Harmodius song' is well known to everyone, mentioned several times with different variations: e.g. *Ach.* 978f., 1093; *Wasps* 1224; fr. 444 K.–A. (*Pelargoi*). They might later become political slogans (Taylor (1981)).

[60] It is usually thought that they originated soon after the events they mention and that the whole collection of skolia in Athenaeus was made from a fairly narrow period: e.g. Bowra put it shortly after the Persian Wars. Our first reference to the Harmodius song is in the *Acharnians* (425 B.C.). See most recently Day (1985) and Page (1981).

[61] Cf. Podlecki's objection ((1966), 134) that if Cleisthenes adopted the tyrannicides, nothing was left for the rival opposition to claim. But that might be precisely the point!

[62] Pleket (1972).

[63] The aristocratic meaning cannot be proved from the skolia alone: for which see Fornara (1970), 337ff, and Pleket (1972).

phrase *isonomia* or developed its meaning and fostered the tyrannicides as symbols of his new constitution.

The actual train of events suggests forcibly why the tyrannicides were convenient and innocuous symbols for all Athenian groups. The Alcmaeonids had bribed the Pythia to tell Sparta to free Athens. Sparta had eventually succeeded in doing this, then Cleisthenes took the demos into partnership. Cleomenes expelled Cleisthenes and seven hundred families as accursed and tried to restore the tyranny but was besieged on the Acropolis. Finally, Cleisthenes and the rest could be recalled. Delphic corruption, Sparta's armed intervention and the expulsion of a leading family because it was accursed do not amount to an inspiring tale of liberation. The corruption shocked Athenians as well as Spartans, and later traditions diminished Sparta's role. Sparta's attempt to restore Hippias probably helped this. Herodotus (v 90.1) also says that the Spartans were angry at being tricked and because they had received no gratitude for their help. Perhaps, then, they received little recognition at the time. Surely the immediate glorification of the tyrannicides was an implicit rejection of the debt to Sparta. They were a convenient symbol for everyone in Athens as they stressed the Athenian role in the liberation. Indeed, Taylor has recently shown how powerful an heroic symbol they provided for the Athenian democracy of implacable opposition to tyranny.[64] At the time of the expulsion, they provided a far more inspiring symbol of the end of tyranny than the dubious and confusing events surrounding the real expulsion. No wonder the Athenians embraced them.

They were an even more convenient symbol for the Alcmaeonids. For, contrary to Jacoby's view, the Alcmaeonids could not at the time point to a glorious achievement on their own part. It is occasionally recognized either that the family's actions at this time were hardly praiseworthy or that they had good reason to foster the tyrannicides, or both. But curiously not for adequate reasons.[65] The circumstances of the expulsion were as awkward for Cleisthenes as for the city. But a further element, not mentioned at all, was disastrous – the Alcmaeonid curse, which left them polluted and exposed to threat of expulsion. Strangely neglected, this must be the most compelling reason for Cleisthenes to adopt the tyrannicides.[66] The most extensive Alcmaeonid exile was that enforced by Cleomenes because of the curse. It was the Athenians who defeated

---

[64] Taylor (1981), Day (1985).

[65] Ehrenberg (1956); Bowra ((1936), 394) argued Alcmaeonid support of the tyrannicides, because Sparta's role was awkward.

[66] Demanded by Fornara (1970) against Ehrenberg's view or by Jacoby against Bowra's. Cf. Jacoby's insistence (with Podlecki) that the Alcmaeonids were proud of liberating Athens 'by persuading Delphi' and because they suffered from Sparta's perfidy.

Cleomenes, then summoned the Alcmaeonids back. In exile as accursed, the Alcmaeonids were merely peripheral in this second victory.[67] The tyrannicides were not only excellent symbols for the whole city; for Cleisthenes they could also divert attention from the dubious role he and his family had played. The encouragement of their cult may well have been an extremely astute political move by Cleisthenes, for there was ample reason for everyone to welcome the tyrannicides as symbols of liberation.

The honours to Harmodius and Aristogeiton were certainly official, in so far as anything was official in Athens: the cult and statues were sanctified by the democracy. What is interesting, then, is that their honours and memorials still do not seem to have prompted an 'official tradition' remembering their action alone (at least not till the very late fourth century). The very existence of 'official traditions' in Athens is doubtful, and the term often misleading.[68] But beyond this, Athens' oral traditions were far more complex and fluid than they have been taken to be. Fifth-century popular tradition, family and polis tradition had a more accurate idea of the period than has always been assumed. In fact, it was essential to remember those actions in which individuals other than the tyrannicides took part. Memory and oral tradition were too complex and long-lived to permit the facile idea that it was the tyrannicides alone who freed Athens. They were, however, the only participants in the tangled complexity of events who could be honoured without enhancing aspects of the liberation which no one wished to emphasize.

How, then, did the Alcmaeonid family tradition itself deal with these difficult elements, and what could the fifth-century Alcmaeonid family 'defence' actually have said?

5.4 The Alcmaeonid family tradition again

The curse was an acute embarrassment to the family. Nearly two hundred years after its origin the Spartans even invoked it against Pericles, pressing for his exile at the start of the Peloponnesian War. For

---

[67] This significance of the curse is not even noticed by G. W. Williams (1951 and 1952a and 1952b), nor its general importance in the late sixth century by any of the discussions. Yet, characteristically from a different perspective, Parker (1983), 16f. and 206 points out how the family were able to counteract the curse's taint by their political claims. There may have been extensive traditions, now lost, about the curse in the late sixth century: Plato, *Laws* 642d, refers to a purification of Athens by Epimenides, *c.* 500, not in Cylon's time as in all other sources (see further, Ch. 5, n. 127). Bicknell (1972), however, discusses the ostracisms in the early fifth century, the significance the curse had then, and the label 'friends of the tyrants' (Arist. *Ath. Pol.* 22.6), referring to cooperation *before* the end of the tyranny.

[68] As Fornara (1970), 160 points out; however his 'vulgate', deduced from Thucydides' objections ((1968b), 401ff.), still implies a fairly standard or coherent version. See

Pericles was of Alcmaeonid descent on his mother's side. As we saw (Ch. 2.4.3), the family tradition presented in Isoc. xvi had by the early fourth century transferred some of the effects of the curse to a secular and ideological setting. The 'continuous exile' throughout the tyranny was a tradition which probably originated in the exile provoked by the curse *after* Athens had expelled the tyrants but before the Cleisthenic democracy was established. The curse was eventually smoothed over to produce a fine tradition of democratic sympathies. I would suggest that it was this, rather than the tyrannicides, which was the main problem for family tradition.

What form, then, did the Alcmaeonid defence and family tradition take earlier in the fifth century? It is sometimes suggested that the conventional 'Alcmaeonid defence' (taken to be similar to Jacoby's 'Alcmaeonid tradition') was only necessary in the decades after the expulsion when memories were fading: in the family's decline after Marathon the family began to be attacked for medism and support of tyranny (Hdt. vi 121).[69] So they had to reassert their part in the liberation, for the tyrannicides' cult had too effectively obscured their own part.[70] But Herodotus' Alcmaeonid excursus (vi 121–31) cannot simply be taken as representative of the Alcmaeonid defence as Jacoby thought (p. 248 and Ch. 5.5 below). The tyrannicides were, in fact, probably fostered by Cleisthenes himself as a symbol convenient both for the family and Athens in general.

Certainly Herodotus' passage suggests that an Alcmaeonid defence of the family's democratic sympathies was current by the time he was writing. But what could they actually say in their defence? And can the tyrannicides really explain neglect of the family's true role when polis and family traditions continued to remember the military intervention? It tends to be assumed in most discussions that the 'Alcmaeonid defence' was both true and decisive, that they had a perfect and unquestionable case.[71] But surely the main necessity for the defence was first, because there were some very disreputable elements in the Alcmaeonid role before and after the liberation, and secondly, because what they had to say in any defence was historically untrue.

While Herodotus' Alcmaeonid excursus is not representative of the family defence as it stands, those elements in it that recur in Isoc. xvi

---

Ch. 4.1 for discussion of the various terms; even 'popular traditions' may include different emphases.

[69] It is puzzling, though, that none of the ostraka naming Megacles (supposedly in the mid-480s) mention treachery so far, although they mention the curse – perhaps a sign that the Marathon betrayal story was not yet current, D.M. Lewis (1984), 605. 'Son of Koisyra' may denote treachery, however, since Koisyra had Eretrian connections (see Davies, *APF*, p. 380).

[70] Ehrenberg (1956); Fornara (1970).   [71] Esp. Jacoby, *Atthis*, followed by Podlecki.

must have been part of the early Alcmaeonid defence of the mid-fifth century against their detractors. They show that certain parts of the defence were simply false. In both we find the claims that the Alcmaeonids were *misotyrannoi* ('tyrant-haters') (Hdt. VI 121.1; Isoc. XVI 25f.), in continuous exile during the tyranny (Hdt. VI 123.1, Isoc. XVI 26) and that they liberated Athens (though Herodotus stresses the bribery as the means). None is strictly true. The later defence in Isocrates bears little relation to Herodotus' detailed narrative and we must remember that family defence usually offers not an apology but simply an alternative. It is probable that the fifth-century defence also took a very surprising form.

The Alcmaeonids' continuous exile is not only false (Ch. 2.4.3), its implications could obscure highly damaging elements of family history. It could gloss over Cleisthenes' archonship, the probable periods of residence in Athens under the Peisistratids, and the short-lived marriage alliance of Megacles with Peisistratos' daughter. Isocrates' defence illustrates well how the constant exile could deal with the awkward marriage alliance ('though the Alcmaeonid were kinsmen and able to share Peisistratos' power, yet they preferred exile to seeing the demos enslaved'). It could also attract attention away from the great exile enforced because of the curse. The exile tradition combined with the catchword *misotyrannoi* were also necessary to deal with Cleisthenes' descent from the tyrant of Sicyon (of which Herodotus reminds us twice) and the connection with Croesus, as well as any friendship with Peisistratids. Both traditions were extremely successful, entrenched already by Herodotus' day and conclusively destroyed only with the modern discovery of the archon list.

As for the last positive claim that they expelled the tyrants and liberated Athens, I need hardly stress by now that it was at least an exaggeration of the truth. In fact, it was a gross simplification which glossed over the crucial role of Sparta, instructed by Delphi. Alcmaeonid participation there was small, except for the bribery. Then they were expelled as accursed. It was the 'demos' who besieged Cleomenes and, when successful, brought back the exiles (the reverse of the family tradition in Isocrates). Thucydides may even hint that the Alcmaeonid return was still disregarding their pollution (I 126.12, 'Nevertheless they returned . . .'). Despite Cleisthenes' constitutional importance, full Alcmaeonid responsibility for – even full participation in – the liberation is doubtful.

By the mid-fifth century the family tradition could have become almost unrecognizable, if one compares the fourth-century family defence of Aristocrates' descendants only sixty years after Aristocrates' main achievement (Ch. 2.4.1). I suspect – though it cannot be proved – that by *c.* 450 the Alcmaeonid tradition could well have telescoped together Hippias' expulsion and the victory over Cleomenes on the Acropolis and the establishment of the democracy. This would omit the awkward period of stasis after 510 and so could transfer the accursed exile of the family to the long period of tyranny. If the Alcmaeonids were said to lead the returning exiles (as in Isocrates) there was, moreover, no need for Sparta's help.

Even this slight evidence reveals steadfast avoidance of the curse, its implications and connected events. According to Herodotus, both the Peisistratid alliance failed and the great exile of seven hundred families was enforced precisely because of the curse. Exile for democratic reasons smoothed over both and left no room for the curse. The curse continued to be a powerful weapon, used against Pericles and still well remembered in the later fifth century (Ch. 5.5). It meant the Alcmaeonid 'liberation' was less straightforward than usually imagined: they could not simply present the truth and still less under this taint could they boast of having bribed Delphi. The main elements of their fifth-century defence obliterated any hints of the curse. And anxiety to avoid its mention can largely explain why it was so difficult for them to produce a satisfactory defence when their patriotism began to be questioned after Marathon.

So, already after Marathon, and certainly by the mid-fifth century, a defence that was misleading and often simply untrue was being developed. The Alcmaeonids needed their defence because their part had not been entirely praiseworthy. They depended a great deal on the broad claim of being tyrant-haters and continually in exile during the tyranny. This claim eventually became the family tradition, the only tradition the family knew. Indeed, it was successful enough to have passed to Herodotus and Thucydides (VI 59) and become one of the accepted 'facts' of sixth-century Athenian history.

5.5 Alcmaeonid early history and the 'Alcmaeonid tradition'

Several traditions were preserved about the Alcmaeonid family in the archaic age, even about the very origin of their curse in the late seventh century. Most occur in the second part of Herodotus' 'Alcmaeonid excursus' (VI 125–31), and they are usually simply taken to be Alcmaeonid family tradition, straight from a supposed 'Alcmaeonid source'. But again, on closer examination they seem to have a wider and more varied provenance. They give us an intriguing insight into the much older oral traditions of Athens, how and why they were preserved and how Herodotus treated them. The nature of these traditions is closely bound up with problems of fifth-century historiography.

I shall mainly be interested first in the character of the tales Herodotus presents from the Alcmaeonid past (whether they are family tradition or have a popular and wider provenance); secondly, in his intentions in presenting them. The whole excursus has, as we have seen, been taken as 'the Alcmaeonid tradition', even a panegyric of the family. This is partly because it is thought to glorify the Alcmaeonids, partly simply because it is about them. That is bound up with the assumption that Herodotus must have been a wholehearted supporter of Pericles and Periclean Athens (which, in turn, is largely adduced from this passage).[72] But as we have seen, in the first part of the excursus (VI 121–4) Herodotus defended the Alcmaeonid role in overthrowing the tyrants by information which the family could not stress and which he expressly attributed to 'the Athenians' (Ch. 5.1 above). The undoubted fact that Herodotus is saying the family could not have shown the shield at Marathon is extended into a pro-Alcmaeonid 'bias' and read into the second part of the excursus also. In fact, the conventional idea of his views on Pericles and Periclean Athens relies considerably on the single mention of Pericles here at the end of the excursus. It can at least be questioned, as can the close identification of Pericles with the Alcmaeonids.[73] We must also separate clearly Herodotus' views about the role of Athens in the Persian Wars and what he might think about Athens some decades later. His belief that it was in fact most responsible for the defeat of Persia, a view he knows will be unpopular (VII 139.1), does not automatically imply full approval of Athenian development since then. Such a view and its inherent confusions have been fully dissected and demolished by Fornara.[74]

It has been occasionally noticed that the second half of the excursus (VI 125ff.) contradicts or undercuts the apparent defence of the first. Strasburger has argued forcibly that the implications of the stories Herodotus gives do not further the family glorification or defence and therefore that Herodotus has deliberately chosen those stories which would undermine the defence of §§121–4 and omitted or left unemphasized aspects of the family history that could have furthered the family's

---

[72] Jacoby (1913), 238 and *Atthis* 161, 'Herodotus got everything from Pericles or from the circle around Pericles.' Similarly, e.g., Aly (1921), 158, Ehrenberg (1950), G.M.E. Williams (1980), Murray (1987) and many others. Most systematically criticized by Strasburger (1965); also Hart ((1982), 2ff.), who stresses that Herodotus used Alcmaeonid sources critically; less subtly, Devlin (1985) (against Herodotus' partiality for Alcmaeonids).

[73] Strasburger ((1965), 574ff.): Herodotus' stress on Athens' service in the Persian Wars need not extend to Athens in the time of its empire; cf. esp. VIII 3.2 on Athens' hegemony. Pericles' probable honouring of the tyrannicides (*IG* I³ 131, with Ostwald (1951), Fornara (1970)) is problematic for those who see the traditions in Jacoby's terms and illustrates the inherent contradictions in the theory.

[74] Fornara (1971a), ch. 3 (and cf. Schwartz (1969), 369). Herodotus' investigation could be *used* by propagandists for the empire but he was not a propagandist himself.

glorification. Perhaps he is introducing an ironic 'defence' which in fact shows up the inadequacies of the Alcmaeonid claims to be *misotyrannoi*.[75] One cannot simply attribute the contradiction to Herodotus' naivety – often overstressed – which is itself undercut by the modern theories that he is presenting an 'Alcmaeonid defence'.[76]

So Herodotus declares that the family were tyrant-haters and could not have medized (i.e. gone over to the Persian side) at Marathon and continues with an outline of their ancestors from Alcmaeon (§§125–31). First he describes Alcmaeon's visit to Croesus, then the wooing of Agariste, daughter of Cleisthenes of Sicyon. Then he traces Megacles' descendants through Cleisthenes, Hippocrates, Megacles and Agariste to Pericles.

The Alcmaeonids were illustrious (*lamproi*) even before Alcmaeon, Herodotus tells us, but from the time of Alcmaeon and Megacles they were very distinguished indeed. The famous story of Alcmaeon's visit to Croesus is introduced as the reason for their increased distinction. 'The house thus became very wealthy and Alcmaeon himself was able to keep horses for the chariot race and won at Olympia' (§125.5). This has a slightly different emphasis from the later family tradition of Isocrates xvi which merely implied ancestral wealth.[77] Nor does Herodotus include Isocrates' boast that Alcmaeon was the first Athenian ever to win the chariot race at Olympia, which bears the mark of family pride. The family tradition in Isocrates does not even presuppose the tale of Alcmaeon's visit to Croesus. This reinforces one's impression that the whole tale in Herodotus has a popular provenance, not a family one.

As Herodotus tells the tale, Alcmaeon is summoned to Sardis by Croesus and, in return for his services at Delphi, offered as much gold as he can carry. Alcmaeon tries to stuff as much as possible about his person and staggers out. Croesus laughs and gives him the same amount again. Thus the house became wealthy. Even taken at its face value, the story is amusing, and amusing at the expense of Alcmaeon, a boorish Greek displaying his greed before the wise and generous king of Lydia.[78] At a deeper level, it hardly glorifies the Alcmaeonid house to be introduced to

---

[75] Strasburger (1965), 595: 'Herodotus lost no chance of including unfavourable material'; cf. also Bornitz (1968), Hart (1982), Ubsdell (1982); cf. How and Wells on vi 121: 'Herodotus' attempt to prove Alcmaeonid hatred of the barbarian and of the tyrant is illogical and unconvincing.'

[76] See, e.g. Strasburger's analysis (1965) of the Sosikles scene and the Corinthian tyrant stories in Hdt. v 90ff. and the Alcmaeonid 'defence' itself, which shows considerably more subtlety in Herodotus' treatment; cf. also Bornitz (1968), Ubsdell (1982) and now Raaflaub (1987).

[77] This passage, only mentioned by Strasburger, considerably strengthens his argument (see Ch. 2.4.3).

[78] Cf. Strasburger's description (1965), 596: 'Diese drollige Heldentat'; Aly (1921), 158f.

its eponymous ancestor in Croesus' treasury. As Strasburger points out (1965, 598), the situation reminds one of Solon's remarks when shown the treasury by Croesus (I 30ff.) about the vanity of wealth and the real nature of happiness. So its presentation in this form may be a further sign of what Herodotus himself wishes us to think. But in Book I the wealthy Croesus was discomforted by Solon's moralizing. Here, while the vanity of wealth may remain in the background for Herodotus and his audience, the laugh is against Alcmaeon, and Croesus is the fabulously rich but generous Lydian king able to rise above greed. In this story (in its Herodotean form at least) the credit goes to Croesus rather than Alcmaeon. The moralizing note working against Alcmaeon would be inappropriate in family tradition.[79]

The tale reflects badly on the family's wealth. It also undercuts their 'defence' against medism and favouring tyranny. For we now read that the eponymous ancestor gained the family's wealth from a Lydian king, both a barbarian and in some sense a tyrant. We are even told explicitly that Alcmaeon was an 'assistant' (συμπρήκτωρ) to Croesus at Delphi, which prompted the reward in the first place (VI 125.2).[80]

But we can be more precise about the nature and origin of the story. A common type of tale explains a person's wealth by some sudden stroke of luck, one sudden find, rather than by any long-term explanation. It is particularly common in some peasant societies. It has been explained by the difficulty of accumulating wealth simply through hard work in a subsistence economy. Moreover, that kind of accumulation would be thought to harm the rest of the community and thus cause envy. So wealth has to be attributed to something external, a sudden find of treasure or a windfall.[81] One might also add that a story of the sudden finding of wealth would be more easily remembered, embedded in a memorable tale and repeated.

The popular milieu of this kind of tale confirms that the Croesus story was not the family's own version of the origin of its riches, though the family might have known it. It also means that this stylized explanation cannot necessarily be translated into a rationalized version of the origins of the family wealth.[82] There are other similar stories about the wealth of

---

[79] Chronologically, the visit 'should' have been to Alyattes. Like synchronisms of the Seven Sages, there is probably very little basis in historical fact; How and Wells (*ad loc.*); cf. Davies, *APF* 371; Forrest (1956), 48ff. suggested the visit was connected diplomatically with the Sacred War.

[80] Bornitz (1968), 42f.; cf. Macan *ad loc.* who declares that the significance of Alcmaeonid relations with Lydia was 'not realized by the storyteller'.

[81] Forster (1965); hence he explains the popularity of lotteries in countries such as Mexico.

[82] Meyer, e.g., thought it reflected Alcmaeonid trade with Sardis. It may reflect some connection with Croesus or Lydia or Delphi, but this would need to be confirmed from elsewhere.

Athenian aristocratic families. Comedy and oratory show a preoccupation with the wealth of certain families, how they gained it and (in particular) how they lost it (Ch. 2.2). Tales of the origins of Hipponikos' great wealth are reminiscent of the Alcmaeon story. Variations centred on the finding of buried Persian gold by Callias in a pit or *lakkos* either at Marathon or after the battle of Salamis.[83] Plutarch's version (*Arist.* 5.8) said the story explained their nickname in comedy, *lakkoploutoi*, referring to 'pit-wealth'. It is probably unwise to rationalize the nickname into a reference to mining wealth.[84] The tales dispense with the more prosaic method of gaining money and focus on a colourful and memorable tale of discovery in the Persian Wars. A similar moral element may even be compared with the Croesus tale. For in Plutarch's tale the greed of Callias (who acquires the gold) contrasts with the modesty of Aristeides. In such aetiological tales the family concerned need not emerge with credit. Here the moral superiority belongs to the side which is *not* acquiring the gold. These tales are simply unsuitable for family tradition. They seem to be a product of curiosity and rumour about a certain family's great prosperity and are not untinged with moral censure.[85]

Herodotus continues with the next generation of the family (§126.1): 'Afterwards, in the next generation, Cleisthenes, the tyrant of Sicyon, raised it to much greater eminence (Κλεισθένης μιν ὁ Σικυώνιος τύραννος ἐξῆρε), so that it was much more distinguished among the Greeks than before.' And he tells the story of the wooing of Agariste, daughter of Cleisthenes, tyrant of Sicyon. Many distinguished suitors were gathered together for Cleisthenes to choose the best for his daughter. Hippokleides was the favourite, until he 'danced away his marriage' by undignified behaviour and Agariste was given instead to the Alcmaeonid Megacles. Having reminded us that the Alcmaeonids gained their wealth from their friendship with the Lydian king, Herodotus now emphasizes their second rise to fame and wealth achieved with the help of the tyrant Cleisthenes. The form of words (above) stresses both that Cleisthenes of Sicyon was the patron and that it was a tyrant's patronage.

---

[83] All references (Ch. 2, n. 45) are fairly late, though Plutarch is known to have used the dialogue *Callias* by Aeschines of Sphettos (*Arist.* 25.9). Alciphron (1 9) uses the word *lakkoploutoi* as proverbial of a rich man. Another example of this kind of story surrounds the oracle 'move every stone' (references in Parke and Wormell (1956), 109): there was a rumour that Mardonius had buried some treasure below his tent at Plateia; a certain Polycrates buys the site and digs, finds nothing and receives the oracle.

[84] See Davies, *APF* 7826 VII (p. 260): their mining interests are given explicitly by two other sources, of which Xen. *Poroi* IV 15 is reliable (also Nepos, *Cim.* 1 3). But *sudden* acquisition is necessary to this kind of tale, so one cannot automatically rationalize it into a sudden strike in the mines.

[85] Cf. Dover (1974), 109ff. and 170ff., esp. for connection of wealth with hubris.

Again, the tale does not form a clear glorification of the Alcmaeonid Megacles, though he is the one who wins Agariste. Hippokleides' spirited retort to the tyrant Cleisthenes, 'Hippokleides doesn't care' (οὐ φροντὶς Ἱπποκλείδῃ), caught popular imagination enough to become a proverb, as Herodotus tells us, and as he gives it the tale revolves around Hippokleides. If we think of the tale from the point of view of the proverb, there is a hint that Hippokleides' retort is approved and the success of Megacles, who was only second best, less admired. The laugh is against the Alcmaeonid, or at least not necessarily against Hippokleides.[86] There may even be a hint of anti-tyrant sentiment.

The real origin of the whole story is puzzling as it seems to have archaic and poetic elements combined with the tale of Hippokleides' undignified behaviour which would be more appropriate in a popular milieu. So, some think it has a poetic source,[87] whereas Strasburger (for instance) saw it as a 'sarcastic anecdote' suitable for a symposium.[88] But no one origin is convincing when we find both an archaic list of suitors in the grand epic style and the amusing débâcle of Hippokleides' suit.[89] And in fact any tale's narration may concentrate on different aspects depending on its aim and audience.[90] What one can stress is that from Herodotus' own presentation it is not unambiguously favourable to the Alcmaeonids; and that it was crystallized in a proverb, thus it had popular circulation. Indeed, it is one of the few (extant) oral traditions explicitly connected with a proverb.[91] This second rise in the family fortunes was, as Herodotus stresses, under the patronage of a tyrant and only made

---

[86] As Strasburger (1965), 595 on these two tales: 'Die anschliessende Familienchronik wird zu mehr als neun Zehnteln von zwei köstlichen Schwänken eingenommen'; against Luria (1930), *RE* VIII 1773 'Hippokleides' (Swoboda), and by implication all works already cited which see the excursus as glorifying the family.

[87] Stein, commentary *ad loc.*, suggested a Pindaric source; Macan suggests (curiously) that the number of 'Italiote' suitors could be explained if the story was first coined around the date of the founding of Thurii.

[88] Strasburger (1965), 596; Aly ((1921), 160) sees it as a 'folk narrative' because of its prolixity and folktale characteristics (e.g. three dances), but does not really explain the obscure list of suitors.

[89] To describe the motif simply as one of 'loss of expected success' or 'loss of suit' (Aly and Macan suggesting an eastern parallel) obscures the moralizing element. Note Hippokleides' introduction in the list of suitors (§127.4), 'the most wealthy and handsome of the Athenians'. For Megacles we are only reminded that it was his father who went to Croesus.

[90] See the commentaries of How and Wells, and of Macan for the obscure names in the suitor list, which may indicate poetic transmission; but the anachronisms in the collection of heroes who could never have met is to be expected in such tales of 'wooing' as in many other popular tales (Aly (1921)). By strict calculation of generations, the wedding of Agariste 'should' have been before Croesus' accession and therefore not in the second generation, as Herodotus says (§125.3). This is even without the complexities of Orthagorid chronology (see Griffin (1982), 43ff.).

[91] Murray (1980), 203.

possible through Hippokleides' cavalier cession of first place. It is plausible neither as the Alcmaeonid family tradition nor as part of any claim that they were tyrant-haters.

Herodotus then rapidly traces the family's descent down to Pericles (VI 131): Cleisthenes who established the tribes and democracy of Athens is born of Megacles and Agariste. Herodotus reminds us, however, how Cleisthenes 'took his name from his maternal grandfather of Sicyon' (§131.1). This seems a deliberate allusion to the passage where Herodotus described Cleisthenes' establishment of democracy and declared its precedent in the actions of Cleisthenes, his maternal grandfather and tyrant of Sicyon (V 66–9).[92] There Herodotus seems to present as his own opinion the similarity in manipulation of the tribal system by both men, Cleisthenes of Sicyon to exalt his own tribe at the Dorians' expense, Cleisthenes of Athens despising the Ionian ones (V 69.1): 'The Athenian Cleisthenes, who was grandson of the Sicyonian Cleisthenes through his mother and was named after him, decided, through contempt of the Ionians as it seems to me, that his tribes should not be the same as theirs and so copied his namesake Cleisthenes.' That is, we are reminded again, quite deliberately, of the relation of both Cleisthenes and his democracy to the tyrant Cleisthenes.[93] Though Herodotus is not criticizing the democracy itself, he is reminding us of tyrannical connections unsuitable for the straightforward glorification of the family or the initiator of the democracy itself.

After the list of names we come to the final tale of the Alcmaeonid excursus, the dream of Agariste that she would give birth to a lion. A few days later Pericles is born (§131.2); the excursus ends with his name: 'Another Agariste, who took her name from the Agariste, daughter of Cleisthenes, married Xanthippos, son of Ariphron; and when she was pregnant she had a dream in which she seemed to give birth to a lion; a few days later she bore Xanthippos a son, Pericles.' Much hinges on the interpretation of this dream.[94] Its position at the end of the excursus with the only mention of Pericles shows that it is meant to be important. But in what direction? Pericles' presence has usually been taken to be the *raison d'être* of the whole excursus. Certainly there is a sense here of leading up to a figure who needs no explanation. But does this necessarily imply unadulterated admiration and eulogy? Themistocles' entry into Herodotus' text (VII 143.1) is taken in exactly the opposite way.

---

[92] Strasburger (1965), 596 (rather differently), Bornitz (1968), 46ff.
[93] Compare G.W. Williams' difficulty ((1952a) 11), who, believing in the Alcmaeonid source, suggests that the information on Cleisthenes' debt to the tyrant dates back to the time of the reforms and represents the substance of the aristocratic charge against Cleisthenes of aiming at tyranny.
[94] Strasburger (1965), 596–8.

Then there is the meaning of the lion symbol of which, as Strasburger points out, we understand very little. If the tenor of the rest of the excursus is ambiguous, it cannot help us much in interpretation. The dream is usually taken as complimentary to Pericles, even though the lion could possibly be identified with royal power. Yet, against the Alcmaeonid claim of tyrant-hating and contemporary criticisms of Pericles' one-man rule,[95] one might equally see in this motif a sinister reference to Pericles' absolute rule within the democracy.[96]

The precise symbolism clearly depended on the type of lion. In Herodotus it could stand for courage (v 56.1). But Kypselos was denoted in the oracle by a savage lion, perhaps ambiguously (v 92 β 3).[97] More significant for Pericles himself, Aristophanes parodies this kind of oracle in the *Knights* (1037): 'There is a women who will bear a lion in sacred Athens.' Paphlagon is foretelling a saviour of the demos – thus a demagogue – and a pun next made on the theme brings out its appropriate application to tyrants as well.[98] In the *Frogs*, Aeschylus gives the advice that it is unwise to rear a lion in the city, but if you must, you had better humour its ways (1431f.). We are reminded of the passage in the *Agamemnon* (717ff.) where Paris is likened to a lion which is reared in the house and then destroys it. Clearly the metaphorical rearing of the lion could be dangerous and destructive.[99] The lion dream could be ambiguous, and perhaps Athenians could take it differently from non-Athenians.[100] Even royal power, if symbolized by a lion, could have good or bad overtones. It is not a clear glorification of Pericles and, like the rest of the excursus, could even be read as a deliberate piece of irony to undercut the Alcmaeonid defence, following on suitably from the help of Croesus and the influence of Cleisthenes, tyrant of Sicyon.

The idea that Herodotus was a fervent supporter of Pericles and

---

95 In comedy Pericles' followers were sometimes called the New Peisistratids (Plut. *Per.* 16.1); cf. Thuc. II 65.

96 Symbol of royal power suggested by How and Wells, yet they see the excursus as exalting Pericles *c.* 432–430 B.C. when the curse was being used against him. But it is important to remember the supreme necessity of *democratic* defence; exaltation was not enough.

97 See *RE* s.v. 'Löwe', 984ff. (Steier) and Strasburger for the lion's character as beast of prey in poetry and fable. Artemidorus' *Dream Book* stresses the significance of the type of lion.

98 An important addition to Strasburger's argument. The dialogue continues with a pun on lion and 'Antileon': the demos ask (1044), 'And how did you become an Antileon without my noticing?', where Antileon must mean 'a tyrant', since Antileon was an early tyrant of Chalkis (Arist. *Pol.* 1316a29–32; Lloyd-Jones (1975), 197). Cf. *Wasps* 1232–5 where Cleon is indirectly compared to another tyrant, Pittacus. Comedy was clearly aware of how demagogues could be akin to tyrants, and perhaps the similarity is implicit in the lion oracle.

99 Cf. also Eurip. *Suppl.* 1222f., where the symbol is used of the Epigonoi of Thebes. Val. Max. VII 2.7 took the passage in the Frogs to be Pericles' advice.

100 Hart (1982), 13.

Periclean Athens is based largely upon the excursus and this final laconic reference to Pericles.[101] So, to interpret the dream and excursus according to Herodotus' approval of Pericles is unwise. Clearly Herodotus' attitude to Pericles is not as obvious as usually assumed. Certainly he regarded Pericles as important, but that is very different from being his fervent admirer. If one examines the precise tenor, content and stress of the second part of the excursus, it is hard to escape the conclusion that Herodotus' 'defence' of the Alcmaeonids against the charge of medism and support of tyranny is 'a dazzling piece of irony'.[102] He tells us that the family derived its wealth and distinction first from a barbarian and absolute ruler, then from a Greek tyrant. We are reminded of the tyrannical antecedents of Cleisthenes and his democracy, and we end up on an ambiguous and ominous note with Agariste's lion dream.

So, far from presenting us with a straightforward Alcmaeonid defence, Herodotus provides the information we need to discern its falsity. He can hardly have had direct Alcmaeonid sources. Further examination suggests that the Alcmaeon and Hippokleides tales are popular tales of some sort, both amusing, both mildly derogatory of the Alcmaeonid family, both suggestive of moral disapproval of greed for wealth and tyrannical fame. We cannot know how widespread either were, but both could, by their subject-matter, have had wider circulation than Athens alone. As for the story of the bribery and the 'trick' by which Cleisthenes freed Athens, Herodotus tells us himself that this is what the Athenians say. Both the actual content of these traditions and the use Herodotus makes of them tell against their supposed origin in Alcmaeonid family tradition – and still more against Pericles himself as Herodotus' source.[103]

Finally, we return to the curse itself and the story of its remote origin in the conspiracy of Cylon, *c.* 630 B.C. Both Herodotus and Thucydides tell the tale, with slight variations. Again the 'Alcmaeonid source' and 'Alcmaeonid version' are the only explanations seriously considered for either the preservation of the story or its general 'bias'.[104] It is usually assumed that Herodotus' account follows the Alcmaeonid family tradi-

---

[101] Indeed, Strasburger argues forcefully (1965), 598ff. that the reference is intended as an ominous forecast of the growth of the empire under Pericles at the expense of the liberty won in the Persian Wars. It is naive to assume that an excursus which begins with Marathon and ends with Pericles ought to be a panegyric of the family.

[102] Hart (1982), 13.

[103] Nor is it clear why Pericles should identify himself completely with the family (and cf. Ch. 5, n. 73 above).

[104] Main discussions: *Atthis* 186f.; Gomme, *HCT* on I 126; Macan, commentary on Hdt. v 71; G.W. Williams (1951); Jameson (1965) on the significance of the festival of the Diasia, trying to reconstruct events; Lang (1967) starts from the premise that everything in Thucydides but not in Herodotus is a later piece of 'mythologizing' since Herodotus' time: this disregards the nature of oral tradition; Jordan (1979) and (1970); Devlin (1985) has too simple a view of transmission.

tion,[105] and less frequently that Thucydides also presents a version favourable to the family, a view easily confused with a belief that he was using an Alcmaeonid source or tradition.[106] It has even been suggested that 'Cylon's attempt belonged to the history of the Alcmaeonid house who might well preserve a reasonably accurate tradition.'[107] But these views are not grounded in a systematic consideration of either the evidence or the character of the oral traditions from which it derived. As for Herodotus, there is little reason to assume he was automatically following an Alcmaeonid source or defence.

The Alcmaeonid curse continued to be used against the Alcmaeonids right down to the late fifth century. Even the Spartans knew of it and used it against both Cleisthenes and Pericles. The tale of the Cylonian conspiracy is one of the earliest traditions about Athens that is historically acceptable. It has a remarkable lifespan of at least two hundred years. But can this preservation be attributed to Alcmaeonid family tradition alone? For such an ancient tradition the picture is extremely complicated and often confused, and we have a very incomplete knowledge of the various traditions. However, the Alcmaeonid defence dealt with the curse by omitting it and leaving no room for its effects (Ch. 2.4.3 and 5.4 above). They probably even named themselves after Alcmaeon to dissociate themselves from Megacles in the previous generation. Can one, then, really attribute to them the preservation of the detailed tale of Cylon's conspiracy for nearly two hundred years? I shall attempt to argue that the tale was widely known in Athenian popular tradition and perhaps partly preserved by the shrine where the sacrilege was committed. The preservation of this early tradition interested a far wider group than the Alcmaeonids alone. The final picture may be rather confused, but that indicates something of the complexity of these early traditions. To assume a single, identifiable source like Alcmaeonid family tradition is attractive and simple but misleading.

Herodotus is prompted to explain the origin of the curse by its invocation by the Spartan king Cleomenes (v 70–2), Thucydides by its later invocation against Pericles (1 126). Plutarch (*Sol.* 12) gives a rather different version, thought to come from the *Ath. Pol.* which begins (in our text) with the end of the trial of the Alcmaeonids for sacrilege.[108]

In Herodotus' brief account (§71), Cylon, Olympic victor and Athen-

---

[105] E.g. *Atthis* 186f. (Herodotus knows about the magistracy because it is part of the Alcmaeonid defence); Gomme, *HCT* on 1 126 (with caution); G.W. Williams (1951); Lang (1967).

[106] G.W. Williams (1951); Jacoby (who insists that Thucydides also wanted to absolve the Alcmaeonids and so omitted Megacles' name). But at the same time Thucydides is seen as correcting Herodotus.

[107] Adcock (1926), 661 (curiously as proof of the accuracy of dating).

[108] Rhodes on Arist. *Ath. Pol.* 1; Gomme, *HCT ad loc.*, Jacoby, *Atthis* 186f.

ian, attempted to establish tyranny. He failed and became a suppliant with his companions at the altar on the Acropolis. The 'presidents of the naukraroi' (οἱ πρυτάνεις τῶν ναυκράρων) raised them up promising that they would not be punished by death. But they were murdered and this was blamed on the Alcmaeonids.

Thucydides' longer version seems to be correcting Herodotus. We are told more about Cylon, his relation to Theagenes and his visit to Delphi which encouraged him to attempt to become a tyrant. But he mistook the meaning of the oracle. The Athenians resisted him and besieged him on the Acropolis. Cylon escaped, but the rest remained as suppliants. Matters were entrusted to the archons. They promised the suppliants their safety but took them out and killed them. Therefore the Athenians expelled the accursed.

Plutarch's account has a trial and a cunning stratagem in addition. Megacles the archon (an Alcmaeonid) persuades the suppliants to stand trial. They descend from the Acropolis holding a cord linking them to the altar, and when it breaks, Megacles and his fellow archons kill them. Apparently all the archons are guilty in this version, but Solon (some time later) arranges a trial which declares Megacles' family guilty. They are expelled with the bones of their ancestors.

Attention usually focuses upon the different magistrates said by Herodotus and Thucydides to be involved and moves from there to the family 'source' and bias. But this emphasis obscures other variations and their implications for the oral traditions. In fact, most points of difference between Herodotus and Thucydides centre around Cylon rather than the Alcmaeonids. Thucydides tells of Cylon's marriage alliance with Theagenes and help from him, the encouragement from Delphi, Cylon's actual seizure of the Acropolis and his escape with his brother. We thus have a tale we might rather expect from Herodotus, with a visit to Delphi, a deceptive oracle and failed coup because the oracle was misinterpreted. Reminiscent of many tales in Herodotus, the motif of the ambiguous oracle is common in legends and popular stories. The type of tale is memorable, intriguing and carries an implicit religious moral. The implication of Thucydides' version is that Cylon would have succeeded had he understood the oracle correctly.[109] One would think this moral would counteract any use of the tale as narrow political propaganda. Surely it had wider circulation and popularity in Athens than in family tradition alone.[110]

---

[109] Recently used with other examples to show that the rational Thucydides did in fact believe in oracles, but they had to be interpreted correctly, Marinatos (1981).

[110] This kind of tale where an oracle is proved right is usually seen as part of 'Delphic tradition', not usually considered in Cylon's case (except by Forrest (1956)). Many have an odd meaning which is easily misinterpreted to be favourable. It is possible that

Other details that Thucydides gives confirm that Cylon was remembered in his own right by some kind of popular tradition. For he is a glorious figure in Thucydides, an Athenian Olympic victor, well-born and married to the daughter of the Megarian tyrant (1 126.3): 'Cylon was an Athenian, a victor at the Olympic games, well-born and powerful, and he had married the daughter of Theagenes . . . who was at that time tyrant of Megara.' These were extravagantly valuable assets. Cylon must have been one of the most powerful Athenians of the time. His Olympic victory, which must have carried great prestige, was a vital fact about him. Herodotus, too, introduces him with the epithet *Olympionikēs* ('Olympic victor'), which cannot be derogatory. Alcmaeon's chariot victory of which the Alcmaeonids were so proud, was about fifty years later.[111] Cylon was a powerful and admired figure. This is reflected in our sources and it points to traditions of wider currency than a partisan Alcmaeonid tradition. Victories in the games were remembered particularly carefully by the victor's family and city (Ch. 2.2).

There is also a curious remark of Pausanias (1 28.1) about a statue of Cylon on the Acropolis. This, too, may be expressive of popular traditions about Cylon. He is openly puzzled that the Athenians should have a statue of someone who plotted tyranny: 'I cannot say for certain why they set up a bronze statue to Cylon though he plotted to establish a tyranny.' And he suggests that it may be because Cylon was beautiful, distinguished, an Olympic victor and Theagenes' son-in-law. Here is crucial evidence for a statue of Cylon, presumably archaic.[112] It could

Delphi preserved Delphic tales, though there was no priestly caste to make this easy and one should not envisage a massive propaganda machine. People tend to remember only prophecies which come true. But nor did Delphi alone have an interest in remembering tales involving the oracle. If we consider the process more from the point of view of the poleis and individual consultants (as does Parker (1985)), then they, too, obviously had reason to remember the successful oracles and accompanying events. To attribute *all* oracle tales to a Delphic source is like saying that athletic victors and their poetic commemorations were *only* remembered by the great shrines themselves. Moreover, the motif of the prophecy and oracle is ubiquitous, a convenient and neat addition to many a tale that did not necessarily originate in Delphi: Fontenrose (1978), ch. 2 makes this clear (p. 68 on Cylon's oracle), though his general arguments about Delphi can be questioned (e.g. review by Robertson).

[111] Moretti (1957), no. 56 for Cylon in the *diaulos* (640 B.C.). Cylon can be placed in the late seventh century. Chronology starts from the victory, the archonship of Megacles and the rough succession of events: the Atthis (or *Ath. Pol.*) put the conspiracy before Drakon's code. Aristotle put the trial in Solon's time – thus the conspiracy must belong to the late seventh century. An old view originated by Beloch (1913, vol. I, part 2, pp. 302–9) that the conspiracy was more likely in the mid-sixth century dismisses too much evidence and takes anachronisms in Plutarch too seriously; cf. also the recent down-dating by Levy (1978).

[112] I can see no reason for its erection later; dismissed by Jacoby (as he must) who doubted the ascription to Cylon (*Atthis* 369, n. 88), but as Pausanias' surprise shows it was too unusual to be an invention.

have reinforced memories of Cylon, which were kept alive in any case by the curse's continued importance.[113] It also helps redress the balance still more in Cylon's favour. The Alcmaeonids were not necessarily the main focus of attention. Cylon himself was an interesting figure. The statue was probably an expiatory offering for the sacrilege. The practice has several parallels and a statue for a victory so early is unlikely.[114] There is even evidence, though very slight, that there was a precinct to Cylon, called the *Kylonion*.[115] That might suggest that Herodotus was right to say that Cylon himself was a suppliant. We must remember that Cylon was – at least in Herodotus' version – a victim as well as a very distinguished figure.

What then of the sacrilege itself? We tend to see the sacrilege from the point of view of Alcmaeonid guilt, but it concerned a far wider group than Alcmaeonids alone. It harmed the whole city, the pollution required the expulsion of the entire family, dead or alive, perhaps Epimenides' intervention to purify the city and the erection of a statue in atonement. And the tale is in all our versions essentially one of sacrilege, a fact obscured by our preoccupation with Alcmaeonid guilt.[116] The clear, religious moral was one of more interest to the Athenians than the Alcmaeonids. For instance, two accounts are preserved by Pausanias and a scholiast of Aristophanes, not usually quoted since they are late and derivative. They focus on the basic tale of Cylon's attempt and the suppliants' murder.[117] The murderers' identity is omitted, though it is stressed that they and their descendants were accursed. They remind us that the tale can be one essentially of sacrilege and punishment. The fact that Alcmaeonids are not named is a sign not of Alcmaeonid sympathy in the sources but of a difference in emphasis. Such a tale must have belonged to some kind of wider polis tradition. It was perhaps remem-

---

[113] The presence of a monument by itself does not, however, prove the existence of detailed traditions to go with it: cf. those connected with Cimon, Ch. 4.2, p. 216.

[114] Jameson (1965), stressing the sacrilege (and he argues counter-sacrilege on Cylon's part). Cf. the two statues of Pausanias erected by the Spartans in the temple as expiatory offering for their murder of him, Thuc. I 134.4.

[115] Jameson (1965), 171, n. 1: a κυλώνιον, if Müller's emendation of the text's κυδώνιον is accepted in Polemon (Schol. Soph. *O.C.* 489), τὸ ἱερόν ['Ησύχου] ἐστι περὶ τὸ Κυλώνιον ἐκτὸς τῶν ἐννέα πυλῶν. Travlos (1971), 2 and fig. 5 puts it a little way down from the main entrance to the Acropolis.

[116] If Cylon himself committed sacrilege (as Jameson and Jordan suggest) an attempt to absolve the Alcmaeonids might stress it. But it comes in neither Herodotus nor Thucydides.

[117] Paus. VII 25.3, introduced as a contrast to the proper treatment of suppliants in Codrus' time; schol. Ar. *Kn.* 445, commenting on the Aristophanic parody of an accusation of being accursed. Thucydides' omission of the Alcmaeonids' name hardly absolves them from blame, when he explicitly blames the archons, describes how the accursed were exiled and explains how Pericles was related to them.

bered also in the shrine where the sacrilege occurred, that of the Semnai, which was kept by the Hesychidai.[118]

Indeed it is difficult to see why the whole tale of the conspiracy has been thought to belong to the Alcmaeonid family tradition, still less why they who of all people lost most from the episode should have preserved a 'reasonably accurate tradition'. With the famous figure of Cylon, the misinterpreted oracle, sacrilege and curse, it is simply a different type of tale, unsuitable for any defence and far indeed from a family defence that might, for instance, have stressed that the Alcmaeonid archon acted to prevent tyranny. Cylon's statue and precinct emphasized the figure of Cylon and the sacrilegious murder of suppliants. The tradition was kept alive for the remarkable span of 200 years partly because the curse was periodically used against the Alcmaeonids. It was known to the Spartans, and Aristophanes could parody an accusation of being accursed (*Knights* 445) as if everyone was familiar with the charge against Pericles. Everyone knew which family was accursed. Presumably the other great families remembered it well and used it against the Alcmaeonids. It was not a sufficiently obscure tradition to need an esoteric family source to preserve it.

If we return to Herodotus' account, most of it, then, could well derive from popular tradition. He has nothing of Cylon's visit to Delphi, but says Cylon was an Olympic victor, and he has the bare bones of the attempt on the Acropolis and the supplication. Thucydides' longer account was clearly intended to correct and enlarge on Herodotus.

However, Herodotus introduces one detail, the responsibility of the 'presidents of the *naukraroi*'. This peculiarly detailed piece of information about an archaic board of officials demands explanation. He tells us how the suppliants were murdered (v 71.2): 'The presidents of the naucraries, who at that time governed Athens, raised them up on condition that they were liable to any penalty except death; but they were murdered and the blame was attached to the Alcmaeonids.' (τούτους ἀνιστᾶσι μὲν οἱ πρυτάνιες τῶν ναυκράρων, οἵ περ ἔνεμον τότε τὰς Ἀθήνας, ὑπεγγύους πλὴν θανάτου· φονεῦσαι δὲ αὐτοὺς αἰτίη ἔχει Ἀλκμεωνίδας.) The passage is usually explained thus: Herodotus is

---

[118] On the Hesychidai and the Semnai, see Toepffer (1889), 170–5 and Farnell (1909), vol. v 440. The Eupatrids had no share in their sacrifice according to Polemon (schol. Soph. *O.C.* 39). S. Humphreys has suggested to me that the Hesychidai were chosen to take care of the cult in the confusion of the Cylonian conspiracy precisely *because* they were not Eupatrid, and therefore neutral. Farnell (with D.L. 1 112, who mentions Epimenides) supposes a late sixth-century reorganization of the ritual, probably to do with purification (Epimenides was also supposed to have purified Athens of the curse, see Ch. 5, n. 127 below). The role of genos traditions in preserving traditions connected with shrines may have been important, since the priest did belong to a genos. They probably dwelt mainly on legendary origins of the genos.

trying to absolve the Alcmaeonid archon Megacles by stressing that a different board of magistrates was to blame and by not mentioning either the archons or Megacles himself.[119] But Herodotus neither says nor even implies this. In the Greek, the μὲν and δὲ clauses contrast the promise of safety with the eventual murder, rather than the naucraric presidents and the Alcmaeonids. Read thus, the sentence does not imply that the presidents of the *naukraroi* were responsible for the sacrilege. They were responsible only for the offer of safe conduct. Without preconceptions, one could even read in this a deliberate contrast between the rightful acts of the presidents and the sacrilegious murder by the Alcmaeonids.[120] The whole passage hardly defends the Alcmaeonids unequivocally. Yet it is the sole foundation for the idea that the Alcmaeonids defended themselves by blaming another magistracy.

Thucydides, on the other hand, is careful to stress that the archons were responsible for the siege and killed the suppliants (1 126.8):

> Most of the Athenians . . . left, entrusting to the nine archons the duty of keeping guard and full powers to arrange everything as they thought best. In those days the nine archons carried out most political functions . . . [Cylon and his brother escape] . . . The Athenians who were charged with the duty of keeping guard, when they saw them [the rest of the suppliants] at the point of death in the temple, raised them up on the understanding that no harm would be done to them, led them out and slew them.

This reads like a deliberate refutation of Herodotus' mention of the naucraric officers, as the whole section is trying to correct the record.[121] But with its firm stress on the archons we still find a clear assertion of Alcmaeonid guilt. It is hard to see how Thucydides can be said to absolve the family here.[122] There is little point here in trying to ascertain the original 'events' or the officials involved,[123] and that is probably impossible from such a tradition. It is more helpful to recognize that fifth-century Athenians probably did not really know which magistrates were

---

[119] Macan, Stein, and How and Wells, commentaries *ad loc.*, Jacob *Atthis* 186f.

[120] Recognized by Lang (1967), but she thinks Thucydides' insistence on the archons' responsibility gives respectability to the murder. This makes no difference to the sacrilege.

[121] Jordan ((1970), 156), however, thinks the two sets of officials merely complemented each other, therefore that Herodotus and Thucydides are not incompatible. But it does not read like that.

[122] His narrative implies that they were all guilty, and therefore all should be exiled. The problem has been 'solved' by supposing that only the eponymous archon was responsible, hence the Alcmaeonid exile.

[123] See Jameson (1965) and Jordan (1970) and (1979), with n. 125, below.

responsible, since Herodotus and Thucydides disagreed. In fact, Thucydides may have corrected Herodotus simply on the grounds of which magistrates were in charge of the city, since both historians describe the magistrates they name as 'in charge' of the city at the time.[124]

We can be more certain about the remarkable mention of the presidents of the naucraries. One would not expect this archaic and obscure office to be remembered in oral tradition or understood in the fifth century, hence its significance.[125] For when oral tradition preserves an obscure element which is no longer relevant or understood by the tradition's narrators, that element is likely to be a genuine memory from an earlier time, even if it is not historically accurate.[126] The naucraric presidents must represent, whatever their provenance, some genuine memory or at least a much older stage in the tradition.

How was this detail remembered? The Alcmaeonids are the least likely source since the reference to the officials does not absolve them from blame. If pressed, they could produce a better defence, for instance that they had tried to prevent tyranny or that the city had been purified. Plutarch's tale of the cord attached to the altar reads more like a justification of the murders, since the cord helped to evade the spirit of the religious law (as it was bound to break at some point) while following its 'letter'.[127] We must look elsewhere, to the polis traditions which remembered so much about Cylon or the traditions connected with the shrines involved in the sacrilege. As I have said, the curse continued to be invoked. It was the concern of the whole city, which needed purification, and of the other leading families. It was presumably also the concern of the shrines where the sacrilege took place. The temple of Athena is implied and Thucydides also mentions the altar of the Eumenides. The archaic and surprising detail of the naucraric presidents may have come

124 Thucydides' use of the anachronistic *autokratōr*, a fifth-century term first attested in Aristophanes and Thucydides, would support this: he is clearly trying to explain what the traditions said in familiar constitutional terms.

125 Arist. *Ath. Pol.* 8.3, 21.5, on *naukraroi* responsible for provision of ships, levies and contingents, replaced by demarchs under Cleisthenes. They cannot be identified with archons (Gomme, *HCT ad loc.*). Jordan ((1970) and (1979), 56ff.) sees them as like *tamiai* but with religious duties at first.

126 Vansina (1973), 83; *OTH* 83ff. on 'meaning'; Yoder, *APS* 84, Miller, *APS* 38.

127 Cf. Orestes' purification, esp. in the *Eumenides* (Dover (1957) notes Alcmaeonid parallel). There is much confusion and parallelism between the accounts of the seventh-century conspiracy and aftermath and the end of the sixth century: especially with the periods of exile; the casting out of bones (in the seventh or the sixth century or both – for which see Gomme, *HCT* and G.W. Williams (1951)); the purification associated by Plutarch with Solon is put to *c*. 500 by Plato (*Laws* 642d). We cannot reject either version categorically: this is exactly the kind of duplication to expect in oral tradition.

from there. The tale of conspiracy and sacrilege was remembered despite the main culprits' attempts to forget it.

However, the whole episode was vastly simplified and distorted by the fifth century. We find very blurred chronology. Herodotus only says the incident occurred 'before the Peisistratids'. For oral tradition did not record exact chronology, only a rough sequence of associated events, if that.[128] Plutarch's more detailed account shows a duplication of elements said to occur at the end of both the seventh and sixth centuries. There is also a crystallization of events around the later figure of Solon. Plutarch places both the trial and Epimenides' purification under his auspices. Solon, the wise sage and lawgiver, has attracted the tale in a manner common in oral tradition.[129] Reconstruction of chronology and original events is quite impossible. What is interesting is the complexity of the traditions and their transmission over so long a period. The tale probably belonged to the polis traditions and the shrines where the sacrilege took place, connected with Cylon's statue and perhaps his precinct. It was kept alive so long by the continued invocation of the Alcmaeonid curse. But though the family obviously knew something of the origin, the traditions were preserved and transmitted through so many generations by others, rival aristocratic families, priests and demos.

The cumulative effects of this re-examination of early Alcmaeonid history are startling. Mostly preserved by Herodotus, these tales, too, have been interpreted as Alcmaeonid tradition and fitted into the overall schema of Alcmaeonid, as opposed to popular and official, tradition. But they are representative rather of wider popular and polis traditions which proffered information highly damaging to the family. The Alcmaeonid tradition, like other family traditions, smoothed over embarrassing elements and eventually forgot them. Most significant, memories about the curse were preserved by polis, shrine and demos and – helped by its continued relevance – transmitted in some form for over two hundred years. Far from parroting the family tradition, Herodotus was able to pick up these other traditions and treat them with considerable independence of mind. This reminds us forcefully, first, that family tradition may be the last place to look for accurate memories about its less admirable history; secondly, that if there were reason enough to remember, oral

---

[128] Cf. the phenomenon of 'telescoping' (Ch. 3.2). For archaic Athens, it is optimistic to think that events which were important at the time were remembered along with the interval of years separating them (as does Fornara (1971a), 2, following Jacoby), and more likely that many were remembered in chronological isolation. Compare the vagueness of dating which Thucydides, trying to improve on Hellanicus, offers us for the Pentekontaëtia, and Heidbüchel (1957) with Ch. 2 n. 138.

[129] A 'culture hero' in anthropological terms. See Henige (1982), 87ff., Millers, *APS* 15f. ('ascending anachronisms'), Vansina, *OTH* esp. 22f.

traditions of popular circulation in demos and polis could be complex and resilient.

*

This chapter has examined as a case history the complex of sources and traditions concerning the 'liberation' of Athens from tyranny and the Alcmaeonid family. They have previously been interpreted in terms of opposed family tradition and official tradition. On closer scrutiny, the picture of Alcmaeonid family tradition and its influence is mistaken. The real Alcmaeonid tradition implies very different mechanisms for family tradition. The opposition of Alcmaeonid and official tradition misrepresents both the complex of traditions that existed then and the manner in which the oral traditions developed. The idea of 'official' tyrannicide tradition suggested extremely simple and naive traditions and an exaggerated importance for the monuments. But the traditions of the community – the polis traditions – were a great deal more complex than that. Not only can we be certain that the demos did *not* think the tyrannicides ended the tyranny, but we find different layers and emphases and surprising complexity in the popular traditions alone. In addition, it cannot be overemphasized how the traditions changed with time. Because of their age, for instance, probably very little in the traditions of the Cylon conspiracy is historically accurate. But it is notable how remarkably long the traditions did continue – and in wide circulation – and this must partly reflect the continued importance of the curse on one of the most prominent Athenian families.

The traditions were living ones which therefore altered because of contemporary preoccupations, the needs of defence and the failing of memory. One of the essential factors in the changes was simply democratic patriotism appropriate for one of the great landmarks of Athenian democratic history. It is also crucial to recognize the complexity with which different oral traditions interact. Family traditions are much influenced by the general tenor of the polis traditions and gradually reduced to stereotypes. No traditions or memories are recorded in complete isolation. The traditions slowly change under these various pressures to become simpler and more stereotyped representations of Athens' liberation.

The background of oral tradition affects our understanding of the Greek historians and the problems they faced. The oral traditions about the liberation and early Alcmaeonid history were much simplified and fading rapidly by the fourth century. But later historians at least had the use of Herodotus' account, and their methods must be considered against both the older, written histories and the contemporary, oral traditions. The traditions were still varied and complex, however, when Herodotus was writing. If various traditions were combined, careful enquiry could still reveal much in the mid- to late fifth century. Herodotus' methods emerge in a better light. He seems to have avoided merely repeating any one version. He balanced the Alcmaeonid defence against highly damaging information which he got from wider popular or polis traditions. He succeeded in producing a far more complex and detailed account of the 'liberation' itself than we would expect from any one source. He was surely well aware of the pitfalls of the patriotic and family traditions.

EPILOGUE

Oral tradition in Athens was of the most fluid kind, its transmission casual, and its lifespan usually short. Apart from much earlier oral poetry, the strict mechanisms for accurate transmission found by anthropologists are absent. The same is probably true of the rest of Greece. This means that memory and oral tradition were peculiarly prone to change and selection according to later beliefs and ideals. In evaluating the reliability of oral tradition as evidence, one must therefore ascertain above all the means of transmission and the length of time since the incidents referred to took place. Large vacuums of ignorance and dramatic telescoping of chronology occur only three or four generations back.

Living oral traditions continued to be transmitted alongside the written histories of the classical period, apparently unaffected by them. The Athenian democracy encouraged a new emphasis on the recent past as a source of prestige more important than legendary origins. Family tradition now had to remember the historical period, and it recorded it with greater precision than the wider traditions. But official tradition and ideals fostered an image of Athens' past in the old aristocratic mould, acquiring for the demos an aristocratic legendary ancestry. Combined with certain democratic ideals, this produced a bare and anonymous past, rendering much of Athens' history irrelevant. However, the popular and general polis traditions maintained much more variety and detail. Between them they could produce traditions of some complexity for perhaps three or four generations. Family traditions were also important in preserving individual memories which were not stereotyped. But these, too, eventually grew closer to the simpler polis traditions by the sheer process of memory and the need for democratic ancestry. We can occasionally watch the transformation.

The processes of memory and change reveal much about those transmitting the memories and the values of the society in which they repeat them. Many of the oral traditions examined here are not valuable as evidence for the past events they record: next to the detailed contemporary account of Thucydides, for example, they can add little. But they provide valuable evidence of a different sort. Since oral traditions closely reflect contemporary ideals and beliefs, they can be very valuable in highlighting them. The tenor of family traditions in the democracy was surprising and brought out the somewhat archaic, somewhat aristocratic side of democratic Athens. The fourth-century oral traditions about the sixth-century tyranny had lost most of the specifically archaic elements of that time and saw events in a much simplified, contemporary manner. The gathering of anachronisms is hardly confined to oral traditions about the past. But in the conditions of oral transmission where contemporary written evidence either does not exist or is ignored, there is almost no check on the accumulating changes and distortions, almost no way of halting the transformations or getting behind them to earlier and historically more accurate memories. The process of change is irreversible. It is therefore all the more tempting – and possible – to reconstruct the past, whether legendary or recent, according to beliefs or presumptions about the relation of the past to the present. Similarly with what we would call deliberate distortions: when, say, a speaker in the assembly improves or even deliberately falsifies some family history, that itself is one stage in the transmission of oral tradition and it may shape the family tradition decisively. What if this version is transmitted in good faith, as it were, by the next generation? Such distortion is simply part of the continuing processes of oral tradition, and it may well be backed up again by certain ideals and general beliefs about the past. Compare, for example, the idea that legendary ancestry had great relevance for the character of the present.

The Greek historian enquiring of the past was faced with a constantly changing spectrum of memories which were disappearing fast – and for many periods with a simple vacuum. Chronology was vague or distorted and it might be telescoped drastically. Ancient historians needed much elaboration and 'reconstruction' to fill in the Greek past back to the Trojan War, for all traditions had an immense 'gap' between the recent past and the legendary origins. We must not underestimate the extent of apparently logical and ahistorical 'reconstruction', both at the very start of Greek historiography (and proto-history) and later when historians could foist some responsibility on the authority of their predecessors' written crystallization of oral tradition.

However, it is clear that Herodotus and Thucydides only achieved the detail and quality of their information by exceedingly careful investigation and collection of different versions. The later fourth-century had different problems. By then the oral traditions corresponding to Herodotus' and Thucydides' accounts were either dead or much changed, but at least they had the earlier written texts to work from. We can only appreciate their work (mostly fragmentary) against this more literary background. Herodotus and Thucydides, however, were mostly writing things down for the first time, so the problems of oral tradition and of writing down oral tradition concern their work to an exceptional degree.

I would particularly stress the implications for Herodotus' achievement. He has always been notorious for his extraordinary stories, the unlikely and unsophisticated tales about the figures of early Greece. Many of these are impossible to wed with the recent discoveries of archaeology, for example, or complex theories of archaic Greek politics. But that is partly because Herodotus was at the mercy of oral tradition – and only what oral tradition had chosen to remember, select and simplify. Oral traditions would not, for instance, record the long drawn-out changes and subtle implications of archaic warfare. Nor, presumably, would Herodotus be able to find oral traditions about the many trading posts or incipient colonies in the Mediterranean which archaeology reveals, but which had not lasted down to his own day. Traditions of early colonization could only survive if there was continuity and people to remember the traditions.

Thucydides, on the other hand, was able to talk to actual participants. The greater detail and sophistication of his analysis of the Peloponnesian War arises partly (though only partly) from the great wealth of detail and knowledge of contemporary events still in existence. When he returns to accounts of Pausanias and Themistocles in the 480s and 470s, the calibre of his information changes markedly. We suddenly encounter colourful and dramatic elements which we would rather associate with Herodotus. Yet these men lived only about fifty years before Thucydides began writing his Histories. We surely see here the effect of oral tradition, the selection, simplification and transformation of memory.

The implications for modern study of Greek history are far-reaching. Like the Atthidographers, modern scholars can use the written works of earlier Greek historians, as well as the surviving contemporary written sources. But understanding the nature of the historians' sources is therefore essential, both for evaluating the sources and for appreciating the historians' methods of using them. Where those sources were oral tradition, it is necessary to consider the length and manner of transmission and the reasons for remembering the traditions which would introduce change. 'Anomalous' elements which do not fit the supposed tenor of the tradition sometimes point to earlier layers or perhaps original memories. It is also necessary to appreciate what the historians may have done with the oral traditions, whether they have shaped them or combined them with others. It is suggested that Herodotus and Thucydides at least made careful and critical use of a wide range of oral sources.

The presence of literacy and writing complemented the oral traditions but did not destroy them. The case of classical Athens prompts a reconsideration of the nature of literacy and its uses. We should consider not the mere presence of literacy nor its 'extent', but how and where it was used. The background of extensive oral methods of communication, proof, and record influenced fundamentally the very use or adoption of writing. In other words, writing might not have the significance and content we expect of a written document. Nor would classical Athenians treat it in the ways we take for granted. The stone documents of Greece cannot be interpreted adequately without appreciating the oral background to the ancient use of writing. We can therefore trace a development in the use of writing. Athens was only beginning to be document-minded in the fourth century. By the second half of the fourth century, there are finally signs that people were starting to think oral tradition was not enough: for real and striking proof one needed written documentation. That is symptomatic of the increasing use of written documents in more and more areas and thus of its increasing familiarity and acceptance.

A more subtle relation between writing and oral tradition can also be discerned which deserves much further investigation. In the most straightforward sense, the written accounts of historians seem to have had little effect on the living oral traditions, which continued unabashed and ever more simplified. But we can trace the application of writing and written scholarship to oral traditions, elaborating them and imposing a chronological schema. When we know more about the nature of oral tradition we can understand better the development of early 'historiography' and related subjects, the historians' methods and use of their evidence, and the way that oral evidence was itself affected by being written down.

The classical period offers plentiful enough evidence to examine in detail the character of its oral traditions and the role of the written word. The essential factors in oral tradition, such as the nature of transmission, are clear and their effects visible. We can see how oral traditions changed constantly and why they were changing. The relation between the general values of the society and the emphases and omissions of their traditions are interesting and complex. In particular, it is possible to understand how genuine memories of original occurrences can gradually be transformed from personal reminiscences into simplified oral traditions which bear slight relation to the original memory and which have acquired conventional or idealized elements, clichés and stereotyped form. We know what to expect of oral tradition and how to treat it. We can therefore apply these insights to the earlier periods for which our evidence is not only slighter, but the product of very long and complex transmission.

APPENDIX: EARLY GREEK LISTS

The suggestions of Chapter 3 obviously have some bearing on other early Greek lists. I can only outline some points here which need further development.

What we can suggest from the anthropological studies discussed in Chapter 3.2 is that we could well expect one of the earliest uses of writing to be the recording of lists. Those in the religious sphere (e.g. sacred laws, calendars) might be the first (Ch. 1.1). The aims of such lists might not be the ones *we* tend to assume: the initial incentive need not have been preoccupation with dating by officials. Given the continuing use of memory even where written documents did exist (Ch. 1.2), we cannot assume that there must be written lists where there are eponymous officials – especially since eponymous officials are mnemonic aids in themselves. But once lists are started, such dating would be easier (cf. Jeffery (1976), 34–6, and *LSAG* 59ff. on use of early lists for dating, and below). We have already seen striking examples where documents are not used for the documentary purposes we would expect (Ch. 1.2.2). Nor should we be surprised to find bare lists without any comment at all (Jacoby, *Atthis* 58f. stresses bareness; contrast surprise of ML no. 6, p. 10).

That applies to the keeping of lists with each successive official. But what about the earlier reaches of the lists which correspond to periods before they were kept in writing? There was much room here for speculation and manipulation. Compare the list of priests which went back to Telamon (*Syll.*[3] 1020), or the archon list which extended to an archon in the year 683/2. In other examples, too, where there was no recorded list in writing, we must assume literate and scholarly organization and expansion – though 'additions' were not necessarily regarded as falsifications (see Ch. 1.2.4 and 3). In this, men of the sophistic generation seem to have played a large part. Hippias was said to have compiled the Olympic victor list and he could recite the archon list 'back to Solon' for anyone who wished to hear (*Hipp. Mai.* 285e). Hellanicus used a list of *karneonikai* (victors at the Karneia festival) and based his universal history round the list of priestesses of Hera at Argos (*FGH* 4 F85–6). He also constructed a list of kings of Athens (Jacoby, *Atthis* 58f., and *FGH* 4, (Hellanicus) 'Introduction') and used the archon list in his *Atthis*. In part these men may have been publishing lists that already existed in documentary form of some kind, but common sense tells us that even where that occurred, some expansion and manipulation was necessary at least for the early reaches of a list. Besides this, these activities seem to be indicative of a new interest in this kind of document or reconstructed document – mainly for dating and a chronological schema – thus of a more sophisticated extension of the organization and use of genealogies for chronological reckoning and a more complex use of written record.

For the Olympic victor list, Plutarch doubted that Hippias had any reliable evidence for his compilation (*Numa* 1 6, *FGH* 6 F2). Certainly, it is doubtful if there existed any list at all before Hippias (*Atthis* 58f.). What one can point out, though, is that there were probably many memories of victories preserved by families and cities which Hippias could use at least for recent periods (Ch. 2.2). This does not seem to have been the case with Athenian archonships.

What then of the archon list? Its contents can give us some hints. Though it may have been inscribed as late as 425, it has names of archons under the tyrants. This suggests to me that a list was being written down in some form by the end of the sixth century because (i) family tradition did not remember archonships carefully (Ch. 2.2) and more important (ii) it especially did not remember archonships held under the tyrants (e.g. those of Cleisthenes and Miltiades). Family tradition dealt unscrupulously with awkward memories from the Peisistratid period (Ch. 3.1, p. 169 for the Philaids, Chs. 2.4.3 and 5.4 for the Alcmaeonids). So, how would anyone in the mid-fifth century know from oral tradition alone that Cleisthenes (for example) had been archon? The archon list as it appears in the 420s must have been based partly on some form of written record, not necessarily inscribed, which was being kept by the Peisistratid period.

But manipulation and imaginative 'reconstruction' could also be involved in order to get back to Kreon, not simply to Solon (Bradeen (1963), 17). Elaboration and publication of the list in *c.* 425 could still be the product of a new scholarly attention to lists and other written records. Again, the list was not necessarily intended primarily as a dating system (*pace* Stroud (1978), 32ff., who argues for a written list from earliest times). For in that case it would be remarkable that it took so long for archon dates to be used at all consistently (cf. Ch. 1.2.3, p. 79). Since it is not usually supposed that lists of priests had an obvious and primary function as a dating system, perhaps that analogy might help in considering other possible functions for the archon list (cf. for instance, the 'daduchs' at Eleusis, Ch. 3, n. 101, listed by a descendant to show how his *eugeneia* was inherited from his predecessors in long succession). Similarly, it is misleading to talk of 'inscribed public deception' (as does Stroud) of the partially reconstructed list, for it probably would not have been regarded as such. But the keeping of a public list of state officials does imply some awareness of polis cohesion or identity. (Cf. also Cadoux (1948), 80f., who suggests that memory of early archons was connected with some event; Plommer (1969), arguing that the list was drawn up for the first time in 425, and *Atthis* 58f. on official lists.) One may perhaps compare the significance of the inscribed public laws of the polis.

CHRONOLOGICAL TABLE

Almost all dates before 500 are approximate, and those between 478 and 431 may vary by one to three years. The dates of ancient writers and their works are also notoriously inexact or sometimes unknown: I have indicated the rough period of activity, death or publication depending on the state of our knowledge.

B.C.

1600–1200	Mycenaean Palace Culture in Greece.
1220	Destruction of Troy VIIa.
c. 1200	Destruction of Mycenaean palaces in Greece.
	Beginning of Dark Ages.
1050–950	Ionian colonization of coast of Asia Minor.
8th c.	'Greek Renaissance'.
776	First Olympic Games (conventional date).
By 750	Adaptation of Greek alphabet from Phoenician script.
	Foundation of trading post at Pithecusae, W. coast of Italy.
735–700	Greek colonies founded in Sicily.
c. 730–710	Sparta conquers Messenia and the Helots.
By 700	Wide diffusion of alphabet.
	Homeric *Iliad* and *Odyssey*.
c. 700	Hesiod.
683/2	Athenian archon list begins.
c. 680–640	Archilochus of Paros.
655–585	Tyranny at Corinth: Kypselos and Periander.
c. 650	Tyranny of Orthagoras at Sicyon.
c. 650–600	Earliest Greek law on stone from Dreros, Crete.
640	Theagenes tyrant of Megara.
632	Cylon's conspiracy at Athens; origin of Alcmaeonid curse.
630	Cyrene founded in N. Africa by Therans.
621	Drakon's law code at Athens.
620–570	Pittakos' tyranny at Mitylene.
	Alcaeus, Sappho.
late 7th c.	Tyrtaeus, Alcman, Steisichorus.
By 600	Greek foundation of Naukratis and intensification of Greek contacts with Egypt.
600	Cleisthenes becomes tyrant of Sicyon.
595	First Greek coinage (Aegina).
594/3	Solon archon of Athens; Solonian law code.
c. 592	Alcmaeon (the Alcmaeonid) wins victory at Olympia.

c. 572	The 'wooing of Agariste' arranged by Cleisthenes of Sicyon.
c. 566	Reorganization of Panathenaia at Athens.
c. 561	Peisistratos' first tyranny at Athens.
560–546	Croesus king of Lydia.
559–556	Miltiades (oikist) founds colony in Chersonese, Thrace.
556	Birth of Simonides (556–468).
546	Cyrus conquers Lydia.
546–528	Peisistratos' final tyranny at Athens.
	Supposed Alcmaeonid exile.
528/7	Hippias takes over tyranny at Athens.
525	Cleisthenes archon at Athens.
c. 521–491	Cleomenes king of Sparta. Further expansion of Spartan power.
514	Harmodius and Aristogeiton murder Hipparchus at Athens.
510	Overthrow of Peisistratid tyranny at Athens.
508/7	Isagoras archon; expels Alcmaeonids and 700 families.
507	Cleisthenes implements his reforms at Athens: Cleisthenic democracy.
late 6th c.	Theognis of Megara, Xenophanes, Pythagoras.
c. 500	Hecataeus of Miletus active (geographer and logographer).
499–494	Ionian revolt from the Persians.
492	Miltiades (the general) returns to Athens; prosecuted for tyranny.
490–479	Persian Wars.
490	First Persian expedition: battle of Marathon.
489	Miltiades is fined for misconduct, and dies.
487/6	Athenian archons chosen by lot.
480	Second expedition: battles of Artemisium, Thermopylae, Salamis.
479	Battles of Plateia, Mycale.
478	Delian League against Persia founded by Greeks under Athenian leadership. Origin of Athenian Empire.
470s	Establishment of Athenian public funeral orations.
472	Aeschylus' *Persae*.
468	Sophocles' first victory in tragedy.
467–66	Greeks under Cimon defeat Persians at Eurymedon.
465	Revolt of Thasos from Delian League.
464	Earthquake and Helot revolt in Sparta. Athenian help dismissed.
461	Cimon ostracized.
	Ephialtes' reforms at Athens: radical democracy.
	First Peloponnesian War between Athens and Sparta (461–446).
459	Athenian expedition to Egypt.
458	Battles of Oinophyta and Tanagra: Athenian conquest of Boiotia.
	Aeschylus' *Oresteia*.
456	Death of Aeschylus.
454	Athenian disaster in Egypt.
451/0	Pericles' citizenship law.
450s–420s	Protagoras, early sophist, active.
450?	Five Years Truce between Athens and Sparta.

450–449	Athens' and allies' expedition to Cyprus: death of Cimon.
?449	'Peace of Callias' between Athens and Persia: conventional marker of the end of war with Persia.
447	Parthenon is begun in Athens.
	Athenian defeat at Koroneia and loss of Boiotia.
446	Revolt of Euboia.
	Thirty Years Peace between Sparta and Athens and their allies.
c. 446	Last dateable ode of Pindar.
443	Thurii founded in S. Italy by Athenians.
	Thucydides, son of Melesias, ostracized.
	Pericles holds generalship regularly for next 14 years.
440s–430s	Herodotus active (dies in 420s).
441–439	Samos revolts from Athens.
441	Euripides' first victory.
?441	Sophocles' *Antigone*.
431	Second Peloponnesian War begins (431–404).
	Thucydides begins writing his *Histories* at the start of the war (died probably in 390s).
	Medea of Euripides.
430	Outbreak of plague at Athens.
429	Death of Pericles.
428–427	Revolt of Lesbos.
427	Athenian expedition in Sicily.
	Gorgias the sophist visits Athens.
c. 427	Plato born.
425	Athenians capture Spartiates at Pylos.
	Aristophanes' *Acharnians*.
424	Battle of Delion: Boiotians defeat Athenians.
	Knights of Aristophanes.
	Thucydides, the historian, is exiled.
422	Brasidas and Cleon killed outside Amphipolis.
	Wasps of Aristophanes.
421	Peace of Nicias between Athens and Sparta.
418	Spartans defeat coalition at Mantinea.
415–413	Athenian expedition to Sicily.
415	Mutilation of Hermae at Athens: Alcibiades implicated and recalled from Sicilian expedition.
414	Aristophanes' *Birds*.
412	War resumes in mainland Greece; Spartan treaties with Persia.
411	Aristophanes' *Lysistrata* and *Thesmophoriazusae*.
	Oligarchic coup of the Four Hundred at Athens; replaced by the Five Thousand, then by democracy in 410.
?410–405	Metroön established as the city archive.
410–400/399	Revision of the laws at Athens.
406	Athenian victory at Arginusae.
	Death of Euripides and Sophocles.

405	Spartans destroy Athenian fleet at Aigospotamoi. Aristophanes' *Frogs*.
404	Athenian siege and capitulation to Spartans.
404–403	Oligarchy of Thirty Tyrants at Athens.
403	Democracy restored.
403	Lysias XII, *Against Eratosthenes* (Lysias active as orator *c.* 407–*c.* 380).
401–399	Expedition of Cyrus and Ten Thousand against Persian King.
401	Sophocles' *Oedipus Coloneus* produced.
399	Death of Socrates. Andocides I, *On the Mysteries* (active: before 415–392/1).
397	Isocrates XVI (Isocrates active 390s–338).
396–394	Agesilaos' campaigns in Asia Minor.
395	Corinthian War starts.
394	Persians defeat Spartan fleet at Cnidus.
388	Aristophanes' *Wealth*.
386	Peace of Antalcidas (King's Peace) between Persian King and Greeks.
?385	Plato's *Menexenus*.
384	Birth of Demosthenes and Aristotle.
380	Isocrates IV, *Panegyricus*.
379–8	Liberation of Thebes.
378–377	Second Athenian League established.
371	Thebans defeat Spartans at Leuctra: conventional end of Spartan predominance.
370–361	Theban invasion of Peloponnese.
369	Helots establish separate state (Messenia).
367	Aristotle joins the Academy.
362	Thebans defeat Spartans at Mantinea.
359	Philip II becomes king of Macedon.
357	Philip captures Amphipolis.
357/6	Social War breaks out between Athens and its allies. War between Philip and Athens.
356	Sacred war begins.
c. 355	Xenophon dies (before 425–*c.* 355).
355	Isocrates VIII, *On the Peace*. Demosthenes XX, *Against Leptines*: Demosthenes publicly active from now on.
355/4	Athens defeated in Social War.
348	Philip captures Olynthus and reduces Chalcidice.
347	Plato dies (*c.* 427–347).
346	'Peace of Philocrates' between Philip and Athens.
343	Trial and acquittal of Aeschines: Demosthenes XIX and Aeschines II (*On the Embassy*).
339	Isocrates' *Panathenaicus* (XII).

338	Philip defeats Athenians and Thebans at Chaeronea. Conventional end of Greek 'liberty'. Isocrates dies.
337	Corinthian League founded under Philip's leadership: declares war on Persia. Beginning of Lycurgus' control of Athenian finances.
336	Philip assassinated, Alexander (the Great) succeeds.
335	Alexander and Macedonians destroy Thebes. Aristotle settles at Athens.
334	Alexander sets off on Persian expedition.
331	Foundation of Alexandria in Egypt.
330	Demosthenes XVIII, *On the Crown*; Aeschines III, *Against Ctesiphon*; Lycurgus I, *Against Leocrates*.
325/4	Death of Lycurgus.
324	Demosthenes exiled.
323	Death of Alexander.
323–322	Lamian War: Athens is defeated by the Macedonians.
322	Hypereides' *Funeral Oration*. Change of Athenian constitution: oligarchy and Macedonian garrison imposed. Death of Aristotle (384–322), Demosthenes (384–322), Hypereides.

BIBLIOGRAPHY

ADCOCK, F.E. (1926) 'Chronological Notes: The Date of Cylon's coup d'État', *CAH*, IV, 1st edn, 661–2.

ADKINS, A.W.H. (1960) *Merit and Responsibility: A Study in Greek Values* (Oxford).

ALEXIOU, M. (1974) *The Ritual Lament in Greek Tradition* (Cambridge).
  (1984/5) 'Folklore: An Obituary?', *Byzantine and Modern Greek Studies* 9, 1–28.

ALY, W. (1921) *Volksmärchen, Sage und Novelle bei Herodot und seinen Zeitgenossen* (Göttingen).
  (1929) *Formprobleme der frühen griechischen Prosa, Philologus* Suppl. vol. 21 (3).

ANDREWES, A. (1976) 'Androtion and the Four Hundred', *PCPS* 22, 14–25.
  (1982) 'The Tyranny of Peisistratus', *CAH*, III.3, 2nd edn, 392–416.

ANDREWES, A. and D. LEWIS (1957) 'Note on the Peace of Nicias', *JHS* 77, 177–80.

ATKINSON, K.M.T. (1939) 'Athenian Legislative Procedure and the Revision of Laws', *Bull. of J. Rylands Library* 23, 107–50.

AUSTIN, C. (1973) Review of MacDowell's edition of the *Wasps* of Aristophanes, *CR* 23, 133–5.

AUSTIN, R.P. (1938) *The Stoichedon Style in Greek Inscriptions* (Oxford).

AVERY, H.C. (1963) 'Critias and the Four Hundred, *CPh* 58, 165–7.

BADDELEY, A.D. (1976) *The Psychology of Memory* (New York).
  (1979) 'The Limitations of Human Memory: Implications for the Design of Retrospective Surveys', in Moss and Goldstein (eds.) (1979).
  (1983) *Your Memory: A User's Guide* (Harmondsworth).

BADIAN, E. (1971) 'Archons and Strategoi', *Antichthon* 5, 1–34.

BAINES, J. (1983) 'Literacy and Ancient Egyptian Society', *Man* 18, 572–97.

BARNES, J.A. (1967) 'Genealogies', in A.L. Epstein (ed.), *The Craft of Social Anthropology*, (London), 101–28.

BARNS, J. (1953–4) 'Cimon and the First Athenian Expedition to Cyprus', *Historia* 2, 163–76.

BARRON, J.P. (1962) 'Milesian Politics and Athenian Propaganda', *JHS* 82, 1–6.

BAYNES, N.H. (1955) 'Isocrates', in *Byzantine Studies and other Essays* (London), 144–67.

BEARD, M. (1985) 'Arval Acta', *PBSR* 53, 114–62.

BELOCH, J. (1905) 'Griechische Aufgebote I', *Klio* 5, 341–74.
  (1913–27) *Griechische Geschichte*, 4 vols., 2nd edn (Berlin and Leipzig).

BERNARDI, B. and C. PONI and A. TRIULZI (eds.) (1978) *Fonti orali. Antropologia e storia* (Milan).

BERVE, H. (1937) *Miltiades: Studien zur Geschichte des Mannes und seiner Zeit*, *Hermes* Einzelschriften 2.

BETHE, E. (1935) *Ahnenbild und Familiengeschichte bei Römern und Griechen* (Munich).

BICKERMAN, E.J. (1952) 'Origines gentium', *CPh* 47, 65–81.

BICKNELL, P.J. (1970) 'The Exile of the Alkmaeonidai during the Peisistratid tyranny', *Historia* 9, 129–31.

(1972) *Studies in Greek Politics and Genealogy*, *Historia* Einzelschriften 19.

BLASS, F. (1887–98) *Die attische Beredsamkeit*, 2nd edn (Leipzig).

BLOCH, M. (1981) 'Tombs and States', in Humphreys and King (eds.) (1981), 137–47.

BODIN, L. (1932) 'Isocrate et Thucydide', in *Mélanges G. Glotz* I (Paris), 93–102.

BOEDEKER, D. (ed.) et al. (1987) *Herodotus and the Invention of History*, Arethusa 20.

BOEGEHOLD, A.L. (1972) 'The Establishment of a Central Archive at Athens', *AJA* 76, 23–30.

BOETHIUS, A. (1942) 'On the Ancestral Masks of the Romans', *Acta Archaeologica* (Copenhagen), 226–35.

BOGAERT, R. (1968) *Banques et banquiers dans les cités grecques* (Leiden).

(1976) *Epigraphica 3. Texts on Bankers, Banking and Credit in the Greek World* (Leiden).

BOHANNAN, L.A. (1952) 'A Genealogical Charter', *Africa* 22, 301–15.

BONNER, R.J. (1905) *Evidence in Athenian Courts* (Chicago).

(1908) 'The Use and Effect of Attic Seals', *CPh* 3, 399–407.

BORNITZ, H.-P. (1968) *Herodot-Studien: Beiträge zum Verständnis der Einheit des Geschichtswerkes* (Berlin).

BOURGET, M.N. and L. VALENSI and N. WACHTEL (eds.) (1986) *Between Memory and History*, in *History and Anthropology* 2 (London, Paris, New York).

BOURRIOT, F. (1976) *Recherches sur la nature du genos: étude d'histoire sociale Athénienne – périodes archaique et classique*, 2 vols. (Lille).

BOWIE, E.L. (1974) 'The Greeks and their Past in the Second Sophistic', in M.I. Finley (ed.) (1974), 166–209. (Originally in *Past and Present* 46 (1970)).

(1986) 'Early Greek Elegy, Symposium and Public Festival', *JHS* 106, 13–35.

BOWRA, M. (1936) *Greek Lyric Poetry from Alcman to Simonides* (Oxford).

(1938) 'The Epigram on the Fallen of Coronea', *CQ* 32, 80–8.

BRACCESI, L. (1970) 'L'epitafio di Iperide come fonte storica', *Athenaeum* 48, 276–301.

BRADEEN, D.W. (1963) 'The Fifth-Century Archon List', *Hesperia* 32, 187–208.

(1964) 'Athenian Casualty Lists', *Hesperia* 33, 16–62.

(1967) 'The Athenian Casualty List of 464 B.C.', *Hesperia* 36, 321–8.

(1969) 'The Athenian Casualty Lists', *CQ* 19, 145–59.

BRAUN, K. (1970) 'Der Dipylon-Brunnen B1: die Funde', *Ath.Mitt.* 85.

BRINGMANN, K. (1965) *Studien zu den politischen Ideen des Isocrates*, *Hypomnemata* 14 (Göttingen).

BRISSON, L. (1982) *Plato, les mots et les mythes* (Paris).

BRUNNSÅKER, S. (1971) *The Tyrant-Slayers of Kritios and Nesiotes: A Critical Study of the Sources and Restorations*, 2nd edn (Stockholm).

BRUNVAND, J.H. (1981) *The Vanishing Hitchhiker. American Urban Legends and their Meanings* (New York and London).

BUCHNER, E. (1958) *Der Panegyrikos des Isocrates*, *Historia* Einzelschriften 2 (Wiesbaden).

BURKERT, W. (1985) *Greek Religion: Archaic and Classical*, transl. J. Raffen (Oxford).

BURN, A.R. (1935) 'Dates in Early Greek History', *JHS* 55, 130–46.

BURNS, A. (1981) 'Athenian Literacy in the Fifth Century B.C.', *Journal of History of Ideas* 42, 371–87.

CADOUX, T.J. (1948) 'The Athenian Archons from Kreon to Hypsichides', *JHS* 68, 70–123.

CALHOUN, G.M. (1914) 'Documentary Frauds in Litigation in Athens', *CPh* 9, 134–44.

(1919) 'Oral and Written Pleading in Athens', *TAPA* 50, 177–93.

CAMERON, A. (1940) 'An Epigram of the Fifth Century B.C.', *Harv.Theol. Rev.* 33, 97–130.

CARTLEDGE, P. (1976) 'A New Fifth-Century Spartan Treaty', *LCM* 1, 87–92.

(1978) 'Literacy in the Spartan Oligarchy', *JHS* 98, 25–37.

(1979) *Sparta and Laconia: A Regional History, 1300–362 B.C.* (London and Boston).

CHADWICK, J. (1973) 'The Berezan Lead Letter', *PCPS* 199, 35–7.

CHAMBERS, J.T. (1975) 'The Fourth-Century Athenians' View of their Fifth-Century Empire', *Par.Pass.* 30, 177–91.

CLAIRMONT, C.W. (1983) *Patrios nomos. Public Burial in Athens during the Fifth and Fourth Centuries B.C. The Archaeological, Epigraphic-Literary and Historical Evidence* (Oxford).

CLANCHY, M.T. (1979) *From Memory to Written Record* (London).

CLAVAUD, R. (1980) *Le Ménexène de Platon et la rhétorique de son temps* (Paris).

CLAY, Diskin (1982) 'Epicurus in the Archives of Athens', *Hesperia* Suppl. 19, 17–26.

CLINTON, K. (1974) *The Sacred Officials of the Eleusinian Mysteries* (Philadelphia).

(1982) 'The Late Fifth-Century Revision of the Athenian Law Code', *Hesperia* Suppl. 19, 27–37.

COLE, M. and S. SCRIBNER (1981) *The Psychology of Literacy* (Cambridge, Mass.).

COLIN, G. (1933) 'La déformation d'un document historique dans une argumentation d'orateur', *Rev.de Phil.* 7, 237–60.

(1938) 'L'Oraison funèbre d'Hypéride', *REG* 51, 209–66 and 305–94.

CONNOR, W.R. (1963) 'Theopompus' Treatment of Cimon', *GRBS* 4, 107–14.

(1968) *Theopompus and Fifth-Century Athens* (Washington D.C.).

(1970) 'Theseus in Classical Athens', in A.G. Ward (ed.), *The Quest for Theseus* (London), 143–74.

(1971) *The New Politicians of Fifth-Century Athens* (Princeton).

(1984) *Thucydides* (Princeton).

CRAWFORD, O.C. (1941) 'Laudatio funebris', *CJ* 37, 17–27.

CROMEY, R.D. (1979) 'Kleisthenes' Fate', *Historia* 28, 129–47.

CROSBY, H. (1936) 'Athenian History and the Athenian Public', *Classical Studies Presented to E. Capps* (Princeton), 72–86.

CURTIUS, C. (1868) *Das Metroon in Athen als Staatsarchiv* (Berlin).

DAVIES, J.K. (1971) *Athenian Propertied Families, 600–300 B.C.* (Oxford) (=*APF*).

(1978) *Democracy and Classical Greece* (London).

(1981) 'The Reliability of the Oral Tradition', in Lin Foxhall and J.K. Davies (eds.) *The Trojan War. Its Historicity and Context. Papers of the First Greenbank Colloquium, Liverpool 1981* (Bristol).

(1984) *Wealth and the Power of Wealth in Classical Athens* (Salem, N.H.).

DAVISON, J.A. (1962) 'Literature and Literacy in Ancient Greece', *Phoenix* 16, 141–56 and 219–33.

DAVREUX, J. (1942) *La Légende de la prophétesse Cassandre* (Liège and Paris).

DAY, J.W. (1980) *The Glory of Athens. The Popular Tradition as Reflected in the Panathenaicus of Aelius Aristides* (Chicago).

(1985) 'Epigrams and History: The Athenian Tyrannicides, a Case in Point', in Raubitschek (1985), 25–46.

DENNISTON, J.D. (1927) 'Technical Terms in Aristophanes', *CQ* 21, 113–21.

DEVLIN, R. (1985) 'Herodotus and the Alcmaeonids', in Starr (1985), 125–39.

DEWALD, C. (1987) 'Narrative Surface and Authorial Voice in Herodotus' Histories', in Boedeker (1987), 147–70.

DILLER, H. (1962) 'Freiheit bei Thukydides als Schlagwort und als Wirklichkeit', *Gymnasium* 69, 189–204.

DOVER, K.J. (1957) 'The Political Aspect of Aeschylus' *Eumenides*', *JHS* 77, 230–7.

(1968) *Lysias and the Corpus Lysiacum* (Berkeley and Los Angeles).

(1974) *Greek Popular Morality in the Time of Plato and Aristotle* (Oxford).

DRERUP, H. (1980) 'Totenmaske und Ahnenbild bei den Römern', *MDAI* (R) 87, 81–129.

DUMVILLE, D.N. (1977) 'Kingship, Genealogies and Regnal Lists', in P.H. Sawyer and I.N. Wood (eds.), *Early Medieval Kingship*, (Leeds), 72–104.

DUNBABIN, T.J. (1948) 'The Early History of Corinth', *JHS* 68, 59–69.

DUNCAN-JONES, R.P. (1977) 'Age-Rounding, Illiteracy and Social Differentiation in the Roman Empire, *Chiron* 7, 333–53.

EHRENBERG, V. (1947) 'Polypragmosyne: A study in Greek Politics', *JHS* 67, 46–67.

(1950) 'The Origins of Democracy', *Historia* 1, 515–48.

(1956) 'Das Harmodioslied', *Wiener Studien* 69, 57–69.

(1966) *Ancient Society and Institutions: Studies Presented to Victor Ehrenberg on his 75th Birthday* (Oxford).

ELIOT, C.W.J. (1967) 'Where did the Alkmaionidai Live?', *Historia* 16, 279–86.
ELIOT, C.W.Th. and M.F. MCGREGOR (1960) 'Kleisthenes: Eponymous Archon 525/4 B.C.', *Phoenix* 14, 27–35.
ENTRETIENS HARDT 18 (1972) *Pseudepigrapha* 1 (Vandoeuvres-Geneva).
ERMATINGER, E. (1897) *Die attische Autochthonensage bis auf Euripides*, (diss. Berlin).
EVANS, J.A.S. (1982) *Herodotus* (Boston).
FAIRWEATHER, J. (1974) 'Fiction in the Biographies of Ancient Writers', *Anc.Soc.* 5, 231–75.
FANTUZZI, M. (1980) 'Oralità, scrittura, auralità. Gli studi sulle techniche della communicazione nella Grecia antica (1960–1980)', *Lingua e Stilo* (Milan), 15, 593–612.
FARNELL, L.R. (1896–1909) *The Cults of the Greek States*, 5 vols. (Oxford).
FEHLING, D. (1971) *Die Quellenangaben bei Herodot* (Berlin).
    (1972) 'Erisichthon oder das Märchen von der mündlichen Überlieferung', *Rh.M.* 115, 173–96.
FERGUSON, W.S. (1898) *The Athenian Secretaries* (Ithaca, N.Y.).
    (1938) 'The Salaminioi of Heptaphylai and Sounion', *Hesperia* 7, 1–74.
FIGUEIRA, T.J. (1986) 'Xanthippos, father of Perikles, and the Prutaneis of the Naukraroi', *Historia* 35, 257–79.
FINE, John V.A. (1951) '*Horoi. Studies in Mortgage, Real Security and Land Tenure in Ancient Athens*', *Hesperia* Suppl. 9 (Baltimore).
FINGARETTE, A. (1971) 'A New Look at the Wall of Nikomachos', *Hesperia* 40, 330–5.
FINKELSTEIN, J.J. (1961) 'Ammisaduqa's Edict and the Babylonian "Law Codes"', *Journal of Cuneiform Studies* 15, 91–104.
FINLEY, M.I. (1952) *Studies in Land and Credit in Ancient Athens 500–200 B.C. The Horos Inscriptions* (New Brunswick).
    (1962) 'The Athenian Demagogues', *Past and Present* 21, 3–24 (repr. 1974, 1–25).
    (1965) 'Myth, Memory and History', *History and Theory* 4, 281–302 (repr. 1975, 11–33).
    (1968) 'The Alienability of Land in Ancient Greece', *Eirene* 7, 25–32 (repr. 1975, 153–60).
    (1971) '*The Ancestral Constitution*', Inaugurai Lecture (Cambridge); (repr. 1975, 34–59).
    (1973) *Problèmes de la terre en Grèce ancienne: recueil de travaux* (Paris).
    (1974) (ed.) *Studies in Ancient Society* (London).
    (1975) *The Use and Abuse of History* (London).
    (1982) 'Le Document et l'histoire économique de l'antiquité', *Annales (Economies, Société, Civilisations)* 37, 697–713 (repr. 1985).
    (1983) 'The Ancient Historian and his Sources' in Momigliano (1983), 201–14 (expanded version, 1985).
    (1985) *Ancient History, Evidence and Models* (London).
FINNEGAN, R. (1970a) *Oral Literature in Africa* (Oxford).
    (1970b) 'A Note on Oral Tradition and Historical Evidence', *History and Theory* 9, 195–201.

(1975) *Communication and Technology* (Milton Keynes).

(1977) *Oral Poetry. Its Nature, Significance and Social Content* (Cambridge).

(1981) 'Orality and Literacy: Some Problems of Definition and Research', unpublished article (quoted extensively by Street (1984) esp. 95ff.); to be published as ch. 8 in R. Finnegan (1988) *Literacy and Orality* (Oxford).

FIRTH, R. (1961) *History and Tradition in Tikopia* (Wellington, N.Z.).

FITZGERALD, T.R. (1957) 'The Murder of Hipparchus: A Reply', *Historia* 6, 275–86.

FLASHAR, H. (1969) *Der Epitaphios des Perikles. Seine Funktion im Geschichtswerk des Thukydides* (Heidelberg).

FLORY, S. (1980) 'Who Read Herodotus' Histories?' *AJP* 101, 12–28.

FONTENROSE, J. (1978) *The Delphic Oracle* (Berkeley).

FORNARA, C.W. (1966) 'The Hoplite Achievement at Psyttaleia', *JHS* 86, 51–4.

(1968a) 'Hellanicus and an Alcmaeonid Tradition', *Historia* 17, 381–3.

(1968b) 'The "Tradition" about the Murder of Hipparchus', *Historia* 17, 400–24.

(1970) 'The Cult of Harmodius and Aristogeiton', *Philologus* 114, 155–80.

(1971a) *Herodotus: An Interpretative Essay* (Oxford).

(1971b) *The Athenian Board of Generals from 501 to 404 B.C.*, *Historia* Einzelschriften 15.

(1983) *The Nature of History in Ancient Greece and Rome* (Berkeley).

FORREST, G. (1956) 'The First Sacred War', *BCH* 80, 33–52.

(1969) 'The Tradition of Hippias' Expulsion from Athens', *GRBS* 10, 277–86.

FORSTER, G.M. (1965) 'Peasant Society and the Image of Limited Good', *American Anthropologist* 67, 293–315.

FRANCISCIS, Alfonso de (1972) *Stato e società in Locri Epizefiri (L'archivio dell' Olympeion Locrese)* (Naples).

FRÄNKEL, H. (1975) *Early Greek Poetry and Philosophy* (Oxford).

FRENCH, A. (1972) 'Topical Influences on Herodotus' Narrative', *Mnemos.* 25, 9–27.

FRIEDLÄNDER, P. (1938) 'Geschichtswende im Gedicht. Interpretationen historischer Epigramme', *Studi italiani di filologia classica* 15, 89–120.

FRITZ, K. von (1967) *Griechische Geschichtsschreibung, von den Anfängen bis Thukydides* vol. 1 (Berlin).

FUKS, A. (1953) *The Ancestral Constitution* (London).

(1972) 'Isocrates and the Social-Economic Situation in Greece', *Anc.Soc.* 3, 17–44.

FURET, F. and J. OZOUF (1982) *Reading and Writing: Literacy in France from Calvin to Jules Ferry* (Cambridge).

GABBA, E. (1981) 'True History and False History in Classical Antiquity', *JRS* 71, 50–62.

GAGARIN, M. (1986) *Early Greek Law* (Berkeley and Los Angeles).

GENTILI, B. (1984) *Poesia e publico nella Grecia antica da Omero al V secolo* (Bari).

GERNET, L. (1938) 'Sur les actions commerciales en droit athénien', *REG* 51, 1–44 (repr. 1955, 173–200).

(1955) *Droit et société dans la Grèce ancienne* (Paris).

(1968) *Anthropologie de la Grèce antique* (Paris).

GILL, C. (1977) 'The Genre of the Atlantis Story', *CPh* 72, 287–304.

GITTINS, D. (1979) 'Oral History, Reliability and Recollection', in Moss and Goldstein (eds.) (1979).

GOMME, A.W. (1945–81) *Historical Commentary on Thucydides* (*HCT*), 5 vols., vols. IV and V completed by A. Andrewes and K.J. Dover (Oxford)

(1948) 'The Eion Epigram', *CR* 62, 5–7.

(1954) *The Greek Attitude to Poetry and History* (Berkeley and Los Angeles).

(1962) 'Herodotus and Marathon', in *More Essays* (Oxford), 29–37.

GOODY, J. (1968) (ed.) *Literacy in Traditional Societies* (Cambridge).

(1977) *The Domestication of the Savage Mind* (Cambridge).

(1986) *The Logic of Writing and the Organization of Society* (Cambridge).

(1987) *The Interface between the Written and the Oral* (Cambridge).

GOODY, J. and WATT, I. (1968) 'The Consequences of Literacy', in Goody (ed.) (1968), 27–68 (first published 1962–3).

GRAFF, Harvey J. (1981) (ed.) *Literacy and Social Development in the West* (Cambridge).

GREENE, W.C. (1951) 'The Spoken and the Written Word', *HSCP* 60, 23–59.

GREENWALT, W. (1985) 'The Introduction of Caranus into the Argead King List', *GRBS* 26, 43–9.

GRIFFIN, A. (1982) *Sicyon* (Oxford).

GRIFFITH, G.T. (1966) 'Isegoria in the Assembly at Athens', in Ehrenberg (1966).

GROSSMAN, G. (1950) *Politische Schlagwörter aus der Zeit des Peloponnesischen Krieges* (diss. Basel).

HABICHT, C. (1957) 'Samische Volksbeschlüsse der hellenistischen Zeit', *Ath.Mitt.* 72, 152–274.

(1961a) 'Falsche Urkunden zur Geschichte Athens im Zeitalter der Perserkriege', *Hermes* 59, 1–35.

(1961b) 'Neue Inschriften aus dem Kerameikos', *Ath.Mitt.* 76, 127–48.

HAEDICKE, W. (1936) *Die Gedanken der Griechen über Familienherkunft und Vererbung* (Halle).

HALBWACHS, M. (1925) *Les Cadres sociaux de la mémoire* (Paris).

(1950) *La Mémoire collective* (Paris), transl. 1980, *The Collective Memory* (New York).

HAMMOND, N.G.L. (1956) 'The Philaids and the Chersonese', *CQ* 6, 113–29.

HANSEN, M.H. (1983) *The Athenian Ecclesia. A Collection of Articles 1976–1983* (Copenhagen).

(1986) *Demography and Democracy: The Number of Athenian Citizens in the Fourth Century B.C.* (Herning, Denmark).

HARDING, P. (1973) 'The Purpose of Isocrates' *Archidamos* and *On the Peace*', *Californian Studies in Classical Antiquity* 6, 137–49.

(1974) 'The Theramenes Myth', *Phoenix* 38, 101–11.

(1976) 'Androtion's Political Career', *Historia* 25, 186–200.

(1977) 'Atthis and Politeia', *Historia* 26, 148–60.

HARRIS, W.V. (1983) 'Literacy and Epigraphy', *ZPE* 52, 87–111.

HARRISON, A.R.W. (1955) 'Law-Making at Athens at the End of the Fifth Century B.C.', *JHS* 75, 26–35.

(1968) *Law of Athens I. Family and Property* (Oxford).

(1971) *Law of Athens II. Procedure* (Oxford).

HART, J. (1982) *Herodotus and Greek History* (London).

HARVEY, A.E. (1955) 'The Classification of Greek Lyric Poetry', *CQ* 5, 157–75.

HARVEY, F.D. (1966) 'Literacy in the Athenian Democracy', *REG* 79, 585–635.

(1985) 'Dona ferentes: Some Aspects of Bribery in Greek Politics', in de Ste Croix (1985), 76–113.

HAUVETTE, A. (1898) 'Les "Éleusiniens" d'Éschyle et l'institution du discours funèbre à Athènes', *Mélanges Henri Weil* (Paris), 159–78.

HAUVETTE-BESNAULT, A. (1885) *Les Stratèges athéniens* (Paris).

HAVELOCK, E.A. (1963) *Preface to Plato* (Oxford).

(1982) *The Literate Revolution in Greece and its Cultural Consequences* (Princeton).

(1986) *The Muse Learns to Write: Reflections on Orality and Literacy from Antiquity to the Present* (New Haven and London).

HAVELOCK, E.A. and J.P. HERSHBELL (eds.) (1978) *Communication Arts in the Ancient World* (New York).

HEATH, S.B. (1982) 'What No Bedtime Story Means: Narrative Skills at Home and School', *Language and Society* 2, 49–76.

(1983) *Ways with Words* (Cambridge).

HEIDBÜCHEL, F. (1957) 'Die Chronologie der Peisistratiden in der Atthis', *Philologus* 101, 70–89.

HENDERSON, M.M. (1975) 'Plato's *Menexenus* and the Distortion of History', *Acta Class.* 18, 25–46.

HENIGE, D.P. (1974) *The Chronology of Oral Tradition. Quest for a Chimera* (Oxford).

(1980) 'The Disease of Writing: Ganda and Nyoro Kinglists in a Newly Literate World', in *APS*, 240–61.

(1982) *Oral Historiography* (London, New York, Lagos).

HENRY, A.S. (1977) *The Prescripts of Athenian Decrees, Mnemos.* Suppl. 49 (Leiden).

(1979) 'Archon Dating in Fifth-Century Attic Decrees: The 421 Rule', *Chiron* 9, 23–30.

HERMAN, G. (1987) *Ritualized Friendship and the Greek City* (Cambridge).

HESS, H. (1938) *Textkritische und erklärende Beiträge zum Epitaphios des Hypereides* (Leipzig).

HEUSS, A. (1934) 'Abschluss und Beurkundung des griechischen und römischen Staatsvertrages', *Klio* 27, 14–53 and 218–57.

HIRSCH, M. (1926) 'Die athenischen Tyrannenmörder in Geschichtsschreibung und Volkslegende', *Klio* 20, 129–67.

HOBSBAWM, E. and T. RANGER (eds.) (1983) *The Invention of Tradition* (Cambridge).

HOMOLLE, T. (1902) 'Monuments figurés de Delphes. Les frontons du temple d'Apollon', *BCH* 26, 587–639.

302   Bibliography

HONDIUS, J. (1922) 'Quid sit τὸ κοινὸν γραμματεῖον', *Mnemosyne* 50, 87–90.
HOPPER, R.J. (1960) 'A Note on Aristophanes' *Lysistrata* 665–70', *CQ* n.s. 10, 242–7.
HOW, W.W. and J. WELLS (1928) *A Commentary on Herodotus*, 2nd edn, 2 vols. (Oxford).
HUDSON-WILLIAMS, H.Ll. (1948) 'Thucydides, Isocrates and the Rhetorical Method of Composition', *CQ* 42, 76–81.
— (1951) 'Political Speeches in Athens', *CQ* 1, 68–73.
HUMPHREYS, S.C. (1978) *Anthropology and the Greeks* (London, Boston, Melbourne).
— (1980) 'Family Tombs and Tomb Cults in Ancient Athens: Tradition or Traditionalism?', *JHS* 100, 96–126.
— (1983a) *The Family, Women and Death: Comparative Studies* (London).
— (1983b) 'The Date of Hagnias' Death', *CPh* 78, 219–25.
— (1985a) 'Social Relations on Stage: Witnesses in Classical Athens', *History and Anthropology* 1, 313–69.
— (1985b) 'The Discourse of Law in Archaic and Classical Greece', Symposium (unpublished): Wenner-Gren Foundation for Anthropological Research (Bellagio, Italy).
— (1985c) 'Lycurgus of Butadae: An Athenian Aristocrat', in Starr (1985), 199–236.
HUMPHREYS, S.C. and H. KING (1981) *Mortality and Immortality: The Anthropology and Archaeology of Death* (London).
HUNTER, V.J. (1973) *Thucydides the Artful Reporter* (Toronto).
— (1974) 'Athens Tyrannis: A New Approach to Thucydides', *CJ* 69 (1973–4), 120–6.
— (1982) *Past and Process in Herodotus and Thucydides* (Princeton).
HUTCHINSON, G. (1984) 'Propertius and the Unity of the Book', *JRS* 74, 99–106.
HUXLEY, G.L. (1962) *Early Sparta* (London).
IMMERWAHR, H.R. (1964) 'Book Rolls on Attic Vases', *Classical, Medieval and Renaissance Studies in Honour of B.L. Ullman*, vol. 1, 17–48.
IRGOIN, J. (1952) *Histoire du texte de Pindare* (Paris).
JACOBY, F. (1909) 'Über die Entwicklung der griechischen Historiographie', *Klio* 9, 80–123 (=Jacoby (1956), 16–64).
— (1913) 'Herodotus', *RE* Suppl. II, 205–520 (repr. in *Griechische Historiker* (Stuttgart 1956), 7–164).
— (1923–58) *Die Fragmente der griechischen Historiker* (Berlin), (=*FGH*).
— (1944a) 'Patrios Nomos: State Burial in Athens and the Public Ceremony in the Kerameikos', *JHS* 64, 37–66.
— (1944b) 'ΓΕΝΕΣΙΑ: A Forgotten Festival of the Dead', *CQ* 38, 65–75.
— (1947) 'The First Athenian Prose Writer', *Mnemos.* 13, 13–64 (=Jacoby (1956), 100–43).
— (1949) *Atthis. The Local Chronicles of Ancient Athens* (Oxford).
— (1956) *Abhandlungen zur griechischen Geschichtsschreibung* (Leiden).
JAEGER, W. (1932) *Tyrtaios über die wahre Arete'*, Sitzungsberichte Berlin.

JAMESON, M. (1960) 'A Decree of Themistokles from Troizen', *Hesperia* 29, 198–223.

(1962) 'Revised Text of the Decree of Themistokles from Troizen', *Hesperia* 31, 310–15.

(1963) 'The Provisions for Mobilization in the Decree of Themistokles', *Historia* 12, 385–405.

(1965) 'The Sacrificial Calendar from Erchia', *BCH* 89, 167–72.

JEBB, R.C. (1893) *The Attic Orators from Antiphon to Isaeus* 2nd edn, 2 vols. (London).

JEFFERY, L.H. (1961) *The Local Scripts of Archaic Greece* (Oxford).

(1967) '᾿Αρχαῖα γράμματα: Some Ancient Greek Views', *Europa: Festschrift . . . E. Grumach* (Berlin), 152–66.

(1976) *Archaic Greece. The City States c. 700–500 B.C.* (London).

JEFFERY, L.H. and A. MORPURGO-DAVIES (1970) ΠΟΙΝΙΚΑΣΤΑΣ and ΠΟΙΝΙΚΑΖΕΙΝ: A New Archaic Inscription from Crete', *Kadmos* 9, 118–54.

JOHNSTON, A. (1983) 'The Extent and Use of Literacy; The Archaeological Evidence', in R. Hägg (ed.) *The Greek Renaissance of the Eighth Century B.C.: Tradition and Innovation* (Stockholm), 63–8.

JONES, A.H.M. (1957) *Athenian Democracy* (Oxford).

JORDAN, B. (1970) 'Herodotus v 71.2 and the Naukraroi of Athens', *Californian Studies in Classical Antiquity* 3, 153–77.

(1979) *Servants of the Gods*, *Hypomnemata* 55 (Göttingen).

JOST, K. (1936) *Das Beispiel und Vorbild der Vorfahren bei den attischen Rednern bis Demosthenes*, *Rhetorische Studien*, vol. XIX, (Paderborn).

KAHN, C. (1963) 'Plato's Funeral Oration: The Motive of the *Menexenus*', *CPh* 58, 220–34.

KAHRSTEDT, U. (1938) 'Untersuchungen zu athenischen Behörden', with appendix, 'Das athenische Staatsarchiv', *Klio* 31, 25–32.

KARAVITES, P. (1977) 'Realities and Appearances, 490–480 B.C.', *Historia* 26, 129–47.

KENNEDY, G.A. (1959) 'The Earliest Rhetorical Handbooks', *AJP* 80, 169–78.

(1963) *The Art of Persuasion* (Princeton).

KENYON, F.G. (1951) *Books and Readers in Ancient Greece and Rome* (Oxford).

KIERDORF, W. (1966) *Erlebnis und Darstellung der Perserkriege, Studien zu Simonides, Pindar, Aeschylos und den attischen Rednern*, *Hypomnemata* 16 (Göttingen).

KINZL, K.H. (1974) 'Philochorus *FGrHist*. 328 F115 and Ephorus: Observations on Schol. Pind. *Pyth.* 7, 9B', *Hermes* 102, 179–90.

(1975) 'Herodotus-Interpretations', *Rh.M.* 98, 193–204.

KIRK, G.S. (1972) 'Aetiology, Ritual, Charter: Three Equivocal Terms in the Study of Myths', *YCS* 22, 83–102.

KLAFFENBACH, G. (1960) *Bemerkungen zum griechischen Urkundenwesen*, Sitzungsberichte Berlin.

KLEIN, M.A. and G.W. JOHNSON (1972) (eds.) *Perspectives on the African Past* (Boston).

KNOX, B.M.W. (1985) 'Books and Readers in the Greek World', in P. Easterling and B.M.W. Knox (eds.) *Cambridge History of Classical Literature* (Cambridge), Ch. 1.1.

KROLL, J.H. (1977) 'An Archive of the Athenian Cavalry', *Hesperia* 46, 83–140.

LACEY, W.K. (1968) *The Family in Classical Greece* (London).

LAMBRINUDAKIS, W. and M. WÖRRLE (1983) 'Ein hellenistisches Reformgesetz über das öffentliche Urkundenwesen von Paros', *Chiron* 13, 283–368.

LANDMANN, G.P. (1974) 'Das Lob Athens in der Grabrede des Perikles (Thuc. II 34–41)', *Mus.Helv.* 31, 65–95.

LANG, M.L. (1954–5) 'The Murder of Hipparchus', *Historia* 3, 395–407.
(1967) 'The Kylonian Conspiracy', *CPh* 62, 243–9.
(1982) 'Writing and Spelling on Ostraka', *Hesperia* Suppl. 19, 75–87.
(1984) *Herodotean Narrative and Discourse* (Cambridge, Mass.).

LATTIMORE, R. (1958) 'The Composition of the "History" of Herodotus', *CPh* 53, 9–21.
(1962) *Themes in Greek and Latin Epigrams* (Urbana, Illinois).

LEISI, E. (1907) *Der Zeuge im attischen Recht* (diss. Zurich).

LEVY, E. (1978) 'Notes sur la chronologie athénienne an VIe siècle', *Historia* 27, 513–21.

LEWIS, D.M. (1963) 'Cleisthenes and Attica', *Historia* 12, 22–40.
(1966) 'After the Profanation of the Mysteries', in Ehrenberg (1966), 177–91.
(1973) 'The Athenian rationes centesimarum', in M.I. Finley (ed.), *Problèmes de la terre en Grèce ancienne* (Paris), 187–212.
(1980) Review of F. Ferlanto, *Il testo di Tucidide e la traduzione latina di Lorenzo Valla* (Palermo), *CR* 30, 276–8.
(1984) Postscript to A.R. Burn, *Persia and the Greeks*, 2nd edn (London).

LEWIS, I.M. (1962) 'Historical Aspects of Genealogies in Northern Somali Social Structure', *Journal of African History* 3, 35–48.
(1968) 'Literacy in a Nomadic Society: The Somali Case', in Goody (ed.) (1968).

LIEURY, A. (1975) *La Mémoire. Résultats et théories* (Brussels).

LLOYD, G.E.R. (1979) *Magic, Reason and Experience: Studies in the Origin and Development of Greek Science* (Cambridge).

LLOYD-JONES, H. (1975) 'More about Antileon, Tyrant of Chalcis', *CPh* 70, 197.

LOENEN, D. (1926) 'De nobilitate apud Athenienses', *Mnemos.* 54, 206–23.

LORAUX, N. (1981a) *L'Invention d'Athènes* (Paris), transl. (1986), *The Invention of Athens. The Funeral Oration in the Classical City* (Harvard).
(1981b) *Les Enfants d'Athéna* (Paris).

LORD, A.B. (1960) *The Singer of Tales* (Cambridge, Mass.)
(1967) 'Homer as an Oral Poet', *HSCP* 72, 1–46.

LÖWENCLAU, I. von (1961) *Der platonische Menexenos* (Stuttgart).

LURIA, S. (1930) 'Der Affe des Archilochos und die Brautwerbung des Hippokleides', *Philologus* 85, 1–22.

MACAN, R.W. (1885) *Herodotus. The fourth, fifth and sixth books*, 2 vols., with introduction, text, apparatus, commentary, appendices, indexes, maps (London and New York).

(1908) *Herodotus. The seventh, eighth and ninth books*, 2 vols. with introduction, text, apparatus, commentary, appendices, indexes, maps (London and New York).

MACDOWELL, D. (1959) 'Leogoras at Ennea Hodoi', *Rh.M.* 102, 376–8.

(1962) *Andocides. On the Mysteries*, text and commentary (Oxford).

MCGREGOR, M.F. (1981) *Classical Contributions. Studies in Honour of M.F. McGregor*, G.S. Schrimpton and D.J. McCargar (eds.) (New York).

MACLEOD, C. (1983) *Collected Essays* (Oxford).

MACMULLEN, R. (1982) 'The Epigraphic Habit in the Roman Empire', *AJP* 103, 233–46.

MACVE, R.H. (1985) 'Some glosses on "Greek and Roman Accounting"', in de Ste Croix (1985), 233–64.

MAHIEU, W. DE (1979) 'A l'intersection de temps et de l'espace du mythe et de l'histoire – les généalogies: l'exemple Komo', *Cultures et Développement* 11, 415–37.

MARG, W. (1965) (ed.) *Herodot: Eine Auswahl aus der neueren Forschung*, Wege der Forschung 25, 2nd edn (Darmstadt).

MARINATOS , N. (1981) 'Thucydides and Oracles', *JHS* 101, 138–40.

MARROU, H.I. (1956) *A History of Education in Antiquity* (London).

MASSON, O. (1964) 'Notes d'onomastique Chypriote', *Kypriakai Spoudai* 28, 3–12.

(1974) 'L'Inscription généalogique de Cyrène (*SDGI* 4859)', *BCH* 98, 263–70.

MATTHIEU, G. (1914) 'Survivances des luttes politiques de ve siècle chez les orateurs attiques du ive siècle', *Rev.de Phil.* 38, 182–205.

(1918) 'Isocrate et Thucydide', *Rev.de Phil.* 42, 122–9.

(1926) *Les Idées politiques d'Isocrate* (Paris).

MEIGGS, R. (1972) *The Athenian Empire* (Oxford).

(1984) Review of Meister (1982), *Gnomon* 56, 35–8.

MEIGGS, R. and D.M. LEWIS (1969) *Greek Historical Inscriptions to the End of the Fifth Century B.C.* (Oxford) (=ML).

MEISTER, K. (1982) *Die Ungeschichtlichkeit des Kalliasfriedens und deren historische Folgen* Palingenesia 18 (Wiesbaden).

MERIDIER, L. (1931) Introduction to *Plato, Menexenus*, 1st edn, vol. v (Paris).

MERITT, B.D. (1939) 'Greek Inscriptions', *Hesperia* 8, 48–82.

(1940) *Epigraphica Attica* (Cambridge, Mass.)

(1960) 'Greek Inscriptions', *Hesperia* 29, 1–77.

(1967) 'Greek Historical Studies', *University of Cincinnati Classical Studies*, vol. 1=*Semple Lectures* 1961–5, 118–32.

(1977) 'A Proxeny Decree Restudied (*IG* I² 85)', *ZPE* 25, 289–95.

MEYER, E. (1899) 'Die Biographie Kimons', *Forschungen zur alten Geschichte* (Halle), 1–87.

MEYER, E. (1937) *Geschichte des Altertums, III: Der Ausgang der altorientalischen Geschichte und der Aufstieg des Abendlandes bis zu den Perserkriegen*, 2nd edn (Stuttgart).

MILLER, J.C. (ed.) (1980) *The African Past Speaks: Essays on Oral Tradition and History* (Folkstone) (=*APS*).

MILLER, M. (1970) *The Sicilian Colony Dates* (Albany).

MILLETT, P. (1982) 'The Attic Horoi Reconsidered in the Light of Recent Discoveries', *Opus* 1, 219–30.

MITCHEL, F. (1956) 'Herodotus' Use of Genealogical Chronology', *Phoenix* 10, 48–69.

MITCHELL, B.M. (1975) Herodotus and Samos', *JHS* 95, 75–91.

MOMIGLIANO, A. (1957) 'Perizonius, Niebuhr and the Character of Early Roman Tradition', *JRS* 47, 104–14.

(1966a) *Studies in Historiography* (London).

(1966b) 'Historiography on Written and Oral Tradition', in Momigliano (1966a), 211–20 (London) (first publ. 1961).

(1966c) 'Time in Ancient Historiography', *History and Theory* 6, 1–23 (repr. in Momigliano (1977), 179–204).

(1971a) 'L'excursus di Tucidide in VI 54–59', *Studi di storiographia antica in memoria di Leonardo Ferrero* (Torino), 31–5.

(1971b) *The Development of Greek Biography* (Boston).

(1972) 'Tradition and the Classical Historian', *History and Theory* 11, 279–93 (repr. in Momigliano (1977)).

(1977) *Essays in Ancient and Modern Historiography* (Oxford).

(1983) *Tria corda, scritti in onore di Arnaldo Momigliano* (ed. E. Gabba) (Como).

MORETTI, L. (1957) *Olympionikai, i vincitori negli antichi agoni olimpici* (Rome).

MORRIS, I. (1986) 'The Use and Abuse of Homer', *Classical Antiquity* 5, 81–128.

MOSS, Louis and H. GOLDSTEIN (eds.) (1979) *The Recall Method in Social Surveys* (London).

MOXON, I.S. and J.D. SMART and A.J. WOODMAN (eds.) (1986) *Past Perspectives. Studies in Greek and Roman Historical Writing* (Cambridge).

MUNRO, J.A.R. (1926) 'Marathon', CAH IV, Ch. VIII.i–v.

MURRAY, O. (1980) *Early Greece* (Brighton).

(1983a) 'The Greek Symposium in History', in Momigliano (1983), 257–72.

(1983b) 'The Symposium as Social Organization', in R. Hägg (ed.) *The Greek Renaissance of the Eighth Century B.C.: Tradition and Innovation* (Stockholm), 195–9.

(1987) 'Herodotus and Oral History', in H.W.Am. Sancisi-Weerdenburg and A. Kuhrt (eds.), *Achaemenid History II: The Greek Sources* (Leiden).

NAGY, G. (1987) 'Herodotus the *Logios*' in Boedeker (1987), 175–84.

NILSSON, M.P. (1951) *Cults, Myths, Oracles and Politics in Ancient Greece* (Lund).

(1952) 'Über die Glaubwürdigkeit der Volksüberlieferung mit besonderer Berücksichtigung der Alten Geschichte', *Opuscula Selecta*, vol. 2 (Lund).

NIMSCH, M. (1924) *Genealogie und Familientradition bei den ältern Historikern* (diss. Leipzig).

NOTOPOULOS, J.A. (1938) 'Mnemosyne in Oral Literature', *TAPA* 69, 465–93.

NOUHAUD, M. (1982) *L'Utilisation de l'histoire par les orateurs attiques* (Paris).

OLIVER, R. (1955) 'The Traditional Histories of Buganda, Bunyoro and Ankole', *Journal of the Royal African Institute* 85, 111–17.

ONG, W. (1982) *Orality and Literacy* (London).

OPPENHEIM, A. Leo (1975) 'The Position of the Intellectual in Mesopotamian Society', *Daedalus: Journal of the American Academy of Arts and Sciences* 104, 37–46.

OPPENHEIMER, K. (1933) *Zwei attische Epitaphien* (diss. Berlin).

OSBORNE, J.M. (1981) 'Some Attic Inscriptions', *ZPE* 42, 172–4.

OSBORNE, R. (1985) *Demos: The Discovery of Classical Attika* (Cambridge).

OSTWALD, M. (1951) 'The Prytaneion Decree Reexamined', *AJP* 72, 24–46.

(1969) *Nomos and the Beginnings of the Athenian Democracy* (Oxford).

(1986/1987) *From Popular Sovereignty to the Sovereignty of Law. Law, Society and Politics in Fifth-Century Athens* (Berkeley).

PAGE, D. (1963) 'Archilochus and the Oral Tradition', *Entretiens Hardt* 10, *Archiloche*.

(1981) *Further Greek Epigrams* (Cambridge).

PARKE, H.W. and D.E.W. WORMELL (1956) *The Delphic Oracle*, 2 vols. (Oxford).

PARKER, R. (1983) *Miasma. Pollution and Purification in Early Greek Religion* (Oxford).

(1985) 'Greek States and Greek Oracles', in de Ste Croix (1985), 298–326.

PARRY, M. (1930) 'Studies in the Epic Technique of Oral Verse-Making. I. Homer and Homeric Style', *HSCP* 41, 73–147.

(1932) 'Studies in the Epic Technique of Oral Verse-Making. II. The Homeric Language as the Language of an Oral Poetry', *HSCP* 43, 1–50.

(1971) *The Making of Homeric Verse*, ed. A. Parry (Oxford).

PEARSON, L. (1941) 'Historical Allusions in the Attic Orators', *CPh* 36, 209–29.

(1942) *The Local Historians of Attica* (Philadelphia).

(1949) 'Note on a Digression of Thucydides (VI 54–59)', *AJP* 70, 186–9.

PEEK, W. (1938) 'Das Epigramm auf die Gefallenen von Koroneia', *Hermes* 68, 353–6.

(1939) 'Ein Seegefecht aus den Perserkriegen', *Klio* 33, 289–306.

(1940) 'Die Kämpfe am Eurymedon', in *Athenian Studies Presented to W.S. Ferguson*, 97–120.

PERLMAN, S. (1961) 'The Historical Example, its Use and Importance as Political Propaganda in the Attic Orators', *Scripta Hierosolymitana* 7, 150–66.

(1963) 'The Politicians in the Athenian Democracy of the Fourth Century B.C.', *Athenaeum* 41, 327–55.

(1964) 'Quotations from Poetry in Attic Orators of the Fourth Century B.C.', *AJP* 85, 155–72.

(1967) 'Political Leadership in Athens in the Fourth Century B.C.', *Par.Pass.* 22, 161–76.

PERSON, Y. (1972) 'Tradition orale et chronologie', *Cahiers d'études africaines* 7, 3 (1962), 462–72 (repr. in Klein and Johnson (1972)).

PFEIFFER, R. (1968) *History of Classical Scholarship* (Oxford).

PFISTER, F. (1912) *Der Reliquienkult im Altertum*, vol. II (Giessen).

PHILIPPSON, P. (1944) *Genealogie als mythische Form* (Basel).
PLEKET, H.W. (1972) 'Isonomia and Cleisthenes: A Note', *Talanta* 4, 63–81.
PLOMMER, W.H. (1969) 'The Tyranny of the Archon List', *CR* 19, 126–9.
PLUMB, J.H. (1969) *The Death of the Past* (London).
POCOCK, J.G.A. (1971) *Politics, Language and Time: Essays on Political Thought and History* (New York).
PODLECKI, A. (1966) 'The Political Significance of the Athenian "Tyrannicide" Cult', *Historia* 15, 129–41.
POHLENZ, M. (1948) 'Zu den attischen Reden auf die Gefallenen', *Symbol. Osl.* 26, 46–74.
POSNER, E. (1972) *Archives in the Ancient World* (Cambridge, Mass.)
POST, L.A. (1932) 'Ancient Memory Systems', *CW* 25, 105–110.
PRAKKEN, D.W. (1943) *Studies in Greek Genealogical Chronology* (Lancaster).
PRINGSHEIM, F. (1950) *Greek Law of Sale* (Weimar).
    (1955) 'The Transition from Witnesses to Written Transactions in Athens', in Pringsheim (1961), vol. II, 401–9 (= *Festschrift Simonius* (1955), 287–97).
    (1961) *Gesammelte Abhandlungen*, 2 vols. (Heidelberg).
PRITCHETT, W.K. (1960) 'Marathon', *University of California Publications in Classical Archaeology* 4, 137–90.
    (1985) *The Greek State at War*, Part IV (Berkeley).
RAAFLAUB, K.A. (1983) 'Democracy, Oligarchy and the Concept of the "Free Citizen" in late Fifth-Century Athens', *Political Theory* 11, 517–44.
    (1985) *Entdeckung der Freiheit*, Vestigia 37 (Munich).
    (1987) 'Herodotus, Political Thought and the Meaning of History' in Boedeker (1987), 221–48.
RAUBITSCHEK, A.E. (1941) 'The Heroes of Phyle', *Hesperia* 10, 284–95.
    (1949) *Dedications from the Athenian Acropolis* (Cambridge, Mass.)
    (1955) 'Zur attischen Genealogie. Andocides I 106, II 26. Isoc. XVI 25–26' *Rh.M.* 98, 258–62.
    (1981) 'Andocides and Thucydides', in McGregor (1981), 121–3.
    (1985) *The Greek Historians: Literature and History. Papers presented to A.E. Raubitschek*, ed. W.R. Connor (Saratoga).
REINER, E. (1938) *Die rituelle Totenklage der Griechen* (Stuttgart and Berlin).
RHODES, P.J. (1972) *The Athenian Boule* (Oxford).
    (1976) 'Peisistratid Chronology Again', *Phoenix* 30, 219–33.
    (1980) 'Athenian Democracy after 403 B.C.' *CJ* 75, 305–23.
    (1981) *Commentary on the Aristotelian Athenaion Politeia* (Oxford).
    (1986) 'Political Activity in Classical Athens', *JHS* 106, 132–44.
RIEPL, W. (1913) *Das Nachrichtenwesen des Altertums, mit besonderer Rücksicht auf die Römer* (Leipzig and Berlin).
ROBERT, L. (1938) *Études épigraphiques et philologiques* (Paris).
    (1961) 'Epigraphie', in *L'Histoire et ses méthodes*, ed. Ch. Samaran (Encyclopédie de la Pléiade, Paris), 453–97.
ROBERTSON, N. (1976) 'False Documents at Athens: Fifth-Century History and Fourth-Century Politics', *Historical Reflections* III 1, 3–25.
    (1982) Review of Fontenrose (1978) in *Phoenix* 36, 358–63.
ROMILLY, J. de (1956) *Histoire et raison chez Thucydide* (Paris).

(1963) *Thucydides and Athenian Imperialism*, transl. P. Thody (New York).

ROSENMEYER, T.G. (1949) 'The Family of Critias', *AJP* 70, 404–10.

RUSCHENBUSCH, E. (1958) 'Patrios politeia', *Historia* 7, 398–424.

(1966a) *Solonos nomoi*, *Historia* Einzelschriften 9.

(1966b) 'Ephialtes', *Historia* 15, 369–76.

(1979) *Athenische Innenpolitik im 5. Jahrhundert v. Chr. Ideologie oder Pragmatismus?* (Bamberg).

(1981) 'Atthis und Politeia', *Hermes* 109, 316–26.

STE CROIX, G.E.M. DE (1956) 'Greek and Roman Accounting', in A.C. Littleton and B.S. Yamey (eds.) *Studies in the History of Accounting* (London) 14–74.

(1985) *Crux, Essays in Greek History presented to G.E.M. de Ste Croix on his 75th Birthday*, eds. P.A. Cartledge and F.D. Harvey (Exeter).

SAKELLARIOU, M.B. (1958) *La Migration grecque en Ionie* (Athens).

SANDBACH, F.H. (1985) *Aristotle and the Stoics* (Cambridge).

SCHACHERMEYR, F. (1938) 'Philaidai', *RE* 19, cols. 2113f.

SCHADEWALT, W. (1929) *Die Geschichtsschreibung des Thukydides* (Berlin).

SCHAEFER, A. (1885–7) *Demosthenes und seine Zeit*, 3 vols. 2nd edn (Leipzig).

SCHEPENS, G. (1975) 'Some Aspects of Source Theory in Greek Historiography', *Anc.Soc.* 6, 257–74.

SCHMID, W. (1933) *Geschichte der Griechischen Literatur* I, in I. von Mueller (ed.) *Handbuch der klassischen Altertumswissenschaft*, vol. VII 1, 2nd edn.

SCHMITZ-KAHLMANN, G. (1939) *Das Beispiel der Geschichte im politischen Denken des Isocrates*, *Philologus* Suppl. 31.4.

SCHOFIELD, R.S. (1968) 'The Measurement of Literacy in Pre-industrial England', in Goody (ed.) (1968), 311–25.

SCHROEDER, O. (1914) *De laudibus Athenarum a poetis tragicis et ab oratoribus epidicticis* (diss. Göttingen).

SCHULLER, W. (1984) 'Wirkungen des ersten Attischen Seebundes auf die Herausbildung der athenischen Demokratie', in J.M. Balcer et al., *Studien zum Attischen Seebund*, Xenia 8 (Constance), 87–101.

SCHWARZ, E. (1938) 'Über das Verhältnis der Hellenen zur Geschichte', in *Gesammelte Schriften* I (Berlin), 47–67.

SCHWARZE, J. (1969) 'Hérodote et Périclès', *Historia* 18, 367–70.

(1971) *Die Beurteilung des Perikles durch die attische Komödie, und ihre historische und historiographische Bedeutung* (Munich).

SCHWEIGERT, E. (1938) 'Inscriptions from the North Slope of the Acropolis', *Hesperia* 7, 264–310.

SCOBIE, A. (1983) *Apuleius and Folklore* (London).

SEALEY, R. (1960) 'Regionalism in Archaic Athens', *Historia* 9, 155–80.

SHEAR, T.L. (1963) 'KOISYRA', *Phoenix* 17, 99–112.

(1973) 'The Athenian Agora: Excavations of 1971', *Hesperia* 42, 121–79.

SHERWIN-WHITE, S.M. (1985) 'Ancient Archives: The Edict of Alexander to Priene, a Reappraisal', *JHS* 105, 69–89.

SHILS, E. (1981) *Tradition* (London and Boston).

SIEWERT, P. (1972) *Der Eid von Plataiai*, Vestigia 16 (Munich).

(1977) 'The Ephebic Oath in Fifth-Century Athens', *JHS* 97, 102–11.

SIMONDON, M. (1982) *La Mémoire et l'oubli dans la pensée grecque jusqu' à la fin du Ve siècle avant J.C.* (Paris).

SLATER, W.J. (1972) 'Asclepiades and History', *GRBS* 13, 317–33.

SMITH, S.P. (1921) *Hawaiki, the Original Home of the Maori* (Auckland).

SNODGRASS, A.M. (1971) *The Dark Age of Greece: an archaeological survey of the Eleventh to the Eighth Centuries* (Edinburgh).

(1980) *Archaic Greece: The Age of Experiment* (London).

SOLMSEN, L. (1944) 'Speeches in Herodotus' Account of the Battle of Plateia', *CPh* 39, 241–53 (repr. in Marg (ed.) (1965) 645–67).

(1966) Review of Havelock, *Preface to Plato*, *AJP* 87, 99–105.

STARR, C.G. (1962) 'Why did the Greeks Defeat the Persians?' *Par.Pass.* 17, 321–32.

(1985) *The Craft of the Ancient Historian: Essays in Honour of C.G. Starr* (Lanham, London, New York).

STEIN, H. (1856–1908) *Herodotus* (Berlin).

STRASBURGER, H. (1956) 'Herodots Zeitrechnung', *Historia* 5, 129–61 (repr. in Marg (ed.) (1965), 677–725).

(1958) 'Thukydides und die politische Selbstdarstellung der Athener', *Hermes* 86, 17–40.

(1965) 'Herodot und das perikleische Athen', in Marg (ed.) (1965), 574–608 (first publ. in *Historia* 4, 1955, 1–25).

(1966) *Die Wesensbestimmung der Geschichte durch die antike Geschichtsschreibung* (Frankfurt).

STREET, B. (1984) *Literacy in Theory and Practice* (Cambridge).

STROUD, R.S. (1968) *Drakon's Law on Homicide*, University of California Publications in Classical Studies 3.

(1978a) 'State Documents in Archaic Athens', in *Athens comes of Age. From Solon to Salamis*, Papers of a Symposium of Archaeological Institute of America (Princeton), 20–42.

(1978b) *The Axones and Kyrbeis of Drakon and Solon*, University of California Publications in Classical Studies 19.

STUART, D.R. (1928) *Epochs of Greek and Roman Biography* (Berkeley).

STUPPERICH, R. (1977) *Staatsbegräbnis und Privatgrabmal im klassischen Athen* (diss. Münster).

SYKUTRIS, J. (1928) 'Der demosthenische Epitaphios', *Hermes* 63, 241–58.

SYME, R. (1972) 'Fraud and Imposture', in Entretiens Hardt XVIII, Pseudepigrapha 1 (Vandoeuvres-Geneva).

TAYLOR, M.W. (1981) *The Tyrant Slayers: The Heroic Image in Fifth-Century B.C. Athenian Art and Politics* (New York).

THOMPSON, Homer A. (1937) 'Buildings on the West Side of the Agora', *Hesperia* 6, 1–226.

THOMPSON, P. (1978) *The Voice of the Past. Oral History* (Oxford).

THOMPSON, W.E. (1967) 'Andocides and Hellanicus', *TAPA* 98, 483–90.

(1970) 'The Kinship of Perikles and Alkibiades', *GRBS* 11, 27–33.

(1976) *De Hagniae hereditate, an Athenian Inheritance Case*, *Mnemos.* Suppl. 44.

(1981) 'Athenian Attitudes towards Wills', *Prudentia* 13, 13–23.

TODD, M.N. (1947) *Greek Historical Inscriptions*, 2 vols. (Oxford).

TOEPFFER, J. (1889) *Attische Genealogie* (Berlin).

TRAVLOS, J. (1971) *Pictorial Dictionary of Ancient Athens* (London).

TUPLIN, C.J. (1985) 'Imperial Tyranny: Some Reflections on a Classical Greek Political Metaphor', in de Ste Croix (1985), 348–75.

TURNER, E.G. (1952) *Athenian Books in the Fifth and Fourth Centuries* (London); see also 2nd edn (1977) with addenda.

UBSDELL, S. (1982) Herodotus on Human Nature. Studies in Herodotean Thought, Method and Exposition, unpubl. thesis (Oxford).

VAN BAAREN, T.P. (1972) 'The Flexibility of Myth', in *Ex orbe Religionum. Studia G. Widengren*, Part II (Leiden), 199–205.

VANDERPOOL, E. (1952) 'The Ostracism of the Elder Alkibiades', *Hesperia* 21, 1–8.

VAN GRONINGEN, B.A. (1953) *In The Grip of the Past: An Essay on an Aspect of Greek Thought* (Leiden).

VANSINA J. (1973) *Oral Tradition. A Study in Historical Methodology* (Harmondsworth). (Originally publ. in French, 1961, first Engl. edn 1965.)

(1974) 'Comment: Traditions of Genesis', *Journal of African History* 15, 317–22.

(1980) 'Memory and Oral Tradition', in *APS*, 262–76.

(1985) *Oral Tradition as History* (London and Nairobi) (=*OTH*).

VESSBURG, O. (1941) *Studien zur Kunstgeschichte der römischen Republik*, 2 vols. (Lund).

VEYNE, P. (1983) *Les Grecs ont-ils cru à leurs mythes?* (Paris).

VLASTOS, G. (1953) 'Isonomia', *AJP* 74, 337–66.

VOLLGRAFF, W. (1952) *L'Oraison funèbre de Gorgias* (Leiden).

VOLLMER, F. (1891) 'Laudationum funebrium Romanarum historia et reliquiarum editio', *Jahrbuch für classische Philologie* Suppl. 18, 445–528.

(1924) *RE* 'Laudatio (2) funebris', vol. 12, cols. 992–4.

WACHTEL, N. (1986) Introduction to M.N. Bourget and L. Valensi and N. Wachtel (eds.) (1986), 207–24.

WADE-GERY, H.T. (1933) 'Classical Epigrams and Epitaphs. A Study of the Kimonian Age', *JHS* 53, 71–104.

(1951) 'Miltiades', *JHS* 71, 212–21 (repr. 1958).

(1952) *The Poet of the Iliad* (Cambridge).

(1958) *Essays in Greek History* (Oxford).

WALLACE, M.B. (1970) 'Notes on Early Greek Epigrams', *Phoenix* 24, 95–105.

WALSH, J. (1981) 'The Authenticity and the Dates of the Peace of Callias and the Congress Decree', *Chiron* 11, 31–63.

WALZ, J. (1936) *Der lysianische Epitaphios*, *Philologus* Suppl. 29, 1–55.

WARDMAN, A.E. (1960) 'Myth in Greek Historiography', *Historia* 9, 403–13.

WEBER, L. (1935) *Solon und die Schöpfung der attischen Grabrede* (Frankfurt).

WEIL, R. (1959) 'L'Archéologie de Platon', *Etudes et Commentaires* 32 (Paris).

WEISS, E. (1923) *Griechisches Privatrecht auf rechtsvergleichender Grundlage* I (Leipzig).

WELSKOFF, E. (1965) 'Elitevorstellungen und Elitebildung in der hellenischen Polis', *Klio* 43–5, 49–64.

WENDLAND, M.P. (1890) 'Die Tendenz des platonischen *Menexenos*', *Hermes* 25, 171–95.

WEST, M.L. (1985) *The Hesiodic Catalogue of Women* (Oxford).

WEST, S. (1985) 'Herodotus' Epigraphical Interests', *CQ* 35, 278–305.

WEST, W.C. (1970) 'Saviours of Greece', *GRBS* 11, 271–82.

WESTLAKE, H.D. (1977) 'Thucydides on Pausanias and Themistokles: A Written Source?' *CQ* 27, 95–110.

WHITEHEAD, D. (1983) 'Competitive Outlay and Community Profit: φιλοτιμία in Democratic Athens', *Classica et Mediaevalia* 34, 55–74.

(1986) *The Demes of Attica, 508/7–ca. 250 B.C.* (Princeton).

WILAMOWITZ-MOELLENDORF, U. VON (1886) 'ΙΑΜΟΥ ΓΟΝΑΙ', in *Isyllos von Epidauros*, *Philologische Untersuchungen*, vol. 9 (Berlin), 162–85.

(1893) *Aristoteles und Athen* 2 vols. (Berlin).

WILCKEN, U. (1899) *Griechische Ostraka aus Ägypten und Nubien* 1 (Berlin and Leipzig).

WILHELM, A. (1909) 'Über die öffentliche Aufzeichnung von Urkunden', Supplement to *Beiträge zur griechischen Inschriftenkunde* (Vienna), 229–99.

WILLIAMS, G.M.E. (1980) 'The Image of the Alkmaionidai between 490–487/6', *Historia* 29, 106–10.

WILLIAMS, G.W. (1951) 'The Curse of the Alcmaeonidai I', *Hermathena* 78, 32–49.

(1952a) 'The Curse of the Alcmaeonidai II', *Hermathena* 79, 3–21.

(1952b) 'The Curse of the Alcmaeonidai III', *Hermathena* 80, 58–71.

WISEMAN, T.P. (1974) 'Legendary Genealogies', *GR* 21, 153–64.

(1986) 'Monuments and the Roman Annalists', in Moxon et al. (eds.) (1986), 87–100.

WOODBURY, L. (1976) 'Aristophanes' *Frogs* and Athenian Literacy: *Ran.* 52–3, 1114', *TAPA* 106, 349–57.

WRIGHT, R. (1979) 'How Credible are Plato's Myths?' in *Arktouros, Hellenic Studies presented to B.M.W. Knox* (Berlin and New York), 364–71.

WYCHERLEY, R.E. (1957) *The Athenian Agora III, Literary and Epigraphical Testimonia* (Princeton).

WYSE, W. (1904) *The Speeches of Isaeus*, commentary (Cambridge).

YODER, J.C. (1980) 'The Historical Study of a Kanyok Genesis Myth: The Tale of Citend a Mfumu', *APS*, 82–107.

YOUTIE, H.C. (1971a) 'ΑΓΡΑΜΜΑΤΟΣ: An Aspect of Greek Society in Egypt', *HSCP* 75, 161–76.

(1971b) 'βραδέως γράφων: Between Literacy and Illiteracy', *GRBS* XII, 239–61.

ZADOKS-JOSEPHUS JITTA, A.N. (1932) *Ancestral Portraiture in Rome and the Art of the Last Century of the Republic* (Amsterdam).

ZIOLKOWSKI, J.E. (1981) *Thucydides and the Tradition of Funeral Speeches* (New York).

INDEX

accounting, 82 n.218
administration: and documents, 37, 53ff.,
69; not valued, 111–15; traditions of,
203 n.22
Adrastus, 207f., 211f.
Aelius Aristides, 206, 227 n.114
Aeschines: and Demosthenes, 112f., 125;
family tradition of, 125 n.96; family
transmission of history, 101; oratory,
101; use of records, 69ff., 83ff.
age, knowledge of, 79 n.207
Agariste, 'wooing of', 268ff.
agathoi, 114, 178; used of demos, 217–20
Agathon of Zakynthos, genealogy, 159 n.9
Agoratos, 65, 86 n.237, 87
Aigina, in tradition, 120–3, 203 n.24, 227f.
Aigospotamoi, 67, 116, 134, 230
Ajax, 162–4, 183
akoē, versus *opsis*, 3 n.3, 201 n.14, 243f.
Akousilaos, 182–3, 184; *see also*
genealogists
Alcibiades, 52f., 145; family tradition of,
108f., 110 n.47, 151f., 159 n.7, 183; *see
also* Alcmaeonids
Alcmaeon, 98, 130, 145f., 266f.
Alcmaeonids: 'Alcmaeonid tradition',
239ff., 247ff., 257, 264–82; curse of,
130f., 145, 149f., 152f., 249, 261ff.,
272ff.; exile of, 148ff., 252ff.; family
tradition, 111, 116, 130–1, 144–54, 238,
247–50, 261–82; friendship with tyrants,
147, 169 n.31, 263, 267–8; and Pindar,
104 n.33, 107 n.39
alphabet, impact of, 20, 22–3; *see also*
writing, literacy
Amazons, 201 n.14, 207–8, 211–12
amnesty, of 403 B.C., 52
anagegrammenos, 67 n.173
ancestors: celebration of, 103–5; of
democracy, 217–20; documentation of,
83ff.; emulation of, 50–1, 83ff., 101,
196–237; range of meaning, 100, 126;

relation to present, 175–9; tombs of, 50,
99f., 101, 102ff.; *see also* legendary
ancestors, genealogy
Andocides: 67–8, 112; family of, 119–20;
family tradition, 108, 111, 115–16, 130,
139ff., 159, 182–3; knowledge of
history, 119ff., 201, 204, 232 n.126; use
of documents, 87
anthropology, on oral tradition, 5–6; on
genealogy, 186ff.
Antiphon: use of documents, 87; family
tradition, 251
archaic traditions, of Athens, 161ff., 264ff.
archives: before Metroön, 39, 53, 73ff.;
democratic significance, 69–71;
development of, 38–40, 46, 68ff.;
Hellenistic period, 76, 78; modern
conceptions of, 37, 45–6, 52–3, 72–4;
organization, 72–83; for private
documents, 46; relation to inscriptions,
35, 45–6, 65 and n.166, 74, 76; reference
to, 78–83; *see also* Metroön, temple
archives
archonship: 63–4, 105, 278–9;
archon-dating, 79 n.209; archon list,
148, 153, 287–8; in oral tradition,
112–15, 169, 171 and n.36
aretē: 113–14; in Athenian democracy,
211–12, 213ff., 221, 224, 227, 231; effect
on official traditions, 231–2, 233–5
Arginusae, 136, 138, 230
Aristeides, family tradition, 101, 110
Aristophanes: *Lysistrata*, 245ff.; on
Persian Wars, 225–6; and writing, 19–20
Aristotle, *Ath.Pol.,* use of records, 91
Aristocrates: family tradition of, 127,
132ff., 254; in popular tradition, 137
Arthmios of Zeleia, stele of, 84–5, 87
n.239, 88, 91
assembly: list of members, 82 and n.220
Athenian democracy, *see* democracy
Athenian empire: justification of, 208,

313

forgery: ease of, 29; of historical documents, 83ff.

fratry, and ancestry, 179

freedom, in Athenian ideology, 211, 214, 217 n.79, 219–20, 223, 227, 229, 231, 233–5

funerals: archaic, 103–5; speeches at, 103–4; and oral tradition, 100–5; public, 200, 207, 211, 216, 219; *see also* epitaphios, tombs

games: lists of victors, 288; victories at, 111, 114–15, 133, 145–6

genealogists: 158–9, 181ff.; and chronology, 184–6; written methods of, 183ff.

genealogy: relation to the present, 175ff., 187–9; critics of, 174–5; and father–son succession, 191–3; linear, 163, 165–70, 172–3, 191ff.; manipulation of, 168–9, 173; memory of, 127–8, 130–1, 139–44, 145, 151–2, 156–9, 165ff., 169–70, 180; and modern expectations, 157 n.2, 179, 187–8; and 'pedigree', 157 n.2, 178, 180 n.62, 188 n.87; reliability of, 161, 168–9, 172–3, 177–8; role of, 156, 160, 168–9, 172ff., 182, 187–9; role of writing in, 170–1, 181ff., 186ff.; symbolic meaning of, 175ff., 188 n.86; time span of, 185–6

generals: in family tradition, 116–17; in polis tradition, 202–3; in official tradition, 205, 213–15, 224

generation-counting, 185 and n.78

genos; 179, 192–3; traditions of, 277 n.118

Goody, Jack, 3, 20–2, 24ff., 30, 34, 189

Gorgias, epitaphios of, 209

graffiti: 31–2; spelling in, 47 n.109

Grammata, range of meaning, 35 n.66, 73 and n.182

Hagnias, 63, 111

handwriting, 41, 42 n.88

Harmodius, *see* tyrannicides

Havelock, 17 n.2, 32 n.61

Hecataeus, 156, 160, 181, 183; *see also* genealogists

Hellanicus, 181–2, 184, 243–4, 287

Heraklids, 207–8, 211–12

Heraclitus, 31

Hermae, mutilation of, 55, 243–4

Herodotus: and Alcamaeonids, 247ff., 255 n.43, 256 n.46, 264–82; and Athens, 265; calibre of, 7, 280–2, 284–5; and chronology, 185 n.78, 186 and n.79, 193; and inscriptions, 90; oral sources of, 3–4, 96, 98, 171–2, 198 n.5, 235, 280–2; on Peisistratids, 240–1, 247ff.; and Pericles, 265, 270–2; on Philaids, 165–72

Heropythos of Chios, 156, 159, 169, 189 n.90, 190

Hesiod, 174–5, 182, 183 n.71

Hesychidai, 276–7

Hipparchus, and stele of traitors, 65–6

Hipparchus (tyrant), 148, 149 n.153, 238–9, 242–4

Hippias, sophist, 109 n.44, 174, 287–8

Hippias, tyrant, 148, 169, 238, 242–3, 260; in comedy, 244

Hippokleides, 115, 167–8, 171, 268ff.

Hippokrates, doctor, 159–60, 178 n.57

historiography, general: development of, 287–8, *see* genealogists; and oral tradition, 284, 286; and use of documents, 89ff.; versus oral tradition, 7

Homer, 2–3, 9; genealogies in, 174

Homeric ancestors; *see* legendary ancestors

Horoi, 46 n.101, 55–9; Solon's, 57 n.139, 58 n.143

Hypereides, epitaphios of, 210

Iamids, 107, 178

illiteracy, 17, 18 and n.9, 23, 31; 79 n.207

inscriptions; abbreviated, 48; destruction of, 52–3; false additions to, 62 n.157, 65–6; function expressed of, 46 and n.103, 51, 61 n.151, 64–5, 75–6; historians' use of, 89ff.; legibility of, 51 n.121, 61 n.151; and literacy, 16, 31; as memorials, 49ff., 65, 75–7, 84ff.; 'non-literate' features of, 35ff., 45–60; orators' use of, 49ff., 64ff., 83–94; pre-403, citation of, 73–4 and n.187; public accessibility, 51, 60–1, 66ff.; reading of, 51, 64ff.; symbolic, 49ff.; *see also* archives, lists

Ionian migration, 160 n.10, 164–5, 185 n.77

Isocrates, use of history, 87, 90, 201 n.14, 202 n.19, 203 n.26, 220, 254